Baseball

FOR

DUMMIES

A Wiley Brand

4th Edition

by Joe Morgan
Hall of Fame player

and

Richard Lally
Sportswriter and author

FOR

DUMMIES

A Wiley Brand

Baseball For Dummies® 4th Edition

Published by: **John Wiley & Sons, Inc.,** 111 River Street, Hoboken, NJ 07030-5774, www.wiley.com

Copyright © 2014 by John Wiley & Sons, Inc., Hoboken, New Jersey

Published simultaneously in Canada

For general information on our other products and services, please contact our Customer Care Department within the U.S. at 877-762-2974, outside the U.S. at 317-572-3993, or fax 317-572-4002. For technical support, please visit www.wiley.com/techsupport.

Wiley publishes in a variety of print and electronic formats and by print-on-demand. Some material included with standard print versions of this book may not be included in e-books or in print-on-demand. If this book refers to media such as a CD or DVD that is not included in the version you purchased, you may download this material at http://booksupport.wiley.com. For more information about Wiley products, visit www.wiley.com.

Library of Congress Control Number:

ISBN: 978-1-118-51054-4

ISBN 978-1-118-51052-0 (ebk); ISBN 978-1-118-51059-9 (ebk)

Manufactured in the United States of America

10 9 8 7 6 5 4 3 2 1

Contents at a Glance

Table of Contents

Introduction

Welcome to *Baseball For Dummies,* 4th Edition, a book dedicated to the proposition that no one's education is complete unless it includes a thorough grounding in the principles of the greatest sport ever created. This book is much like a baseball game: orderly but spontaneous, filled with nuance and surprise, and packed to the brim with cutting-edge information — and fun. We hope you enjoy reading it as much as we enjoyed writing it.

About This Book

We wrote this book to appeal to fans of every level, from the novice who just recently purchased his first pack of baseball cards to the loyalist who has been sitting in the same seat at the ballpark since the Coolidge administration. Whether you participate on the field or just watch, our mission is to increase your baseball pleasure by a factor of ten.

As a spectator, you'll have an easier time watching and appreciating baseball's finer points after you finish our book. You will not only know what the players on the field are doing, but you'll also know why they are doing it. If an extraterrestrial dropped out of the skies, we would hope it could read *Baseball For Dummies,* 4th Edition, today and attend its first baseball game tomorrow without experiencing any confusion.

The new edition is even better than its predecessors. It can keep you abreast of not only what's changed on the field — including the stadiums themselves — but it can push open the doors on the Major League front office and reveal the behind-the-scenes movers and shakers. You can get hip to the latest in advanced statistics, rules, and baseball lingo; find out why the amateur draft is so important to building a winning team; and get the scoop on the Steroid Era, from the beginning to the present day. If all that weren't enough, we also guide you in finding the best in baseball news and analysis on the Internet and in print.

If you're a player, there isn't any component of your game that can't be elevated by studying this volume. Pitching, hitting, fielding, and baserunning — we cover it all with the aid of some of the game's legendary players. It doesn't matter if you're taking your first cuts in Little League or already sitting in a big-league dugout; you can find something in this book to make you a better player.

Within this book, you may note that some web addresses break across two lines of text. If you're reading this book in print and want to visit one of these web pages, simply key in the web address exactly as it's noted in the text, pretending as though the line break doesn't exist. If you're reading this as an e-book, you have it easy — just click the web address to be taken directly to the web page.

Foolish Assumptions

When we wrote this book, we made the following assumptions about you. All of them or just one may apply to you:

- ✔ **You're a novice and want a quick primer on the ins and outs of the game.** No other book can offer you such a comprehensive introduction to the national pastime.

- ✔ **You're a diehard fan who already knows a lot about the sport and you just want to uncover as much as you can about it.** We show you how the great outfielders are able to get a good jump on the ball, where the first baseman should stand to receive a cutoff throw, how many stitches are in a baseball, and who manufactures bats that meet Major-League standards. Plus, we provide a look at all levels of the game, from T-ball to the Major Leagues. This book is chock-full of inside tips and insights that you rarely encounter anywhere below the professional ranks.

- ✔ **You're a parent of a baseball-playing child.** You want know exactly what's transpiring on the field during every moment of the game.

No matter whether one of these assumptions addresses you, we're confident that you can find tons of useful information to help you love the game even more.

Beyond This Book

Your baseball education won't stop when you finish this latest print version of *Baseball For Dummies*. In addition to the material in the print or e-book you're reading right now, this product also comes with some access-anywhere goodies on the web. No matter how much you glean from this book, while following the game, you'll likely come across a few instances where you don't have a clue. Check out the free Cheat Sheet at www.dummies.com/ cheatsheet/baseball.

You can also find more bonus material online at www.dummies.com/ extras/baseball. We discuss perhaps the most important skill involved in hitting: pitch recognition. We show you how Major League Baseball is organized and how its season progresses and culminates in post-season play. We also provide you with a myriad number of ways to follow the game — on radio, TV, print, and the Internet. As if all that wasn't enough, we have added a few bonus Part of Tens lists. Finally, you can find a bonus chapter full of different defensive plays.

Icons Used in This Book

These icons that appear in the book's margins can help you navigate your way through the book. Here is what they mean.

Talk like this and the folks in the bleachers will have no trouble understanding you.

This icon cues you to some "must have" books to start or enhance your baseball library.

This icon signals tips from the Hall of Famer himself.

This icon gives you valuable information that can prevent you from making a bonehead play on or off the field.

This icon alerts you to sage advice from the greats of the game, signals an insight that can enhance your baseball viewing (whether you are in the stadium or in front of the TV), and alerts you to advice that comes from a coach and can be passed on by a coach.

Beware! This icon warns you that a situation can be dangerous.

You can find lots of additional information for free online. This icon points you in that direction.

Where to Go from Here

If you don't have a strong understanding of baseball, we suggest that you start with Chapter 1 and read your way through the book, front to back cover. However, if you're familiar with the sport, you can peruse through the table of contents or index, find the topic that interests you, and read that chapter. Feel free to reference this book during the season as you're watching a game or during the offseason when something, such as an odd statistic or a term, doesn't make sense.

Part I
Getting Started with Baseball

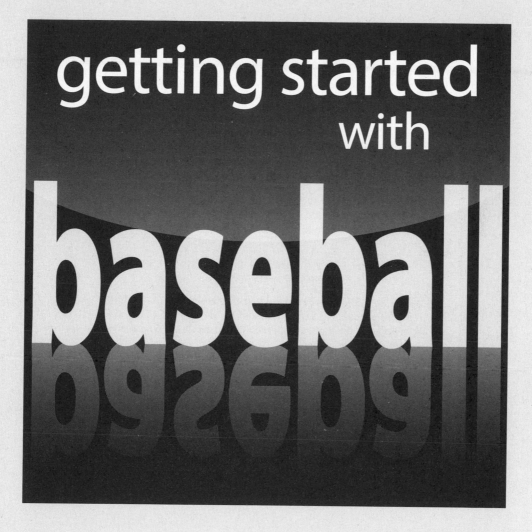

 Go to www.dummies.com/cheatsheet/baseball for more informative tidbits about the ins and outs of baseball.

In this part...

- Examine the history of baseball, including how the game started and how it has evolved into America's pastime.

- Identify the tools of the trade so you can take the field properly equipped, know where you can acquire them, and discover how to take care of your bats, balls, and gloves so they can take care of you.

- Review the rules of baseball so you don't commit any *faux pas* on or off the field, such as running the bases in the wrong direction or failing to tag up before scoring on a would-be sacrifice fly.

- Know how to use the proper glove for your position, so that you don't wear a catcher's mitt in the outfield.

- Make sure that you stay in foul territory when you reach third base — if you don't and your teammate strikes a fair ball that hits you, you'll not only be called out, but you'll also incur the wrath of your teammate for robbing him of a possible hit.

- Look closer at the strike zone so that you don't mistake for strikes pitches high over your head or low enough to bounce past the catcher. And understand that although there's supposed to be a uniform strike zone, each umpire has his own interpretation of it, so you had better pay close attention to the zone.

Chapter 1

The Lowdown on Baseball

For people who still believe that Abner Doubleday invented baseball in Cooperstown, New York, we bring you a line from the gangster movie *Donnie Brasco:* "Fuhgedaboudit!" Abner didn't invent nuttin'. No one person actually conceived of the sport. Baseball evolved from earlier bat and ball games including town ball, rounders, and one o'cat. Although there's no denying that the English game of cricket was also an influence, baseball is as singular an American art form as jazz. (Although during the early 1960s, the Soviet Union claimed baseball was a Russian creation. We should note, however, that Soviets were also taking credit back then for the invention of the telephone and the electric light.)

This chapter gives you a quick overview to America's pastime. Whether you've been a fan your entire life or just started showing an interest in the sport, this chapter can help you start.

Tapping into the Roots of the Game

If anyone invented baseball, it was Alexander Joy Cartwright. This gentleman bank teller founded the New York Knickerbockers, America's first organized baseball team, in 1842. Three years after that, Cartwright formulated the sport's first codified rules (which included three strikes per out and three outs per half-inning). Cartwright's game included a pitching mound that was only 45 feet from home plate and base paths spaced 75 feet apart. Baseball's lawmakers have altered these distances while modifying other rules over the years.

The pitcher's mound is now 60 feet, 6 inches, from home, and the bases now sit 90 feet apart. But the bank teller's guidelines remain the basis of the modern sport. If a time machine were to transport Cartwright to a present-day Major-League ballpark, it would only take him an inning or two to acclimate himself to the action on the field. That's because the most fundamental aspects of the game haven't changed since Cartwright's Knickerbockers first suited up. Most importantly, the objective of a baseball game is still for a team to win its game by outscoring its opponent.

Understanding the Game's Structure

In the Major Leagues, a game is divided into nine units of play called *innings*. Almost all leagues play nine-inning games, except some youth leagues that play only five to seven innings. An inning consists of a turn at-bat and three outs for each team. Visiting teams bat in the first half (called the *top*) of an inning; home teams bat in the second half (called the *bottom*) of the inning.

While one club (the offensive team) is at-bat, the other (the defensive team) plays in the field. Nine players compose each team's lineup. The defensive team consists of the pitcher, catcher, first baseman, second baseman, third baseman, shortstop, left fielder, center fielder, and right fielder. Check out Figure 1-1 of the playing field to see the basic positions for each of the defensive players. (Table 1-1 gives you the abbreviations for these players.)

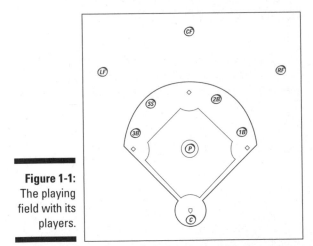

Figure 1-1:
The playing field with its players.

Illustration by Wiley, Composition Services Graphics

Table 1-1	The Players
Abbreviation	*Player*
P	Pitcher
C	Catcher
1B	First baseman
2B	Second baseman
3B	Third baseman
SS	Shortstop
LF	Left fielder
CF	Center fielder
RF	Right fielder

When nine isn't really nine

Many baseball games are finished before the completion of nine full innings. If the home team leads after the top of the ninth, it wins the game without taking its turn at-bat in the bottom of that inning. The home team can also win the game in less than nine innings if it scores the winning run during the last inning before the third out. For example, the Toronto Blue Jays come to bat in the bottom of the ninth inning of a game against the Detroit Tigers. The Tigers lead 3–2. With two men out, Blue Jays' Jose Reyes hits a two-run homer off Tiger starter Justin Verlander. Toronto won 4–3. The game is over even though the two teams combined for only 8⅔ innings. (Remember, a team doesn't complete an inning until it makes the third out.)

This example illustrates a difference between baseball and other major team sports. Either team can win a game that ends in regulation time in football (four quarters), basketball (four quarters), and hockey (three periods). In baseball, the home team can never win any game that lasts the full nine innings (except in the event of a forfeit).

Going extra innings

Games that are tied after nine innings go into *extra innings*. The two opponents play until they complete an extra inning with the visiting team ahead or until the home team scores the winning run.

Introducing the Playing Field

Baseball is played on a level field divided into an infield and an outfield. The infield (also known as the *diamond*) must be a square 90 feet (27.45 meters) on each side. Home plate sits at one corner of the square, and the three bases rest at the other corners. Moving counterclockwise from home, you see first base, second base, and third base.

Base lines run from home plate to first base, as well as from home to third. Base lines also extend from first base to second and from second to third. However, only the base lines extending from home to first and home to third are marked by white chalk. The lanes connecting the bases are the base paths. Runners must stay within them while traveling around the diamond. Should a runner step out of the base path to elude a tag, the umpire can call him out.

Foul lines extend from the first-base and third-base lines and run straight to the outfield walls. The section of the outfield beyond first base is called *right field*, the outfield section behind second base and shortstop is *center field*, and the outfield section beyond third base is *left field*.

Coaches pass on advice to players from the *coach's boxes*, the chalk rectangles in foul territory near first and third. When the players are not on the field, they sit in shelters in foul territory called *dugouts*. Between the dugout and home plate is the *on-deck circle*, where the next hitter awaits his turn at-bat. (See Figure 1-2.)

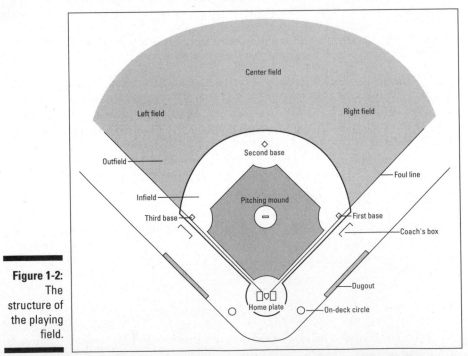

Figure 1-2:
The structure of the playing field.

Illustration by Wiley, Composition Services Graphics

Major League rules require the distance from home plate to the nearest fence or wall in fair territory to be at least 250 feet (76 meters). Home plate must be a 17-inch (43-centimeter) square with two of its corners removed to leave a 17-inch edge, two 8½-inch (21.5-centimeter) adjacent sides, and two 12-inch (30.5-centimeter) sides angled to a point. The result is a five-sided slab of white rubber. A regulation pitching rubber is a 24-x-6-inch (61-x-15.5-centimeter) rectangle made of white rubber, set in the middle of the diamond 60 feet, 6 inches (18.4 meters) from the rear of home plate (refer to Figure 1-3).

Figure 1-3: Home plate and the pitching rubber.

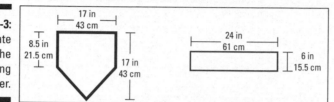

Illustration by Wiley, Composition Services Graphics

Getting into the Action of Play

The pitcher is the player who stands at the middle of the infield diamond on the hill called the *mound,* where the pitching rubber is located. He throws the baseball toward the catcher, a teammate who squats behind home plate. When the pitcher throws the ball to the batter at home plate, he is said to be *delivering a pitch.*

Each batter comes to the plate according to a specific order (the batting order or *lineup*) designated by the manager or head coach. The opposing team's batter (hitter) stands in one of two batter's boxes on either side of home plate. If he's right-handed, he stands in the box to the left of the plate (as viewed from behind). If he's left-handed, he stands in the box to the right of the plate. As the ball reaches the home plate area, the batter tries to hit it with a club called a *bat.* The batter tries to hit the ball into *fair territory* — that part of the playing field between the first- and third-base lines, from home base to the outfield fences — where it is either *fielded* (caught) for an out or drops in safely for a *base hit.* (We describe the various ways a batter makes an out or reaches base safely in Chapter 3.) A hit can take four forms:

- ✔ A *single* delivers the batter to first base.
- ✔ A *double* is hit far enough that the batter reaches second base.
- ✔ A *triple* gets the batter to third base.
- ✔ A *home run* means the batter circles all three bases and touches home plate for a run.

  Home runs usually travel over the outfield fence in fair territory. If a batter hits a ball that stays on the field, but he is able to circle the bases and touch home before he can be called out, he has hit an *inside-the-park home run.*

Game called because of . . .

Umpires can *call* (end) games because of inclement weather, power outages, earthquakes (don't laugh — a tremor postponed the 1989 World Series between Oakland and San Francisco), a disciplinary action (a mob of fans runs on the field and refuses to vacate; no matter which team is ahead, the umpire forfeits the game in favor of the visiting club), or some other event that renders play impossible or dangerous. To be an *official game* (one that counts as a win or a loss in the league standings), the two teams must play at least five full innings. Exceptions to this rule occur whenever the top of the fifth concludes with the home team ahead or if the home team scores the winning run during that fifth frame.

Coming Home (Eventually)

Players score runs by getting on base and then moving around (and touching) all three bases in order before crossing home plate. They must reach home before the offensive team tallies three outs in its half of the inning. When a club's hitters make three outs, its half-inning ends. Then it takes the field (moves to defense) and the opposing team comes to bat. (Chapter 3 has all the details on how an out is made.)

You can advance on the bases (move from first to second, second to third, or third to home) at any time, but you do so at your own peril. If you're off base when a member of the defensive team (a *fielder*) tags you with the ball, you are out. The exception to this occurs when the umpire calls "Time" (timeout). At that moment, the ball is considered dead. You may step off base without being put out, but you may not advance. Umpires may call time at the request of either team, when an injury occurs, or if some circumstance threatens the flow of the game (for instance, a cat running across the field).

Knowing Who Is in Charge

In professional baseball, *managers* are the team leaders. (At some other levels, such as college and high school baseball, this person may be referred to as the *head coach*.) Managers plot strategy and decide which team members play which positions. They also determine a club's batting order. Most importantly, they decide which players to put on the field in the first place. In essence, they're *personnel* managers.

Managers have assistants, called *coaches,* who help them train and discipline the team. Managers also use the first- and third-base coaches to pass
along instructions to players through a series of signs. In recent years it has
become fashionable for managers to employ a dugout coach. This coach
is usually a savvy baseball veteran with whom the manager plots strategy
throughout the game.

Enforcing and Scoring: Umpires and Official Scorers

On-field officials known as *umpires* enforce the rules of play. In the Major
Leagues, four umpires — one for each base and home plate — are assigned
to each game. They decide whether a batted ball is fair or foul and whether
a player is safe or out. The home-plate umpire also calls balls and strikes
during the pitcher-batter confrontation. Umpires have complete authority
over the game. They can eject anyone from the field who violates the rules of
conduct. (Lower levels may have only two or three umpires.) (See Chapter 15
for more information about umpires.)

All professional games also have *official scorers.* The league hires these
people to record on a scorecard all the events that take place on the field
during a game. Scorers can't overrule an umpire, nor can they affect the
outcome of a game. They do, however, often rule on whether a batted ball
should be labeled a hit or an error for the official record. (In high school and
college games, the home team provides a scorer, who usually consults with
the visiting team scorekeeper on a close call.)

More than history: Baseball's Hall of Fame

To discover more about the history and evo-
lution of this great game, there's only one
place to visit: the National Baseball Hall of
Fame and Museum in Cooperstown, New
York. The museum has more than 6,500 arti-
facts, including examples of the earliest bats,
balls, and gloves (see the following figure of
historic baseballs). Many of the exhibits are
interactive. The Hall's library and archives
boast the world's most comprehensive collection of printed baseball matter, including
box scores from the late 1800s.

(continued)

(continued)

Photo courtesy of National Baseball Hall of Fame Library, Cooperstown, N. Y.

The Hall of Fame gallery is this institution's Valhalla, the place where baseball's immortals are commemorated in bronze. Members of the Baseball Writers Association of America elect honorees from a list of players with ten years or more of major-league service. All candidates must be retired from baseball for at least five years before they can be considered for induction. Every two years, the Hall of Fame Veterans Committee votes for managers, pioneers of the sport, baseball executives, umpires, players from the Negro Leagues, and players who missed election their first time through the Baseball Writers Association of America voting process. A candidate must collect 75 percent of all ballots cast by either the writers or the Veterans Committee to earn a plaque in the gallery.

The Hall reserves the right to exclude anyone who is on baseball's ineligible list — for example, Pete Rose or Joe Jackson — from its ballots. Players on the ineligible list are disqualified from holding jobs with any Major-League teams. Rose was ruled ineligible because he bet on baseball games while serving as manager of the Cincinnati Reds. Though deceased, Jackson's name remains on the ineligible list because he actively participated in a conspiracy with gamblers and seven Chicago White Sox teammates to deliberately lose the 1919 World Series.

The Hall features permanent exhibits such as *Viva Baseball* (tracing Latin American contributions to the game), *Chasing the Dream* (about the legendary Hank Aaron's career), and *One for the Books* (baseball's records and the stories behind them). At various times of the year, the Hall of Fame also showcases special temporary exhibits. It has the Barry Halper Gallery, a showcase for a vast array of memorabilia, which includes such rare items as a camelhair overcoat formerly worn by one George Herman (Babe) Ruth that Mr. Halper had previously displayed in the basement of his New Jersey home. The gallery also hosts traveling exhibits on a revolving schedule, such as a 2011 show exploring the historic connection between cricket and baseball. The Hall of Fame also features online exhibits.

You can get ticket, schedule, and exhibit information for the Hall by calling 888-425-5633 or visiting its website at www.baseballhall.org.

Chapter 2

Suiting Up: Equipment

· ·

· ·

*W*hen Pittsburgh Pirates shortstop Dick Groat was hitting his way to a batting title and MVP award in 1960, his manager Danny Murtaugh claimed, "Groat could hit .300 using a piece of barbed wire as a bat." Perhaps Groat could, but no one expects you to attempt that feat. When you take the field, you should take along the best equipment available, which this chapter discusses. You don't need to spend vast sums to purchase top-quality accessories as long as you know what to look for and where to find it. Hence, as the late sportscaster Howard Cosell would say, this chapter tells it like it is.

Choosing Your Weapons: Balls, Bats, and Gloves

Unless you're under ten years old, buy equipment that meets all the Major-League specifications. Equipment licensed by a reputable body such as Major League Baseball, the NCAA, or the Little League offers you some quality assurances.

These sections show you how to shop for the basic tools you need in order to play the game effectively and keep yourself protected both on the field and in the batter's box. With the right ball, bat, and glove, your chances of success on the playing field can increase dramatically.

Baseballs that last (and last and last)

A baseball must meet the following criteria:

- ✔ Have a circumference between 9 and 9¼ inches (22.9cm and 23.5cm)
- ✔ Weigh between 5 and 5¼ ounces (141.8g and 148.8g)
- ✔ Have an outer covering constructed from two pieces of white horsehide or cowhide stitched together with red thread
- ✔ Have a cork core surrounded by two layers of rubber and wrapped in yarn

Figure 2-1 shows a standard baseball.

Figure 2-1:
A standard
baseball.

Illustration by Wiley, Composition Services Graphics

You don't have to go to your local sporting goods store armed with a tape measure, scale, and scalpel (for filleting the ball to check its innards) to make sure you're buying a baseball that conforms to Major-League standards. Rawlings (877-977 2391, www.rawlings.com) is the only company licensed by both Major Leagues to manufacture their official baseballs. So if you buy one of their balls, you know you're getting the genuine article. Rawlings' baseballs carry the designation "Official Baseball of the American (or National) League" and are signed by the commissioner of baseball. You can buy first-rate baseballs that other companies manufacture, but you have no way of knowing whether these products are of Major-League quality.

If you plan to lose a lot of balls bashing homers during batting practice, you may want to invest in a bagful of Rawlings' Recreational Play baseballs. Constructed of synthetic leather with a rubber center, these balls have the same weight and dimensions as the official league balls at a fraction of the cost.

Rawlings tests its baseballs by injecting them into an air gun and firing them against a wall nearly nine yards away. To pass muster with the company's ballologists (yes, we made that word up), the hurtled sphere must rebound at 51.4 to 54.6 percent of its original velocity. Other machines roll each ball for 15 seconds to ensure roundness.

A ball whose insides are poorly wrapped rapidly becomes misshapen with use. If your baseball is poorly stitched or constructed from inferior leather, it will fall apart. Avoid balls made with synthetic leather wrapped around a core of hard plastic. This kind of ball makes a good toy or first ball for a toddler, but if you're a young adult or older, you'll tear its cover off in one good afternoon of batting practice. The toy balls are also so light that you risk throwing out your arm if you use one for a serious game of catch.

Want to rip a few line drives inside a gymnasium during the dead of winter? Several companies manufacture balls with nylon covers and cloth centers so your best line drives won't shatter any windows. Honing your batting eye after dusk? Shop for orange-colored baseballs — a brainchild of Charlie Finley, the late, innovative owner of the Oakland A's — specifically designed for nighttime play. And for those of you who like to play through rain delays, Elite Sports (www.elitesportsupply.com) is one of several companies that offer waterproof baseballs.

Reducing injuries with innovative baseballs

Many baseball-playing youngsters live in fear of being struck by a batted or thrown ball. Likewise, many parents fret while watching their children face live pitching for the first time. To ease such fears, Worth, Inc. manufactures Sof-Dot Reduced Injury Factor (RIF) baseballs — softer balls that reduce the peak force of impact, lessening the chance of serious injury. Although slightly spongier, a RIF ball has the exact size and weight of a regulation baseball, giving children a realistic training tool that reduces the chance of head trauma by as much as 70 percent.

Worth manufactures three types of RIF baseballs with varying injury protection:

- **Level 1,** the softest of the three, is recommended for players age 5–7 or as a training ball for all ages.

- **Level 5,** a medium-firm ball, is recommended for players age 8–10.

- **Level 10,** the firmest RIF baseball, is recommended for players age 11 and up.

You can find Worth's RIF baseballs at many sporting goods stores; check www.worthsports.com for the Worth dealer nearest you.

Bats that really swing

Although pro players are required to use wooden bats, many people prefer the power that aluminum can offer. In this section, we cover how to buy a bat that will last, how to care for it after you've made your purchase, and what to expect if you choose the metal version rather than your standard lumber.

Professional wood

A Major-League bat must be a single, round piece of solid wood, no more than 2¾ inches (7 centimeters) in diameter at its thickest point and no more than 42 inches (1.06 meters) long. Figure 2-2 shows what a standard bat looks like.

Figure 2-2:
A standard baseball bat.

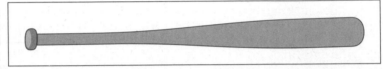

Illustration by Wiley, Composition Services Graphics

Choose a bat that you can swing comfortably with control and speed (see Chapter 5 for more details), but also look for one that will last. Bats made of white ash have greater durability than bats constructed from less dense woods. When you choose a bat, look for one with a wide grain, the mark of an aged wood. These bats are more resistant to breaking, denting, chipping, or flaking than bats made from less mature wood.

Hillerich & Bradsby (800-282-2287, www.slugger.com), the official bat manufacturer for Major-League baseball, makes the Louisville Slugger, a bat that remains the bludgeon of choice among Major-League hitters. Their TPX Pro Composite features barrel grooves filled with resin to impart greater durability for those teams that don't want broken bats breaking their budgets. Former batting champion and Hall of Famer George Brett owns Brett Brothers Bats (509-891-6435, www.brettbats.com), which produces a laminated ash bat with what the company has dubbed a *boa constrictor handle*. Laminating increases the wood's durability, and the boa handle decreases the likelihood that your bat will come flying out of your hands during a particularly strenuous plate appearance. Martial arts buffs might be in the market for their lethal-sounding Bamboo Dragon, a bat constructed with a bamboo core and a maple exterior.

For the color-coordinated among you, Glomar Enterprises (626-359-8707, www.justbats.com) sells a customized white ash bat that you can have stained in your favorite hue and with your name printed on the middle line of the barrel. Hoosier (800-228-3787, www.hoosierbat.com) manufactures an ultradurable bat made of three types of glued wood: ash for the handle, maple for the barrel, and hickory at the *sweet spot* (a spot four to eight inches from the end of the barrel, where the ball can be hit most solidly). They also make a birch bat, which is more durable than ash, but doesn't break as much as maple. Former big-league pitcher Bill Lee will handcraft a bat for you on his lathe if you email him for prices and specifications at spaceman@vtlink.net.

Powerful aluminum

Aluminum bats are currently popular in many levels of nonprofessional baseball. More than 4.1 million are made in the United States each year. The choice of aluminum over wood is largely an economic one. Most non-pro leagues find that the cost of regularly replacing broken wooden bats can bust their budgets. It costs about $1,200 to buy an entire team's worth of aluminum bats that will last up to five seasons, whereas that same amount may not be enough to buy one season's worth of wooden bats.

Hitters love aluminum bats because they're hollow and light yet they have more hitting mass than heavier wooden bats. Also, balls fly off aluminum bats faster — up to 8 miles per hour. What the scientists call their *batted ball speed* can reach almost 107 miles per hour. This combination enables the hitter to generate greater bat speed and power. Balls that are routine outs when struck by a wooden bat are out of the park when launched by aluminum.

An aluminum bat's *sweet spot,* the launching point for so many base hits, is twice the size of that found on a wooden bat. Pitchers dislike these war clubs for obvious reasons.

Aluminum bats have a longer game-life than wooden models, but they aren't immortal. After 600 hits or so, metal fatigue becomes a factor.

If your league insists that you use an aluminum bat, buy one that rings or lightly vibrates when you strike its barrel on something hard, such as the BBCOR bats, the new standard in metal bats for high school and college play.

Picking your lumber

The bat you choose should feel comfortable. Big-league bats generally weigh between 32 and 36 ounces (around 1 kilogram). If you can snap a 36- to 38-ounce bat through the strike zone with control and velocity, go for it. When a pitched ball collides with a heavyweight bat, it travels farther.

However, don't choose a large, heavy bat thinking it will magically transform you into a power hitter. Big bats don't necessarily produce big hits. If you can't control your bat, your swing becomes awkward and long. You may have to start your swing early in the pitcher's delivery — and after you get it

The aluminum bat controversy

Aluminum bats were introduced in 1974, and as fast as hitters came to love them, other people wanted to ban them. The anti-aluminum side felt that they gave the hitters a huge advantage that distorted the balance between offense and defense. They also felt that the ping of an aluminum bat hitting a ball inflated batting averages and game scores, made games longer, and induced young players to *go yard* (hit a home run).

Even more concerns focused on the safety of players, especially pitchers and infielders, because the anti-aluminum side claimed that aluminum bats made the game more dangerous. A pitch thrown at 90 mph could come back off a lively aluminum bat at 108 mph and reach the pitcher 0.375 seconds later, leaving him a nanosecond to defend himself.

Over the years, aluminum bat manufacturers took advantage of loopholes in the rules to create even springier bats. These turbocharged clubs led to an increase in incidents in which pitchers were hit by line drives. *Comebackers* became potentially fatal — and sometimes actually so.

In 2003, an 18-year old American Legion pitcher was killed by a line drive. Seven years later, a Little League pitcher also died after being hit in the head by a batted ball. Other players' careers were ended by a ping.

Since 1985, a leading aluminum bat manufacturer introduced the Black Magic bat sparked a controversy in the National Collegiate Athletic Association (NCAA) over the safety of aluminum bats. In 2009, the organization changed the way it certified bats. It decided that the existing system that measured the speed a baseball has after being hit by a bat — known as Ball Exit Speed Ratio (BESR) — was inadequate and switched to one that measures the bounciness of the ball and the bat. This is known as Ball Coefficient of Restitution (BBCOR) or known to players as the *trampoline effect*. (For more info, visit www.acs.psu.edu/drussell/bats/NCAA-stats.html.)

In response, bat makers shifted to composite bats constructed with the same aluminum exterior, but with a graphite wall on the inside. High school governing bodies quickly adopted the system.

It may be too soon to tell if the new bats will reduce the number and severity of injuries, but already they've severely decreased run scoring and drastically changed how the game is played. Those fly balls struck by aluminum bats that would've reached the bleachers now settled safely in outfielders' gloves, and *small ball* (playing for one run at a time by sacrifice bunts, hit-and-run plays, and steals) displaced the home run–derby style that preceded it. That little bit of graphite created a new dead ball era in college ball. (See Chapter 12 for more on the growing interest in collegiate ball.)

going, it's hard to stop. Pitchers, taking advantage of that swing, can continually fool you with breaking stuff. Pretty soon, you won't be hitting for power, you won't be hitting for singles, you won't be hitting *period*. You may as well use that big bat for kindling.

Bats come in various shapes. Find one that suits you. For instance, a bat with a medium handle and large barrel offers more hitting surface. However, you won't be able to snap it through the hitting zone as quickly as a bat with a very thin handle and a large barrel. Throughout most of my career, I swung an average-sized bat — it weighed 32 ounces (907 grams) and measured 34½ inches (87.6 centimeters) long — yet I still managed to lead the National League in slugging in 1976. It had a thin handle and a large barrel. Bat speed was the key to my power. With my light bat, I could wait longer on the ball, which allowed me more time to recognize the pitch. I could whip through the strike zone with a quick, compact swing. The large barrel added momentum and gave me all the hitting surface I wanted.

Some big-league hitters change bats depending on the pitcher. I would occasionally go to a heavier bat against soft-throwing left-handers. I knew I didn't have to be quite as quick against them, and the bat's additional mass helped me drive the ball. Other than those instances, however, I stayed with my regular bat. It gave me the bat speed, control, and balance I needed to cope with most situations.

If you're a younger player, you may want to think light. If you're not sure what precise bat weight is right for you, simply choose a bat that's comfortable.

Caring for your wood bat

Eddie Collins, a Hall of Fame second baseman with the Chicago White Sox and Philadelphia A's, reportedly kept his bats stored in a manure pile during the off-season to ensure their freshness. (When we told that to our resident left-handed sage Bill Lee, he quipped, "Well, at least Eddie knew no one would steal them.") We're not suggesting you do anything quite so exotic to keep your wooden bats in the swing of things (and won't your teammates be thankful). Instead, perform the following maintenance:

✔ Clean your bat with rubbing alcohol every day, especially if you cover its handle with pine tar. Cleansing prevents pine tar and dirt buildup.

✔ Keep the bat away from dampness. Absorbed moisture adds weight to your bat, which is why Ted Williams never, ever placed his bats on wet ground. If your bat gets wet, dry it off immediately and rub it with linseed oil.

✔ *Bone* your bat to maintain its hard surface. Rub it hard along the grain using another bat or a smooth piece of bone (any kind of thick bone will do — a thick steak bone or a turkey leg bone works great).

✔ Store your bats vertically, barrel down, in a dry place.

Gloves that fit the job

Major League Baseball rules regulate the size of gloves at each position. Most leagues for young adults and older players adhere to these directives. Keep the following in mind when choosing your glove:

- ✔ Catcher's mitts can be no more than 38 inches (96.5 centimeters) in circumference and no more than 15½ inches (39.4 centimeters) from bottom to top. The webbing should be no more than 7 inches (17.8 centimeters) across the top. It should also extend for no more than 6 inches (15.2 centimeters) to the base of the thumb.

- ✔ The first baseman's mitt must be no longer than 12 inches (30.5 centimeters) from top to bottom and no more than 8 inches (20.3 centimeters) wide across the palm. The web of this mitt — which can be a lacing, a lacing through leather tunnels, or an extension of the palm with lacing — cannot exceed 5 inches (12.7 centimeters) from top to base or 4 inches (10.2 centimeters) in width.

- ✔ Pitchers' and other fielders' gloves must not measure more than 12 inches (30.5 centimeters) long from the base to the tip of any one of the four fingers and no more than 7¾ inches (19.7 centimeters) wide. If you work on the mound, your opportunity to make a fashion statement is limited: Pitchers' gloves must be a solid color other than white or gray (which could serve as camouflage for the ball).

All Major League gloves and mitts are made of leather. Children can get by with using vinyl gloves and plastic balls, but when you're playing serious baseball, leather is the only way to go. Pick a glove that conforms to the major-league standards and fits your hand comfortably. Pitchers can benefit from gloves with closed webbing, which allows them to better hide their pitches).

MLB licenses Wilson Team Sports (800-874-5930, www.wilson.com) to manufacture fielding gloves (see Figure 2-3). The Wilson SOG series features a slip-on glove that shapes itself to the player's hand without the use of straps or other adjustments, a real hi-tech breakthrough. Akadema, Inc. (973-304-1470, www.akademapro.com) produces gloves with names straight out of the latest sci-fi flick. The Reptilian-Mantis series includes the Praying Mantis Catcher's mitt whose features include a patent-pending Stress Wedge to soften the impact of your pitcher's most blazing fastball. The craftspeople at Barraza BBG, Inc. (877-753-2552, www.barrazpro.com) customize a glove for you that fits like, well, a glove.

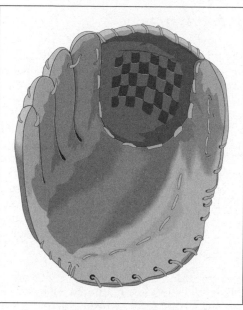

Figure 2-3:
A left-
handed
fielder's
glove.

Illustration by Wiley, Composition Services Graphics

Ballplayers didn't always wear gloves to capture scorching line drives. During the sport's early days, athletes bravely fielded their positions barehanded. It wasn't until 1869 that Doug Allison, a catcher for the Cincinnati Red Stockings, set up behind the plate wearing a mitt (for which Joe's teammate, Hall of Fame backstop Johnny Bench, would be eternally grateful). Allison's leather accessory, however, didn't become all the rage until the mid 1880s, when a livelier, faster-moving baseball finally convinced players that they needed some padding to keep their digits intact.

Caring for your leather glove

The best way to break in a leather glove is to play catch with it frequently. You can also make it more pliable by rubbing it with linseed oil, saddle soap, or — here's a Helpful Hint from Heloise — shaving cream (though you may want to avoid shaving gels, which tend to dry out quickly). If your glove gets wet, let it dry naturally. Placing it on a radiator or some other heat-producer cracks the leather. When your glove is idle, place a ball in its pocket, and then tie the glove closed with a leather strap or wrap a rubber band around it to maintain its catching shape.

Wearing the Right Shoes

Your shoes should fit properly and offer your feet adequate support; otherwise you risk damaging the connective tissue in your lower legs. Choose a sturdy shoe with support that runs its entire length. Because your shoes stretch with use, choose a pair that fits snugly when you first wear them.

Most nonprofessional players give little thought to their shoes; they just put on whatever they can. In fact, standard baseball shoes are no longer obligatory for many pro players. I (Joe) have seen former Chicago White Sox slugger Frank Thomas hit in tennis shoes. But I'm a traditionalist in this area. I believe you should buy a light shoe with metal spikes so that you can get maximum traction in the batter's box and on the base paths. (Slipping in the batter's box, on the bases, or in the field could cost your team a ballgame.) If you don't want to wear spikes, at least get shoes with rubber cleats so you can grip the playing surface as you run.

Adidas (800-982-9337, www.adidas.com) and Nike (800-806-6453, www.nike.com) produce reliable spikes (the shodding of choice when you're playing on natural grass) and rubber cleats (preferably worn on artificial turf).

Equipping Yourself for Safety

Baseball isn't as limb threatening as football, with its 300-pound human condominiums hurtling themselves into each other. However, you do face some risk of injury whenever you step onto the baseball field. You can minimize the chances of getting hurt by buying the proper protective equipment. The following can help you select the best equipment.

✔ **Catchers' gear:** Besides their gloves, catchers have to wear this equipment to survive behind the plate (as shown in Figure 2-4):

- Chest protector

- Mask

- Shin guards

- Protective helmet

- Throat guard

- Neck protector

If these items are of questionable quality, you're jeopardizing your health every time you drop into your crouch. Diamond Sports (714-415-7600, www.diamond-sports.com) produces major-league-quality catcher's gear, including a chest protector with an ergonomic shoulder design that alleviates stress on the upper body.

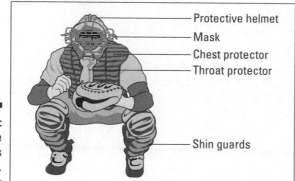

Protective helmet
Mask
Chest protector
Throat protector

Shin guards

Figure 2-4:
The
catcher's
equipment.

Illustration by Wiley, Composition Services Graphics

✔ **Batting helmets:** Major-league rules require hitters to wear batting helmets with at least one *earflap* (which protects the side facing the pitcher). Anytime you go to bat against live pitching without wearing a batting helmet, you should have your head examined. And if you're unlucky, that is exactly what you will have to do. Even a low-grade fastball can permanently damage or even kill you if it collides with your unprotected cranium. A solid batting helmet with double earflaps is the best insurance policy a hitter can buy. Rawlings and Wilson Team Sports both manufacture batting helmets of superior quality that meet industry safety standards.

To offer effective protection, your helmet should

- Fit squarely on your head

- Feature ear holes that center over each of your ears

- Extend far enough to cover the delicate *mastoid region* (behind the ear)

Light plastic batting helmets, such as the freebies that major-league teams give away on Helmet Day at the stadium, are too flimsy to protect your head from an errant fastball. Don't wear them to the plate.

✔ **Batting (and sliding) gloves:** Batting gloves protect a hitter's most important tools — his hands — from painful blisters, cuts, and scrapes. Runners can wear them on the base paths to protect their hands while sliding; fielders can don them under their fielding gloves to reduce the sting of hard-hit balls. Pro-Hitter Corp. (845-634-1191, www.prohitter.com) has created a doughnut-shaped rubber accessory that fits over and protects your thumb, the digit most susceptible to injury when you're working in the batter's box. It can be worn over your batting glove.

The way you wear your hat

We're not sure who wrote the major-league rulebook, but it surely wasn't Ralph Lauren. The rule makers frown on any attempt at an on-field fashion statement that even hints at individuality. (As Jim Bouton, the irreverent pitcher for the New York Yankees and Seattle Pilots during the 1960s, once observed, "When baseball says it wants its players to show some flair, it means it wants us to wear our caps on a jaunty angle.")

Baseball rules demand that teammates wear identical uniforms. Try to stand out by wearing different colored socks or donning a white fox cape, and the umpires won't permit you on the field. Home team uniforms must be white; visiting teams are required to wear a darker color. This requirement is meant to help fans, umpires, and especially players distinguish the teams from one another. If you have a base runner trapped in a rundown play and you slap the ball on a player whose uniform is the same hue as yours, you just tagged out your own third baseman.

- ✔ **Sweatbands:** When the temperature is scorching and perspiration soaks your body, sweatbands help keep your hands dry at the plate. Wilson Team Sports and Easton Sports (800-345-8140, www.eastonsports.com) produce the wristbands many major leaguers wear. *Remember:* Make sure you clean those sweatbands regularly, or the aroma they exude will clear out entire stadiums.

- ✔ **Jock straps and cups:** Male ballplayers should never take the field without wearing jock straps (athletic supporters) and protective cups. You don't really need to ask why, do you?

Donning Your Caps and Uniforms

Safety isn't the only consideration when dressing for the field — style and comfort matter, too. Want to dress your head like a Major Leaguer? Consider doing with the following:

- ✔ New Era Cap Company (866-338-1365, www.neweracap.com) is an official manufacturer of caps. Most major retail sporting goods chains, which include Foot Locker, Modells, Lids, Sports Authority, and Sears, carry baseball headwear. Your cap should fit snugly enough that the bill doesn't droop over your eyes to block your vision.

✔ Russell Corporation (270-781-6400, www.russellcorp.com) has an MLB license to manufacture uniforms, batting practice jerseys, and baseball undershirts.

Wilson and Rawlings also manufacture uniforms for several major-league teams. Uniform fit is a matter of personal comfort; your pants and jersey should permit unrestricted movement at the plate and in the field.

Evolution of the uni

Major Leaguers weren't always clothed in the sleek, form-fitting uniforms they sport today. Believe it or not, in 1869, when the Cincinnati Red Stockings — the first big-league club — took the field, they wore woolen uniforms. Doing so was probably appropriate, given the wild and wooly atmosphere of early baseball when there were no fences and fans strolled through the field or fought the players, the umps, and each other, but they sure must've been *hot*. In the beginning, and for almost a century, teams had just two uniforms — for home games (mostly white) and road games (mostly gray). They weren't durable, and they shrank, like wool normally does.

By the 1940s, uniforms had become lighter, wool-cotton flannels, but the invention of synthetic fibers such as nylon in the post-World War II era led to an evolutionary leap that culminated in the early 1970s with double-knit unis (pullover jersey and beltless trousers) that were lighter and more comfortable. They lasted longer and led to an era in which players strutted their stuff by wearing garish color combinations, psychedelic jerseys (like the infamous rainbow unis worn by the 1975 Houston Astros), and yes, even shorts (Chicago White Sox in the early 1980s).

In the 1990s, MLB realized that the uniforms their players wore were a potential goldmine and started heavily licensing caps and jerseys to the public. Unis proliferated; some teams now have not only standard home and away uniforms, but also special Sunday game uniforms, such as the San Diego Padres' camouflage unis (presumably worn to conceal themselves from their fans), batting practice unis, and ensembles worn on special events. Some MLB teams hold Turn Back the Clock Day, regularly scheduled games in which they donned throwback uniforms in the retro styles of their predecessors or Negro League teams.

Today's unis are made of high-tech space-age materials that wick away moisture and keep players cool in July and warm in October. Most players wear their pants loose and long, down to their cleats, foregoing the stirrup sock look that had lasted for decades. (*Stirrups* were colored socks with no bottom, just a loop that fit under the instep, and worn over long white socks called *sanitaries*.)

Today's media-savvy players sometimes get to pick what combination of uni elements they wear, and it's possible that in some Major League clubhouse, a burly slugger may turn to a lithe shortstop and asked, "Does this uniform make me look fat?"

Preparing the Field for Practice and Play

After you've equipped the players for some baseball action, your team may want to better equip its field and practice facilities for serious training and playing. In that case, consider contacting some of the companies listed in Table 2-1 that equip the professionals.

Table 2-1		Training and Field Equipment	
Equipment	**Manufacturer**	**Web Address**	**Phone Number**
Backstops	L.A. Steelcraft Products	www.lasteelcraft.com	626-798-7401
Bases	C&H Baseball	www.chbaseball.com	800-248-5192
Batting cages	Lanier Rollaway Cages	www.lanierbatting cages.com	800-248-5192
Field covers (tarpaulins)	Vantage Products International	www.vpisports.com	800-244-4457
General field equipment	Diamond Sports	www.diamond-sports.com	714-415-7600
Netting	C&H Baseball	www.chbaseball.com	800-248-5192
Pitching machines	JUGS Sports	www.jugsports.com	800-547-6843
Portable pitching mounds	Jaypro Sports	www.jaypro.com	800-243-0533
Radar guns	Stalker Sports Radar	www.stalkerradar.com	888-782-5537
Scoreboards	Sportable Scoreboards	www.sportable scoreboards.com	800-323-7745
Seating	Southern Bleacher Company	www.southern bleacher.com	800-433-3116
Wall padding	Promats Athletics	www.promats athletics.com	800-617-7125
Wind screens	Covermaster	www.cover master.com	877-470-7891

HEADS UP

Play with the best equipment you can find

Remember, you don't always have to spend a lot of money to equip yourself well and to have fun. The great Willie Mays used to play stickball, and he seems to have done pretty well for himself. Who knows? In an attic or a garage somewhere, your family may have some good equipment just waiting to see daylight again. (And if you run across the following old baseball spikes, you've just found some shoes worn by Hall of Famer Ted Williams.)

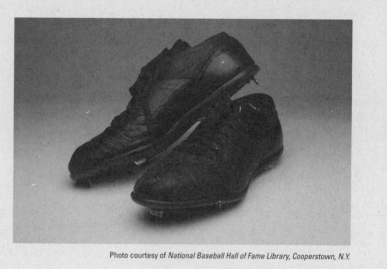

Photo courtesy of *National Baseball Hall of Fame Library, Cooperstown, N.Y.*

Chapter 3

Tackling the Rules of Baseball

. . . .

In This Chapter

▶ Making plays: How a batter gets out or gets on base

▶ Knowing the strike zone

▶ Enacting the designated hitter rule

▶ Being savvy on the base paths

▶ Keeping the pitcher in line

▶ Outlining the role of the umpire

. . . .

ajor League Baseball has rules — lots and lots and lots of rules. We considered presenting all of them to you, but then we glanced through an abridged version of the official rulebook. It was over 120 pages long. We could jam them into this chapter only if we switched to the following font size:

A batter is out when the catcher legally catches a third strike.

And, of course, the whole chapter would have to be single-spaced and would be three times as long. Not very practical, huh? You can just imagine the mountain of lawsuits our publisher would face from readers who suffered eyestrain while trying to discern the balk rule. So instead, we provide you with Major League's Baseball most important rules: the regulations you have to know if you want to understand what is happening out there on the field.

Play Ball! Starting the Game

Actually, the umpire doesn't have to be that verbose when ordering a game to begin. He just has to call "Play," after first ensuring that each member of the defensive team (the hometown team in this case, because the visiting club always bats first in an inning) is in position and that the hitter is in the batter's box.

When an umpire calls "Play," the ball is considered *alive*. No, it doesn't start tap dancing. The term just means that players can use the ball to make outs or get on base. Whenever the ball is alive, runners may advance on the base paths at their own peril; the team in the field can also tag them out. If the umpire calls "Time," the ball is *dead*. No action can take place on the field until the umpire again calls "Play." The ball is also rendered dead whenever a fielder falls into the dugout or the stands while making a catch. If the fielder steps into the dugout and makes the catch without falling, the ball is alive, and runners can proceed at their own peril.

Batting by the Book

Both team managers must present the home-plate umpire with their respective lineups before play begins. A hitter bats according to the order of that lineup throughout the entire game unless the manager removes him for a substitute.

After the pitcher comes to his set position or begins his windup, the hitter can't leave the batter's box unless the umpire grants his request for "Time." (See Chapter 8 for details on pitchers.) If the hitter leaves the box without the ump's permission, the pitcher can deliver a pitch, which may be called a strike. If a batter refuses to get into the batter's box, the umpire can order the pitcher to pitch. In that situation, the rules require the ump to call every pitch a strike regardless of whether it passes through the strike zone.

Making an out

If you're batting, you can be called out in the following situations:

- A fielder catches your fair or foul ball before it touches the ground. (The exception to this rule is a *foul tip* to the catcher with less than two strikes. See Appendix A for an explanation of the foul tip rule.)
- After you hit the ball, a fielder holding the ball tags either you or first base before you touch first base.
- The catcher catches a third strike while you are at-bat.
- A ball that was initially hit or bunted fair hits your bat a second time while you are in fair territory.
- While running outside the foul lines, you obstruct a fielder's throw.
- You hit the ball with one or both feet outside the batter's box, or you step from one batter's box to the other while the pitcher winds up.
- You obstruct the catcher from fielding or throwing.

✔ You use a bat that has been tampered with in defiance of league specifications.

✔ You bat out of turn in the lineup. (*Note:* The umpire calls this out only if the opposing team protests.)

✔ You hit a foul tip that the catcher catches for strike three.

A foul ball that isn't caught counts as a strike against the hitter. However, the umpire can't call a third strike on any *uncaught* foul. If a foul isn't caught, the hitter's at-bat continues.

Defining fair and foul

Right about now, you may be wondering which is fair territory and which is foul territory. Put simply, fair territory is that part of the playing field between and including the first- and third-base lines, from home plate to the outfield fences. Foul territory is the section of the playing field outside the first- and third-base lines and behind home plate. (See Figure 3-1.)

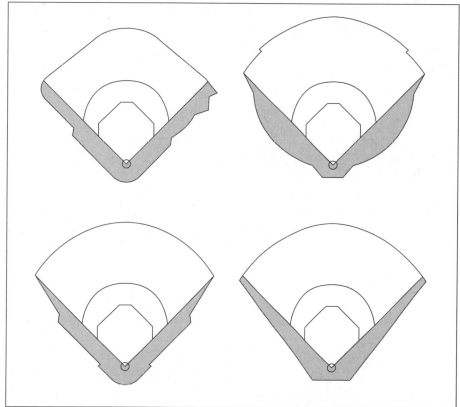

Figure 3-1: Foul territory (shaded here) varies from stadium to stadium — just like fair territory does.

Illustration by Wiley, Composition Services Graphics

Getting on base

Now that we've depressed all the hitters in the audience by revealing how many ways you can fail, it's time for a little positive feedback. You can get on base in the following situations:

- You hit a fair ball that is not caught by a fielder before it touches the ground.
- You hit a fair ball that touches the ground before a fielder catches it, and you reach base before the ball does (meaning the fielder's throw doesn't beat you to a base).
- You earn a walk when the umpire calls four pitches *balls* during your at-bat. (Balls are pitches thrown out of the strike zone that you do not swing at.)
- A thrown pitch hits you without first touching your bat.
- The catcher obstructs your swing.
- You hit a fair ball beyond the playing field (a *home run*).

- You hit a fair, catchable ball, but the fielder makes an *error* (drops the ball or throws it past another fielder).
- The pitcher throws a third strike, but the catcher misses or drops the ball and you reach first base before the ball does.

- You hit a fair ball and a base runner is tagged out, or *forced out*, at another base, but you are safe at first base. (See Appendix A for the definition of a force-out.)

Eyeing the Strike Zone

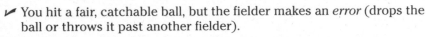

Pitchers try to throw the ball through a *strike zone*, an imaginary box that, according to the rules, is the width of home plate and extends from the bottom of the batter's kneecap to the uniform letters across his chest (see Figure 3-2). Any pitch that passes through the strike zone without being struck by the batter is a strike — provided that the umpire calls it a strike, that is.

Figure 3-2:
The strike
zone.

Illustration by Wiley, Composition Services Graphics

Pitches outside the strike zone are called *balls,* as long as a batter doesn't swing at them. If a batter does swing at a ball outside the strike zone and misses it, he registers a strike, regardless of where the pitcher threw the ball.

During an at-bat, if a batter tallies three strikes before the pitcher throws four balls, the umpire declares the batter out. If the pitcher throws four balls (which the batter doesn't swing at) before registering three strikes or before the ball is hit in fair territory, the umpire awards the batter a *walk* — a trip to first base.

If a batter hits a pitch into foul territory (no matter where the batter makes contact with the ball, in or out of the strike zone), it counts as a strike against him. The only exception to this rule occurs when a batter has tallied two strikes; at that point, he can hit foul balls indefinitely without any of them counting as the third strike. (Just to make things more confusing, the foul tip rule is an exception to this exception; check Appendix A for an explanation of the foul tip rule.)

Baseball's strike-zone controversy

Despite the fact that the strike zone is at the very core of the game, it doesn't really exist — at least not as a physical object. It's more like a conceptual design, an "imaginary box in the umpire's mind," according to Baltimore Orioles closer Jim Johnson. If you were to draw it, it would look like a type of *heptahedron* (a seven-sided figure — something you may have studied in geometry class). This hypothetical zone hovers directly above the 216.75-square-inch rubber slab known as *home plate.* The strike zone has the same official width as the plate, 17 inches.

Major League Baseball's 2013 Official Baseball Rules further defines the strike zone as "that area over home plate, the upper limit of which is a horizontal line at the midpoint between the top of the shoulders and the top of the uniform pants, and the lower level is a line at the hollow beneath the knee cap. The strike zone shall be determined from the batter's stance as the batter is prepared to swing at the pitched ball." Seems pretty clear, doesn't it? If a pitch is over the plate and arrives between a batter's knees and the team letters across his chest, it should be a strike, right? Only if the umpire enforces the rule as it's written. However, nearly every umpire in the big leagues brings his own interpretation of the strike zone to each game. So-called "pitcher's umps" call strikes on pitches that don't quite pass through what you may think of as the traditional strike zone. Other umps have a strike zone that favors the hitter.

As long as these umps consistently call the same zone for both sides, pitchers and hitters can function. However, some umpires have elastic zones that seem to change from batter to batter. Others have different strike zones for right- and left-handed hitters. Adapting to their idiosyncrasies is almost impossible.

In 1999, Sandy Alderson, Major League Baseball's director of operations, tried to create a uniform strike zone by issuing a directive that required all umpires to call balls and strikes by the rulebook. In his memo, Alderson declared, "the upper limit of the strike zone will extend *two inches above the top of the uniform pants.*" Alderson's interpretation further confused matters because it clearly contradicted the existing rules. Though some umpires altered their strike zones, most of them refused to follow the directive; they continued to call balls and strikes as they had in the past. The disagreement over what constitutes balls and strikes heightened the long-standing tensions between team owners and the umpires union. Relations between the two sides got edgier still when in 2001, MLB installed a system made by a digital media company named QuesTec that used pitch tracking technology to review the performance of home plate umpires during games. Both umpires and players balked (no pun intended) at QuesTec's Umpire Information System, which consisted of four cameras strategically placed around stadiums to record the location of pitchers, then fed into a computer network. The results were made into CDs for MLB executives and umpires to review.

After a few years straightening out the kinks — and reassuring alarmists who thought the UIS would ruin baseball — the game's VIPs concluded that the system was fulfilling its mission: to return the strike zone to the dimensions specified in the rulebook.

Then in 2009, they changed their minds and introduced a new system. Zone Evaluation, a video tool, was installed at all 30 MLB ballparks that records a ball's position more than 20 times before it reaches home plate. Although most umpires score between 95 and 98 percent on the

Zone Evaluation System, and each one of the 68 full-time MLB umps meet or exceed league standards for the machine, the gradual encroachment of technology has frayed umps' nerves. (You'd be on edge, too, if your every move was being recorded and instantly replayed and analyzed by multiple cameras in front of millions of fans.) The new technology has strained relations between players and umpires, who feel that the all-seeing eye has undermined their authority.

But 15 years after Alderson's ruling, baseball's strike zone is as elusive as ever, a magic box that causes consternation among players, managers, and everyone who follows the game. Orioles manager Buck Showalter created a spreadsheet he posts on the wall that ranks all umpires from the most pitcher-friendly to those whose zone is thinner than a model after a sauna visit.

If an umpire calls a large percentage of strikes, even on balls that seem slightly out of the strike zone, players refer to him as "hunting

for strikes." With a "hunter" behind the plate, hitters will be more aggressive and swing at pitches earlier in the count. If batters know an umpire doesn't hunt, they'll take their normal approach to an at-bat.

Hitters and pitchers who are extremely disciplined can influence an umpire by demonstrating a thorough knowledge of the strike zone. Because umpires realize that players like Joey Votto, Miguel Cabrera, Clayton Kershaw, and "King" Felix Hernandez know the zone so well, they tend to call close pitches in their favor whenever one of these craftsmen is at work. However, if a pitcher is consistently wild or a batter comes to the plate swinging at anything, umpires generally will call the close pitches strikes.

The strike zone continues to be a hot debate, and it may not be resolved for many seasons to come.

Grasping the Designated Hitter Rule

The *designated hitter* (DH) bats for the pitcher throughout the game without taking the field to play defense. Managers can let their pitchers hit, but if they do, they can't use a DH for the entire game. If a *pinch hitter* bats as a substitute for the DH, or if a *pinch runner* replaces the DH on base, the substitute becomes the DH. If a manager puts his DH in the field at some point in the game, the pitcher must bat in place of the substituted defensive player. After this move takes place, the DH role is terminated for that game.

The DH rule currently applies only to the American League or during interleague play, when an American League team is the home team. (For more about interleague play, see Chapter 13.) During the World Series, the DH only applies when the American League representative is the home team.

What if you hit a ball that strikes a fielder?

It depends on how the ball reacts after it bangs into him. On April 5, 1998, Joe broadcast a game between the Arizona Diamondbacks and the San Francisco Giants that treated spectators to an unusual play. With his team down 3-1 in the fourth inning, Giants left fielder Barry Bonds led off the inning with a double off Arizona pitcher Andy Benes. Bonds advanced to third when teammate Jeff Kent grounded out.

Giants first baseman J. T. Snow followed with a line-drive up the middle that appeared to ricochet off the pitcher's mound to Arizona shortstop Jay Bell, who promptly threw Snow out at first base while Bonds scored, or so Bonds thought. With Bonds sitting in the dugout, Diamondbacks skipper Buck Showalter signaled third baseman Matt Williams to retrieve the ball and tag third before another pitch was thrown. Williams complied, and umpire Randy Marsh ruled Bonds out. The inning was over, and the run didn't count.

Marsh ruled Bonds out because, unbeknownst to nearly everyone except the umpire and the Arizona manager, the ball never touched the mound or playing field. It had ricocheted from the pitcher's foot. Snow was out as soon as Bell snared his line drive. Bonds was called out for leaving his base without tagging up (touching the base he occupied) after Bell's catch. (No one can blame Bonds, one of the smartest players in the game, for that. Like nearly everyone else, he was certain the ball had struck the mound before Bell caught it.) Had the ball dropped to the field after colliding with Benes's foot, Bonds would have been safe at home, and the inning would have continued. But because a fielder grabbed it before it touched the field, Snow and Bonds were both retired. A 1-6-6-3-5 double play if you were scoring at home — a combination that you probably won't witness twice in 10,000 games.

Adhering to Baserunning Protocol

BASEBALL SPEAK

Running the bases is much more dangerous than it may appear. Unfortunately, you can be *retired* (called out) on the base path in many, many ways. Chapter 6 offers more details about how to run bases effectively, but here are some basic rules to keep in mind:

- ✔ If a fielder tags you with a live ball while you're off the *bag* (or base), you're called out. However, no one can tag you out if you overrun or overslide first, provided you return immediately to that bag without making a turn toward second.

- ✔ If your teammate hits a ball that touches you in fair territory without first touching or passing any fielder except the pitcher, you're retired. When that happens, the ball is dead, and no other runners can advance or score on the play.

- ✔ If an umpire judges that you have hindered a fielder from making a play, you're called out.

- ✔ If you run the bases in reverse order to confuse the defense (or if you are confused yourself!), you're retired.

Going into reverse gear

You can run the bases backwards, provided you circle them in the proper first-to-home order. New York Mets outfielder Jimmy Piersall did just that in 1963 to celebrate hitting his 100th career home run. However, his manager, Casey Stengel, released him shortly after the stunt, so maybe it's not such a good idea.

✔ If a batted ball forces you to advance to another base, and the fielder possessing the ball tags that base before you reach it, you are called out. This occurs, for example, when you are on first base and the batter hits a ground ball to an infielder; you have no choice but to try to advance. (The following rule explains why.)

✔ Generosity is a virtue, but if you share a base with a teammate while the ball is alive, the defense can tag out the runner who should have advanced to the next base.

✔ If you pass another runner on the base path, you're called out.

✔ When advancing from base to base, you must tag each bag in its proper order, even when you hit a home run. If you miss a base and the defense notices it, they can get you out on an appeal play. (See Appendix A for an explanation of how an appeal play works.)

When you can't stray from the base line

The base line is a direct line running from home plate to first base, from first base to second base, from second base to third base, and from third base back to home plate. Between first and second, and between second and third, the base line isn't marked — but it still exists. Normally, you need not worry about staying near the base line when running the bases. In Chapter 6, you can find out the best way to round first base and go directly to second and how to lead off third base by moving into foul territory away from the base line.

In these and other situations, you're allowed to wander from the base line because no opposing player is pursuing you with the ball. However, when someone is chasing after you with the ball trying to tag you out, you need to stay near the base line. You aren't permitted to stray more than three feet (about a meter) outside the base line to avoid being tagged. If you do, you're called out. Do you think that this base line specification is unfair to runners? Just attend any Little League game, and you'll soon see baserunning chases that convince you of the wisdom of this ruling.

Eyeing the Rules That Govern the Pitcher

Baseball mandates that the pitcher can throw from only two positions: the *set* and the *windup*. The set position is the stance a pitcher holds when he is turned sideways to home plate (facing either first or third base, depending on whether he throws right or left handed)) and has the baseball tucked into his glove. The windup is the motion a pitcher goes into (such as lifting his front leg and pulling his throwing arm back) prior to releasing a pitch. (See Chapter 8 for more details on choreographing a pitch.)

After each pitch, the umpire insists that the catcher promptly throw the ball back to his pitcher. With no runners on base, the pitcher must throw the ball to home plate within 20 seconds of receiving it from either the umpire or the catcher. If the pitcher fails to do so, the umpire may (but seldom does) call a ball.

These sections explain the different rules in greater depth that focus on the pitcher.

Avoiding the balk

With runners on base, after the pitcher goes into his windup or makes any movement associated with delivering the ball to home, the pitcher must not interrupt his motion or the umpire can call a balk. A *balk* occurs when a pitcher tries to catch a runner off base with a pickoff throw after he has started his delivery to the batter. To avoid balking, a pitcher standing on the rubber cannot raise either foot from the ground toward home plate unless he is starting his delivery. The umpire also calls a balk if the pitcher drops the ball while trying to deliver a pitch. A balk does not occur if the pitcher is in his set position when he throws to a base. (See Chapter 8 for more information on how to avoid a balk.)

Warming up

When the pitcher comes to the mound at the start of an inning or when he enters a game in relief, the umpire can allow him no more than one minute to throw eight warm-up pitches. Play is suspended during these warm-ups. An exception to this rule occurs when a pitcher relieves an injured teammate; then, he can take as long as he needs to finish his warm-ups.

The reasoning behind this rule is that unless a pitcher is taking over in an emergency situation, such as an injury to the previous pitcher, he should have been warming up in the *bullpen* (the practice area) prior to taking the field.

Visiting the mound

A manager or his coaches may visit the mound to consult with the pitcher only once each inning. If a manager or coach visits a second time during the inning, the pitcher must leave the game. However, if a manager, coach, or trainer goes to the mound because the pitcher has apparently suffered an injury, the umpire doesn't count it as an official visit. If a coach goes to the mound and removes a pitcher, and the manager then visits the mound to talk to the newly-arrived pitcher, those two visits count as one trip to the mound for that inning.

After a manager or coach leaves the 18-foot circle surrounding the pitcher's rubber, the umpire considers the mound visit officially concluded.

Catchers or fielders can visit the mound to discuss strategy with the pitcher at any point during an inning. Though the rules don't limit the number of these confabs, a good umpire will keep them to a reasonable minimum.

Throwing spitballs (and other pitches that go bump in the night)

Any wet or rough spot on a baseball can make that ball move more than usual — sometimes in unpredictable ways. At one time, a pitcher could touch his lips with his pitching hand while he was on the pitcher's mound. Heck, he could shove his whole hand and the ball into his mouth if they would fit. However, since Major League's spitball ban of 1920, a pitcher cannot touch his mouth as long as he is on the mound. He may not apply any foreign substance (such as mud or petroleum jelly) or spit to his hand, ball, or glove.

Regulations also forbid pitchers from defacing the ball in any way. For instance, some pitchers try to make their breaking balls drop or curve more sharply by nicking them with nails or scratching them with sandpaper. Some pitchers would bring a power saw out to the mound if they could figure out a way to hide it from the umpires.

If the ump catches you throwing a doctored pitch, he can automatically call the pitch a ball even if it passes through the heart of the strike zone. The rules then require him to warn you of the consequences if a second infraction occurs during that game. What happens if you throw another illegal pitch? The ump boots you from the field and the commissioner lightens your wallet with a large fine. You might even earn a suspension.

Immediate ejection is also the penalty if the umpire finds you in possession of a foreign substance on the mound, even if you don't apply it to a pitch (so leave those tubes of hair mousse in your lockers).

You may get away with throwing a pitch close to a batter to back him away from the plate, but deliberately hitting a player with a pitched ball is a no-no. If the umpire decides that a pitcher has intentionally thrown at a batter, he can expel the offender, as well as his manager, from the game even if the ball makes no contact with the batter. Or the umpire may warn the pitchers and the managers of both teams that another such pitch from either side will result in an immediate expulsion. As the Major League's rules note, throwing at a batter's head is "unsportsmanlike and highly dangerous. It should be condemned by everybody."

Knowing an Umpire's Authority

You occasionally see two umpires reach conflicting decisions on the same play. When that happens, the umpire-in-chief (the fellow standing behind the catcher at home plate) gets the final say.

Any time anyone participating in the game — including the managers, coaches, and trainers — violates a rule, the umpire must report the infraction to the commissioner's office within 12 hours. The commissioner then decides what penalties, if any, to impose.

If a manager believes an umpire's decision violates the rules of baseball, he can protest the game to the league. He must declare his protest to the umpire immediately following the disputed decision and before the next play begins. Upon hearing the protest, the commissioner can order the game replayed if he believes the umpire was wrong and that his error adversely affected the protesting team's chances of winning the game. It rarely, if ever, happens, though, even when the league admits the umpire made the wrong call.

The umpire can throw any player, manager, coach, or trainer out of a game if that person's voiced disapproval of a decision is, in the umpire's opinion, excessively violent or profane. Any voiced disapproval over a ball or strike call is grounds for automatic ejection. You can, however, dispute the umpire's "judgment" calls, such as whether a player is safe or out or whether a ball is hit fair or foul. Bumping or making any other violent contact with an umpire is a definite no-no. Most leagues levy severe penalties against players, coaches, or managers who assault any ump. Refer to Chapter 15 for more specifics about the umpires' roles during a game.

Part II
Taking Your Swings — Playing Offense

Knowing the strike zone

Head to www.dummies.com/extras/baseball for how you can help your team by being a better hitter.

In this part...

✔ Shape up your hitting game and discover how to approach hitting *before* the pitcher tosses his first pitch — knowing how to choose the appropriate bat, tailoring your stance, getting comfortable, and giving you the best chance at taking a good swing.

✔ Examine the most important element in hitting — plate discipline — and figure out how to read the pitcher and size up both your own strike zone — and an umpire's.

✔ Understand some important nuances, including how to hit to all fields and smooth out the kinks in your swing to maximize your bat speed.

✔ Check out the small but important ways that you can help your team win, such as bunting (both to sacrifice a runner and to bunt for a base hit) and executing the hit-and-run and the run-and-hit.

✔ Refine the way you accelerate out of the box, take a proper lead, run the bases most efficiently, and slide without risking life and limb.

✔ Discover how to read the pitcher to get a good lead, when and how to steal a base, and how to break up the double play.

Chapter 4

Preparing to Swing the Lumber: Life in the Batter's Box

· ·

· ·

*W*e could talk about hitting for five minutes or five hours without repeating ourselves. Advice on the subject can be as complex as an in-depth explanation of hip rotation or as simple as saying, "See the ball, hit the ball." Ted Williams once said, "Hitting big-league pitching is the most difficult thing to do in sports." Coming from the greatest hitter of the past 60 years, that statement may seem like bragging. However, most athletes who have taken their cuts on a baseball diamond would agree with Williams. Just ask Michael Jordan how hard it is to get good wood on the ball. The greatest basketball player of our time — perhaps of all time — struggled to hit .220 during his season in the minor leagues. Bo Jackson was a football superstar, and as a Major-League baseball player, he was a fine outfielder with great speed, a prodigious arm, and awe-inspiring power. But Jackson's lifetime batting average was a modest .250. Jim Thorpe, undoubtedly the finest athlete in Olympic history, also hit little more than .250 during his six-year stint in the Major Leagues.

What makes hitting so difficult? Geometry, for one thing. As coaches have reminded hitters since baseball's earliest days, "The game is played with a round ball and a round bat, and you have to hit it square." Geography and physics complicate that challenge. Only 60 feet 6 inches (18.4 meters) separate the pitching mound from the batter's box. The average Major-League pitcher throws his fastball 87 miles per hour, which means it takes the average fastball less than two-thirds of a second to travel from the pitcher's hand to your hitting zone. How quick is that? In the time it takes to think the phrase "two-thirds of a second," strike one is already past you.

So unless the hurler is soft-tossing a *knuckle ball,* a hitter has barely an instant to read the pitch. Is the pitcher throwing a *fastball,* a *slider,* a *change-up,* or a *curve?* If it's a fastball, is it a *four-seamer,* a *two-seamer,* or the dreaded split-fingered version? (Read all about these pitches in Chapter 8.) Where will it cross the plate — inside or out, high or low? Can you pull this pitch down the line, or should you hit it to the opposite field? As you make these assessments, you must move your bat into the hitting zone. Of course, as soon as you make contact, you have eight fielders in front of you (and one behind you) committed to transforming the ball you just hit into an out. No wonder the best hitters succeed only about three times out of ten. This chapter gives you the lowdown on improving your chances of hitting the ball and making it safely on base.

Identifying a Hitter's Tools

If you're willing to put in the hours, you can overcome all these obstacles to make yourself a good hitter. How good depends on what you have to work with. To succeed, hitters need:

- **Excellent vision:** As the baseball adage declares, "You can't hit what you can't see." You need strong vision and depth perception to judge a ball's distance, speed, and spin. However, you don't have to have 20/20 vision in both eyes. Many Major-League hitters have excelled while wearing corrective lenses. Michael Tucker, an outfielder for the 1997 Atlanta Braves, was not quite the nearsighted Mr. Magoo without his contacts, but he was close. Despite his poor uncorrected vision, Tucker hit .283 in 1997 while playing excellent defense. Frank Howard wore glasses as an outfielder/first baseman with the Washington Senators during the 1960s and 1970s. He led the American League in home runs twice.

- **Quick reflexes:** After you recognize (or *read*) the pitch, your hand-eye coordination must be sharp enough to get your bat on the ball. The better your reflexes, the longer you can wait on a pitch.

- **Focus:** When you're up at the plate, fans, players, and coaches are yelling at you (and sometimes their words are not encouraging). Planes may be flying overhead, the wind may be swirling objects across your field of vision, the pitcher may have a funky motion, and you may be tempted to think about the error you made in the last inning. You must block out all these distractions and concentrate on the task at hand.

- **Upper body strength:** To swing a wooden bat (which often weighs two pounds or more) with controlled velocity, you must build up your arms, shoulders, chest, and wrists. You also need strong hands. If you have a weak grip, a pitcher can knock the bat right out of your hands.

- ✔ **Courage:** A fastball is a missile that can maim or even kill you. Hitters face that hard reality every time they step up to the plate, but you can't let it rattle you. If you're afraid of the ball, you're going to back off (or *bail out*) any time a pitch comes near you. You won't stay at the plate long enough to get a good look at the ball. You'll never be able to hit if you can't overcome your fear.

- ✔ **Sound strike zone judgment:** Hitters who come to the plate swinging at every pitch handicap themselves. You need to be able to recognize the strike zone while developing the patience and control not to swing at pitches outside it.

- ✔ **Adaptability:** You opened the season crushing inside fastballs. Now the pitchers around the league have gotten the message. (Trust me, they will. FedEx doesn't operate as quickly as the pitchers' grapevine.) So you're suddenly seeing a steady diet of outside breaking stuff. Adjust to the change — or your batting average will plummet.

- ✔ **Hitting hunger:** Some batters get two hits in their first two at-bats and think, at least subconsciously, that they're done for the day. Great hitters are never content. As Stan Musial, the former St. Louis Cardinals outfielder and batting champion, has repeatedly said, "When I got two hits in a game, I came up wanting a third. If I got a third, I had to get a fourth. I never knew when I might go 0 for 4, so I was always *hungry* for more base hits."

That last item is something you either have or you don't, but you can develop the other attributes. We help you work on most of them throughout this chapter.

Holding the Bat

The first thing you should consider when gripping a bat is *to glove or not to glove*. Almost all big-leaguers wear batting gloves — some because it gives them a better hold on the bat, others because they have large endorsement contracts with glove companies. I *didn't* wear a glove when I hit because I liked the feel of the wood against my fingers. (I did, however, wear a golf glove when I was on base to protect my hands while sliding.) Whether you wear batting gloves is a matter of personal preference. If gloves improve your grip, wear them. (Some players prefer substances such as resin or pine tar to improve their grip.) Keep these tips in mind when batting.

Getting a grip

When you hold your bat, your hands should touch so they can work as a unit. Begin by placing your bat handle at the base of the fingers of both hands. Grip the bat with your fingers rather than in your palm; holding it with your palm deprives you of wrist action, flexibility, and bat speed. Align the middle knuckles of your top hand between the middle and lower knuckles of your bottom hand.

Choking up on the bat gave me better control. I would slide my hands an inch or two above the knob of the bat. Many people believe that choke hitters can't generate power, but Ted Williams choked up, and he has over 500 career home runs on his résumé. You *do* sacrifice some power with an extreme choke (five or more inches above the knob). See Figure 4-1 for an illustration of both grips.

If you're strong enough, you can slide your hands down to the knob without surrendering any control; this grip gives you a tad more plate coverage. Some sluggers bury their little fingers beneath the bat knob; they believe doing so helps their wrists and hands to work in better sync. You have to be extremely powerful to do this, though. Most hitters should stick with one of the more conventional grips.

When you're at-bat, hold the bat firmly but don't squeeze it; tension slows down your wrists and hands. Your grip automatically tightens as you swing. Hold the bat more firmly with your bottom hand than with your top one. Your bottom hand pulls your bat through the hitting zone.

As kids, we were told that our bats would break if we hit a ball on the bat label. That's an old wives' tale, but you should keep the label turned away from the pitcher anyway. The grain side of the bat gives you a harder hitting surface.

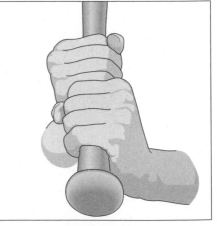

Figure 4-1:
The basic bat grip and choking up.

Illustration by Wiley, Composition Services Graphics

Positioning the bat and your body

Now that you have your bat in your hands, how close should you hold it to your body? Again, let comfort dictate your choice, but it should be no less than 5 inches and no more than 7 inches from your torso (about 13 to 18 centimeters). Holding your hands near your body keeps you on the inside of the ball. If you hold the bat out farther than that, your swing has too large an arc; you lose leverage and find it difficult to coordinate your hip and arm into your swing. If you bring the bat in too close, you restrict your movement and lose bat speed; your swing has a large loop, and it requires a long push to get your bat into the hitting zone. By the time you get the bat where you need it, that fastball is already past you (see Figure 4-2).

Figure 4-2:
Holding your hands too near or too far from your body changes your swing.

Illustration by Wiley, Composition Services Graphics

Hold your hands somewhere between the letters on your uniform front and your shoulders. Your elbows should be away from your body (as shown in Figure 4-3).

Figure 4-3:
The proper way to hold your bat.

Illustration by Wiley, Composition Services Graphics

JOE SAYS

On chicken flaps and other eccentricities

Whenever I brought my arms too close to my body, I tended to uppercut the ball. The result? Too many fly-outs. That habit was tough to break. The late Nellie Fox, a Hall of Fame second baseman and a player/coach when I played with the Houston Astros, suggested I flap my elbow whenever I was at the plate as a reminder to keep my arms away from my torso. I was only supposed to do this for a few days, but the "chicken flap" became part of my hitting routine. It kept my elbows out and also got me ready to hit.

Will flapping your elbows make you a better hitter? If you have the same problem I did, it may. However, rather than emulate my or some other player's quirk, you must develop your own method for getting comfortable at the plate. My Cincinnati Reds teammate Tony Perez — one of the best clutch hitters I ever saw — used to continually regrip his bat. First, the fingers of one hand would open and close on the handle, and then the fingers of the other would do the same. It was as if he were playing a flute as he waited for the pitch. This method was nothing more than a rhythmic device that relaxed Tony while preparing him to hit.

Some players step out of the box after every pitch to windmill their bats. Next time you watch a game, pay attention to the hitters as they enter the batter's box. You'll probably detect a different idiosyncrasy with each player.

The point of all this is that you can do anything you want with the bat *before you start your swing*. However, as you attack the ball, your stride must carry you into your hitting zone. Stan Musial had a peek-a-boo crouch at the plate that made him look like a man peering around a corner (see the following figure). Carl Yastrzemski, the great

Photo courtesy of National Baseball Hall of Fame Library, Cooperstown, N.Y.

Boston Red Sox outfielder and batting champion, stood nearly upright at home — he only slightly flexed his knee and hip — while holding his bat high above his left ear. (Yaz was a left-handed hitter.) He looked like he was ringing a church bell. Musial and Yastrzemski had dissimilar stances, but their strides and hip rotations left them in the same position as they made contact with the ball.

So however you choose to carry your bat to the plate — on your shoulders, close to your body, parallel to the ground — is fine, as long as it allows you to quickly reach your ideal hitting position. And you can't know what impact your quirk has on your swing until you get into the batter's box to practice.

Stepping Up to the Plate

When you come up to hit, the first thing you must decide is where to stand in the batter's box. Placement in the box is a matter of personal preference. Edgar Martinez, former great hitter for the Seattle Mariners, stood so far back in the box he was almost in Tacoma. That stance gave him more time to look over each pitch. Other batters stand in the rear of the box but far from the plate, up in the box and near the plate, or up in the box and far from the plate.

Any number of combinations is possible. I have short arms, so I stood close to the plate. This position gave me a better opportunity to reach strikes on the outside corner. (If your stance doesn't allow you access to those outside pitches, find another one.) Because I had a very quick bat, I felt comfortable standing far up in the batter's box. To discover what serves you best, hit from various positions in the box against live pitching and check out these tips.

Being up-front: The advantages

When you stand at the front of the box (see Figure 4-4), your stride brings you in front of home plate. Anything you hit in front of the plate has a better chance of staying fair. Standing in front also helps you against sinkerball and breaking ball pitchers; you're able to hit the ball before it drops below your swing. If you stand deep in the box against a good sinkerballer, you're giving him an advantage; his ball has more time to sink.

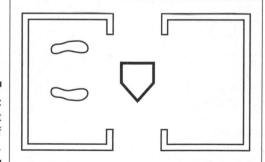

Figure 4-4: Standing at the front of the box.

Illustration by Wiley, Composition Services Graphics

Standing at the front of the box also allows you to hit the curveball before it fully breaks. Even knuckle balls are easier to hit from this location; they have less time to dance. (I used to move as far up in the batter's box as I could against certain breaking ball pitchers; it took their best weapons away from them.)

Fastballs provide your up-front stance with its ultimate test. The closer you are to the pitching mound, the faster pitches reach you at the plate. If you can't handle fastballs from the front of the batter's box, you need to step back.

To develop bat speed and strength, I would swing a lead bat only with my front (right) arm. This exercise strengthens your front side, which pulls the bat through the hitting zone. I would do this 50 times a day during the off-season and 10 times before a game. Your daily regimen should also include 25 full swings with a bat that's heavier than the one you normally use in a game.

Stuck in the middle

Some batters take their swing from the middle of the box (see Figure 4-5). Hitting from the middle gives you a little more time to catch up with the fastball — but curveballs, sinkers, and knucklers also have more time to break. If you have only medium bat speed (something a coach can tell you), this is the place for you (at least until you develop a faster bat).

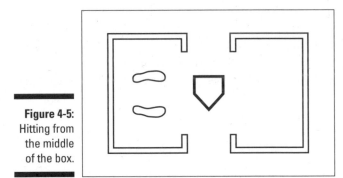

Figure 4-5: Hitting from the middle of the box.

Illustration by Wiley, Composition Services Graphics

Tales from the deep

Obviously, standing deep in the box allows you the maximum time to cope with the fastball. But you have to be a great breaking ball hitter to consistently succeed in this location; you're giving the curve, sinker, and knuckler the best opportunity to work their magic. Because you'll be hitting balls on the plate and the angle of your bat is toward foul territory, their trajectory may carry more of them into foul territory. If you stand deep in the box and far from the plate, you may find it difficult to hit outside pitches (see Figure 4-6).

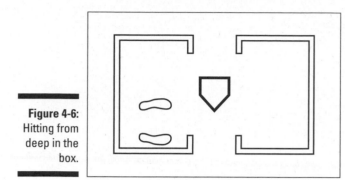

Figure 4-6:
Hitting from
deep in the
box.

Illustration by Wiley, Composition Services Graphics

Up close and personal

The toughest pitch to hit is the ball out and away from you. After getting in the batter's box, swing your bat to make sure you have full plate coverage. Stand close enough to home to reach pitches 4 inches (10 centimeters) off the outside corner. When you're close to the plate, the outside part of it becomes your middle, and you take away a strength from the pitcher. Sure, the pitcher can throw even farther outside, but if you're a disciplined batter you can take those pitches for balls. In the ninth inning of the 1975 World Series final game, I drove in the winning run when Red Sox left-hander Jim Burton threw me a slider that broke down and away. It would have been a perfect pitch *if I had been standing farther off the plate.* Because I was close to the dish, I was able to reach over and hit it into left center field.

Tailoring Your Stance

As a hitter, you can choose from three basic stances:

- ✓ **The open stance:** Your back foot is closer to the plate than your front foot.

- ✓ **The even or square stance:** Both feet are equidistant from the plate.

- ✓ **The closed stance:** Your front foot is closer to the plate than your back foot.

Figure 4-7 illustrates these stances for a right-handed hitter.

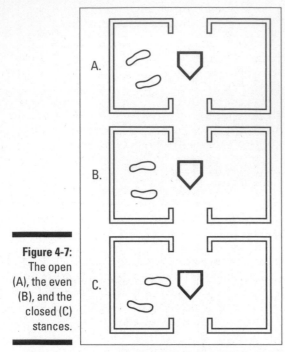

Figure 4-7:
The open
(A), the even
(B), and the
closed (C)
stances.

Illustration by Wiley, Composition Services Graphics

I always preferred the closed stance. Only hitters who can't rotate their hips out of the way properly need a somewhat open stance. (Your coach can tell you whether you have the right hip action.) The open stance frees your upper torso and automatically opens your hips, allowing you to drive your body and hands through the hitting zone while generating bat speed. The open stance also lets you turn your head so it faces the pitcher, which allows you to use both eyes simultaneously.

Everybody rotates away from the ball in order to hit. Open-stance hitters are already a half step away from the plate. They must, therefore, remind themselves not to pull off the pitch (move away from the plate a split second too soon) or they won't be able to hit the ball with any authority. For that reason, most Major Leaguers choose the closed stance or square stance.

Novice hitters should start with an even stance. It helps you keep your weight distributed evenly on the balls of both feet. (Now you know how the stance got its name.) As you gradually develop balance, reduce your stance an inch at a time until you find the stance that generates the most power.

Positioning Your Body

Your shoulders are slightly closed in a closed stance and more squared in the even or open versions. No matter which stance you choose, point your face toward the pitcher's mound so you can see the pitcher with both eyes.

Young hitters often make the mistake of looking out of only one eye. Sometimes they slightly cock their heads to the side so that one eye is closer to the pitcher than the other. This stance alters your depth perception. You need both eyes on a parallel plane if you are going to read the ball's spin and speed as quickly as possible. Tucking your chin behind your shoulder also limits your vision. Keep your head square and still throughout your stride and swing. You may hear broadcasters discuss how a hitter keeps his head down throughout his swing. That's always good policy. Keeping your head down keeps your eyes on the ball. Move your head, and your eyes and body follow — and your swing suffers.

When taking your stance, bend your knees slightly to allow greater freedom of movement. An erect stance restricts your lower body's maneuverability. How far you spread your legs apart is a matter of personal preference. I always felt more balanced with my feet spread slightly more than shoulder width (see Figure 4-8).

Figure 4-8: A balanced batting stance.

Illustration by Wiley, Composition Services Graphics

Crouch for comfort

Bending too much from the top hinders your swing; as you straighten up during your stride, you lose sight of the pitch. Stay in your crouch as you stride. If the pitcher takes a long time between pitches, step out of the batter's box to stretch so you don't become rigid.

Some players, like the former outfielder Rickey Henderson, go into an extremely wide crouch to shorten their strike zone. Rickey, the all-time stolen base king and Hall of Famer, is proof that you can be productive hitting from a wide crouch. My former Cincinnati teammate Pete Rose hit out of a deep crouch with his bat on his shoulder. I don't think young players should copy that stance, but Pete used it to get more base hits than anyone in MLB history. It all comes down to comfort and productivity. I recommend a slight crouch with some flex in the knee and your upper body only slightly tilted toward the plate.

Can you dig it?

You hear a lot about *digging in* at the plate. That term simply means the hitter is planting both feet firmly in the batter's box. Digging in gives you more traction and prevents you from slipping. Power hitters do it all the time because they want to rotate off a firm back foot as their hips open. This position helps them to explode into the hitting zone.

Striding for Power

Try hitting without taking a stride. If you stand still and swing, you can't generate any power. Your stride releases your energy and takes you into the pitch. It helps you pivot while bringing your hips, arms, and shoulders into action. You must hit from a strong front side; your stride ensures that you are successful by allowing you to firmly plant your front foot. To increase your power when hitting, keep reading these sections.

Looking before you stride

When I was first learning how to hit, someone gave me a poem that taught me a valuable lesson about strides. It went

> See the ball before your stride / Let it go if it's outside / If it's a curve and should break down / Jack up and hit it downtown.

This poem reminded me that I had to see the ball before starting my stride. If you move too soon, you're going to swing at the pitcher's arm motion instead of the ball. You won't get too many hits doing that. Always remember that you have more time to see and hit the ball than you think.

Some hitters watch the ball from the moment the pitcher puts it into his glove to start his windup. Don't bother with that because different motions may deceive you. Pitchers can rear back as if they are going to throw the ball through a wall, and then deliver a soft change-up. Or they can give you an easy, rocking-chair motion while throwing something hard and nasty.

Start looking for the ball when the pitcher drops his hand behind him to begin his throw to the plate. A pitcher's motion is like a batter's stance. A lot of idiosyncratic bells and whistles may be at the start of it, but eventually the pitcher has to come to a conventional release point. Concentrate on that point — say, the corner of a right-handed pitcher's right shoulder — because the ball comes out of that slot. As soon as you pick up the ball leaving his hand, react. Stride toward the pitch.

To make sure that you don't move too soon, try this exercise. Take batting practice and instruct the pitcher to occasionally complete his delivery *without throwing the ball.* If you find yourself moving into this phantom pitch, you need to discipline yourself at the plate.

Honing the length of your stride

Pitches lose speed from the moment they leave a pitcher's hand. When you stride toward the pitcher, you help the ball get to you quicker by shortening the distance it has to travel. So your stride should not be longer than your original batting stance. A long stride with a narrow stance also makes your head bob. The pitch seems as if it's jumping in and out of view. If your stance is 8 inches (20 centimeters) wide, make sure your stride is no wider than that.

When you over-stride, your upper body becomes unbalanced. Remember, the only purpose of a stride is to get your lower body into hitting position. Because your eyes are focused on the ball (at least they should be!), don't move your head or upper torso toward the pitch; you don't want to throw off your field of vision. Instead, stride into the ball with your lower body. After you stride, your head should still be in the middle of your body rather than leaning forward or backward. A hitter should glide and pop, not leap and sweep.

JOE SAYS

As you move toward the pitch, step away from your hands, or push your hands back, to let your body move forward (see Figure 4-9). If you take your hands with you as you stride, you lose bat speed and power. Keep your hands and shoulders in the same position they held in your stance. I started my stance with my hands at the end of my left armpit, just off my shoulder. They would still be in the same position after I took my stride.

Figure 4-9:
Beginning
your stride.

Illustration by Wiley, Composition Services Graphics

Troubleshooting your stride

You know that your stride is too narrow and that you need to lengthen it when

- ✔ Your front side doesn't feel strong.
- ✔ Your legs collapse in mid-stride.

You know your stride is too wide when

- ✔ You can't generate any hip action.
- ✔ The ball seems as if it's jumping.

Players who overstride can draw a line or lay a bat across the batter's box during practice as a reminder not to stride beyond it. I always thought the best remedy for overstriding was concentration. If you focus, you can eliminate most mistakes from your game.

Dealing with the Strike Zone

The baseball rulebook says the strike zone is a rectangle the width of home plate, extending from the top of the batter's knees to the letters across his uniform jersey. (See Chapter 3 for a diagram of the strike zone.) In practice, however, every player and umpire has his or her interpretation of the strike zone. Most umpires have a strike zone that starts at the bottom of the player's knee and finishes no higher than the top of his belt buckle. Rarely does an ump call a strike on a pitch at the letters.

Because the strike zone is supposed to have the same width as the plate, you wouldn't expect to see too much variance there. Yet some umpires call strikes on pitches 6 inches (15 centimeters) off the plate (mostly pitches on the outer edge, rarely inside). And some umps never call a strike on any ball that just nicks the plate's corners.

When you take batting practice, swing at pitches in your legally defined strike zone; you can adjust to an individual umpire's zone after you determine what it is. The best hitters take most of their swings at pitches in the strike zone. Some players are so strong that they can hit a pitch that is 1 or 2 inches off the plate. However, these so-called "bad-ball" hitters are rare. Discipline yourself to swing only at strikes.

To get a sense of your strike zone without swinging a bat, play catch with someone. Stand 60 feet (18.3 meters) apart (nearly the distance between home plate and the pitcher's mound), and keep your throws between each other's chest and knees. Move your tosses up and down within this area. Because you are facing the thrower dead-on, you can immediately detect from the ball's trajectory whether it's a strike or a ball. (For more on the strike zone, see Chapter 3.)

After you know your strike zone, find out where your hot hitting spots are within it. In his book *The Science of Hitting* (a must-read for every ballplayer), Ted Williams broke down his strike zone in a diagram, which demonstrated that he batted .400 when he hit pitches down the heart of the plate but only .220 when he hit pitches that were low and outside. This diagram reminded Ted that he shouldn't swing at those low, outside pitches unless he already had two strikes and the ball was over the plate. All athletes must develop that same kind of self-awareness. You can never be a good hitter or player unless you know your strengths and weaknesses. If you aren't a good low ball hitter, lay off that pitch unless you have two strikes.

Judging the First Pitch

Should you swing or take the first pitch you see in an at-bat? It depends on the situation. I remember a minor-league game I played in Durham, North Carolina. My team was facing some rookie pitcher, and I opened the first inning by popping up on his first pitch. When I came back to the bench, my manager, Billy Goodman, a former American League batting champion, asked me, "What does that pitcher have?" Well, I didn't know what the pitcher had other than a fastball, and I couldn't even tell you how hard he threw that. I hadn't seen enough of his pitches. And that was Billy's point: The first time you face a pitcher you don't know, *take* as many pitches as you can. Find out how his curve ball breaks, which way his slider moves. Does he have a change-up? Does he throw every pitch from the same angle?

When you face pitchers you're familiar with, however, there are no hard rules about swinging or not swinging at the first pitch. In that situation, I always went to the plate looking to hit the first good pitch I saw. If it came on the pitcher's first offering, I swung. However, I invariably *took* (didn't swing at) a lot of first pitches simply because so many of them were thrown out of the strike zone.

Chapter 5

Hitting Like a Major Leaguer

. . . .

In This Chapter

▶ Making contact with the ball

▶ Hitting the ball where you want

▶ Bunting and moving runners

▶ Practicing and troubleshooting your swing

▶ Taking some advice from Rusty Staub

. . . .

After the pitch leaves the pitcher's hand, your intention may be to hit the ball and hit it far. On the other hand, you may want to bunt, either for a base hit or to sacrifice a runner. And although you may already know how to prepare and wait for the pitch, we show you how to maintain your stance and plate discipline and avoid falling into bad habits. In short, in this chapter we explain how to practice hitting the right way.

Slapping Down or Cutting Up: Two Approaches to Hitting

Almost everyone agrees that the ideal swing starts about armpit high and levels out as your bat comes to the ball. How much it levels out is a point of divergence.

Some instructors tell you to hit slightly down or even chop at the ball. (Ted Williams has told me that hitters can't hit down on the ball; they can only hit the ball's top half.) When I was playing, Matty Alou, a center fielder with the Pittsburgh Pirates, won a batting title (.342 in 1966) and posted a .307 life-time batting average by slapping the ball on the ground. Matty had a slender, almost frail physique. Power was never going to be his game, so his hitting style suited him perfectly.

The King of Swing, Ted Williams, took the opposite approach from Alou. Ted's swing ended with a slight, upward arc. His swing permitted him to hit for power without hurting his batting average (.344 lifetime). Ted still preaches the slight uppercut swing to every hitter he meets. He persuaded Tony Gwynn, the San Diego Padres outfielder and eight-time National League batting champion, to try it in 1997. Gwynn had his best all-around season at the age of 37; he won another batting title and drove in more than 100 runs and slugged over .500 for the only time in his career. Yet he still managed to bat a league-leading .372, so he didn't sacrifice any base hits.

I'm in the Williams camp. Batters who hit the ball hard are going to put more runs on the board than those who don't. Runs, not hits or batting averages, win ballgames. If you hit down on the ball, it is difficult for you to drive it for doubles or home runs. Keep your swing level; and if you stay behind the ball, your swing will have a slight upward arc as your body rotates into the pitch.

Making Contact

Don't swing as soon as the pitcher releases the ball; wait until you recognize the pitch (its spin and speed) before attacking it. Cock your body with your stride and take that step away from your hands. As you go after the pitch, uncoil everything. Pivot forward, opening your hips as you transfer your weight from back foot to front. Brace your front leg. Bend your rear leg while pivoting your back foot. You know you have shifted your weight correctly if your rear toe ends up pointing directly downward (see Figure 5-1).

Figure 5-1:
The anatomy of making contact.

Illustration by Wiley, Composition Services Graphics

During all this time, your hands and arms direct the bat's movement. Keep your elbows close to your body so that the bat travels in a tight circle. (Your hands and arms don't stay close to your body; good extension creates more bat speed.) Your bottom hand should pull the bat into the hitting zone while your top hand pushes and guides it (see Figure 5-2). The back surface of the bat should rest against your top hand's palm.

Figure 5-2:
Your hands
as you make
contact.

Illustration by Wiley, Composition Services Graphics

Your swing should bring your hands and arms in front of the plate with your bat trailing slightly behind for leverage — think of swinging an axe from the side. Make sure your wrists are firm as the bat moves into the hitting zone. Try to see the bat making contact with the ball. (You probably won't be able to, but just the attempt ensures that you're watching the ball throughout your swing.)

Remember that you want to hit the ball in front of the plate so it has a better chance of staying fair. As you finish your swing, the bat should make an almost complete circle around your upper body; most of your weight should be against your front foot.

Fine-Tuning Your Swing

Depending on a pitch's location, you can make small adjustments to your swing:

- **On pitches inside:** Rotate your hips out of the way quickly so that you can get the bat out in front faster. When you hit an inside pitch, the barrel of the bat should cover the inside of the plate.

- **On pitches outside:** Do the opposite of what you do with inside pitches. Keep your hips closed and go to the ball with your upper body. Try to drive the ball to the opposite field (to left field if you're left-handed, to right field if you're a righty).

- **On low pitches:** You shouldn't have to bend to hit a low strike. Give your swing slightly more arc as you go down to get the pitch.

- **On high pitches:** Many coaches tell you to get on top of the ball, but you can develop bad habits if you take that advice to an extreme. Because your hands should be at the top in your stride just before you start swinging, simply stay level (or high) a little longer and then hit through the ball.

- **When the pitcher has two strikes against you:** In this situation, you have to swing at anything near the plate. You can't count on the umpire calling a ball if the pitch is only an inch or so out of the strike zone. Shorten your stride and cut down on your swing by choking up another half-inch or so.

Following Through

Conventional baseball wisdom holds that the follow-through (shown in Figure 5-3), which occurs after the ball leaves your bat, is the last essential part of your swing. Some coaches tell you that if you don't have the proper follow-through, you can't hit the ball with power. It's true that concentrating on continuing your swing after the point of contact helps you to drive *through* the ball. But I think that people who emphasize the importance of follow-through have things backward. The reason you're not driving the ball with power is because you're not executing one or more of the other elements of your swing that produce a good follow-through. Following-through ensures that you hit *through* the ball, not *to* the ball.

By itself, a good follow-through doesn't help you hit. Why? Because the ball has left your bat! If you've done all the things we've talked about, your swing has already accomplished its purpose. A good follow-through results from properly executed mechanics; it is a finish, important only to the batter, not to the ball. A poorly balanced follow-through may tell you your swing is off, but the weak pop-up you just hit to the catcher already let you know that.

Illustration by Wiley, Composition Services Graphics

Figure 5-3:
The classic follow-through.

Going to All Fields

Being able to hit the ball to all fields is important. Keep the following in mind to master this skill:

- **Hit the ball up the middle or to the opposite field:** If a pitch is thrown away from you, hit it to the opposite field (right field if you're right-handed, left field if you're a lefty). If a pitch travels down the heart of the plate, smack it up the middle of the diamond. If the ball is thrown inside, jerk (or pull) it into left field if you're a right-hander or into right field if you're a lefty.

- **Pull the ball:** Hit the ball early enough so that the bat meets the ball in front of you. Right-handed hitters pull the ball to the left side; left-handers pull to the right. If you're using a closed stance, you're going to naturally pull a lot of balls. (See Chapter 4 for information on your stance.) The more closed your stance, the more you pull the ball. Crowd the plate as much as possible. This position expands the area from which you can pull. Make sure to plant your back foot firmly because you want something stationary to drive from. Planting your back foot also gives your swing more arc. Don't uppercut the ball; let your body, stride, and swing to give the ball power. As you start your swing, shift your weight to your front foot. This shifting keeps your bat level in the hitting zone for a longer period of time. Want to hit for more power? Keep your weight back a little longer.

As you gain experience, you may discover whether you're predominantly a *spray hitter* (a player who hits to all fields, such as the Tigers' Miguel Cabrera, who won the American League Triple Crown in 2012 — the first time any player had done so in 43 years) — or a *pull hitter* (a slugger like Pedro Alvarez). See Figure 5-4 for an illustration.

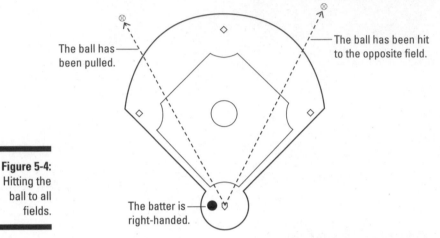

The ball has been pulled.

The ball has been hit to the opposite field.

Figure 5-4:
Hitting the ball to all fields.

The batter is right-handed.

Illustration by Wiley, Composition Services Graphics

I started my big-league career as a spray hitter but developed into a pull hitter as I got stronger. However, as a pull hitter, I could still slap a hit to the opposite field when the situation demanded it. A good spray hitter can pull the ball down the line when he needs an extra-base hit. The bottom line is you want to be as complete a hitter as possible.

Analyzing the Pitcher

Most hitters don't keep written notes on pitchers; they keep mental books documenting how pitchers have come at them in the past. If a pitcher has been unsuccessful trying to get you out with inside fastballs but has been burying you with outside breaking pitches, you can assume he's going to keep throwing those curves. However, you can't necessarily establish a pitching pattern based on any one game. Maybe the pitcher's fastball was sluggish the night he never tried to bust it by you inside. He may have had an unusually wicked curve working that evening. The next time you face him, if his heater is hopping, he may get you out with fastballs inside all night. You may not even see his curveball. So you have to discover what a pitcher has working for him on game day.

JOE SAYS

I usually watched the opposing pitcher warm up in the bullpen to see what pitches he was throwing for strikes. Generally, if a pitcher can't control his slider or curve in the bullpen, he won't be able to control them in the game for at least an inning or two. Take those pitches for balls until he proves he can get them over the plate.

The Dying Art of Bunting

When you *bunt,* hold your bat in the hitting zone and let the ball make contact with it. The idea is to deaden the ball so that the base runners can advance (or you can get to first) while the opposing fielders run in to make a play. There comes a time in every baseball season when anyone — even hulking sluggers like Chris Davis or Adam Dunn — should bunt. For example, say you're playing a game that decides whether you or your opponent clinches a championship. You come to bat with the winning run on first and nobody out in the bottom of the ninth inning. I don't care how many home runs you hit all season, your job is to bunt that runner to second base. Bunts can win ballgames, so everyone who swings a bat should know how to lay them down.

If you're a pitcher, being able to bunt is very important, even if they play in a league that allows designated hitters. Depending on how many substitutions are made during a game, pitchers can be called on to hit even in designated hitter leagues. (For more on this rule, refer to Chapter 3.) Or you may play an interleague game in the home park of a team whose rules don't provide for a designated hitter. These sections help you master the skill of bunting.

In the fourth inning of the second game of the 1997 World Series between the Cleveland Indians and Florida Marlins, Cleveland pitcher Chad Ojea — who had never batted in the Major Leagues because of the designated hitter rule — bunted two teammates to second and third. It was a crucial play. A two-run single then broke open the game, which the Indians eventually won. Had Ojea failed to get the bunt down — or, worse, bunted into a double play — the outcome may have been different.

Choosing your bunting stance

The most commonly used bunting stance is the *pivot.* Take your normal stance at the plate while waiting for the pitch. As the ball comes to the plate, pivot your upper body toward the pitch while keeping your feet in their stance position (see Figure 5-5).

Figure 5-5:
An ideal
bunting
stance.

Illustration by Wiley, Composition Services Graphics

The pivot has several advantages:

- ✔ You can flow into a pivot quickly, maintaining an element of surprise.

- ✔ In the event of a fake bunt — where you "show" bunt to pull in the infielders and then swing away to drive the ball past them — the pivot allows you to easily resume a standard batting stance.

- ✔ With a pivot stance, getting out of the path of errant pitches is easier.

The *squared-stance* is your other bunting option — and perhaps the best option for players just starting out. Bring your feet parallel to home plate and each other while keeping them shoulder-width apart (see Figure 5-6). This stance gives you better plate coverage and a longer look at the ball than the pivot, but it also has its drawbacks. You become more vulnerable to being hit by a pitch, you risk stepping out of the batter's box (in which case the umpire may call you out), and, because you have to get set in this position early, you decrease your chances of surprising the opposition. I prefer the pivot, but you should adopt whichever position is most comfortable for you.

Figure 5-6:
The squared-stance bunt.

Whether you pivot or square around to bunt, make sure you drop into a slight crouch and square your shoulders toward the pitcher. Shift your weight forward as you stand on the balls of your feet. Hold the bat handle firmly with your bottom hand so you can control it, but don't squeeze the handle or you may hit the ball too hard. Slide your top hand up near the bat label. Pinch the barrel with your fingers and thumb, your thumb on top. This action shapes the hand into a U that absorbs any impact when the ball strikes your bat. It also protects your fingers (see Figure 5-7).

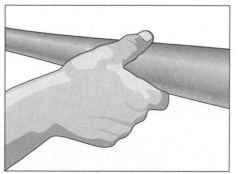

Figure 5-7:
Holding the bat for the bunt.

Many bunters hold their bats parallel to the ground while waiting for the pitch. I think it is better to hold the top of the bat barrel slightly higher than the handle. This strategy keeps you on top of the ball, which is where the bunter has to be. If you come up underneath the pitch, you pop it up. If you hit the ball dead center, you produce a soft line drive that can be converted into a double play.

Hold the bat near the top of your strike zone so you know that any pitch over your bat is a ball. This prevents you from offering at high pitches, which are the hardest to bunt. Try to bunt a low pitch. Watch the ball make contact with the bat in front of you and the plate. Give with the ball, don't push it. You should experience the sensation of "catching" the ball with your bat and guiding it to its destination. Let your bottom hand direct the bat's angle.

Bunting into a sacrifice

With the *sacrifice bunt,* the bunter advances the base runners while giving up a chance for a base hit. With a runner on first, bunt toward the area between the mound and the first baseman. With a runner on second or runners on first and second, bunt toward the third baseman to bring him off the bag (see Figure 5-8).

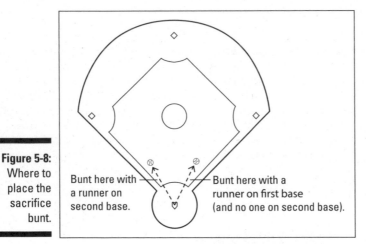

Figure 5-8: Where to place the sacrifice bunt.

Bunt here with a runner on second base.

Bunt here with a runner on first base (and no one on second base).

Illustration by Wiley, Composition Services Graphics

Running the squeeze play

The *squeeze play* is a sacrifice bunt with a runner on third base. If a manager calls for a squeeze play, it's usually during the later innings of a close game with less than two outs. On a *safety squeeze,* the runner breaks for home only after you drop your bunt on the infield. If the bunt isn't good, the runner stays at third. As the bunter, your job is to push the ball away from the pitcher and toward first or third base.

The *suicide squeeze* is a riskier play. It requires the runner to dash toward home plate as the ball leaves the pitcher's hand. *He is coming home no matter what kind of bunt you drop.* You can't take the pitch even if it's out of the strike zone. You must bunt the ball somewhere.

Don't be too finicky about placement. With the runner bearing down on home, just bunt the ball to the ground in fair territory, and you drive in a run. Even if you bunt it foul with less than two strikes on you, the worst that can happen is the runner gets sent back to third. If you don't make contact with the ball, the catcher has the runner dead at the plate (which is why it's called the *suicide* squeeze).

Bunting for hits

To successfully bunt for a hit, you must catch the opposition unaware. This is where the pivot gives you an advantage: It allows you to deceive the infielders longer than the squared-around stance. To bunt for a hit, you should be in motion as the bat makes contact with the ball. You should also grip the bat a little more firmly than you did for the sacrifice.

Left-handed hitters use *drag bunts,* so named because the bunter appears to drag the ball along the first base line as he runs toward first (see Figure 5-9). I beat out a drag bunt to get a hit in the seventh game of the 1975 World Series.

Figure 5-9:
Brett Butler executes the drag bunt.

Photo courtesy of National Baseball Hall of Fame Library, Cooperstown, N.Y.

To execute the drag bunt, shift your weight onto your right foot as you pivot and step toward first base. Hold the bat solidly with its head pointed toward third. Don't pull back the bat or the ball will go foul. You should be moving into your second stride as you make contact with the ball. With your running start, you should beat out the bunt, if it stays fair (see Figure 5-10).

Figure 5-10:
The drag
bunt.

Illustration by Wiley, Composition Services Graphics

Right-handers and left-handers can execute *push* or *dump* bunts for base hits. If you bat right-handed, start with your weight on your right (the rear) foot. As you move to bunt the ball, quickly shift your weight forward into your left foot. Push the ball past the pitcher toward the hole between first and second. Run immediately after making contact. If you're a lefty hitter, reverse your weight shift and tap the ball down the third base line. Run immediately after making contact.

Faking the bunt

You can fake a bunt when a teammate is trying to steal a base. A successful decoy may get the infielders moving in the wrong direction. When you pull back the bat, you force the catcher to stay back so it takes him longer to get to the ball. You can also fake a bunt, pivot back to your hitting stance, and take a short, easy swing (a *swinging bunt*) to slash or chop the ball past the infielders as they mistakenly charge toward home. Square around when you're attempting to help the base stealer; use the pivot stance if you're using the ruse to get a base hit.

Executing the Hit-and-Run

As the batter on a hit-and-run play, your primary responsibilities are to protect the runner and to hit the ball on the ground. Swing and make contact with the pitch, no matter where it's thrown. If the pitch is out of the strike zone, lunge at it and try to get a piece of the ball. The runner takes off without a base-stealing lead, so if you miss that pitch, the catcher will have little difficulty throwing him out. If you hit a line drive at a fielder with the runner moving, it's virtually an automatic double play.

Take your usual swing, but hit slightly down on the ball. You may hit the ball through an area vacated by an infielder who moves to cover second base against the runner breaking from first. The manager usually initiates the play with one or no outs. However, a veteran hitter, suspecting the opposition is going to pitch him a certain way, can call the play with a sign to his base runner.

Turning the Run-and-Hit

The run-and-hit is generally called with a fast runner at first. The play is similar to the hit-and-run, but the hitter's task is less specific. The runner breaks for second after the pitcher commits to throwing the ball toward home. The runner should approach this like a straight steal. You're not obligated to swing at the pitch unless it's a strike (which is why the runner should be fast — if you take the pitch, he has to steal second). You can also put the ball in play anywhere rather than having to hit through the right side of the infield. With his running start, the base runner should be able to get to third on any ball hit out of the infield. An *extra-base hit* (anything more than a single) should score him from first.

Walking Aggressively

You can help your team by getting a base on balls, but you shouldn't go to the plate looking to draw a walk; you may lose your aggressiveness. Instead, work the count against the pitcher by expanding and contracting the strike zone according to the count.

For example, I was a pull-hitter, so I preferred to hit the ball inside. If the first pitch to me was a ball, I shaved 2 inches (5 centimeters) off the outside portion of my strike zone. The next pitch could be a strike, but I wouldn't swing at it if it were on the outer edge of the plate. If it *was* a strike, I'd expand my zone by 2 inches (but I'd never let it become larger than the umpire's strike zone). However, if the ump called it ball two, I'd cut another 2 inches from the outside of my strike zone. On a three-ball and one-strike count, my strike zone would be about half its normal width: from the middle of the plate in. To get me out, the pitcher now had to throw two straight strikes rather than one. That 3–1 pitch had to be exactly where I wanted it, or I wasn't swinging. If the pitcher came inside where I was looking, I could drive that ball a long way. If he threw a strike on the outside corner, I still had another crack at him. Ball four would put me on first base. All the percentages were working in my favor. On a 3–2 count, I'd expand the strike zone out again and protect more of the plate. By altering my strike zone on each pitch, I increased my chances of drawing walks while remaining aggressive at the same time.

Getting the Most Out of Batting Practice

Batting practice is usually divided into rounds. On most of the teams I played for, we would take ten swings in the first round, seven in the second, five in the third, four in the fourth, three in the fifth, and one in the last. Use your first round of batting practice to get loose. Start by laying down two bunts, one as a sacrifice and the other for a base hit. Then work on your swing.

This first round is essentially a warm-up. You're getting comfortable with your timing, stance, and stride while working on your batting eye. Don't try to kill the ball. A lot of hitters are playing *long ball* (trying to hit a home run) when they take batting practice. They're not working on anything in particular; they're just trying to see who can hit the ball farthest. That's a waste of time, especially if you aren't a home-run hitter. Just make contact and aim to hit the ball through the middle.

Starting with the second round, you should be simulating game conditions. Work on every aspect of your hitting. Try to pull the ball on one pitch and hit it up the middle on another. Poke one to the opposite field. Then let a swing rip without caring where the ball goes. Do this on every round.

If you want to play some long ball, do it on your last swing. After taking your last practice swing, trot around the bases to keep loose while practicing your left turns.

Working with Your Batting Practice Pitcher

During batting practice, have the pitcher throw you nothing but fastballs in the first round so that you can get your timing. Then have the pitcher work in some curves, sliders, and change-ups. If you take 30 swings, 8 of them should be against breaking balls. Facing a knuckle-baller in tonight's game? If your pitcher can throw a knuckler, ask to see some of those, too.

You may discover that pitches in a certain location are giving you trouble. Ask the batting practice pitcher to throw to that spot so you can work on them. Usually you know what the pitcher is going to throw. However, every so often you should take a round in which the pitcher can throw any pitch to any spot at any time without telling you in advance. This element of surprise helps hone your concentration and prepares you for actual game conditions.

Considering Other Practice Tips

Besides facing live pitching during batting practice, you can do a number of things outside of the actual games to improve your hitting. Here are some of my favorites.

✔ **Hitting from a batting tee:** Hitting off the tee forces you to concentrate on hitting a particular spot on the ball. It helps to prevent you from *bailing out* (pulling away from the pitch) while quickening your bat.

I used one throughout my career. Adjust the tee's height (see Figure 5-11) and set its position so that you are hitting the ball inside, outside, or down the middle of your strike zone. No matter which side you choose, always set the tee up in front of the plate.

Figure 5-11: The batting tee is a great way to practice.

Illustration by Wiley, Composition Services Graphics

- **Swinging in front of a full-length mirror:** I'm not advocating narcissism here. Swinging in front of a mirror lets you check your entire stance and stride.

- **Playing pepper:** In *pepper,* the batter stands no more than 10 feet (3 meters) opposite several fielders who are lined up side by side. One fielder throws the ball; the batter taps it back. (Don't take a full swing or you may decapitate someone.) The fielder who fields that ball quickly tosses it back toward the hitter, who taps it again. And so on. This game teaches you to keep your eye on the ball and make contact.

- **Working with grips and rollers:** You need strong hands and wrists to hit. Use handgrips and wrist rolls to strengthen them. You can also squeeze a ball of putty to develop your grip.

- **Developing your hand-eye coordination:** I used to punch a speed bag to develop my hand-eye coordination. Playing catch is also great practice. (Playing catch improves your fielding, but learning how to gauge the speed of the ball also helps you at the plate.) Play paddleball, tennis, racquetball, or any sport that demands quick reactions and excellent hand-eye coordination. Table tennis is an excellent choice because the ball moves so quickly toward you and you have to hit it out front, which is precisely what you have to do with a baseball.

Troubleshooting Your Batting

You can work on specific problems during batting practice. Here are some common hitting flaws that often lead to slumps and some suggestions for correcting them:

- **Hitting off your heels:** If you have your weight back on your heels, your body and bat move away from the plate as you swing. Outside pitches and off-speed stuff may give you trouble. You won't be able to hit with any power. **Remedy:** Concentrate on keeping your weight on the balls of your feet while you stride toward the pitcher.

- **Chopping:** Slumping, novice hitters often chop down at the ball just to make contact. Swinging in this manner decreases your hitting area. Also, you can't drive the ball with this swing; you simply hit a lot of grounders (mostly for outs). **Remedy:** Make sure that you transfer your weight properly. When you transfer your weight to your front foot, your bat remains level. Keep your weight on your back foot, drop your rear shoulder (you can't chop with your shoulder down), and take your usual swing.

- **Uppercutting:** When you *uppercut* the ball, you raise your front shoulder while dropping your rear shoulder and dipping your back knee. Batters who uppercut tend to strike out a lot. You can also forget about hitting high pitches with any authority. Raising your front shoulder moves your head out of its level plane, which prevents you from seeing the ball well. **Remedy:** Uppercutters keep their weight on their back foot too long, so level your shoulders and make sure you transfer your weight from front to back. Finish your swing with a slightly upward arc, but avoid any exaggerated uppercutting.

- **Hitching:** If you have a *hitch,* you're dropping your hands just before you swing. A hitch is okay, as long as you can get your hands in good hitting position before the ball arrives. Frank Robinson had a hitch; he dropped his hands below his belt, but he always got them back in time to hit. The last time I checked, his plaque was in the Hall of Fame. Unfortunately, too many hitters compensate for their hitches with rushed, upward swings. This hitch produces the same poor results as an extreme upper-cut. **Remedy:** Keep your hands level and still.

- **Locking the front hip:** Locking your front hip makes it impossible to transfer the weight from your rear foot to your front foot during your swing. You can't pivot properly. This fault significantly decreases your power. **Remedy:** Open your stance and concentrate on stepping toward the pitcher.

- **Lunging:** Batters who *lunge* at the ball step forward toward the pitcher too early. This misstep throws off your timing, power, and bat control. Hank Aaron would occasionally lunge with his upper body, but he could drive the ball because he always kept his hands back. **Remedy:** Be patient. Wait until you read the pitch before you swing. Make sure your stride is no longer than your original stance. *Keep your hands back.*

- **Bobbing your head:** If you bob or turn your head, you lose sight of the ball for a second. When you pick the ball up again (*if* you pick it up again), it is either almost past you or appears to be jumping at you. **Remedy:** Keep your head level and still throughout your stance, stride, and swing. If your stride is making your head bob, shorten it. Remember, your stride should be no longer than your stance.

- **Stepping in the bucket:** *Stepping in the bucket* is another way of saying you're striding away from the pitch. The uneven weight distribution results in a loss of power. Because you're moving away from the plate, you can't hit the outside pitch. **Remedy:** Close your stance and concentrate on striding toward the pitcher.

Some thoughts on slumps

If you go into a slump, take extra batting practice and focus on the hitting fundamentals that I describe in this chapter. Make sure your hands are properly positioned. Are they working together as a unit? Have a coach or teammate observe whether you're over-striding. Practice hitting the ball back through the middle of the diamond. Hitting the ball up the middle prevents you from uppercutting, pulling off the pitch, or hitting it too soon.

If practice doesn't seem to help, take a few days off. You may simply be fatigued. Remember that slumps are inevitable; there isn't a single Hall of Famer who didn't experience them. Babe Ruth was one of the greatest offensive forces baseball has ever produced; he hit .118 in the 1922 World Series. Try to remain confident and optimistic. If you've hit before, you will hit again, so don't lose your aggressiveness. In 1976, I batted .000 in the National League Championship Series against the Philadelphia Phillies. I didn't get a hit or a run batted in (RBI). However, in the World Series that immediately followed, I hit .333 with one home run, three runs scored, and two RBIs in four games. (See photo below.)

Photo courtesy of National Baseball Hall of Fame Library, Cooperstown, N.Y.

Overcoming the Fear of Getting Hit

Some batters stride away from the pitch because they're afraid of being hit by the ball. To be successful, batters must be aggressive. If you can't overcome your fear, you won't be able to hit. I can't tell you how not to be afraid, but perhaps I can calm your concerns with a few facts:

- ✔ **It hurts only for a little while.** Many young players are afraid of getting hit by the ball because it has never happened to them before. They imagine the experience to be much more painful than it actually is. When batters do get hit, it's usually in a fleshy spot. Unless you've broken something (which rarely happens), the pain subsides quickly.

- ✔ **Pitchers don't often hit batters.** I averaged around 600 plate appearances a season and stood way up front in the batter's box and close to the plate. Yet a pitch rarely hit me more than twice a year. Many of those pitches just grazed my uniform. Although pitches have solidly struck me, I was never injured so badly that I had to leave a ballgame or miss any playing time. Ground balls have hit me in the face during fielding practice (is that embarrassing!), but I've never been hit in the face by a pitch.

- ✔ **If your mechanics are sound, you can get out of the way.** Muhammad Ali, the great former heavyweight-boxing champion, once said, "The punch that knocks you out is the one you don't see." Batters should remember that. If you keep your eyes (both of them!) on the ball, it's hard to get hit by a pitch, especially in the head. Your head is the easiest part of your body to move out of harm's way.

- ✔ **Batting helmets work.** Ron Cey, the former third baseman of the Los Angeles Dodgers, got hit in the head by a Goose Gossage fastball during the 1981 World Series. That's like taking a bazooka shell off the old noggin. However, Cey's batting helmet absorbed nearly the entire impact. He not only played the next game, he hit a home run. The moral: Never step up to the plate without wearing your helmet.

However, don't let the helmet give you a sense of false confidence. Getting hit in the head is dangerous and painful. To help prevent this, turn or roll your body away from a pitch at head-level. Besides, if you're going to be hit, your backside is the least uncomfortable place, compared to the ribs or mid-section.

Postscript: Some advice for pinch hitters from Rusty Staub

When your manager asks you to come off the bench cold and go to the plate in a critical situation, he's handing you one of the most difficult assignments in baseball. Pinch-hitting is a specialized skill. I rarely pinch-hit more than ten times in any one season, so I've enlisted an expert to give us some advice on the subject. My good friend and former Houston Astros teammate Rusty Staub wasn't just a great pinch hitter; he was a great hitter, period. He had a disciplined eye, superb bat speed, and excellent balance at the plate. During his career, Rusty amassed 2,716 base hits, 292 home runs, and 1,486 runs batted in while compiling a .279 lifetime batting average. He drove in 100 or more runs three times.

As a pinch hitter for the New York Mets during his final three seasons, Rusty was the top of the line. He led the National League in pinch hits in 1983 and 1984. During the 1983 season, he tied an MLB record with eight consecutive pinch hits; his 24 pinch hits that year also drove in 25 runs. That's delivering in the clutch. So when Staub talks about pinch-hitting, he's like Smith-Barney on investing; we all have to listen.

"More than anything else, a pinch hitter has to be emotionally strong. That season I tied the Major-League record for consecutive pinch hits, people forget that I was 0-for-April. I did walk a few times, but that didn't ease my frustration. It hurt because there were a couple of games we could have won if I had come through. And it's not as though you know you're coming back at the pitchers the following day like you do when you play regularly. A pinch hitter might go four or five games before he gets another at-bat. So you can't let your failures eat at you.

"When you are primarily a pinch hitter, you don't get to take as many batting practice swings as the regulars. Come to the park a little earlier and take extra b.p. (batting practice) as often as you can. Once the game starts, study that opposing starting pitcher intensely because you may be facing him in a later inning. What is working for him today? What is the catcher calling, and what does the pitcher seem to be shaking off? What sort of strike zone is the umpire giving him? If the umpire is giving him the outside of the plate, you have to adjust, not the ump. Just look at what happened during the (1997 National League) playoffs between Atlanta and Florida. You had that game where Eric Gregg was calling strikes on pitches way outside all day. What do you do as a hitter? Complain throughout the game while you go 0-for-4? If you're smart, you move up on the plate and make the pitcher try to get you out inside.

"You should also talk to your teammates after they take their swings against a pitcher. Find out what kind of stuff he has. Then see if you can pick up some nuance that tells you what the pitcher is throwing.

"I picked up enough pitches in my career to know what was coming about 40 percent of the time. It wasn't difficult if you observed closely. For example, Rick Wise (a pitcher with the Philadelphia Phillies and other teams) used to hold the ball with his hand in the glove. Then he put the glove right in front of his chest. If he dropped the glove all the way during the windup, almost to touch his body, he was throwing a fastball. But when he gripped the curveball or his change-up, he would drop the glove only 6 inches. That was blatant. When Tony Cloninger pitched for the Braves, he wore a long sweatshirt, even if it was

110 degrees. When he was at the top of his stretch, that sweatshirt would recede from his wrist. If you saw a lot of wrist, Tony was throwing a fastball. If you saw a little bit of wrist, it would be the curve or slider. No wrist? He was throwing the change. At one time, when Nolan Ryan had to pitch out of a windup, he would look down at the ground before delivering the fastball; if he looked at the catcher, he was bringing the curve. With the stuff he had, that didn't always help, but at least you got a little better shot at him.

"Besides studying the pitcher, you should also examine the park conditions. Is the wind blowing in or out? Is it blowing in different directions in different parts of the park? Is there a sun field (an outfield position that exposes a fielder's eyes to the glare of the sun)? If you hit the ball down the line, is it likely to stay fair or foul? Is the grass slowing down the ball? In Dodger Stadium, when I played, if you bunted the ball off the grass and it hit the mud, it stayed fair. In the old Astrodome, Joe and I knew that if you bunted the ball down the line, the turf moved the ball towards foul territory. Recognizing these idiosyncrasies helps you to bring as many plusses to the plate as you can. Every hitter should know these things, but it is especially important for pinch hitters. You only have that one chance per game; you have to make the most of it."

Chapter 6

The Science of Baserunning

*B*aserunning has always been the most underrated aspect of baseball offense. Teams win or lose more games on the base paths than most fans realize. Clubs that consistently win close games are the ones whose players can go from first to third on singles, break up double plays, score on short fly balls or ground-ball outs, and take the extra base whenever it is offered.

Anyone can become a proficient base runner. You don't need speed; you simply need to be alert, aggressive, and smart. Pete Rose was one of the best base runners I ever played with or against. From the stands, Pete appeared fast because he hustled all the time, but he had only average speed. In a game I played against him in the Houston Astrodome, Pete went from first to third on a sharp single to right. You don't see that happen often on AstroTurf — singles bounce to the outfielders so quickly that base runners usually advance only one base. But Pete executed plays like that all the time because he was hustling from his very first step toward second. He also made it his business to know where the ball was hit and the strength of the outfielder's arm.

Pete went from first to third as well as any player in the Majors because of his head, not his legs. In this chapter, we show you how to take a page from his book by developing your baserunning savvy.

Accelerating Out of the Box

When you get a hit, you should be hustling toward first base the moment the ball leaves your bat. It doesn't matter which foot you lead with as long as you maintain balance and your initial move propels you toward first. Always run in a straight line as close to the foul line as possible so that if a fielder's throw hits you, the umpire won't call you out for obstruction (see Figure 6-1). Don't overstride. Stay low for your first few steps to build acceleration and then explode into your normal running form.

Figure 6-1: The quickest way to first base is a straight line.

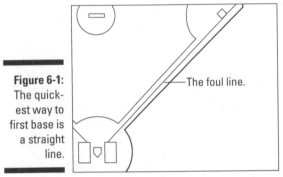

The foul line.

Illustration by Wiley, Composition Services Graphics

If a fielder is going to try to throw you out at first base, don't just run to first base, run *through* it. Always touch the front of the bag as you cross over it. Continue running several steps down the right field line before making your right turn into foul territory. If you do this after touching first, you can't be tagged out for leaving the bag. However, if you turn left toward second base and make an attempt or act with the intent of advancing toward second, the fielder can tag you out before you get back to first. (See Figure 6-2.) As you run through first, glance over your right shoulder to see if you can advance to second on an error. (For instance, the fielder has thrown the ball past the first baseman and into the dugout, so you have enough time to get to second base safely.)

Figure 6-2: The proper way to run to first and beyond.

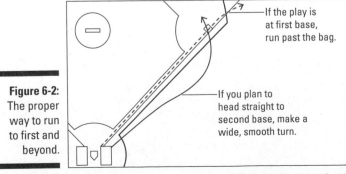

If the play is at first base, run past the bag.

If you plan to head straight to second base, make a wide, smooth turn.

Illustration by Wiley, Composition Services Graphics

Most of the time, you shouldn't bother to watch the ball as you dash toward first. Watching the ball slows you down. The only time you should watch the ball is if it's going toward one of the outfield gaps or over an outfielder's head. You can pick up most of those balls with a quick glance. If you can't, tilt your head slightly (and don't break stride) for a better view. Still can't pick it up? Then rely on your first-base coach to tell you whether you should run through first or turn toward second.

Stay alert after singling to right field. If you make a wide turn at first, a charging right fielder may still get you out by throwing behind you to the first baseman.

You should slide into first base sometimes — for example, if a high throw draws the first baseman off the bag and he has to tag you for the out. If you slide while he's leaping for the ball, it's nearly impossible for him to get the ball down in time to nail you. Some players slide into first on force-outs, but I think this is bad policy. It may feel as if sliding or jumping into first on your final step gets you to the bag quicker, but it actually slows you down.

Taking Your Lead

Baseball is, as they say, a game of inches; you're often safe or out by the barest of margins. Any time you can use your lead to shorten the distance from one base to another, you gain an advantage for your team — you're inching that much closer to your ultimate objective: home plate. These sections give you the lowdown about leading off.

Leading off first

After you're on first, keep your left foot against the bag while you check the alignment of the fielders and pick up any signs from the third-base coach. Remind yourself of the number of outs. Don't move off first until you know the pitcher has the ball. While closely watching the pitcher receive his signs, take several shuffle steps from the bag (do not cross your left foot over your right; you can get tangled if you have to dive back to first on a pickoff). This position is your *primary lead* (refer to Figure 6-3).

Your goal is to gradually get as far from first base as you can without getting *picked off* (thrown out). How far a lead you take depends on a number of factors: whether the pitcher is a righty or lefty, how good his move is, your size, and your reflexes. Tall players can take long leads — but so can short, quick players. Finding your ideal lead length is a matter of trial and error. However, most Major-League runners prefer to be a step or two and a dive away from first.

Figure 6-3:
Taking a
primary
lead.

Illustration by Wiley, Composition Services Graphics

When taking your lead, balance your weight evenly on the balls of both feet. Don't lean toward first or second. Drop into a slight crouch and flex your knees so that you can move quickly in either direction. This stance is known as a *two-way lead*. Your feet should be parallel to each other, shoulder width apart, and pointed toward the pitcher. (Maury Wills, who ran the bases well enough to steal 104 bases for the Dodgers in 1962, used to turn his right foot a little toward second base so he could pivot quicker.)

Let your arms hang loosely in front of you. Keep your eyes on the pitcher the moment you step from the bag. Watch for the pickoff play! Imagine a straight line leading from the outer edge of first base to the outer edge of second. Stand even with that line or a little bit in front of it. Leading off the bag from behind that line costs you extra steps as Figure 6-4 shows. It also makes it appear to the pitcher that there is a wider distance between you and first base than there actually is. You invite additional pickoff throws when you stand too far back.

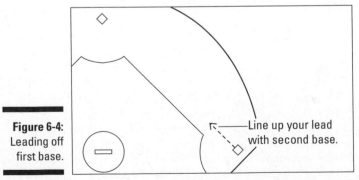

Figure 6-4:
Leading off
first base.

Illustration by Wiley, Composition Services Graphics

As the pitcher throws toward home, assume your *secondary lead.* Take a crossover step and a hop toward second while watching the action at the plate. In a well-timed crossover, your right foot hits the ground a split second before the ball reaches home. When the ball passes the hitter or if the hitter hits the ball in the air directly at an infielder, stop on your right foot, turn, and get back to first. If the ball gets past the catcher or if the batter hits a grounder or a longer fly ball, push off your right foot and run toward second.

Remember: Don't leave the base until you know the location of the ball. Base runners must stay constantly alert for pickoff plays and hidden ball tricks.

Fly balls are tricky; if a fielder catches one, you must get back to first before you get thrown out. If the batter hits a fly ball that looks catchable, you should move far enough off first base that you can make it safely to second (or beyond) if the ball is dropped, but not so far that you can't get back to first safely if the ball is caught. If the batter hits a medium fly ball, run no farther than halfway to second base until you see how the play evolves. You can run farther toward second on a deep fly.

If the outfielder catches the fly ball and the throw reaches the infielder at your base before you return to the bag, you've just run into a double play. (Refer to the later section, "Tagging Up" to make sure you avoid a double play.) As you trot toward your dugout, you'll notice a livid fellow with smoke coming out of his ears and veins in his head threatening to explode. That's your coach.

Leading off second

You can take a longer lead off second than off first. Generally, no one holds you close to the bag because the pitcher can't look directly at you; he has to wheel and turn to pick you off; you rarely see anyone pull off that play.

If you're going to steal, set up in a straight line to third. Otherwise, stay a few feet behind the base line. Take your primary lead. Advance as the pitcher delivers to the plate. You should be 15 to 18 feet (4.6 to 5.5 meters) from second as the ball crosses home plate.

If your team already has two outs, extend your primary lead off second to about 20 feet (6 meters), but set up about 3 to 5 feet (.9 to 1.5 meters) behind second base. This lead puts you in a better position to round third and head for home on a base hit. You don't have to worry about being part of a double play, so you can take off at the crack of the bat. (See Figure 6-5.)

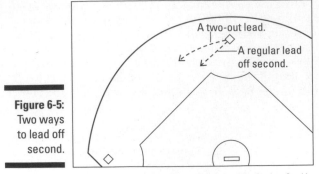

A two-out lead.

A regular lead off second.

Figure 6-5:
Two ways
to lead off
second.

Illustration by Wiley, Composition Services Graphics

Leading off third

Managers and head coaches have exiled base runners to Devil's Island for getting picked off at third base. Therefore, your primary lead off third should put you no farther from the bag than the opposing third baseman. Take this lead in foul territory so you won't be called out if a batted ball hits you (check out Figure 6-6).

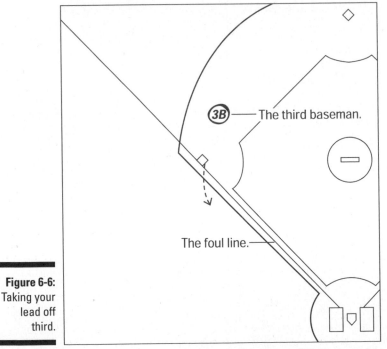

The third baseman.

The foul line.

Figure 6-6:
Taking your
lead off
third.

Illustration by Wiley, Composition Services Graphics

As the pitcher delivers the pitch to his catcher, take a two- or three-step walking lead toward home. You should land on your right foot, ready to break for the plate or return to third, just as the pitch approaches the batter. This movement leaves you in position to score easily on a wild pitch, passed ball, or ground out. It also allows you to pivot back toward third if the catcher handles the pitch cleanly.

Disguising the hit-and-run play

As the base runner on a hit-and-run play, don't depart from your normal lead or you may signal your intentions to the opposition. Timing matters more to the successful execution of this play than the size of your lead does. You must make sure the pitcher delivers the ball before you break from the base. (You can review how to execute the hit-and-run in Chapter 5.)

Reading Your Opposition

Great base runners take the extra base *before* the ball is hit. Prior to your game, watch the opposing fielders during practice to see the strength and accuracy of their arms. When you reach first base during the game, observe how deeply the outfielders are playing the hitter. If the left fielder is playing deep, and your teammate hits a shallow fly in his direction, you can take off without holding up to see if the ball is caught. Notice if the outfielders are leaning in any particular direction. If the outfield is *shaded* (leaning) toward left, and the hitter smacks the ball down the right field line, you can go for at least two bases.

Also observe if any of the outfielders are left-handed throwers. If a left-handed center fielder has to go to his right in pursuit of a hit, he must turn and make an off-balance throw to nail you at third. On a single to right center field, a right-handed center fielder cannot throw to third until he turns completely around. That gives you an extra moment to slide in safely.

Rounding the Bag

All right, you've just pounded a ball into the outfield and you're thinking double all the way. You're not running through first and up the right field foul line on this play. Instead, head straight for first as you normally would. When you're about 15 feet (4.6 meters) from the bag, veer slightly toward foul territory, and then cut in toward the infield. As you pass first base on a nearly straight line toward second, touch the bag with your foot. It doesn't matter which one you use. However, you have a shorter turn to make by touching the inside part of the bag with your left foot, as Figure 6-7 shows. Make sure that you touch enough of first base for the umpire to witness the contact. Scamper to second base.

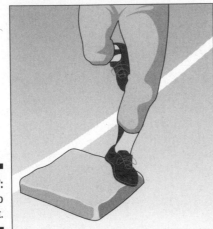

Figure 6-7:
How to
round first.

Illustration by Wiley, Composition Services Graphics

Tagging Up

After a fly ball is caught with less than two outs, base runners must touch the base they occupy before advancing to the next bag. This action is known as *tagging up*. If you are halfway between first and second when a deep fly is hit, you must return to first to touch the bag. Take off for second only *after* the ball and fielder make contact. You can advance in this manner from any base.

When you tag up from first, your right foot should be on the inside edge of the bag. This position leaves your right side open so you can follow the ball's flight more easily. If you're tagging up from third, your left foot should be on the bag. Tagging from second? The situation determines which foot you should place on the bag. On a ball hit to left or left center, it's your right foot. When the ball is hit to right field or right center, switch to your left foot.

As you tag up, drop into a crouch. Extend your front foot 18 to 24 inches (46 to 61 centimeters), depending on your leg length, from the base. Shift your weight forward. Watch the ball! The moment it touches the outfielder's glove, push into your stride toward the next base. You don't have to wait for the outfielder to catch it cleanly.

BASEBALL SPEAK

Focusing on the force-out

Force-out is a term that you need to be familiar with because it occurs frequently in baseball — and the novice player and viewer alike often misunderstand it. (A trip to your local Little League game should convince you of that!) A force-out (or force play) takes place when a batted ground ball forces a runner to advance to the next base, but that base or the runner is tagged by a fielder touching the ball before the runner reaches the base.

Under what circumstances does a batted ground ball force a base runner to advance?

- A runner on first must *always* try to advance to second base.

- A runner on second base must try to advance to third base if another runner is on first base.

- A runner on third base must try to advance home if runners are on first and second base (in this case, the bases are *loaded,* and a force-out is possible at any base, including home).

Of course, if you're the defensive player, it's easier to tag the base in a force play situation (or throw to another fielder who may step on the base) rather than tag the runner — because tagging a runner may knock the ball out of your hand. You don't need to do both. And don't think that you must literally tag the base. Simply step on the base while holding the ball in either your bare or your gloved hand.

Under what circumstances does a base runner not need to advance when the batter hits a ground ball? (If this information seems like overkill, don't forget your visit to the Little League game.)

- A runner on second base need not run if no one is on first base.

- A runner on third base need not run if either first base or second base is empty.

- Runners on both third base and second base need not run if first base is empty.

In the preceding situations, go to the next base only if you can make it safely — and remember that the defensive player must tag you with the ball instead of simply touching the base that you are running to. If you don't think that you can make it to the next base safely, simply stay put!

With two out, don't wait for a fly ball to be touched before you run. If the ball is caught, the inning is over, anyway. Be prepared to run on any fly ball — and hope that the fielder misses or drops it.

Using Your Coaches

You may feel as if you're alone on those base paths; you're not. Think of the base coaches as part of your running team. Use them. When you get to first base, the coach there can be a fount of valuable knowledge. He can remind you how many outs have been recorded (if he doesn't and you're not sure, ask him), reveal a quirk he has detected in the pitcher's motion (so you can get a better lead or steal a base), or tell you something about the outfielders (such as which one seems hobbled or isn't throwing particularly well that day). This is just the kind of information you need to make appropriate decisions on the base paths.

The third-base coach is your beacon. If you've lost sight of the ball or are unsure whether you should advance to the next base, watch his signs. No matter how much experience you have, heed the third-base coach in most situations. He has a better view of the entire field than you do. You may think you're running faster than you are, or you may not realize how quickly an outfielder has gotten to the ball. A good third-base coach can gauge all that for you.

Sliding Safely

You can grab runs and wins for your team if you know how to slide properly. Often, the only difference between the umpire calling you safe or out on the bases is the quality of your slide. These sections explain the different types of sliding you can add to your repertoire.

Practice sliding as diligently as you work on the other aspects of your game. You don't need to do this on a baseball diamond. My brothers and I used to practice in our backyard. Get into a pair of tennis shoes and sliding pads, wet some grass, put down a base, and practice all your slides. It's important to be able to slide on both sides. George Foster, one of my teammates on the Reds, could slide only on one side no matter how a play developed. Many times he could have been safe but was tagged out simply because he couldn't elude the tag. As you practice, you develop a feel for when you should start your slide.

The straight-leg slide

The *straight-leg slide* is my favorite. It gets you to the bag as quickly as possible while leaving you in position to bounce up and advance to another base if a misplay occurs. Because your top leg is straight and aimed at the bag, you have less chance of catching your spikes in the dirt (a leading cause of ankle injuries).

Start this slide about 10 feet (3 meters) from the bag. Push off your rear foot and lift both legs up. Your body should glide forward feet first. Slide straight in (you can do this on either side) with the toe and foot of your top leg pointed in a straight line toward the middle of the bag. Your bottom leg is bent under you as Figure 6-8 demonstrates.

Illustration by Wiley, Composition Services Graphics

Figure 6-8:
The straight-leg slide.

The bent-leg slide

The *bent-leg slide* is a variation of the straight-leg slide. To launch the slide, push off your rear foot and lift up both legs. Then tuck your rear leg under your slightly flexed top leg at a 90-degree angle (this pairing should resemble a figure 4). Maintain a semi-sitting position with your torso arched back and hands held high as you slide. Hold your chin close to your chest so you can see the base and the ball. Aim for the middle of the bag with your top leg. Touch the base with your heel (which prevents your cleats from catching on the bag).

The *pop-up slide* is the bent-leg slide with a wrinkle. You start this slide about 8 feet (2.4 meters) from the bag. Don't lean back. As your top leg hits the base, push up with your bottom foot. The momentum brings you to your feet, ready to advance if a misplay occurs.

Lou Brock, the all-time National League leader in stolen bases, used the pop-up slide to great effect. So do current players such as Brett Gardner (see Figure 6-9). It leaves you in position to take an extra base on a misplay. However, I don't like to see it used unless someone has already overthrown the ball when you start your slide. Too many runners have been called out when they were safe simply because their pop-up slides didn't afford the umpires a long-enough look to make the correct calls.

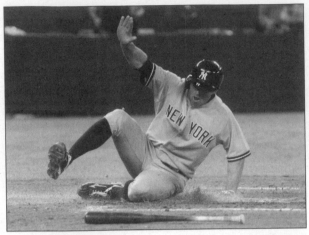

Figure 6-9:
Brett
Gardner
is ready to
pop up and
run some
more in
a misplay.

Photo by Thornhill/Reuters/Corbis

The headfirst slide

This slide is nothing more than a dive into a swimming pool — without any water. You're hurtling yourself at great speed onto a hard surface that has little or no give. Pete Rose slid headfirst for more than 20 years and never even cracked a fingernail. Current players such as Andrew McCutcheon (see Figure 6-10) got so used to it that when he tried switching to the feet-first slide, the latter felt so uncomfortable that he quickly reverted to the headfirst variety — with the blessing of his manager, Clint Hurdle. However, don't let such examples fool you. The headfirst slide can be dangerous. A descending fielder can spike your hands, the ball can hit you in the head, or you can jam your fingers and hands against the base if you hold them too low. In one month alone, Yunel Escobar suffered a concussion, Josh Hamilton injured his shoulder, Ryan Zimmerman strained his abdomen, and Rafael Furcal broke his thumb — all while attempting headfirst slides.

If you're still not dissuaded from going in head first, at least minimize your risk by executing the slide properly. Start the headfirst slide by gradually lowering your body until you are about 8 feet (2.4 meters) from the bag. Extend your arms while you launch yourself off your rear leg. Keep your body straight, but relaxed, so that your forearms, chest, and thighs hit the ground simultaneously (this absorbs the shock). Stay alert and hold up your hands and head while sliding, as Figure 6-11 shows. Should you attempt to execute a literal headfirst slide, you risk a sprained neck, concussion, or worse. I especially don't like to see young players, from high school on down, sliding headfirst. Too much can go wrong.

Photo by David Denoma/Reuters/Corbis

Figure 6-10:
Andrew
McCutcheon
prefers the
headfirst
slide.

Illustration by Wiley, Composition Services Graphics

Figure 6-11:
The head-
first slide.

You may find it difficult to keep your hands up when attempting any type of slide. Wearing sliding gloves offers you some protection from injury.

The hook slide

The *hook slide* was supposedly the brainchild of Mike Kelly. It may have helped inspire that song they wrote about him, but it's basically a desperation play that you should use only when trying to evade a probable tag.

Let me set it up. You're on first. The batter hits the ball to right field. You cruise around second and burst toward third. The right fielder, however, has gotten a perfect bounce and has already fired the ball to the third baseman. As the ball beats you to the bag it pulls the third baseman toward his right. A hook slide to your right (the third baseman's left) is your only hope of avoiding an out.

Always execute the hook slide to the opposite side of wherever the tag will originate. If the throw comes in from the outfield side, slide to your left. Should it come from the infield side, slide to your right.

To hook slide to your left, push off on your right foot and drop to your left side. Your outer calf and thigh absorb the slide's impact. Keep your right leg relatively straight with a slight knee flex (your right leg slides to the right of the bag). Scissor your left leg out toward the base. While sliding past the base, reach out with the toes of your left foot or either hand. Touch the bag at its nearest corner (refer to Figure 6-12).

Figure 6-12:
The hook slide.

Illustration by Wiley, Composition Services Graphics

If the fielder is about to tag your hand as you try to touch the base, you can pull your hand back. As the fielder's momentum carries him to one side, reach out to grab the bag with your other hand.

Remember to stay in contact with the bag until the fielder returns the ball to the pitcher or the umpire calls time.

To hook slide to your right (say, on a throw from the catcher), do everything I just described — only in reverse. Practice the hook slide from both sides. Don't use this slide on force plays; it slows you down when you need to get to the bag as quickly as possible.

Maury Wills was the greatest hook slider I ever saw. He could reach either corner of the base with the tip of his toe. This presented the fielder attempting a tag with the smallest target possible. With most runners, I only had to put the ball in the middle of the base to get them. They would slide right into it. I couldn't do that with Maury. You had to look for him, which is why he was so elusive.

You should also be aware of the risks involved with the hook. Your body's momentum can easily pull you too far past the base or make you miss it completely. Catching your spikes on the bag is another danger. Do this, and you can tear or break something. Keeping your knees slightly bent and both feet sideways offers you some protection. (See me do the hook slide in Figure 6-13.)

Figure 6-13:
Joe Morgan demonstrates a hook slide against the master hook slider Maury Wills.

Photo courtesy of National Baseball Hall of Fame Library, Cooperstown, N.Y.

Keeping safety in mind

To avoid injury while sliding, regardless of which type of slide you use, try to hold both hands in the air. Many Major-League ballplayers hold a clump of dirt in each hand to remind them to hold their hands high on the base paths. (Don't ask me how *that* custom started.) Wearing sliding gloves is a further precaution. And always remember the four cardinal rules of sliding:

- ✔ When in doubt, slide.
- ✔ Never be tentative (half-hearted slides are the most dangerous).
- ✔ It is always better to slide early rather than late.
- ✔ Never slide head first into home or when breaking up the double play (you don't want to expose your head and neck on contact plays).

Breaking Up Is Hard to Do: Preventing the Double Play

Anytime you break up a double play, you snatch an out from the box score; you give your team an extra opportunity to score and win. To execute this maneuver, you must know how to slide properly. You should also know the rules governing the play:

- ✔ You must be on the ground when you make contact with the fielder.
- ✔ You must be able to reach the bag with some part of your body during your slide.

As the runner trying to break up the double play, your assignment is to get to second base as quickly as you can while making a good, hard slide. You're not looking to hurt anyone, so forget about any rolling blocks. (I had one thrown at me in 1968. It crumpled my knee and put me on the disabled list for the entire season. Inflicting that sort of injury is not your objective.) The idea is either to knock the pivot man (the second baseman or shortstop) off-balance or to disrupt his timing by making him leap or hurry his throw.

Start your takeout with your normal straight-leg slide. However, try to hook your top leg's foot under the pivot man's striding foot to knock it out from under him. Keep your weight on your bottom leg. When you take your usual slide, you aim for the base. Your objective here is to reach the fielder. Slide on whatever side of the bag he pivots from.

This type of take-out slide applies only to Major League players; it's illegal for youth and high school players to do it. Such attempts may result in an automatic out being called and the player's ejection from the game. The same caveat applies to running over the catcher.

Though you don't have to hit the pivot man to break up the double play, you should try to do exactly that. This potential collision forces him to jump out of the way. Minimize the chance of injury by sliding with your spikes held below the pivot man's knee. Should you make contact, you will hit his shins or lower, where you won't break anything. Avoid hitting any fielder from the knee up.

In the final game of the 1975 World Series, the Cincinnati Reds and I were losing 3–0 to the Boston Red Sox in the top of the sixth. Pete Rose led off that inning with a single against Red Sox left-hander Bill Lee. With one out, our catcher Johnny Bench hit a sure double-play ball to Boston shortstop Rick Burleson. Burleson shoveled the ball to his second baseman Denny Doyle to start the double play. Doyle attempted to get a throw off to first, but Pete barreled into him just as the ball was leaving his hand. Though Pete was out, his hard (but perfectly legal) slide forced Doyle to throw wildly into the Boston dugout. Bench was safe; the inning, which should have been over, continued. The next batter, Tony Perez, hit a two-run homer that propelled us toward a 4–3 win and a world championship. Our comeback in that game started with Pete's slide.

Colliding with the Catcher at Home Plate

Catchers have this thing about base runners; they don't like to see them sliding across home plate. So good catchers do everything they can to stop you. Catchers are usually built like small condominiums. They wear heavy protective gear, and many of them enjoy a good crunch at the plate. Getting through them can be a daunting task, but you have to do it whenever you have the chance to score a run, particularly in a close game. Take the easy route whenever possible — if you can see the plate and know you can touch it, launch into your slide.

However, if the catcher has the plate completely blocked, you must barrel through him. There is no elegant way to do this. Just get low so you have your center of gravity working with you and keep your head away from the point of contact.

The catcher can block the plate only if he possesses the ball. If he blocks it without having the ball, he is guilty of obstruction, and the umpire will declare you safe at home after the collision.

Profile of a Base Thief

All great base stealers have a love of larceny. They derive joy from picking the opposing team's pockets, especially in pressure situations. To excel as a base thief, you have to be cocky. When you get to first base, your body language and demeanor should announce, "I'm stealing and there's nothing anyone can do to stop me!" You have to embrace the role of intimidator.

Base stealers make things happen. During the 1975 World Series, Boston pitcher Reggie Cleveland walked me to open the sixth inning of the fifth game. He threw over to first base seven times before throwing a strike to the batter Johnny Bench. Then he made four more throws to first. When he delivered another pitch, I took off for second but Bench fouled off the ball. What did Cleveland do then? He made five more tosses to first. This didn't bother me a bit. Cleveland was concentrating more on me than the batter, which is precisely what I wanted. On Cleveland's next pitch, Bench singled, and then Tony Perez came up to hit a three-run homer. The lesson here is that you don't need to steal a base to help your team; just the threat of a theft can rattle a pitcher into making a critical mistake. If the pitcher is playing cat-and-mouse with you, he can't focus fully on the hitter.

Stealing a lot of bases with your team far ahead or behind doesn't mark you as a great thief — many runners can steal in those situations because the opposing pitcher is paying little attention to them. He's either cruising to a win or concentrating solely on getting the batter out. Far more valuable are the runners like Juan Pierre, who ignite their offenses by stealing in the early innings or during the late portions of a close game.

A good base thief should be successful on at least 75 percent of his stolen base attempts. If your percentage is below that, your attempts are hurting your team. These sections can help you become a better base thief.

What every base thief should know: Reading the pitcher

Ninety percent of all stolen bases come off the pitcher rather than the catcher. If you waited until the pitch reached home plate before you tried to steal, you would be thrown out 95 percent of the time. However, if you get a good jump as the pitcher delivers the ball, a catcher can do little to get you out, even if you aren't blessed with exceptional speed. In the fifth game of the 1997 World Series, Marlins first baseman Darren Daulton caught the Cleveland pitcher napping and stole second base. Darren has undergone nine knee operations, which have left him nearly immobile. Yet he got such a good lead that he was able to steal second against Sandy Alomar, one of the best throwing catchers in the business. Had the Indians' pitcher been paying more attention to first base, Darren never would have attempted a steal.

Base runners should study the opposing pitcher the moment he takes the mound. See if he has two distinct motions: one when he throws home and another when he tosses the ball to first to hold a runner on. Watch the pitcher throw to the plate from the stretch; note what body parts he moves first. Then see whether he does anything different when he throws to first base. See if he sets his feet differently on his pickoff move. Try to detect any quirk that can reveal the pitcher's intentions. In his final Major-League season, Yankee outfielder Paul O'Neill stole 22 bases in 25 tries, a fabulous percentage. No one would describe Paul as a speed merchant back then, but he was one of the headiest players around and taught himself to read the pitchers' moves.

Ironically, good pitchers are often the easiest to steal on. Erratic pitchers typically use different release points from pitch to pitch (which is what makes them erratic). You never know when they are going to let go of the ball. The better pitchers have purer mechanics. They establish a rhythm and stick to it. Pedro Martinez, a three-time Cy Young Award winner, did the same thing to hit his release point on nearly every pitch. So a runner may have been able to spot some clue in his motion when he planned to throw to first base (of course, when Pedro was working the mound, getting a runner to first base to begin with is the first challenge).

After you have a pitcher's pattern down, take off for second the moment he moves toward his release point. He might indicate this move with a hand gesture or some slight leg motion. Even a pitcher's eyes can fall into a pattern. Many pitchers take a quick glance toward first before throwing home; when they don't sneak a look toward you, they're throwing to your base.

You can also figure out pitchers by observing their body language. Watch the pitcher's rear leg. If it moves off the rubber, the throw is coming toward you. To throw to the plate, every pitcher must close either his hip or his front shoulder. He also must bend his rear knee while rocking onto his back foot. After the pitcher does any of these things, the rules state he can no longer throw to your base. You should immediately break for the next bag. If the pitcher breaks his motion to throw toward any base, the umpire should call a balk, which allows you and any other base runners to advance.

If you're on first base, left-handed pitchers are traditionally harder to steal on than right-handers because the lefty looks directly at you when he assumes the set position. However, this also means you are looking directly at him so he is easier to read — if you know what to look for. Scrutinize his glove, the ball, and his motion. If a *southpaw* (a left-hander) tilts back his upper body, he is probably throwing to first; a turning of the shoulder to the right usually precedes a pitch to the plate. When he bends his rear leg, he is most likely preparing to push off toward home.

When a righty is on the mound, observe his right heel and shoulder. He cannot pitch unless his right foot touches the pitching rubber. Throwing to first requires him to pivot on that foot. If he lifts his right heel, get back to the bag. An open right shoulder also indicates a throw to first.

Lead — and runs will follow

Base thieves can choose between a *walking lead* and a *stationary lead*. Lou Brock, the former Cardinal outfielder, used a walking lead. Brock was faster than most players, but he wasn't especially quick out of his first few steps (most taller players find it difficult to accelerate from a dead stop). He would walk two or three small steps to gain momentum before taking off toward second base. If you require a few steps to accelerate, this is the lead for you. A walking lead does, however, have one disadvantage: A good pitcher can stop you from moving by simply holding the ball. If you continue to stroll, the pitcher can pick you off.

For that reason, I prefer the stationary lead, when a batter takes a few strides off first base then stands still while the pitcher prepares to throw. The pitcher can still hold the ball, but the batter is not budging until the pitcher makes his first move to the plate.

Remember: Whichever baserunning lead you choose, use the same one whether you're stealing a base or not. Set up the same way on every lead. You don't want to telegraph your intentions to the pitcher. He's watching you for clues as closely as you're watching him.

The key to stealing third

Stealing third is generally easier than stealing second. You can take a bigger lead at second than at first without drawing many throws. If your timing is good, you can also take off from second before the pitcher actually releases the ball.

Pitchers generally find it more difficult to pick runners off at second than at first; the timing between the pitcher and his fielder must be precise. To catch you at second, either the second baseman or the shortstop has to cover or *cheat* (lean) toward the bag; this leaning opens up a hole for the batter. Alert coaches let you know when the fielders are sneaking in on you.

The potential to steal third depends on the batter at the plate. If a right-handed hitter is at-bat, you have an advantage because the catcher must throw over or around him to get the ball to third. But never try to steal third with a lefty at the plate, unless you get such a good jump that even a perfect throw cannot beat you.

Stealing third isn't a good gamble unless your success rate is 90 percent or better. Because you're already in scoring position at second, getting picked off can devastate your offense. And making the first or last out of an inning at third, whether through an attempted steal or simply by running the bases, is considered a big mistake.

The only reason to steal third with fewer than two outs in a close ballgame is so you can score on a fly ball or ground out. However, if you're a proficient base thief, it does makes sense to steal third with two outs; being on third rather than second in that situation offers you nine more opportunities to score. Memorize the following list and dazzle your friends with your baseball erudition.

If you are on third, you can score on

- A balk
- An infield hit
- A wild pitch
- A passed ball
- A one-base infield error
- A fielder's choice (where the hitter and any other base runners are safe)
- Baserunning interference
- Catcher's interference
- A steal of home

Home, stolen home

Speaking of stealing home (how's that for a segue?), think long and hard about it — the odds are against you. If you must, only attempt a steal of home during the late innings of a close, low-scoring ballgame with two men out and a weak hitter at the plate. Obviously, home plate is the one base you steal entirely on the pitcher, because the catcher makes no throw on this play. Your best victims are pitchers with unusually slow deliveries or long windups.

Having a right-handed batter at the plate when you attempt to steal home provides you with two advantages. First, the hitter obstructs the catcher's view of you at third. Second, if the batter remains in the box until just before you arrive at home, he can prevent the catcher from getting in position for the tag.

Delayed, double, and fake steals

With the *delayed steal,* slide-step into your regular lead when the pitcher releases the ball and then count 1-2-3. This should slow your takeoff just long enough to persuade the catcher and infielders that you aren't stealing. Race for second after you finish counting. (You may also first break out of your

JOE SAYS

Stealing: Know when to say "No"

The 1975 World Series serves as a great setting for a base-stealing lesson. In the bottom of the ninth inning of the fourth game, I was batting while our center fielder, Cesar Geronimo, was on second and Pete Rose was on first. We were trailing 5–4. Right-hander Luis Tiant was pitching for Boston. I was trying to concentrate on Tiant, always a difficult task because he had a thousand different herky-jerky moves and hesitations with which he distracted hitters.

Geronimo suddenly raced toward third just as Tiant went into his delivery. His unexpected movement pulled my attention away from the pitcher for a split second. By the time I looked back toward Tiant, the ball was nearly down the heart of the plate. A perfect pitch to drive

for extra bases. However, that momentary lapse of concentration left me with little time to swing. My weak, late swing produced an inning-ending, rally-killing pop-up. That was the best pitch I'd seen all night. I blew it.

Cesar should not have been running at that point. He was already in scoring position, we were trailing by a run, and Tiant was tiring (he threw an arm-wringing 163 pitches in that game). Given those circumstances, a base runner has to give his team's number three hitter — usually an RBI man — a chance to drive him in. To be a great base stealer, you must be aggressive, but you also have to know when to throw on the brakes for the good of the team.

lead and return to first to camouflage your intentions.) Another general rule is to get your usual secondary lead when the pitcher releases the ball and then take off for second after the ball hits the catcher's mitt. Catchers have no way of knowing who will cover second base on a delayed steal until either the second baseman or shortstop moves toward the bag. If you've caught those two infielders napping and no one covers second, the catcher has to hold onto the ball or risk throwing it into the outfield.

Double steals are possible whenever two bases are occupied. With runners on first and second, this play is nothing more than two straight steals occurring simultaneously. With only one out, the catcher will probably try to erase the lead runner heading to third. With two out, he may go after the slower of the two base stealers.

With runners on first and third, double steals become more complex. Imagine you're the runner on third. Your teammate on first should break full-out for second as the pitcher delivers the ball. You move down the line toward home. Halt as the catcher receives the pitch. Don't move until the catcher commits to throwing the runner out at second. Be alert in case he fakes a toss to the bag and instead throws to his pitcher, who fires back the ball for a play at the plate. The throw's *trajectory* should tell you if it's going to second base or to the pitcher — the throw will be higher if it is going all the way to second base, so hesitate long enough to see this. Dash home as soon as the throw bound for second base leaves the catcher's hand.

If you're the runner on first for this play, your primary goal is helping your teammate at third score. You may break for second while the pitcher is in his set position. Should your movement distract the pitcher, he may balk (see Chapter 3 for details on the balk). In that case, both runners advance one base. Attract a throw to first, and you can force a rundown. While you jockey to elude the tag, the runner on third can score.

Fake steals open the infield for the batter at the plate. You can bluff the opposition by taking two and a half quick strides out of your primary lead before coming to a halt. Your movement should draw the infielders out of position, because one of them must cover second base.

Sprinting for home

When you're ready, stand at home plate as if you're at-bat. (You can use a real bat or an imaginary one.) Swing, and then sprint to first as if you're trying to beat out a close play. Jog back to home plate, swing again, but this time sprint to second. Retrace your steps with another jog, swing, and sprint at top speed to third. Catch your breath, and then sprint for home as if a teammate has just hit a sacrifice fly and you're challenging outfielder Jeff Francoeur, one of baseball's deadliest arms. Finish the rotation by hitting an inside-the-park homer and circling all the bases. (If you want to fantasize that Clayton Kershaw delivered the pitch with the score tied in the bottom of the ninth of a World Series seventh game, that's all right.) Do one complete circuit and then work up to two.

You can add variations to your sprinting drill. Stand at first and pretend to be stealing second or sprint to third on a ball hit into the gap. Start at second and try to score on a single to left-center. By recreating these game situations, you're building speed while practicing your game.

Part III
The Ball in Play — Playing Defense

Knowing about the infield fly rule

Umpires may invoke the infield fly rule only when all three of the following conditions are met:

- There are less than two outs.
- Base runners occupy first and second base; or first, second, and third.
- The batter hits a fair fly ball to the infield, which the umpire believes can be caught by an infielder making "an ordinary effort."

By yelling "infield fly" (usually while waving his arms), the umpire automatically rules the hitter out, even if the ball isn't caught. The runners may advance only at their own peril.

Why have such a rule? When a pop fly is hit to the infield, the runners assume the ball will be caught, so they stay anchored at the bases. If there were no infield fly rule and the fielder deliberately dropped the ball, the runners would be forced to advance (to make room on the bases for the hitter). Because they couldn't begin running until the ball came down, the runners' late starts could make them easy victims of a double or even a triple play. Baseball's rule makers saw this as "stealing outs through deception," so they enacted the infield fly rule in 1895.

Go to www.dummies.com/extras/baseball for some underappreciated roles of a pitcher and how mastering those roles can help your team. At the same URL, you can also read a bonus chapter that will serve as your defensive playbook.

In this part...

- Determine which position is right for you, know what to do when the ball is hit to you, and field the ball correctly in order to get the out.

- As a catcher, uncover how to handle your pitcher, catch a diving split-finger fastball, block a curveball in the dirt, gun down daring base runners, and catch pop-ups, swirling in the wind tunnel around home plate.

- Combat the sun, wind, screaming crowd, and intrusive fans looking for a souvenir when you're playing defense.

- Get some extra zip on your fastball, more curve on your curveball, more slide on your slider, and stymie batters that you face when you're pitching.

- Know how to grip and throw the ball, figure out to whom you should throw the ball after you field it to record an out, and find out how you can get it there as rapidly and accurately as possible.

- Figure out how to get in proper position to field every manner of ground ball — from the grass-cutter hit right at you, to the rocketing smash to your right or left, and to the dribbler you have to charge — and know how to position yourself for the strongest, most accurate throw to the *right* base.

- Turn the double play, including where to go before the ball is hit and the best way to feed a second baseman or shortstop so that a sprinting base runner doesn't mow down him — or you.

- Discover the joys and perils of tracking a fly ball, whether it's a 400-foot monster shot over your head or a tricky pop-up in between the infield and outfield, read the ball hit right off the bat, run to the right spot for the catch, and be in position to uncork an unerring throw

Chapter 7

Knowing the Players and Plays

- -

In This Chapter

▶ Discovering the requirements for each position

▶ Getting your arm ready

▶ Fielding and positioning

- -

*W*inning teams play good defense. We tend to think of power pitchers and sluggers as the dominant forces on a baseball diamond, but a great defensive player can be just as intimidating. When the Detroit Tigers' Austin Jackson defies the earth's pull to make yet another leaping, rally-crippling snatch of what appears to be a sure double, watch how many shoulders sag in the opposing dugout. Plays like that can slaughter hope before it gains full maturity, deflating the victimized hitter and his club while elevating the team on the other side of the field.

Jackson, third baseman Chase Headley, and second baseman Darwin Barney are among the premier fielders playing today. These Gold Glovers have sure hands, fast reactions, and strong, accurate arms. They get to balls that other fielders merely wave at. While many great defenders are blessed with natural ability, you also can become a great defender by working at it.

Making your hands good and quick

No matter which position you play, you need to have what ball players call *good hands*. However, *quick hands* and *soft hands* would be more accurate terms. If you have them, your hands adjust swiftly to bad hops, erratic bounces, or wild throws. Some people are born with quick hands, but most of us must develop them.

One way to develop quick hands is to play the game *short hop.* Stand 4 to 5 feet (1.2 to 1.5 meters) apart from a partner. Throw the ball to each other so that the ball bounces on a short hop, forcing the fielder receiving the throw to reach and adjust on every toss. Keep score to make the drill interesting. The first player to miss three short hops loses the round. Start again until you complete a five-round game. While practicing this drill, concentrate on using both hands for every catch. Training your hands to work in unison makes you a more coordinated fielder.

This chapter starts with the information you need to find the right position for you. We then provide some general fielding tips and go around the diamond discussing the ins and outs of each position, concluding with some mental coaching about how to handle the plays you've just botched.

Picking a Position

Want to know which position is right for you? These sections examine the particular qualities that each position requires so that you can see how you measure up.

Catcher

You must have a high threshold of pain to be a catcher. Foul balls are going to ricochet off your fingers and feet, you may take an occasional fastball or bat on the mask, and you can count on an occasional home-plate collision every week. Catchers must have strong legs — you spend half the game squatting while wearing extra equipment. If you're going to play the position properly, you must possess a powerful, accurate arm, although you can compensate for an average throwing arm with a quick release.

If you want an example of how a strong arm can completely neutralize base stealers, just watch Yadier Molina and Matt Wieters intimidate a team from behind the plate. They both throw out a high percentage of potential base thieves, but more impressive is how few runners attempt to steal against them.

Besides having physical stamina, catchers must be mentally tough. Catching is draining work; you are in on every pitch of the game. If your pitcher takes the mound without his best stuff, you're the one who has to improvise a strategy to retire batters with his secondary pitches. With every hitter, that computer between your ears is working in overdrive, trying to recollect or decipher the hitter's weaknesses and strengths.

Are you immersed in a batting slump? No matter how many hitless games you've had, you need to put your hitting woes out of your mind the moment you squat behind home plate. You must place your entire focus on aiding your pitcher in the battle against the hitter.

Finally, you have to be a practical psychologist — if your pitcher is getting battered, you have to know whether he needs a pat on the back or a good swift kick in the rear.

What's glove got to do with it? (With apologies to Tina Turner)

Your glove (or mitt) is your most important fielding tool. It should fit snugly enough that it wouldn't come off when you catch a ball in its tip. However, your glove should not be so tight that it restricts wrist flexibility or movement. How big should your glove be? That depends on what position you play.

- Catcher's mitts are always large, but yours shouldn't be so big that you cannot control it. Choose a mitt that you can open and close in a split second. (See Chapter 2 for some preliminary details on gloves and how to select them.)

- At first base, catching the ball is your primary concern. Digging the ball out of the mitt to get off your own throw is a secondary issue. Your first baseman's mitt should be as long as you can comfortably manage so that you can snag wide, errant tosses in the glove's webbing.

- Third basemen should also opt for large gloves. Balls are hit so quickly to third that you often only have time to block the ball or knock it down. You also have to field many

balls hit wide to your left and right. A big glove helps you cover more territory.

- Second base is the position of quick throws; use the smallest glove possible here so that the ball won't stick deep in its pocket. Choosing a small glove to play second is also a matter of self-preservation — at times you may have 220 solid pounds of seething base runner bearing down on you to break up the double play (as well as any part of your anatomy he can reach). In these cases, you don't want to spend a split second more time than necessary searching for the ball before unleashing your throw.

- Shortstops must get the ball out of their gloves quickly, too. But they must also be able to catch grounders cleanly when they range wide in the hole. A medium-sized glove is in order for this position.

- Outfielders are primarily interested in catching the ball. They have little need for a quick release. If you're playing the outfield, use the longest glove that the rules permit. (See Chapter 2 for rules about gloves.)

Ideally, catchers should have a low center of gravity, like the 5-foot, 8-inch former great Ivan Rodriguez or 5-foot, 10-inch Russell Martin. This body type gives the pitcher a better target and also offers the umpire a clearer perspective of each pitch. For example, seeing over a tall catcher like 6-foot, 4-inch Joe Mauer can be difficult for an umpire; that size may occasionally cost his pitcher a low strike. But Joe more than compensates for it. He's the only catcher in MLB history to win three batting titles and also three Gold Glove awards.

First base

Left-handed throwers have an advantage playing first base. As a first baseman, all your throws to the infield go to your right; if you throw left-handed, the play is always in front of you. Right-handed throwers often have to whirl completely around before they can toss the ball to another base. First basemen don't need particularly strong arms; they rarely throw more than 60 feet (18.3 meters). But your arm must be accurate, particularly on the 3-6-3 (first-to-short-to-first) double play when you're throwing into the runner.

First basemen should have enough range to cover their half of the hole between first and second. You need quick reactions and agility to cope with the opposition's bunting game. (Watch how Albert Pujols of the Los Angeles Angels pounces on bunts with the nimbleness of a middle infielder.) First basemen catch more throws than any other fielders, with the exception of the catcher. Depending on how the thrower grips the ball prior to release, those throws can sink, rise, or dart to either side of you. You have to be prepared to gather in tosses from every angle. If catching the ball is a liability for you, move to another position.

Second base

Second base is a paradox. I've played enough of it to know that this can be the easiest infield position for catching the ball — you don't have to cleanly catch a ground ball to record an out. Your proximity to first base allows you plenty of time to simply knock the ball down and make the short toss to the bag.

However, second base is also the most difficult position because you're a sitting duck on the double play. You often wait for a throw with your back to some runner who is eager to tear you in half with his slide. (Think football and hockey players are the only athletes who relish a little hard contact? George "Boomer" Scott — a hulking bruiser of a base runner when he played with the Boston Red Sox and Milwaukee Brewers during the 1970s — often wore a necklace, which he gleefully claimed was constructed from retired second basemen's teeth. And George was one of the more genteel of baseball's crash artists.) Your attitude has to be, "The double play takes priority over my physical well-being. I'm going to turn the play first and *then* look for the runner."

Too many otherwise-skilled second basemen hurt their teams by letting their fear of injury prevent them from *turning two* (getting both outs on a double play). The key to not getting creamed is to catch your shortstop's ball cleanly so you have time to plant your left foot on the bag. When you throw toward first base, you gain the momentum to leap out of the way of the base runner. Second basemen who bobble that toss from the shortstop tend to freeze for a split second before they recover. This hesitation leaves them prone to collision.

In addition, a second baseman needs to be a take-charge type, an infield captain who can direct where a play should go. (Between pitches, the second baseman can indicate where the ball should be thrown if hit by the batter.) Because you move around so much — for example, when you have to cover first base on a bunt — you must concentrate on positioning a little more than the other infielders. Brandon Phillips of the Cincinnati Reds is an excellent example of a second baseman who positions himself well on every hitter.

Because most of your throws are short, you don't need a powerful arm to play second base. However, your throws must be precise and quick (particularly when you are relaying an outfield throw to another base) and you must be able to throw under pressure (being exerted by that base runner bearing down on you).

Shortstop

Shortstop is the most difficult infield position to play. Shortstops must be able to field grounders cleanly because they rarely have time to knock a ball down and throw out the runner. Because you have more territory to cover than any other infielder, you have to be far ranging.

Tall, lean players, like Derek Jeter (6-feet, 3-inches) and the Braves' star-in-the-making Andrelton Simmons (6-feet, 2-inches), are ideally built to play shortstop; they can stretch out over more ground and reach out farther than smaller infielders. However, a relatively short player like 5-foot, 9-inch former Met Rey Ordonez could outplay almost anyone at this position because he was so quick. This position demands a powerful throwing arm to make the throw from the hole (near the third-base side of the infield) or from deep behind second base.

Third base

Like the catcher, a third baseman must be willing to absorb a few body blows. You play close to home plate; if a right-handed hitter pulls the ball sharply, you often won't have time to get your glove into fielding position. That's when you have to throw your body in front of the ball, block it, get to your feet, and throw out the runner. That's why third basemen like Adrian Beltre are studies in black and blue by midseason. You take a lot of punishment at third base.

Great third basemen usually have powerful arms; they need them to make long throws across the diamond. If you can throw with velocity, you can make up some of the time you lose blocking the ball and picking it up. However, Brooks Robinson, who won more Gold Gloves than any other third baseman, had an average arm at best. He compensated with a quick release and by positioning himself so that he seldom had to make the long throws required of most third basemen.

Third base is a reflex position; you must be able to react quickly to balls hit sharply to either side of you. A great third baseman, such as Adrian Beltre, can go to the line to his right as well as to the hole on his left. That agility is one of the reasons he has several Gold Gloves sitting on his mantel.

Left field

Left field is the easiest position to play. Of the three outfielders, the left fielder makes the shortest throws, so he can get by with a below-average arm. Fly balls hit to left don't curve as much as fly balls hit to right. When batters hit the ball to the opposite field, it tends to *slice*. Because so many more hitters bat right-handed than left-handed, the left fielder doesn't have to handle many sliced balls (those fly balls that seem to keep moving farther away from the pursuing outfielder no matter how hard he runs).

Left fielders must be able to *charge the ball* (catch it while running toward it) properly; their close proximity and direct angle to home offer them numerous opportunities to throw out runners at the plate. Charging the ball gives them the momentum to unleash strong throws. The Dodgers' Carl Crawford — nick-named "The Perfect Storm" — demonstrates the gifts a left fielder must have to excel. He's fast, goes back well on balls hit over his head, expertly plays balls hit down the line, and has a powerful arm that rarely misses its target. Watch how he lines up his entire body behind a throw. He's a walking — make that running — clinic on left-field play.

Center field

Center fielders should have accurate, strong arms; they're going to run down more balls than the other two outfielders and consequently have to make more throws. (***Note:*** If you charge the ball quickly and have a quick release, you can get by without having a strong arm.)

Speed and quickness are two more requisites for center field. (A relatively slow player who positions himself well, on the other hand, can play either left or right field.) You cannot play center unless you can run; you have too much territory to cover. In addition to chasing after fly balls, you back up your fellow outfielders on any fly balls or grounders hit your way.

Center fielders must be able to get a good jump on the ball; they need to react and accelerate quickly. Players like Carlos Gomez and Austin Jackson move at the crack of the bat. Excellent lateral movement is another must. The Yankees' Brett Gardner and Denard Span of the Washington Nationals are among the best at going to either side to make a catch.

As a center fielder, you also have to understand your limitations. If you don't go back on the ball well, don't play too shallow. If you have trouble coming in, don't play too deep. A great center fielder like Andrew McCutcheon, who has no difficulty coming in or going out, plays deep to steal extra base hits from the opposition.

Finally, the center fielder must be assertive — the entire outfield is your domain. If you call for a catch, the other outfielders must give way. On balls hit to the left or right fielders, you direct the play. (For more on where to go on a particular play, check out some handy defensive plays at www.dummies.com/extras/baseball.)

Right field

The first thing that managers look for in a right fielder is a strong arm. Right fielders have to make longer throws than anyone else on the diamond, sometimes throwing from deep in the right-field corner to third or home. (Jeff Francoeur does that as well as anyone; he has a howitzer of an arm.) Because hits to right tend to curve or fade away from the fielder, you must be proficient at reading the ball's angle.

Pitcher

For this chapter, we look at the pitcher solely as a defensive player. You're 60 feet, 6 inches (18.4 meters) away from the hitter, so you must have quicker reactions than anyone else in the infield. For your own safety, you should be able to catch the ball cleanly, but this skill isn't a requirement. If you can simply knock the ball down in front of you, you usually have plenty of time to throw out even the fastest runners.

Young pitchers often ignore fielding fundamentals; they seem to think all they need to win ballgames is a lively arm. However, most of baseball's elite pitchers — players such as Gold Glovers Adam Wainwright and Clayton Kershaw — are excellent fielders. They know how to execute — to do those little things that help them win close ballgames. That's one of the reasons they're among their league's pitching leaders year after year. (Refer to Chapter 8 for the ins and outs of throwing pitches.)

Loading the Cannon: Getting Your Arm Ready for the Field

A poor throw can undermine the best glove work. Before exploring any other aspect of fielding, here we discuss the mechanics of throwing. To start, you need to warm up your arm. You and your throwing partner should stand 10 feet (3 meters) apart and gently lob the ball to each other. As your arm starts to feel loose and warm, gradually increase the velocity of your throws. If you're a young adult, toss the ball from four throwing angles:

- Over the top
- Three-quarters
- Sidearm
- Underhand

After you feel completely loose, stretch and strengthen your arm by gradually increasing the distance between you and your throwing partner.

Players under the age of 16 should throw only overhand or three-quarters to develop arm strength. Resist any temptation to throw sidearm or underhand.

Getting a grip

When you grip the ball, your middle and index fingers should be approximately 1 inch (2.54 centimeters) apart, *across* the seams. Place your thumb on the ball's underside, directly below your middle finger. Press the ball with your thumb and middle finger. Because you want your throws to travel straight and true, always throw with your fingers across the seams (see Figure 7-1). Placing your fingers *with* the seams causes the ball to sink or sail (a no-no unless you're a pitcher throwing to a hitter).

Make sure that you hold the ball out in your fingers because, if you hold the ball back in your palm as you throw, you won't generate enough velocity. Don't squeeze the ball; hold it just firmly enough to maintain control. Practice grabbing the ball and finding your across-the-seams grip without peeking.

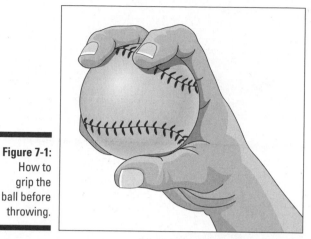

Figure 7-1:
How to
grip the
ball before
throwing.

Illustration by Wiley, Composition Services Graphics

Delivering the throw

How you throw the ball depends on the position you play. Most outfielders throw the ball overhand for maximum power. The exception occurs on a *shoe-string catch* (a ball caught, usually on the run, near your feet). If a runner is trying to advance on that play, the outfielder has to throw underhand or side-arm, or he won't get rid of the ball quickly enough.

Infielders rarely have time to straighten up and throw over the top; whenever you rear back to throw, you concede about 12 feet (3.6 meters) to the base runner. So you should throw three-quarters, sidearm, or underhand depending on the situation. On the double play, a second baseman or shortstop must throw from wherever he catches the ball. If you catch it high, throw overhand; if you catch it low, throw underhand.

To make an accurate, powerful overhand throw:

1. **Start the throw by squaring yourself toward your target and swinging your throwing arm back to your side in an arc.**

   Tilt your upper torso back on your throwing side, while keeping your other shoulder (and your eyes) pointed toward your target. Your wrist should be cocked and ready to throw.

2. **Step and thrust forward as you swing your arm directly over your shoulder and toward your target.**

   Make sure you extend your arm fully. Keep your elbow higher than your throwing shoulder (see Figure 7-2).

Figure 7-2:
Making the
overhand
throw.

3. **Plant your front (striding) foot while pushing off your rear (pivot) foot. To get maximum velocity on your throw, snap your wrist downward as you release the ball.**

 Your arm should continue to sweep in front of you and down to your side. As you follow through, your glove hand should come up behind you for balance. Allow your lower body to follow your upper body's momentum toward the target.

4. **Bring your pivot foot forward until it is parallel to your striding foot.**

 Use this same motion for the three-quarter throw from the outfield, but bring your elbow around on a 45-degree angle.

Infielders often throw sidearm and don't have time for a lot of motion when they throw. To throw sidearm, bring your throwing arm back in a short arc. Step toward your target and thrust forward as you swing your arm back in an arc that is parallel to the ground. You often cannot get your whole body behind this throw, so put as much shoulder and wrist into it as you can. Aim your throw for the middle of your target's torso.

You usually must throw underhand when you're close to your target or have to quickly toss a ball you have caught below your knees and to the side. Using a bowling motion, flip the ball toward your target's chest. Because you cannot get anything behind this throw, give it a good wrist snap as you release the ball.

Determining how hard is too hard

You don't have to air everything out on every throw you make. I don't believe throwing consistently hard is likely to hurt or tire your arm. However, if you are trying to throw the ball through a wall on every play, you can strain your muscles over the course of a season. Rick Burleson, a first-rate shortstop for the Red Sox and Angels from the mid-1970s to early 1980s, had a cannon arm whose power he demonstrated on nearly every throw. By age 30, a torn rotator cuff (an arm injury more common to pitchers than fielders) finished his career as a starting shortstop.

A Word about Errors

The first thing you have to remember is that every player makes errors. Don't let it get you down, though. On the upside, if you have good range and play aggressively, you're going to commit fumbles on balls that other fielders don't even reach. Most errors come on grounders that are hit directly at you. (If you have any talent for catching a baseball, you rarely muff a fly ball.)

In 1976, for example, I made 13 errors (nearly one every two weeks) while still winning a Gold Glove at second base. In 1980, when I was with Houston, our left fielder Jose Cruz led the National League with 11 errors, and he still managed to catch nearly 97 percent of the balls hit his way. (By the way, Jose was a fine outfielder; he just had one of those years.)

Fielders who fumble grounders tend to freeze for an instant instead of being aggressive. This lack of aggressiveness is what broadcasters mean when they say that the fielder *let the ball play him.* Whenever a ground ball is hit toward you, charge it immediately so you can gauge its hop. If you fail to charge right away, you can misperceive the ball's bounce. Keep reading for some tips about how you can reduce errors.

Don't short-leg

Fear of fumbles can sap you of aggressiveness. Some players, rather than charging a ball, time their approaches so they and the ball arrive at a spot simultaneously. If they catch the ball, it looks like a dazzling play. If they miss it, the official scorer usually deems it a hit instead of an error. It's called *short-legging* the ball, and it is a capital crime. You aren't on the field to look pretty or compile a gaudy fielding percentage. You're there to help your team win. Short-leggers invariably cost their clubs victories. When you're on the diamond, give everything you have to every play.

Avoid mental errors

Mental errors don't appear in anyone's box score, but they are often more costly than physical mistakes. When you commit a *rock* (make a boneheaded play) like throwing to the wrong base, it's usually because you did not anticipate the situation. As each hitter steps up to the plate, review all your options.

For example, you're the second baseman with a man on first and one out. Right away you should not only be thinking double play, but how to execute it. If the ball is hit to the shortstop or third baseman, you have to cover second. Hit to the pitcher? You're backing up the shortstop's play at second base. And so on. Cover all the possibilities so that when the ball hits the bat, you are ready to execute. You don't have to waste a second wondering what to do — you can simply react.

Fielding Grounders: Six Tips

Fielding a ground ball is easy if you have sound fundamentals. To put yourself in position to make a play, you should do the following:

- ✓ **Charge the ball whenever you can.** If you hang back, the ball has more time to take a bad hop. Maintain a short, quick stride rather than one that is long and uncontrollable. You should be able to stop abruptly.

- ✓ **Stay down on the ball.** Keep your body, including your buttocks, low to the ground. Standing straight up makes it difficult to gauge the ball's hop. You want your eyes down low for a good look at the ball. Keep your eyes on the ball; watch it go into your glove. After you catch it, look where you're going to throw it.

- ✓ **Keep your weight balanced evenly on the balls of both feet when you take your fielding stance (unless you're anticipating a specific play).** Having your knees slightly bent allows the freedom of movement you need to burst out of your stance in pursuit of the ball.

- ✓ **Use both hands to field whenever possible.** Catch the ball with your glove near the ground facing up and your bare palm above it facing down. If a ball takes a bad hop, using two hands gives you a better chance to corral it. The ball may drop into your glove after hitting the palm of your hand, or it may drop in front of you. Then you can pick it up in time to throw out the runner. If you use only one hand and the grounder takes a bad hop, the ball will get by you. Using both hands also allows you to get your throws off quickly.

- ✔ **Let your hands "give" a bit when the ball makes contact with your glove.** Cradle the ball in your glove as if you were catching an egg.

- ✔ **Keep your arms extended so that you catch the ball in front of you.** Try to field the ball in the middle of your body so that if the ball hits you on the bad hop, it drops in front of you. If it hits off to your side, the ball can bounce away from you.

Practice your throws so that you can take the ball out of your glove without looking at it. Remember, you want to grab the ball across the seams to ensure an accurate throw. You must be able to get your preferred grip on the ball while looking at your target, *not the ball*.

There will be times when you shouldn't even attempt a throw. For example, suppose that Michael Bourne is speeding toward first on a slow grounder. If you realize that you have no chance to make an accurate throw, hold the ball. Yes, you just put a runner on first, but that decision is better than letting Bourne take second or third (and he will) if you throw the ball wildly.

Positioning Yourself for a Strong Defense

No matter where you play on the field, knowledge and anticipation are the keys to positioning. Prior to the game, your pitcher should have told you and your teammates how he plans to throw to the opposing batters. You need to combine that information with all the data you have on those hitters.

For example, when I was with the Reds, Jack Billingham may have tried to catch Billy Williams (a terrifying left-handed hitter with the Chicago Cubs) off-balance with a slow curve. I knew Billy would probably pull that pitch toward right field. If Jack threw his fastball away, Billy would probably shoot it to the opposite field. However, if Reggie Jackson — a slugger who hit over 500 home runs in the American League — was the hitter, Jack may have thrown a fastball away. Most left-handed hitters would hit that pitch to the opposite field in left. But Reggie was strong enough to pull the fastball away into right field with authority. I had to know all these tendencies so I could position myself accordingly.

After your mental data file on the opposing players is complete, you can reposition yourself for each hitter that comes to the plate; you may even change your position from pitch to pitch. Say that your catcher calls for the fastball inside; you're going to lean to the left or right depending on the hitter's tendencies. Because smart hitters adapt to situations, you must do the same. For example, with the first baseman holding a runner on first, a left-handed hitting genius like Ichiro Suzuki can shoot balls through that big hole on the right side of the infield. If you were playing second in that circumstance, you would lean more toward first to get a better jump on balls hit toward the hole. If no one was on base, you would play closer to second. However, if the pitcher was going inside on Ichiro, you would cheat toward first.

Fielding Line Drives

Catching a line drive is a reaction play — you either catch it or you don't. However, if you can't catch a line drive cleanly, you must knock it down so you have some opportunity to pick it up and throw. Whenever you have to leap for a line drive, watch the ball until it enters your glove (professional players call this "looking the ball into your glove").

Fielding Fly Balls

Here we talk about *pop flies,* those weakly hit fly balls that don't make it out of the infield. On pop flies, you should run to wherever you expect the ball to drop. Catch the ball in front of you on your forehand side. Don't play the ball so that you have to run to catch it at the last moment. If you have to go back on a pop fly, run sideways rather than backpedaling (though you can back-pedal if you're only going a few steps). You don't want to risk tangling your feet. Get stationary so the ball comes straight down into your glove. Position yourself so that if you fail to catch the ball, it hits you in the chest rather than the head or shoulders. Keep your arms extended but loose: That way, if you bobble the ball, you have a second chance to catch it before it hits the ground.

Whenever you see infielders or outfielders collide on a pop fly, you know that someone wasn't paying attention. I always told our outfielders to yell so I could get out of the way if they were going to catch a pop-up. If you both yell for the catch, you won't hear each other. When I was with the Astros, our left fielder, Jesus Alou, and our shortstop, Hector Torres, were both yelling as they went after a pop fly. They collided and Hector nearly choked to death on his tongue. Make sure that you have your signals straight before each game so you can avoid that kind of catastrophe.

With a fast runner on first base, I've seen infielders deliberately drop pop flies so they could get the force-out at second. The idea is to erase a base-stealing threat or replace a speedy runner with a slower one. I don't believe that is ever good policy. Baseballs can take funny hops; if a pop fly hits the ground and bounces away from you, you may not get anybody out.

Chapter 8

Winning the Arms' Race: Pitching Like a Major Leaguer

*P*itching is the most valuable commodity in baseball. Most teams don't reach the postseason without possessing solid *starting rotations* (pitching lineups) backed by deep *bullpens* (relief pitchers). Any manager (or head coach) will tell you that strong pitching is the best insurance against long losing streaks. When your club surrenders only three or four runs every game, you can find a way to win even with the weakest offense. A gifted hitter can galvanize an entire lineup, but a dominant pitcher can do more to elevate a team than any position player can. Even a last-place club can compete like a world champion if it has a top gun on the mound.

Find that opinion hard to believe? Open up a baseball encyclopedia and look up the 1972 Philadelphia Phillies. You'll see a team whose .358 win-loss percentage was the worst in the National League that season. Yet when Steve Carlton pitched for the Phillies, they played .730 ball. No team came within 110 points of that mark. If Philadelphia could have cloned Carlton, the club would have won its division by 22 games.

And Carlton is only one of the many examples we could present to support our point. The record books are filled with the names of men — Randy Johnson, Roger Clemens, Pedro Martinez, Tom Seaver, Walter Johnson, Bob Gibson — who transformed their clubs from victims to predators every time they

Before you take the mound

You can increase the effectiveness of all your pitches if you throw them with the same motion. Have your coaches and teammates watch you on the mound to see if you make any subtle gestures that may reveal which pitch you are about to deliver. Never throw a half-hearted pitch. If you don't agree with the sign from your catcher, shake him off (shake your head "no"). Wait until he calls for something that inspires more enthusiasm or comes out to the mound to discuss the options. Don't let a hitter beat you on your second-best pitch. With the game on the line, go with your best stuff, even if that means matching your strength against the hitter's.

strode to the center of the diamond. Each of these pitchers had powerful arms, sound mechanics, a genius for pitch selection, and an unquenchable competitive spirit. Now, we can't give you Aroldis Chapman's arm, Justin Verlander's drive, or Craig Breslow's brain. But in this chapter we show you the proper way to throw the various pitches you need to get hitters out. The rest you have to develop between the lines.

We've enlisted help from both sides of the mound for this section. Bob Gibson is our right-hander. During his 17-year career with the St. Louis Cardinals, Bob won 251 games, struck out 3,117 batters, posted five 20-win seasons, won two Cy Young Awards, and was named a National League Most Valuable Player — an award few pitchers have on their résumés. And he's also a Hall of Famer.

Bob was a power pitcher, so for help with *off-speed* (non-fastball) stuff, we have Bill Lee. As a member of the Boston Red Sox and Montreal Expos, Bill was one of the leading left-handers of the 1970s. He wasn't overpowering; Bill got hitters out with movement and great control. ***Note:*** For information on special rules for pitchers, see Chapter 3.

Check out www.dummies.com/extras/baseball for more underappreciated aspects of pitching and how you can become a better pitcher.

Delivering Your Pitch: Starting with Your Stance

Stances are as individual as the pitchers who assume them. Find a stance on the mound that leaves you balanced and comfortable. Your weight should be evenly distributed and your hands relaxed. Keep your glove hand and ball hand together so you don't let the hitter see your grip on the ball (it may tip him off to which pitch you intend to throw). As you take the sign from your catcher, your *pivot foot* (right foot for right-handers, left foot for left-handers) must touch the pitching rubber.

If you're left-handed, place your pivot foot on the left end of the rubber. If you're right-handed, do the reverse. Face the plate squarely. After you're in your stance, you want to windup, thrust, release, and follow-through to deliver an effective pitch. These sections can help you with the basics.

Winding up, thrusting, and releasing

Your *windup* should get the full force of your body behind the pitch. Model your windup after these steps:

1. **From your stance, start releasing the momentum by taking a short step back behind the rubber with your striding foot (left foot for right-handers, right foot for lefties).**

   Avoid taking a large step or you'll throw off your balance. You should be gripping the ball in the glove at some point between the top of your shoulder and high above your head. (See Figure 8-1.)

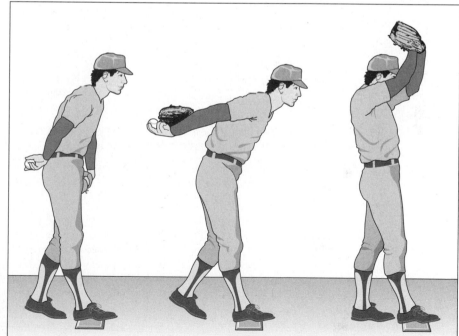

Figure 8-1: Starting the windup.

Illustration by Wiley, Composition Services Graphics

2. **Pivot as you lift your striding foot to bring it back over the rubber and lift your striding knee to your chest.**

   This is your *leg kick,* but if you actually do kick out, you may disturb your balance. Keep your head steady and over your rear foot. (See Figure 8-2.)

Figure 8-2:
Beginning
your leg
kick.

Illustration by Wiley, Composition Services Graphics

3. **Bring your hands down (somewhere between your belt and chest) and separate them. Nearly all your weight should be on your pivot leg.**

   That leg should be slightly bent. As you pivot back, turn your striding foot until it is perpendicular to the rubber. Your hips and shoulders should be closed to the batter.

   "Don't try to copy your windup from some other pitcher. Find out what is comfortable for you. If someone were to give you a ball and tell you to go into your windup, 99 percent of the time that basic motion is what will serve you best because it's what's most natural for you. We may have to alter your mechanics — the positioning of your arm or something like that — but not your natural motion. If you're a coach and you have a youngster who isn't comfortable winding up, don't make him do it. Let him pitch without a windup." — Bob Gibson

4. **Maintain the weight on your back foot until your leg kick is at its highest point and then start shifting your weight forward toward home plate as in Figure 8-3.**

Figure 8-3:
Starting to
come home.

Illustration by Wiley, Composition Services Graphics

5. **Bring down your striding leg and plant it with your foot pointed toward home plate.**

   As the striding foot hits the ground, your hips should open (but keep your front shoulder closed). Your throwing arm should be raised behind your head to its highest point with your wrist cocked back. Your striding leg should be slightly bent. Lower your body and thrust from the pitching rubber.

   "You have to get your hips into this. It's very much like playing golf or hitting. To play golf, you have to turn your hips away from the ball and then bring them back with your swing. To hit, you turn your hips away from the plate, and then come back. Same thing as a pitcher, you bring your hips to the side and then come back forward." — *Bob Gibson*

6. **As you bring your throwing arm around, bring your glove hand forward just above your elbow with the palm up.**

   Keep your elbow high so you can trace a wide arc with your throwing arm. Do not, however, trace so wide an arc that it throws off your balance. To get the most movement on the ball, deliver your pitch with a three-quarters motion.

"If you were to stand erect while facing home plate and point your arm out straight from your shoulder and then put your elbow and hand up at a 90-degree angle, you'd see and feel the proper angle (for delivering a pitch). You'll see pitchers who go higher or lower, but the 90-degree angle is the easiest on your arm. Most pitchers — and a lot of them don't even know they're doing this — will have their arm in this spot just as they begin their thrust." — Bob Gibson

7. **Release the ball with your head over your striding leg and your arm fully extended.**

    Your elbow should be at or above shoulder level and your forearm parallel to the ground. Your pivot foot should come forward with its heel up as your hip (throwing-hand side) drives toward home plate. (See Figure 8-4.)

"Don't try to muscle the pitch to get greater velocity. When you tighten the arm to throw, it's like a hitter trying to hit a home run and swinging too hard. His bat gets very slow. The same thing will happen with your arm. Keep your hand, wrist, and arm relaxed so you can pop the ball at the very last second. You get your velocity in front of the rubber, not behind the rubber. The ideal thing would be for you to use your arm like a whip, but not everyone is capable of doing that." — Bob Gibson

Figure 8-4:
Releasing
the ball.

Illustration by Wiley, Composition Services Graphics

Following through on your pitch

"Follow-through is very important for a pitcher. If you cut off your follow-through, you won't be able to pop the ball for velocity." — Bob Gibson

After you release the pitch, your pivot foot should continue to move forward until it is parallel or slightly in front of your striding foot. Bring the elbow of your glove hand back toward your hip (as if you were elbowing someone behind you). Your throwing arm should sweep across your body on a diagonal and end on the first-base side (if you are right-handed) or third-base side (if you're left-handed) of your knee (refer to Figure 8-5). Ideally, this follow-through should leave you in perfect fielding position: weight balanced evenly on the balls of your feet, knees bent, and your glove ready to field anything hit your way.

Figure 8-5: Following-through with the pitch.

Illustration by Wiley, Composition Services Graphics

"If your follow-through ends with you in perfect fielding position, fine. But don't let it get in the way of your main objective, getting the ball to the plate with location and something on it. If I had tried to come out in perfect fielding position all the time, I probably wouldn't have gotten anybody out because I would have had to cut my follow-through off. I wasn't willing to do that. So I just made sure I recovered quickly enough after my follow-through to field the ball." — Bob Gibson

Gibson's follow-through often ended with him facing first base, but he recovered quickly enough to earn nine consecutive Gold Glove awards.

...g from the Stretch

With runners on, you have to discard your full windup; it leaves your leg in the air so long that opponents are able to steal bases easily. Instead, pitch from the *set* or *stretch* position. Stand sideways with your rear foot against the front edge of the rubber and your front shoulder aligned with home. Your feet should be a little less than shoulder width apart with your front foot's heel even with the rear of your back foot's arch (check out Figure 8-6).

Figure 8-6: Getting into the stretch position.

Illustration by Wiley, Composition Services Graphics

Instead of winding up to deliver the ball, simply stretch your arms above your head and bring your ball and glove hands to a complete stop somewhere between your chest and belt. The rest of the delivery is similar to the one you use out of your windup, except you need less kick and pivot and more push from the pitching rubber.

"Pitching from the stretch is no different from pitching with a windup. You're simply cutting off the windup, but at the point where you rotate your hips you should be in the same position as when you take your full windup." — Bob Gibson

Identifying the Weapons in Your Pitching Arsenal

Ninety-four miles per hour, 100 miles per hour, 105 miles per hour — the numbers reported by the speed-obsessed media may lead you to believe that a fastball's velocity is its most important attribute. It isn't. More critical to a pitcher's success is the fastball's movement and location. Pitchers should also be able to change speeds to throw off the batter's timing. If a fastball doesn't move much, a competent hitter can time it after a few viewings no matter how many speed records it shatters.

Case in point: When Hideki Irabu, the Japanese League pitching star, made his MLB debut with the New York Yankees, his best fastball clocked in at 98 mph. Few pitchers matched his speed. However, during his first season with New York, Irabu's pitches were straight as a string. After opponents got their swings grooved, they were hitting long shots off of him. After Yankee pitching coach Mel Stottlemyre taught Irabu how to make his ball move more (Stottlemyre altered Irabu's grip), the pitcher enjoyed greater success.

"You can teach a pitcher to increase his movement on the ball. It's all a matter of how you hold and release the ball. If you release the ball with your fingers pointed straight up, there's a good chance the ball won't move. But if you just cock the ball to one side or the other, it will move if you work at it." — Bob Gibson

Four-time Cy Young Award winner Greg Maddux, on the other hand, rarely threw harder than 88 mph, which is below average for a Major Leaguer. However, Maddux was so successful because he could put the ball wherever he wanted it. His pitches not only moved, but they moved late. Batters thought they had honed in on a Maddux pitch, only to find that the ball had darted at the very last second. The right-hander rarely threw two consecutive pitches at the same speed. Like most great pitchers, Maddux threw a variety of pitches, including a slider, curve, and change-up.

Every pitcher, no matter how hard he throws, should have at least three strong pitches — something hard, something that breaks, and something off-speed — in his arsenal. In fact, many people feel that the change-up is the best pitch in baseball, and it doesn't add strain to the pitcher's arm. With that advice in mind, take a look at your options in the following sections.

The four-seam fastball

The *four-seamer* is considered the basic fastball. Grip it with your top two fingers across the seams at their widest point. Nestle your thumb under the ball across the bottom seam. Curl your ring and little fingers along one side. Your middle and index fingers should be about a half-inch apart. If they touch, the ball can slide, making it difficult to control. If you spread them too far, you can limit the wrist action you need to pitch. Hold the ball away from your palm with your fingertips (see Figure 8-7).

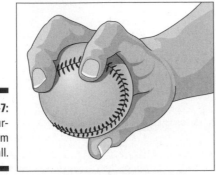

Figure 8-7:
The four-seam fastball.

Illustration by Wiley, Composition Services Graphics

Keeping your fingers in the center of the ball limits its movement. However, if you bring your digits a bit closer together and move them off-center to the left, the ball runs (moves to either side) or sinks. Placing your fingers off-center to the right causes the ball to break in on a left-handed batter and break away from a righty.

The two-seam fastball

The *two-seam fastball* moves more than the four-seamer. To throw it, grip the ball along its two seams with your middle and index fingers. Position your thumb under the ball. Your ring and little fingers are off to the side of the ball, slightly behind your gripping fingers. Exert pressure with your middle finger and thumb. To throw a sinking fastball, move your top fingers so that they hook a seam. Throw the ball like a fastball and let your grip do the rest.

For a variation on this theme, you can grip the ball with your middle and index fingers across the two seams at their narrowest point (the portion of an official baseball that bears the league president's signature). Maintain pressure with your thumb and middle finger. With this two-seam grip, the ball should move more to the side.

Some pitchers turn their hands down and in when they release the two-seamer. This action slows the ball's break, which can throw off a hitter's timing; however, if it doesn't, that pitch is an excellent candidate for a home run.

"As a right-handed pitcher, if I threw the two-seamer to a right-handed hitter, the ball would usually sink or curve into him. If I threw that same pitch to the left-hander, it would sink and move away from him. Most left-handed hitters are low-ball hitters, which means that a two-seamer would be right in their wheelhouse. So I'm going to throw the four-seamer to him; that pitch will ride in on his hands." — Bob Gibson

The slider

A hybrid, the *slider* is part fastball, part breaking ball. We list it with the other fastballs because it's more effective the harder it's thrown. The key to an effective slider is its late break. The pitch should resemble a fastball until it approaches the hitter. Then it should veer sharply to the side.

Grip the slider with the index and middle fingers across the two widest seams. Keep your fingers slightly off-center, toward the outside of the ball. Your thumb should be tucked under the ball, and your ring and little fingers should be off to its side. Exert pressure with your thumb and middle finger, as Figure 8-8 shows.

Figure 8-8:
The slider.

Illustration by Wiley, Composition Services Graphics

When you throw the ball, *keep your wrist loose!* Throwing this pitch with a stiff wrist can strain and damage your elbow.

You also shouldn't twist your wrist as you release the slider (a mistake commonly made by pitchers who think twisting imparts greater spin on the pitch — it does, but it also increases the chances of injury). Instead, throw it like a fastball, but imagine cutting through the ball with your middle finger as you deliver the pitch. Keep your fingers on top of the ball until the moment of release.

"If you twist your wrist like you're throwing a curve, you won't get that extra bite on the pitch. That ball will have a big, slow break. Instead, turn the ball with your first two fingers and your thumb as if you were turning a doorknob." — Bob Gibson

The split-fingered fastball

The *split-fingered fastball* is the child of the *forkball,* a pitch that was thrown with great effectiveness by such relief-pitching stars as Elroy Face and Lindy McDaniel during the 1960s. Pitchers held the forkball between the first two joints of their middle and index fingers. When thrown by a good fastball pitcher, it was more like a good change-up than a power pitch. You don't hold today's split-finger (or *splitter*) as high between your fingers as the forkball, which means you can throw it with greater velocity. Split your middle and index fingers and grip the ball along its seams. Don't jam it past the midway point of your fingers. (See Figure 8-9.)

Figure 8-9:
The split-
fingered
fastball.

Illustration by Wiley, Composition Services Graphics

"Throw the pitch with a fastball motion and plenty of wrist. When properly delivered, the splitter should look like a fastball until it reaches the plate. Then the pitch should dive down as if the bottom has dropped out from under it." — Bill Lee

The curveball

Good *curveballs* (also known as *yakkers, hooks, and deuces*) have put more hitters out of work than all the baseball strikes combined. If you have a hook that you can throw for strikes, batters can't *sit back on* (wait for) the fastball even when the count is in their favor. Hitters never look worse than when they swing at a curve after guessing a fastball.

To throw the curve, grip the ball with your middle and index fingers across the seams at their widest part. Hold it farther back in your hand than the fastball, but don't let it touch your palm or you won't get enough spin. Your object here is to get more of your finger surface in contact with the ball. Curl your ring and little fingers into your palm. Exert pressure with your middle finger and thumb; keep the index finger loose against the ball (refer to Figure 8-10).

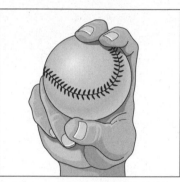

Figure 8-10:
The
curveball.

Illustration by Wiley, Composition Services Graphics

"As you bring your arm forward in your motion, your wrist should be cocked and rotating inward. Your palm and ball should face you as your hand passes your head. While keeping your elbow high, turn your wrist and snap down as you release the ball over your index finger. The back of your hand should be facing the batter as the pitch leaves your fingers." — Bill Lee

Make sure you follow through with your motion, or your curve ball will hang (stay up in the strike zone where a hitter likes it). Pitchers who throw a lot of hanging curves often want to hang themselves because batters tend to smack those pitches a long, long way.

The three-fingered change-up

Change-ups make your fastballs more effective by making them seem faster by comparison. You can use a variety of change-up grips, but the *three-fingered change-up* is the easiest to master. Hold the ball back against your palm with your index finger, middle finger, and ring finger spread across the seams at their widest point. Nestle the thumb and pinky against each other under the ball (check out Figure 8-11).

Figure 8-11:
The three-fingered change-up.

Illustration by Wiley, Composition Services Graphics

"Exert equal pressure with all five fingers. Keep your wrist stiff. Bring it straight down as if you were lowering a window shade. Don't pick a corner with this pitch; throw it down the middle of the plate." — Bill Lee

The circle change-up

Hold the *circle change-up* like the three-finger change-up — only join the index finger and thumb in a circle on the side of the ball, as in Figure 8-12. The best change-ups — like that employed by Justin Verlander — look like fastballs out of the pitcher's hand. However, they take more time to reach home plate and can upset the timing of any hitter looking for something hard and fast.

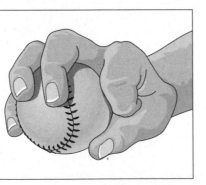

Figure 8-12:
The circle change-up.

Illustration by Wiley, Composition Services Graphics

The palmball

The *palmball* is an off-speed pitch, a change of pace designed to mess with the hitter's rhythm. Unlike all other pitches, the ball is held tight against the palm. Your middle and index fingers rest across the top of the two widest seams. Your ring and little fingers rest against one side; your thumb is slightly raised along the other. Exert pressure on the ball with your ring finger and thumb (look at Figure 8-13). Throw this pitch with your usual fastball motion. As you release the pitch, straighten out your fingers and make sure your hand is behind the ball rather than on top of it. You want the ball to slip from between your thumb and fingers.

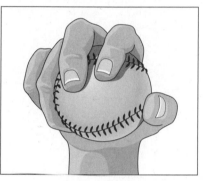

Figure 8-13: The palmball.

Illustration by Wiley, Composition Services Graphics

"Pitchers make the mistake of trying to underthrow their change-ups, reducing their arm's speed to slow the pitch. Throw the ball as if it were a fastball and let your grip and motion do the work." — Bill Lee

The screwball

Throw the *screwball* pitch only at your own peril; this pitch is murder on the arm. A reverse curveball, the *scroogie* is held like a four-seam fastball (see Figure 8-7). The index finger and thumb provide all the pressure, but you release the ball off your middle finger.

Come over the top with this pitch as if it were a fastball. However, just before you release the ball, turn your wrist, forearm, and elbow inward in a corkscrew motion. The rotation should be the opposite of your curveball. When thrown by a left-hander (which most screwballers are), the ball breaks down and away from right-handed hitters. However, it breaks down and in on left-handed hitters, which they like a lot; that's why left-handed hitters usually hit left-handed scroogie artists so well.

The knuckle ball

The *knuckle ball* is the one pitch that is more effective the slower you throw it. Knuckle balls are difficult to control because their movement is so erratic. Often, the pitcher who throws one has no idea how it will move or where. Knucklers dart, dance, jump, break, swerve, and rise. Sometimes these pitches perform two or three of these motions in the same flight. Most batters hate to hit against the knuckler; a good one can throw off their swings for weeks.

The trick to throwing the pitch is to eliminate as much of the ball rotation as you can. Despite its name, the ball is rarely thrown off the knuckles. Instead, dig the tips of your index, middle, and ring fingers (make sure your nails are always trimmed if you are going to throw this pitch) into just below the seams of the ball. Keep your thumb and little finger on the side (refer to Figure 8-14).

Figure 8-14:
The knuckle
ball.

Illustration by Wiley, Composition Services Graphics

TIP

"Don't throw the knuckle ball; push it towards home plate with a stiff wrist out of your usual motion. Imagine you're tossing a pair of socks into the hamper. As you release the ball, extend your fingers straight out towards home plate." — Bill Lee

Playing Defense as a Pitcher

Retiring batters isn't the only responsibility pitchers have. When you're on the mound, you must cover a base or back up a fielder on nearly every play. You have to be quick enough to flag down hot smashes up the middle (or at least get out of their way so one of your infielders can catch them) and pounce on bunts. When runners stray far from the bag, you have to drive them back with a look or a pickoff move. On many infield plays, you're the traffic cop directing your teammates, so you must stay cool and alert.

A word from Bob Gibson on control

"Being able to throw the fastball with as much velocity as you can is important. But the number one thing for any pitcher is control — being able to throw the ball where you want when you want to. Try using the same release point every time. If you don't know where your release point is, your ball is going to be everywhere. You also have to know yourself. For instance, if my ball was high, I knew there were two things I could be doing wrong. One was I had screwed up my release point, the other was I had taken too long a stride. When you understand your error, you can make adjustments on the mound."

Photo courtesy of National Baseball Hall of Fame Library, Cooperstown, N.Y.

For advice on how pitchers can field their position properly, we turn to one of Joe's opponents from the 1975 World Series, Bill Lee. The Red Sox left-hander was one of the smoothest fielders in the game, quick on bunts, fundamentally sound on grounders, and capable of the amazing play. (The behind-the-back catch of line drives hit up the middle was a Lee specialty.)

Getting into fielding position: The follow-through

Ideally, when you emerge from your follow-through, you should be in a position to field anything hit toward you. Your body should be squared toward home plate, your feet should be parallel and shoulder-width apart, and your weight should be evenly distributed over the balls of your feet. Few pitchers on any level come out of their follow-through perfectly positioned to field. However, you should strive to come as close to the ideal as you can.

"Never forget that your number-one concern is getting the hitter out. If you can't come out of your follow-through in the ideal fielding position, you can compensate by keeping your eyes peeled on home plate and watching for the ball off the bat. Then let your reactions take over if the ball is hit towards you." — Bill Lee

Fielding aggressively

Try to field as many balls hit between you and first as you can. Anytime you can keep that first baseman near the bag, you're helping your team's defensive alignment.

- ✔ On bunt plays, charge balls that are hit directly toward you.
- ✔ On balls to the extreme side of you, field only those that look as if they will stop rolling before one of your infielders reaches it.

"As you go after the ball, don't focus on the runner. Instead, watch the ball into your glove. Don't rush your throw after fielding it. Get a good grip on the ball. Keep moving towards your target as you step and throw. If you have to spin and throw, keep a low center of gravity; it will make you quicker. If you're close to the base and the fielder isn't there, lead him to the bag with an underhand toss. However, if your fielder is on or near the bag and you aren't too close, hit the target he gives you with a strong overhand throw. Aim for his chest." — Bill Lee

On plays that require you to cover first base, go to a spot approximately 6 feet (1.8 meters) from first on the base line. Run parallel to the base line as you cut toward first. As you reach the bag, shorten your strides so you can adjust to any bad throws.

"Touch the inside of the base on the home plate side with your right foot. This will prevent your momentum from carrying you into the runner (a must to avoid) or into foul territory." — Bill Lee

Keeping runners close

Anytime you keep a base runner anchored near a base, you not only reduce his chances to steal, you also make it more difficult to take an extra base or score on a long hit. Making numerous pickoff throws will chase a runner back to a base. Bill recommends three other things you can do to hold a runner on without making a throw:

✔ Use the same motion to first as you do to home. Don't give the runner any extra movement to pick up on. Be especially careful that you don't reveal your intentions with slight head or eye movements. Good base runners are studying you constantly and pick up on the tiniest quirks.

✔ Disrupt the runner's timing by altering your rhythm as you move into your set position and go into your windup. Remember you're not changing movement here, just the timing of your movement. Don't fall into any consistent rhythms. Hold the ball during your set position for varying time periods.

✔ If you're left-handed, just watch the runner. If you don't move to throw, he can't go anywhere. (Well, technically he can, but the odds are you'll throw him out.)

Avoiding balks

Deceptiveness is one of the keys to an effective pickoff throw. However, you can't be so deceptive that the umpire calls you for a *balk.* There are many ways to commit a *balk,* but the basic definition is any motion by the pitcher that can be construed by the umpire(s) as trying to trick the base runner(s). (For the official lowdown, visit `www.mlb.com/mlb/official_info/off`.)

You can avoid balking while attempting a pickoff at first by doing the following:

✔ When you're in the set position, take the sign from your catcher with your foot on the rubber and your hands visibly separated.

✔ After you have your sign, bring your hands together and pause one full second before going into your delivery.

✔ If you swing your striding foot past the rear portion of the pitching rubber, you must deliver a pitch.

✔ Move only your head while in the set position. If you shrug your shoulders or move your legs or hands, the umpire can nail you for a balk.

✔ If you make any motion toward a base, throw to it. You must complete any movement you start without interruption until you're in the set position.

✔ Always step directly toward the bag that you're throwing to. You may step and fake a throw to second or third, but you can't fake a throw to first without first stepping off the rubber.

✔ If you want to move out of the set position without incurring a balk, step off the rubber.

✔ Never make a pitching motion unless you have the ball.

✔ Don't drop the ball during your delivery.

"It may sound funny, but don't even scratch your nose or wipe your mouth when you're on the rubber with a runner on first. I've seen guys called for balks for doing just those things. You're concentrating so hard on the hitter, something itches, and you just do the natural thing. Just make sure you step off the rubber first." — Bill Lee

"Always try to be quick to home plate. If the runner does take off, you will save your catcher a stride when he tries to throw the runner out. If you're slow to the plate, your catcher doesn't have a chance against the faster base stealers. He won't be able to get them unless he's Dirty Harry Callahan and he's toting his .44 Magnum." — Bill Lee

Catching the runner off base

You can attempt to pick off a runner anytime your foot is off the pitching rubber (that's to say when you are in the set position or going into your stretch). If you're a right-hander trying to pick off a runner at first, push off your right foot while pivoting toward the bag with your left foot. Keep your upper torso open so you throw overhand rather than across your body, as in Figure 8-15.

Figure 8-15: The right-hander's pickoff move.

If you're a left-hander, you don't need to pivot because you are already facing first. All you have to do is snap off a sidearm throw while stepping toward first. When you raise your striding leg out of the set position, there will be a moment when it points toward first. Unlike the right-hander, you now have the option of throwing to the bag or continuing your motion toward home plate (see Figure 8-16).

Illustration by Wiley, Composition Services Graphics

Figure 8-16:
The left-hander's pickoff move.

Pickoffs at second are more complicated. You can employ a time play by signaling your second baseman or shortstop as you check the runner at second (refer to Chapter 10). On a 1-2-3 time play, the count begins when you turn back to face the hitter. On two, you should turn back toward second as the fielder breaks for the bag. On three, throw the ball at the fielder's knees and over the base. On the daylight play, the fielder sneaks up near the bag. You throw as soon as you see daylight between the fielder (usually the shortstop) and the runner.

"I know Joe prefers the time play, but, as a pitcher, I have to go the other way. I like the daylight play's spontaneity and the fact that you are reacting to your shortstop's movements. Time plays can go awry if you and your fielder aren't synchronized. That was always a problem for me. My middle infielders were usually on Greenwich time and I was on Somalian time." — Bill Lee

You shouldn't attempt many pickoffs at third because it's a bad percentage play. Few runners steal home, and if you throw the ball away, you've just given the opposition a run. To pick the runner off at third, the right-hander and left-hander reverse the mechanics they use when throwing to first.

"Don't even think about this play with two outs. The runner cannot score on an out and no one wants to face his manager after making the inning-ending out on an attempted steal of home. Concentrate on the hitter; he's the one who can hurt you." — Bill Lee

Chapter 9

Behind the Plate: The Catcher

Good catchers are field generals. Because they call the pitches from behind the plate, they dictate a team's defensive strategy. The better catchers can also set a tone for an entire ball club.

All of a game's action flows from the catcher's signs. Because everything starts with this position, it's an appropriate place to begin a catcher's duties. Throughout this chapter, you get tips from the player who redefined the position — Johnny Bench. Johnny came to the Major Leagues with the Cincinnati Reds in 1968 and promptly won the first of his ten consecutive Gold Gloves — a record for Major-League catchers.

Getting Ready: Before the Ball Is Pitched

A catcher must be able to recognize the strengths and limitations of his pitchers and the opposing hitters. His arm must be powerful enough to provide base thieves with some incentive not to run. Catchers are often thought of as slow, blocky types. Most of them aren't speedy, but they need to be quick enough to scurry from behind the plate on bunts.

For example, when Johnny Bench joined the Reds, he brought an intimidating presence to the field that immediately transformed Cincinnati into a cockier, more aggressive team. Joe Girardi, a catcher on three New York Yankee world champion teams was an intense individual who raised his pitchers' concentration level the moment he squatted behind the plate. Yadier Molina boosts the Cardinals in a multifaceted way. Not only does he feel the responsibility to be the leader of his team, but he also calls a great game. And don't even think of running on him.

I could go on for pages about this Hall of Famer's accomplishments, among them two Most Valuable Player Awards and 12 All-Star Game starts. However, no roll of honors or litany of dry statistics can summarize Bench's career better than the words of his former Reds' manager, Sparky Anderson, who proclaimed, "Johnny Bench is the standard against which all other catchers must be compared. As the total package, no one who has ever played the position can touch him."

Setting up

Catchers are the only players in baseball who set up defensively in foul territory. How deeply you position yourself behind the plate depends on the hitter: You should get as close to home as you can without getting struck by the bat. Hitters who stand back deep in the box force you to stay back. If a hitter moves up in the box, you should also move forward. The closer you come to home plate, the better positioned you'll be to handle bunts, foul tips, wild pitches, and would-be base stealers.

Though each player brings a different wrinkle to his job, all catchers assume two basic stances behind home plate. The first is a set-up that puts you in position to deliver signs to your pitcher. Drop into a squat; keep your knees parallel with your weight evenly distributed on the balls of your feet. (See Figure 9-1.) To assume the second stance, put one foot slightly behind the other to help maintain balance. Spread your knees so that they provide a strong but comfortable base. Drop your rump until it is below your knees but slightly above your heels. Your upper body should be straight but never stiff.

"You don't have to follow any 'Spalding Guide' model when you get behind the plate. People have different physical makeups, so they are going to squat differently. If you try to assume a position that doesn't fit your body, it will not work. Do whatever feels comfortable and balanced so that you can move either way on a pitch or block a ball in the dirt. Don't restrict yourself by holding your elbows too far in so that you're blocked from reaching across." — Johnny Bench

Figure 9-1:
A basic catching stance.

Illustration by Wiley, Composition Services Graphics

Flashing signs: The secret language of catchers

To flash signs, extend your right hand between your thighs. Point your right knee at the pitcher; this position shields your signals from the opposition's first-base coach. You can prevent the third-base coach from stealing your signs by holding your glove in front of your left knee. Most catchers give signs by extending one or more fingers. To avoid confusion, keep your signals basic: one finger for the fastball, two for the curve, three for a change-up, four for any other pitch your pitcher throws, such as a slider or screwball. Spread your fingers as wide as you can when you give signs. You want to make sure your pitchers can see each digit clearly as Figure 9-2 shows.

Figure 9-2:
Giving clear signs to your pitcher.

Illustration by Wiley, Composition Services Graphics

"Depending on the shadows and your pitcher's vision, you might want to tape your fingers to give him a better look at what you're flashing. Sometimes you have to improvise. When I was with the Reds, one of our pitchers, Wayne Simpson, had a corneal abrasion on the day he was scheduled to pitch. He couldn't wear his contacts on the mound. I could have painted my fingers in neon and he wouldn't have seen them. So I set the glove on the side of my knee for a fastball, on top of my knee for a breaking ball. Wayne pitched a two-hit shutout." — *Johnny Bench*

You can also transmit signs through the *pump system.* Using this method, you indicate which pitch you want by the number of times you flash the sign. (Pump one fist for a fastball, two for a curve, and so on.) Call for pitch location by holding your palms up (for high pitches) or down (for low). Pointing away from or toward a batter tells your pitchers whether the next pitch should be inside or out.

"You might go to the pump if you have an indication that the other team has stolen your signs, or with a runner on second. Whatever method you use, always make sure you and your pitcher are on the same page. The worst nightmare is to be giving signs during a game and suddenly realize that you have no communication whatsoever with the pitcher." — *Johnny Bench*

After a runner gets to second, where he has almost as good a view of the catcher's signs as the pitcher, things get more complicated. You must alter your signs so the runner cannot decipher them. One way to confuse him is to give several different signs in sequence after first deciding with your pitcher which of these is the genuine article. Or you can prearrange with your pitcher to combine two signs to get the appropriate signal. For example, you can flash one finger (fastball) as your first sign, three fingers (change-up) as a second, and two fingers (curve) as a third. If you and your pitcher have agreed to combine sign one (one finger) and sign three (two fingers) when a runner is on second, the addition produces the three-fingered signal for the change-up. (It's important that your infielders are also privy to your signs in all their various guises so they can set up properly on each pitch.)

"You can use physical signs to indicate an addition. For example, I might go to my mask to add one, or touch my chest protector to add two. Hitters will try to peek at your signs to gain an edge. If you catch them doing it, you can set it up with your pitcher to throw an inside pitch after you call for something outside. And I mean way inside — like around the hitter's neck. That will give him some incentive to stop peeking. If you think he's checking out your location behind the plate, to see if you're setting up inside or out, set up inside — but call for something away. Or stay centered and don't move in or out until your pitcher starts to unwind with his pitch." — *Johnny Bench*

When you give signs, make sure that neither your fingers nor hands extend below your thighs (where an alert opponent can observe them). Keep your elbow as still as possible; if the opposition detects you wiggling your elbow when you call for a breaking pitch, they can feast on your pitcher's fastballs.

When you're ready to catch

After you've given your sign, you can hop from your set-up position into your receiving (or *ready*) stance. Bring your rump up to just below knee level while keeping your thighs parallel to the ground. Stay low to give your pitcher a good target. This alteration shouldn't raise you as much as it makes you more compact. Shift your weight forward onto the balls of your feet until your heels are lightly touching the ground. Your feet should be shoulder width, with your right foot a few inches in front of your left. Turn your knees and feet slightly out, as in Figure 9-3.

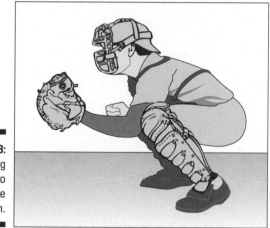

Figure 9-3: Getting ready to receive the pitch.

Illustration by Wiley, Composition Services Graphics

In front of your knee, bend the forearm of your catching hand at a 45-degree angle from your body. Don't lock your elbows or place them inside your knees — if you do, catching pitches far out of the strike zone is nearly impossible. When nobody is on base, protect your bare hand by tucking it behind you. With runners on, keep your bare hand in a relaxed fist behind the webbing of your glove. Grab the pitch with your throwing hand as soon as it is delivered.

Your pitcher should be able to look directly into your mitt after you set up a target. Centering your glove to your body gives the pitcher a clearer view. If you call an inside pitch, you have to shift your target inside; do the reverse for outside pitches. Don't shift your body until the last possible moment or you'll tip off the opposition. Always keep your target within the strike zone. After you set up your target, maintain the target until the ball has left the pitcher's hand.

"You have to know what your pitcher wants to use as a target. For instance, Tom Seaver may have thrown to my shinguards — right shinguard, left shinguard — depending on which side the batter swung from and whether we wanted to go in or out. Or he would pitch to one of my shoulders. Other guys looked to my glove. When you set a target with your glove, do not hold it straight up so your wrist is cocked into a L-shape. Angle the glove so you can stay flexible enough to rotate to the left or right." — Johnny Bench

Receiving the pitch

Catch the ball in the strike zone. If you receive it on the edge of the zone, the pitch's force can move your glove enough to transform a strike into a ball. Don't stab at the pitch; let it come to you. If you must, sway with the pitches on the borders of (or just outside) the strike zone. However, avoid any extreme movements: Any radical body shift may persuade the umpire that the pitch is a ball even if it is in the strike zone.

When a pitch is legitimately outside the strike zone, don't try to steal a call by pulling it back into the zone with your glove. Umpires resent this trick, and they can punish you by refusing to call borderline pitches in your favor for the rest of the game. You can, however, *frame* a pitch by subtly rolling your wrists to rotate the glove up or down. To do this, keep your arm and torso stationary. Rotate the glove down on high pitches, up on low pitches.

"On an outside pitch to a right-handed hitter, keep the largest portion of your glove over the plate while catching the ball in your web. Do just the opposite against a left-hander. Always try to catch the ball in the web." — Johnny Bench

Tracking errant pitches

With runners on base, your pitcher must know he can throw a low pitch without having to worry that you'll let it skip by you. He'll have that confidence after you demonstrate your ability to dig those babies out of the dirt. To do that, you must forget about catching when runners are on base. Instead, concentrate on blocking the ball while anticipating that every pitch will be a bad one.

If the ball in the dirt comes directly to you, drop to your knees and face the ball squarely. Get your hands low and centered. Drop your chin onto your chest to protect your throat. With your shoulders hunched, push forward to smother the ball. Should the pitch look as if it will veer to your right, step toward the ball with your right foot while dropping to your knee with your other leg. Move your glove and bare hand to the space between your foot and knee. Keep both hands between your legs but close to your body. (Refer to Figure 9-4.)

Figure 9-4:
Blocking
balls in
the dirt.

Illustration by Wiley, Composition Services Graphics

On high pitches, raise your glove slightly higher than the ball. Angle your glove downward so that if you miss the catch, the ball drops in front of you. If you keep your glove too low or angled upward, the ball can glance off it and skip in back of you. The runners will like that; it means extra bases for sure.

Catching a thief

Though it's not fair, catchers usually establish their defensive reputations with their throwing arms. (Though a catcher's game-calling ability provides a better measure of his value to a team.) Most teams prize those catchers who can curtail the opposition's running game. Like the other fielders, you must practice gripping the ball and removing it from the glove without looking. Your speed with this maneuver improves with repetition.

"You have to be quick. The good base stealers get down to second in about 3.1 seconds. It takes the average pitcher about 1.5 seconds to get the ball to home plate (from the start of his windup). That leaves you 1.5 seconds to throw the ball 127 feet, 3 inches to a target 6 inches above the bag on the first base side so the infielder has 1/10 of a second to make the tag. And then you have to hope the umpire is in position to make the call." — Johnny Bench

As a catcher, your throws must be straight and true. A proper grip ensures that they are. Grab the ball across the seams where they are widest apart. If your grip is off on your first try, rotate the ball as you cock your arm to throw.

Your grip, cock, and release should constitute one continuous motion. As you grip the ball, bring your glove hand back to your right shoulder while closing your left one. With the ball in hand, bring your right arm slightly above and past your ear. As your right arm comes forward to throw, aim your left shoulder at the target. Keep your glove arm parallel to the ground. Throw overhand; sidearm deliveries tend to tail away from their targets. As you release the ball, snap your wrist downward.

"You can't practice enough the transfer of the ball from glove to hand. You have to keep doing it until reaching in and grabbing that ball across the seams becomes second nature. Practice this even when you are having a simple catch. When you're behind the plate and you make the transfer with your shoulder closed, step straight with your toes pointed towards your target so that your arm follows your body line." — Johnny Bench

To catch today's speediest runners, you have to get the ball off to your fielders quickly. Therefore, you must try to throw while still coming out of your crouch. Major-League catchers generally choose from among three throwing styles:

- ✔ **The step and throw:** Recommended for catchers with average arms, it allows you to put more of your body behind each throw. Just before you catch the ball, step forward about 6 inches (15.2 centimeters) with your right foot while pointing it toward second base. After you possess the ball, turn your hips as you draw back your arm, stride forward with your left foot, and throw.

- ✔ **The jump pivot:** The moment the ball hits your glove, jump to your feet and plant your left foot below the spot where you just gave your target while making a 90-degree turn to plant your right foot. Take a short stride toward second and throw.

✔ **The rock and throw:** This throw requires a powerful throwing arm because it entails little body movement. As you receive the ball, rock back on your right foot. Rise from your crouch with your arm cocked. Shift your weight forward to your left foot and throw.

"When people talk about throwing out base runners, they are almost always thinking about arms, but they should be thinking about feet. A catcher has to have quick feet so he can 'get under himself' and move fluidly from a receiving position to a throwing position. Your feet will get your shoulders turned and in position to throw." — *Johnny Bench*

Derailing the double steal

With base runners on first and third, the catcher must be alert for the *double steal*. On this play, the runner on first breaks for second hoping to draw a throw while the runner on third scores. Before stepping toward second to throw (if that is your choice), check the runner at third. If he has just broken for the plate, throw to third or hold the ball and get him in a rundown. You are virtually conceding second base to the runner on first, so failing to get the man at third leaves you with two runners in scoring position. If the runner on third breaks for home as your throw heads for second, be prepared for your second baseman or shortstop to cut off your throw and return the ball to you at the plate.

Getting help

Catchers should have no difficulty seeing runners break from first when a right-handed hitter is at the plate. However, a left-handed hitter may block his view. Your first baseman has to let you know when the runner is taking off. (You should anticipate the steal on every pitch.)

Neither lefties nor righties can obstruct your view when a runner tries to heist third. However, with a righty at the plate, the angle of the pitch determines the launching point of your throw. On outside pitches, step forward with your right foot and then step toward third with your left so you can throw in front of the hitter. If the pitch arrives inside, throw from behind the hitter. Step to the side with your left foot, shift your weight to your right, step toward third with your left, and throw.

Handling pickoffs and pitchouts

Pitchers aren't the only players who can pick a runner off base. The catcher can also initiate a pickoff play whenever a runner strays too far from a bag. If the count is favorable (one ball or less), you can begin the pickoff play with a *pitchout*. After first signaling your pitcher, step into the opposite batter's box just as he starts to the plate; jump in earlier and you risk committing a balk. Ideally, the pitchout should come to you at your letters, but be prepared for a throw that is either too low or too high. As soon as you get the ball, throw to the fielder covering the targeted base.

When the count is not in your favor, call for a strike on the outside corner to set up the *pickoff*. As your pitcher delivers the ball, step back into throwing position with your right foot. Close your body by bringing both hands to the top of the letters. Pivot off your right foot, step in the direction of your target with your left foot, and throw.

You want the umpire to call a strike, so don't pop up too soon or you may obstruct his view of the pitch.

After the Ball Is Hit

A catcher's job is arduous enough when the batter makes no contact or fails to even swing. It becomes if not more difficult, certainly more hazardous, after a ball is in play.

These sections explain how to avoid base runners trying to part you from the ball to score a run, how to handle force plays at home, how to pounce on bunts, and how to corral foul pop flies twisting in the wind.

Blocking the plate

Throughout the season, the catcher is involved in numerous collisions at home. How well you block the plate determines if you get the out while staying off the disabled list. As the runner steams toward home, spread your legs a little wider than shoulder width and anchor your left foot about 18 inches (45.7 centimeters) in front of the plate as in Figure 9-5.

Figure 9-5:
Blocking the
runner from
scoring.

Illustration by Wiley, Composition Services Graphics

"When you block the plate, remember it is better to be a live coward than a dead hero. I always let the runner see at least half the plate, so he has the option of going around me. If he can't see the plate, he has no alternative but to try to go through you or over you. If you persuade him to slide, you have him on the ground, where you can control what he is trying to do. As you block the plate, keep your toes pointed up the third base line and aimed directly at the runner. Should you angle the leg, the impact of the collision could permanently damage your knee." — Johnny Bench

After you have the ball and the runner has committed to sliding away from you, move your left leg until you block the plate entirely. Grip the ball in your bare hand while turning the back of your glove toward the runner to protect your inner wrist. As the runner slides in, drive down on top of him with your shin guards to prevent him from reaching the plate. With the ball held firmly in the glove, you can tag him with the back of your mitt. If other runners are on base, see if any other plays are developing as soon as you make the tag at home.

These instructions assume that you're handling an accurate throw. If the throw is slightly off to either side, you can pull it in by shifting your right foot without leaving your position. However, if the throw is far off-line, abandon the tagging position and do what you must to get a glove on the ball. If the runner decides to come in standing up, roll away from him as you apply the tag. Avoid head-on collisions.

A catcher can't block the plate unless he is receiving a throw or is already in possession of the ball — otherwise it's obstruction.

Fielding pop-ups

The best way to field pop-ups is to do it by the numbers:

1. **As the ball goes up, turn your back to the field and scan the sky for the ball.**

2. **Move toward the ball with your catcher's mask in your bare hand. (If you throw it too early, you risk tripping over it.)**

3. **After the ball reaches its apex and you sense where it will descend, toss your mask away and move in for the catch.**

4. **Catch the ball over your head with both hands.**

   The fingers of your glove should be slanted upward. Don't stab. Allow the ball to come to you.

After judging where a pop is going to come down, it's usually wise to back up one more step so that the ball doesn't wind up behind you — fouls usually drift back a little more than one expects.

Right-handed hitters usually pop up inside pitches to the right and outside pitches to the left. Left-handed batters do the reverse.

"The pop-up behind home plate reacts like a banana. The ball will drift towards the stands as it goes up and curve back towards the field when it descends. So when the ball is popped up in back of you, turn around quickly, stop, and slowly move towards the ball while remembering it will come back to you a few feet." — Johnny Bench

Thwarting the bunt

The catcher is in the best position to field and throw balls bunted directly in front of the plate. When the ball is bunted in your territory, stay low as you pounce in front of the plate, scoop the ball up with both hands, and then make your throw (refer to Figure 9-6). Your attention should be on the bunt, so call for the ball loudly to avoid a collision with any incoming fielders. When the bunt is beyond your reach, become a traffic cop. Call out which fielder should handle the ball and tell him where to throw it.

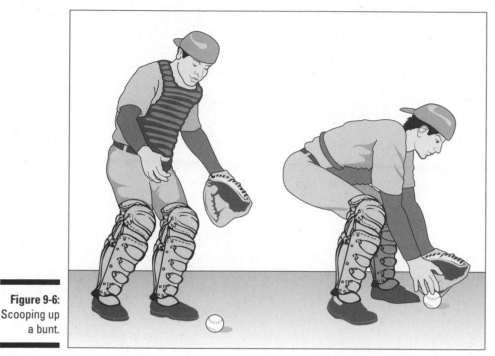

Figure 9-6:
Scooping up
a bunt.

Letting the force be with you

When the bases are *loaded* (a runner on every base) and a ground ball is hit, anticipate that the infielder will throw home for the force-out. You do not have to tag the runner to get the out. You simply must touch home plate while possessing the ball. When a force at home is in order, toss your mask away. Plant your right foot in the middle of home plate so you can move in either direction on a bad throw. Put your left foot in front of the plate. Be prepared to stretch like a first baseman to snare a short throw. With less than two outs, forget about the base runner as soon as you catch the ball. He's out! (Remember, your foot was on the plate.) Immediately pivot to your right, face first, and throw to complete the double play.

Chapter 10

Playing Infield

Winning teams almost always play good defense. Although most fans — and even Major-League managers — prioritize power pitching and dominant slugging, a great defender can be just as intimidating to an opponent. The Red Sox get an adrenaline shot when Dustin Pedroia dives to smother a hot shot in the hole between first and second and turn a single into just another out.

In this chapter, we offer advice on how to play each of the four infield positions. We show you how to prepare to make plays by proper positioning and knowledge of the game situation, and how to execute many of the most common plays.

Playing First Base: No Hiding Allowed

Keith Hernandez and Willie McCovey will act as our guides at first base. I've never seen a better first baseman than Keith; no one could match him covering the hole between first and second or charging bunts. Hernandez won more Gold Gloves (11) than any other first baseman, and in 1979, he shared a National League MVP award with Willie Stargell.

Hall of Famer Willie McCovey played first base for 22 seasons, most of them with the San Francisco Giants and San Diego Padres. Willie won the Rookie of the Year Award in 1959 and was named MVP in 1969. His work at first base earned him the name "Stretch" — an homage to his ability to keep one foot on the bag while reaching wild throws.

"We have to dispel the myth that first base is an old man's position, and that you can put just anybody at the bag and expect them to play it well. The first baseman handles the ball more than anyone on the field except the pitcher or catcher. So you must have good hands. You have to have a little quarterback in you to lead the pitcher with your throws when he goes for the putout at first. A first baseman has to save wild throws from his infielders. Quick reactions are a must. If you charge in on a bunt, and the ball goes to the third-base side, you must immediately retract to get back to cover first. First basemen have so many responsibilities. You cannot hide a defensively weak player at this position."
— Willie McCovey

"You have time to make a methodical decision on what the ball will do: Will it sink, will it run, will it be a short hop in the dirt, will it be over my head, or will it be a long pop? About the only play where you don't have much time is the little chopper to your second baseman. He has to come in running, bare-hand the ball, and throw it to you underhand. That's the toughest throw from the infield. A boom-boom play, he's throwing on the run and he's putting everything on it because it's going to be close. You have to commit before the throw is there and hope he makes the throw somewhere close to you.

"When you're holding a runner on first base, that's when it becomes a hot corner, a little bit like third base. You have to react quickly. My father was a good fielding first baseman and the greatest drill he ever taught me was when I was learning to scoop, which requires good reflexes. He used a tennis ball so that if I got hit in the face I didn't get hurt. Even if you're a Major Leaguer switching to first base and you've never played there before, it's a good way to get over any initial fear. Go to first and have someone throw you short hops, in-between hops, bad throws. You know that tennis ball isn't going to hurt you, so you can concentrate and develop the skills to read the ball and react. As a kid, I also used to throw the ball for hours off the garage door. I'd get closer and closer to the door and throw as hard as I could. That's certainly working your reflexes." — Keith Hernandez

Developing footwork and balance

"You have to be graceful; a first baseman should have loose muscles so he can move easily. Rudolf Nureyev, the ballet star, once came to me after a game and said I moved like a ballet dancer in the field. That was the greatest compliment

I ever received for my fielding. If you're awkward, take a ballet class or study tai chi or some other discipline to improve your balance. If you weight train, make sure you stretch those muscles to stay loose." — Willie McCovey

Taking target practice

First basemen should generally play as deep as they can in the field. However, they must be able to get to the bag and set a target in time for the other fielders to make their throws. Taking those throws while putting your foot on first for the out has to become second nature. Your foot should hit the front inside corner of the bag (refer to Figure 10-1).

Figure 10-1: Taking the throw at first.

Illustration by Wiley, Composition Services Graphics

"Learning footwork is the most difficult transition for anyone just starting to learn how to play first base. You can't master that overnight. First base has to become second nature, an extension of your body. I remember the first drills I had with my father. When you take throws, you're straddling the bag and then you just kind of skip, back left, back right. A little curl-hop back and forth. So one time your right foot is on the corner of the bag on the side facing the catcher, and then you come back and your left foot is on the outfield side of the bag. Back and forth, back and forth. Then do it from two or three steps away. Then you expand it. After a while, I got within five feet of the bag and that would be my last look at it. I knew where it was. You do this drill relaxed. Loose arms, loose legs, like you're dancing. Don't look down. If you have to look down for the bag in the beginning, fine. When you can do it without looking down, you're gaining familiarity with the bag." — Keith Hernandez

You should have your target at first set when the infielder looks up to throw. Keep your weight evenly balanced on the balls of your feet so you can immediately shift to your left or right. Willie says, "A good first baseman will anticipate a bad throw on every play. That way he can easily adjust." Make sure your body is facing the fielder. Don't stretch for a ball until it's in the air and you are sure of its direction.

Handling bad throws

Low throws are usually the toughest to handle. Try to take the low throw before it bounces. If you can't do that, get to it as soon as it hops so it won't bounce away from you. On high throws, you can stay on the bag while stretching for the ball, make a leaping grab off the bag, or move back into foul territory. On a really high throw, avoid stretching out much at all and keep your feet together to reach as high as possible.

"Any time you get a bad throw, your first objective is to catch the ball. Don't worry about keeping your feet on the bag or getting the base runner out. If you catch the ball but it's too late to get the runner, you have a man on first. However, if the ball gets past you because you were stuck on the bag, the runners can advance an extra base." — Willie McCovey

On plays where the pitcher or second baseman is too close to you to make a hard overhand throw, he will probably try to feed you an underhanded toss. Help him by setting a big target with your glove.

"You would be surprised by the number of pitchers who cannot properly throw to first base after making a play. On those soft toss plays, you have to anticipate that the pitcher will throw it over your head." — Willie McCovey

Holding on

When you *hold a runner on,* you shorten his lead off first to deny him a head start to second. Place the back of your right foot against the front inside corner of first while keeping your left foot along the base line. Your feet should be no more than shoulder length apart. Give your pitcher a good waist-high target with your glove.

As the ball is delivered to the plate, cross over with your left foot and bounce as quickly as you can toward second base. Get in a position to cover as much fair territory as possible. As the pitch approaches the plate, you should be in your crouch, facing the batter.

When runners are on first or second, or the man on first is slow, the first baseman can play *behind the runner* rather than hold him on. To play behind the runner, position yourself just inside the runner's left shoulder.

When second base is not occupied, make sure that the pitcher knows when you play behind a runner. Pitchers need to be reminded not to make a pickoff throw. Never assume that the pitcher knows instinctively that you've chosen to play behind a slow runner.

Covering bunts

Play bunts aggressively or you won't play them at all. Charge the plate as your pitcher delivers the ball home. Countless baseball instructional guides advise first basemen to listen for their catchers to tell them where their throws are going (first, second, or third). This advice is fine if you're not playing in a packed stadium where the roar of the crowd makes it impossible to hear yourself think. Under those conditions, you must be able to immediately recognize where the play is developing and throw accordingly.

In some cases, the defending team will call a play when the hitter is likely to bunt. In these instances, the first baseman has a pre-assigned role, such as covering the bag or taking only balls bunted very hard. In other scenarios, he may charge aggressively looking to throw to another bag for a force out.

"Stay aggressive. When someone bunted, I always felt that if I didn't get the lead runner, I failed. I also realized that if a player got down a great bunt, there was only so much you could do. Or if a speed burner was on first like they had on the Cardinals — say Vince Coleman or Ozzie Smith or Tommie Herr — you weren't going to throw one of those guys out unless it was a horrible bunt.

"You come up with the ball ready to throw to second and then you make your decision. If you see there is no play, you have plenty of time to throw to first base. I see so many guys come in on the bunt as if they've already made up their minds to get the easy out (at first base), even when the pitcher's running. Even if a pitcher's running hard, most of them aren't fast. You have time to field that bunt aggressively and in the same motion make as if you are going to throw to second. And if you make your read and there's no out at second, just reset and throw to first." — Keith Hernandez

"Usually everyone in the stadium knows when a bunt is in order. However, there are some players and managers who will try to surprise you with a bunt. (Note: This usually occurs when the batter is trying to bunt for a base hit rather than a sacrifice.) If you study hitters closely, you can pick up some signs that telegraph a bunt is coming. For instance, some batters will look down towards you for an

extra moment or two before bunting the ball your way. Other guys might choke up on the bat a little bit more. Watch what each hitter does when he bunts, and remember any quirks you can detect." — Willie McCovey

Fielding cutoff throws

If runners are in scoring position, the first baseman is responsible for cutting off the throw on balls hit to right or center. The third baseman takes most cutoffs from left, but if he can't get into position, you have to cover for him. Give your outfielder a good target by holding your hand and glove chest high. (All infielders should do this.) Where should you stand to receive the cutoff? Some coaches advise that you take it at a midpoint between second base and the pitcher's mound. Others want you to cut the ball off from behind the mound. And at other times your positioning depends on the strength of the player's arm from whom you're receiving the throw."

"There is an advantage to cutting the ball off between second base and the pitcher's mound. If you are behind the mound, on the home plate side of the diamond, you risk having the ball hit the mound or pitching rubber and bouncing away from you." — Willie McCovey

"You have to read whether the throw is going to clear the mound, or hit the mound and kick up into the air. And you have plenty of time to read it; it's a long throw in. There's no rush to make a judgment. You even have time to check where the runners are." — Keith Hernandez

As you accept the relay from the outfield, wave your arms so the outfielder doesn't waste time trying to find you. Listen for a teammate (usually your catcher) to tell you where your throw is going (or if you should let the ball go through). The instructions should be this simple:

- ✔ "Cut, Cut!" — Cut off the ball and hold it.
- ✔ "Relay! Relay!" — Cut off the ball and throw to a specific base.

If the fielder thinks you should let the ball go through, he shouldn't yell anything. When you are setting up for a relay, line up your body in the same direction as your target. For example, if you are throwing to third, your body should be facing left center.

"Catch the ball on your glove side so you don't have to turn all the way around to throw. Practice catching the ball, taking it out of your mitt, and delivering the throw all in one graceful motion. Too many first basemen break this down into two parts. That extra motion is often the difference between a runner being safe or out." — Willie McCovey

"Once you make up your mind that you are going to cut off the throw, don't wait for the ball to come to you. Commit. Rush to the ball so you cut a second off the throw." — Keith Hernandez

When the pitcher must cover first

If you play deep, the pitcher is going to cover many grounders hit to the right side. He heads to first base in case you can't get there in time to make the tag on your own. If you can get to the ball and field it near first base, make the tag (tag the base) yourself. Make sure you wave off the pitcher so he is out of harm's way.

When fielding the ball takes you too far from first to make an unassisted putout, you must get the ball to your pitcher. If the distance is short enough, lead the pitcher to first with a firm underhanded toss that hits him chest-high. Balls fielded on their way to the second-base hole may require you to throw overhand. Again, you should lead the pitcher to the bag with a chest-high toss.

"A lot of first basemen will catch the ball, stay where they caught it, and then underhand it to the pitcher. Catch the ball and run towards the bag! Give the pitcher a big shovel pass, as if you're throwing a bowling ball. You're shortening the distance between the throw, making it easier for the pitcher. Try to hit him with the throw waist- to letter-high." — Keith Hernandez

Doing the 3-6-3 (first-to-short-to-first double play)

Many first basemen will tell you this play is the most difficult play they make. To initiate this double play if you're left-handed (as most first base-men should be), pivot clockwise — to your glove-hand side — to unleash a throw. If you're right-handed and the ball is hit directly at you, turn clockwise to throw. However, if the ball is hit to your left, you'll probably have to pivot counter-clockwise — that is, turn completely around — before throwing.

Your first throw is the key to making this double play. Nine out of ten times, you field the ball in the same line as the runner going to second. You must be able to throw the ball to your shortstop without hitting that runner. Then you have to get back to the bag for the return throw. Because this play is always going to be close, you need to stretch before catching the ball on the return. (Sometimes this play goes 3-4-3, first-to-second-to-first. If he must throw to the second baseman, the first baseman's responsibilities remain the same.)

"Make sure you get that lead runner. Too many first basemen are so concerned with getting back to the bag to get that second out, they end up throwing the ball away and fail to get anyone. If you don't have a clear shot, take an extra sidestep to create a throwing lane to the shortstop. Try to get the throw to your shortstop in a spot to his liking. (Note: Many favor receiving the ball chest high.) But if you can't do that, make the best throw you can and depend on the shortstop's athleticism to complete the play." — Willie McCovey

"I just realized one day while I was taking ground balls, that I was always looking at my throw to make sure it was perfect. I said to myself, 'Once it's out of my hand, even if it's a bad throw, I can't do anything about it. So why waste my time looking at it.' I wanted to make sure the throw was good so I'd watch it fifteen, twenty feet out of my hand, and that wasted two seconds getting back to the bag. Now the key, obviously, is not to break back to first base too soon, before you get rid of the ball. So I just started working on it. Once that ball was out of my hand, I might have looked at it for a split second but then I got back to the bag." — Keith Hernandez

Focusing on Second Base

Joe couldn't find a second baseman for this team, so he's doing the honors himself. His collaborator, editor, and publishers couldn't be more pleased. From 1973 to 1977, Joe's play at second won him five consecutive National League Gold Glove awards. He was tutored in the field by two of the greatest second basemen in baseball history — Nellie Fox and the Grand Master of the Keystone, Bill Mazeroski.

None of the suggestions in these sections are absolutes. Eighty percent of the time, you execute a play at second in these manners. However, some situations — such as when a throw is off line or the runner arrives at second faster than you anticipated — demand improvisation. When these situations occur, remember that your bottom line is to make the play any way you can. Get the out!

Setting up

A second baseman's stance in the field should distribute his weight evenly on the balls of both feet. This position allows him to move easily to one side or another. As the pitcher goes into his windup, look directly at the batter. But don't look at his body. Instead, imagine he is swinging through a rectangular box that is as wide as home plate and extends from his shoulders to the tops of his toes. Watch that box. The ball will come to you from some spot within it. Make sure you're on the balls of your feet and ready to move when you see the bat and ball collide as in Figure 10-2.

Figure 10-2:
Getting
ready for
the play.

Illustration by Wiley, Composition Services Graphics

"Be relaxed but alert at all times in the field. If you stay in one position too long, your body will tense; this will slow your reactions when the ball is hit. To allevi-ate tension, move your hands while you are in your stance. I often rested my hands on my knees as the pitcher wound up. An infielder has to do that to ensure that he is bending forward far enough. But as soon as the pitcher released the ball, I would raise my hands about 5 inches to give myself greater freedom of movement." — Joe Morgan

Your skills and the situation determine how deeply you play your position. However, if you're fielding on artificial turf, the ball will shoot to you much quicker than it will on grass. Play two to five steps deeper. You should also remember that you can't slide to a ball hit to either side of you on the turf. You have to field the ball and continue moving.

Knowing whose ball it is

On balls stroked up the middle of the diamond, who has first call? The shortstop or the second baseman? That's the shortstop's ball. Because he is moving toward first base on the play, he can make a stronger, more accurate throw than the second baseman (who is moving away from first).

"Just because it's the shortstop's play doesn't mean you don't have any responsi-bility. Get behind your shortstop and be ready to catch the ball in case it gets by him." — Joe Morgan

Blocking the ball

Nellie Fox was a three-time Gold Glove winner who led American League second basemen in putouts nine times. He taught me the best way to stop a ball you cannot catch cleanly from entering the outfield: Get down on one knee and block it with your body. After you knock it down, quickly pick up the ball with your bare hand and throw.

If this posture isn't comfortable, find another way to get down on the ball. With a runner on second, do everything possible — dive in front of it if you have to — to prevent the ball from rolling into the outfield. Your methods may lack grace, but they get the job done.

"Because the second baseman rarely makes a long throw, he doesn't always have to catch a ball cleanly. Always remember that if you simply knock a ball down, you will usually have plenty of time to toss out the runner." — Joe Morgan

Getting the ball to first

When you have to throw the ball to someone like our friend Willie McCovey at first base, aim for an area between his belt buckle and his chest. This strategy allows you some margin of error if your throw is too high or low. Your throws should be on the money as often as possible. If you have to take a throw from a teammate, give him a chest-high target.

In most situations, you can wait until the first baseman reaches his bag before throwing to him. However, if the runner is some flash like Jacoby Ellsbury or Mike Trout, you may not have time to see if the first baseman is in place. Your job in that instance is to throw the ball to the bag; it's the first sacker's responsibility to somehow get to it.

"Make sure any player you are throwing to gets a good look at the ball. Take it out of your glove as quickly as possible so he can see it in your hand. This will help him to better gauge your throw's velocity and trajectory. When you bring back your arm to throw, make sure your glove doesn't block your target's view of the ball." — Joe Morgan

Preventing grand larceny: Defending against the steal

One of the oldest maxims in baseball dictates who covers second — the shortstop or second baseman — on an attempted steal. The shortstop covers if the batter is left-handed. When the batter is right-handed, the second baseman has to make the play. However, like all good rules, this one does have its exception. If the batter is a good hit-and-run man or opposite field hitter like Placido Polanco, the second baseman and shortstop can switch assignments. Placido is a right-handed batter who excels at hitting behind the runner. Any second baseman who covers the bag on every steal attempt is inviting Placido to slap the ball through the vacated hole and into right field. So you have to play the big-league version of cat-and-mouse with him. Your shortstop may cover for a pitch or even two. Then you may cover for the next couple of pitches. Keep switching so he doesn't know whether to pull the ball or go the other way.

"You and your shortstop must communicate to each other who will cover on the attempted steal. Before the game, decide between yourselves who will make the call. Keep the signals simple. Shield the front of your face with your glove. When you want your shortstop to cover second, open your mouth and purse your lips as if you were saying, 'You!' If you are going to take the catcher's throw, keep your mouth closed with your lips tightened to indicate, 'Me!'" — Joe Morgan

Picking runners off

In a *pickoff play,* the pitcher tries to catch a runner off base with an unexpected throw. You're not merely jockeying for an out with this play; you're also attempting to reduce the runner's lead. Just the threat of a pickoff can appreciably change the game. With the runner anchored at the base, your outfielders have a better opportunity to throw him out on a base hit; you have more time to execute plays in the infield.

"If the second baseman is covering the bag on the pickoff play, the shortstop must get behind him to back up any errant throws. If the shortstop is covering, the second baseman must reciprocate." — Joe Morgan

Pickoff plays come in two basic varieties.

- ✔ In the **time play,** the pitcher signals to the infielder covering second by glancing at him before looking toward the catcher. As the pitcher faces home, he and the infielder start counting, "One second, two seconds, three seconds." On three, the pitcher spins and throws; the infielder breaks for the bag. If everything is in sync, the infielder and the throw should arrive at second base simultaneously.

- ✔ **Daylight pickoff** plays don't require a count. The pitcher whirls and throws to second as soon as he sees a large enough space or "daylight" between the infielder and the runner.

"I dislike daylight plays because they can so easily backfire. Suppose you're trying to fake a runner back to the bag. The pitcher might mistakenly think you're breaking for second. If he attempts a pickoff, you have to scramble back to make the play. Often, you can't. The ball flies untouched into center field, the runner races to second or even home. Stick to the time play; there's less opportunity for error." — Joe Morgan

Executing the rundown

Rundowns occur (among other times) when a pickoff traps a runner between two bases. While tossing the ball to each other, you and your teammates chase the runner back and forth until he can be tagged. Making as few throws as possible is the key to an effective rundown. The more throws you make, the greater the chance one of you will toss the ball away.

After the rundown begins, you should try to force the runner back to the base he just left. The fielder with the ball should hold it high and away from his glove so the other fielders can see it. Whoever is waiting to receive the throw must give the player with the ball a target. For example, say a right-handed throwing teammate is chasing the runner back to you at second. You should stand to the left of the incoming runner. This position affords the thrower a clear view of your glove. If the thrower is left-handed, take a step to the other side. By using your glove as a target, your teammate is less likely to hit the runner with the throw.

During rundowns, fielders must stay out of the base line while they await the ball. If you stand in line with the runner, his body may prevent you from seeing your teammate's throw. If the runner crashes into you on the base line when you don't have the ball, the umpire can award him the bag on fielders' interference, also called *obstruction*.

"Never fake a throw during a rundown; you might fake out your teammates as well as the runner. Always hold the ball high so your teammate can see it. Cock your arm back only when you intend to release the ball. When you're not involved in a rundown, choose an unoccupied base to back up. Stay out of the action unless the ball gets by someone and comes in your direction."
— *Joe Morgan*

Tagging the big-league way

When a runner slides into a base you're defending, tag him on his foot, toe, or whatever other part of his anatomy is closest to the bag. Try to tag his hand if he attempts a headfirst slide. Tag a runner who arrives at the base standing up anywhere you can reach him.

Don't attempt a tag with the pocket of your glove facing the runner or he may kick the ball away from you. (And yes, that's a legal play. New York Giants second basemen Eddie Stanky pulled it on New York Yankees shortstop Phil Rizzuto during the 1951 World Series. The ball went trickling into center field. Instead of being called out, Stanky was safe. The Giants went on to score five runs that inning.) Instead, hold the ball firmly as you swipe the runner with the back of your glove.

Covering first

Both your pitcher and first baseman usually try to field any slow-hit balls between first and the pitcher's mound. With first base unattended, the second baseman must cover. You must become a first baseman. Go to the inside of the bag with your rear foot. Lean into the diamond to give the thrower a proper chest-high target with your glove. Maintain your balance so you can spring to either side on a bad throw.

Handling relays and cutoffs at second

You're playing second base. With a man on first, the batter smacks the ball down the right field line. Cinch double. What do you do? Don't stand at second waiting for a throw. Instead, turn to face the right fielder from a point midway between first and second base. If the runner on first tries to score, your job is to relay the right fielder's throw to the catcher at home plate. If the runner is heading toward third when you get the ball, try to nip him at that base.

To study your defensive assignments on some of baseball's basic plays, check out the bonus chapter of basic defensive plays at www.dummies.com/extras/baseball.

Any time the batter drives a ball into the gap (between the outfielders), there's going to be a relay. Make sure the outfielder makes the longest throw; between the two of you, he should have the stronger arm. Go out just far enough for the outfielder to reach you with a throw. After you get the ball, your job is to deliver a short, accurate throw to the appropriate base.

On balls hit to the left or left center field gaps, the shortstop accepts the relay. The second baseman must back up any balls that get by him. You must also let the shortstop know where to throw the ball. If he has to turn and look, he surrenders about 12 feet (3.6 meters) to the runner. While the outfielder's throw is in flight, observe the runners so you can tell the shortstop which base offers the best opportunity for a play. Identify the bag by yelling to the shortstop, "One!" for first base, "Two!" for second, "Three!" for third, and "Four!" for home plate.

Turning two

Ask any infielder: The *double play* (DP) is the greatest play in baseball (other than the triple play, which is so rare you can't even think about it). When you turn a double play in a crucial situation, you immediately become the most popular guy on your club. Teammates shower you with high fives, pitchers want to buy you dinner, and managers name their firstborn after you. Nothing short of a win is more pleasing to a fielder than getting two outs with one ball.

Whenever the opportunity for the double play presents itself — runners on first, first and second, or first, second, and third with less than two out — the second baseman must automatically think about turning two. Move a couple of steps closer to second and in toward the plate. You sacrifice a little range with this positioning, but it enables you to get to the bag quickly.

Charge for the base as soon as the ball is hit to the left side of the diamond. When you get within three steps of second base — and with practice, you instinctively know when you are — shorten your stride. Take choppier, quicker steps to ensure that you don't overrun the bag. You must maintain body control as you reach second, or you'll have trouble adjusting to a poor throw.

If you're a novice at second, look for the bag when you first run toward it. After you know where it is, put your focus on the fielder. Give him the best chest-high target you can. However, stay alert in case the ball veers off on an angle. As the fielder cocks to throw, your attention should go to the ball.

"The double play transpires so quickly, you must eventually learn to locate the bag without looking. When I first came up to the Major Leagues, I would work on starting the double play with our first baseman and shortstop for an hour and a half a day before practice. We did this until I was able to get to the bag without even glancing at it." — Joe Morgan

To complete the double play, you must catch the ball, force-out the runner from first by tagging second base, pivot, and relay the ball to your first baseman. It sounds like several parts, but they're all parts of the same motion held together by your pivot (check out Figure 10-3). You have different ways to pivot on the double play:

Figure 10-3: The pivot for the double play.

Illustration by Wiley, Composition Services Graphics

✔ Many second basemen straddle the bag. As they catch the ball, second base is between their feet. They touch the bag with their left foot while throwing to first.

✔ Second basemen with unusually strong arms sometimes use the push-off method. They catch the ball behind the bag, tag the front of the base with their rear foot, and then push off it as if it were a pitching rubber for their throws to first.

"I learned the quickest and, in my opinion, best way to pivot by studying Bill Mazeroski. As a Gold Glove second baseman with the Pittsburgh Pirates, Maz led National League second basemen in double plays a record eight consecutive seasons (1960 to 1967). He was, and remains, the unchallenged king of the DP. Like Maz, I would catch my shortstop's throw out in front of my body. While crossing second, I would step on the center of the bag with my left foot. Then I would pivot and throw from wherever I caught the ball. If I gloved the ball high, my throw would be overhand or three-quarters. Feed the ball to me at my waist, and I relayed it sidearm. Any ball caught below my waist was delivered to first with an underhand toss. Your primary concern is to get rid of the ball as quickly and accurately as you can. Some players drag their foot across the bag when making the force-out at second. I think that practice upsets a fielder's rhythm on the double play. If you instead step on the center of the bag, your motion continues uninterrupted. This also helps build some momentum behind your throw to first." — Joe Morgan

The care and feeding of your shortstop

Some double plays require a role reversal: Your shortstop makes the pivot. You have to field the ball and then feed it to him for the relay to first. It is important to know where your double-play partner prefers to catch the ball. *Note:* Many second basemen throw to the shortstop backhand in a double play — a backhand throw is less likely to sail high than an underhand toss. If you're close enough to the bag to do so, a backhand throw is preferred.

"For example, when I was with the Reds, our shortstop Davey Concepcion liked to take the throw on the outfield side of second. So I would give it to him chest-high (the easiest ball to handle and throw while on the move) on the bag's outside edge. I've also played with some shortstops who wanted my toss on the inside of the bag. However, no matter what your shortstop prefers, you shouldn't wait to make the ideal throw. If you're off balance, get the ball to your partner any way you can and let him make the adjustment. If your double-play partner hasn't reached the bag, feed the ball to him wherever he is. Never make him wait for the ball or you can disrupt his timing." — Joe Morgan

Dealing with the runner

The second baseman's job is to make the double play before looking for the incoming runner. If you're continually concerned about getting hit at second, you can't play the position. One way to defend yourself against a collision is to get the ball to first as soon as you can. Don't worry about hitting the runner. Your quick throw will compel him to slide that much sooner. The sooner he slides, the longer it takes him to reach you at the base.

Cookin' at the Hot Corner (Third Base)

Third base is called the *hot corner* because the third baseman is so close to home plate he tends to field a lot of hot smashes. The position demands a strong arm, hair-trigger reflexes, and a ton of heart. Keep in mind these points when playing third base:

- ✔ **Stance:** Plays develop so quickly at the hot corner that third basemen must be able to shift out of position in an instant. Many third basemen set up in the lowest crouch on the field so they can spring up to the left or right.

- ✔ **Anticipation:** The greatest third basemen don't rely solely on their reflexes and proper weight distribution to glove the bazooka shots aimed their way. They combine a sixth sense with concrete data to anticipate where the batter is likely to hit the ball.

- ✔ **Preparation:** Before the first game of every away series, the third baseman (as well as the other fielders) should examine how a ballpark's topography may affect play. Never take anything for granted; groundskeepers or the elements may have altered a park since you last played there.

- ✔ **Speed:** Have fast hands for slow rollers. The grab-and-throw on bunts or slow rollers tapped to third is among the most difficult of all infield plays. The third basemen considered the all-time best at shutting down "small ball" are Clete Boyer, Brooks Robinson, and the great Negro Leaguer Ray Dandridge. Figure 10-4 shows you how to bare-hand the slow roller.

- ✔ **Mind games:** Persuade a runner to hang close to third base, and you decrease his chances of scoring on a short fly ball or hard-hit grounder. How do you get a runner to anchor near third? You can employ numerous fakes and moves to keep the runner honest.

- ✔ **Double plays:** Middle infielders usually attempt to get the ball to each other in a particular spot — at the letters, to the inside of the bag — on the double play. Their proximity to each other allows them this luxury. Third basemen don't need to be quite as specific.

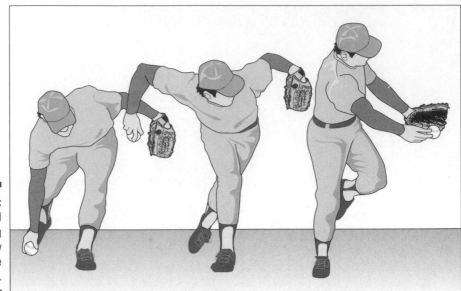

Figure 10-4:
Fielding and
throwing
the slow
roller in one
motion.

Illustration by Wiley, Composition Services Graphics

Ranging Wide: Playing Shortstop

All the infield fundamentals reviewed in this chapter — throwing, field-ing grounders, positioning, and so on — can be applied to this position. Shortstops should also read the section "Focusing on Second Base" for more information. The shortstop is nearly a mirror of the second baseman except he has more ground to cover and must make longer throws.

A second baseman's longest throw to first is barely more than 90 feet. The average throw for a shortstop to the same base is 110 feet. Because of the greater distance, you must be able to catch grounders cleanly or you won't survive at this position. If you knock balls down as a second baseman some-times does, you may not have time to throw out the runner. Because you're responsible for so much territory, you must study the hitters throughout your league so you can position yourself properly in every situation.

Our coaches for this position are two shortstops who have proven they know how to handle big plays. New York Yankees captain Derek Jeter has been a human highlight film in nearly every postseason since he entered the majors in 1996. A 13-time member of the American League All-Star team, Derek has played a pivotal defensive position on Yankee teams that have won 13 divi-sional titles, seven American League championships, and five World Series crowns. In 2004, he played the best defense of his career and earned a place on Rawlings' American League Gold Glove team, which he has made five times.

In 1995, Barry Larkin of the Cincinnati Reds became only the fourth shortstop to win the National League's Most Valuable Player award. Barry also won three Gold Gloves (1994–96), was a 12-time All-Star, and helped lead the Reds to a World Series championship in 1990. In his prime, he earned a reputation as one of baseball's great double-play artists, as well as being one of the best throwing shortstops ever.

Setting up

Because you must roam to either side at short, keep your weight balanced. Your feet should be a little more than shoulder width apart with your legs bent slightly in a semi-crouch. You often have less time than any other infielder to make a play, so you must be continually thinking about how to react if the ball is hit a certain way. It's hard to turn on the jet packs from a stationary position, so put your body in motion by taking two steps forward as the pitch approaches the plate. You have a direct view to home plate. Watching the catcher's signs lets you know what the pitcher is going to throw. If you feel the hitter is going to hit a certain pitch to your left or right, cheat a step in that direction.

"The most important thing is to field the ball cleanly, and — for the advanced player — catch it with your momentum carrying you towards wherever you are going to throw, second or first. You always hear that you should look the ball into the glove, but you should also look at the ball as you remove it from the glove. A lot of times, guys catch the ball and immediately look for their target instead of at the ball — as if someone was going to move first base. Then they have to double-clutch or regrip the ball before throwing, and that can cost outs." — Barry Larkin

"Probably the biggest key for me, because I'm tall, is to stay down. If the ball bounces up, you want to come up with the ball as opposed to going down and stabbing at it. So stay low. Once I have the ball, I try to pick up my target and make sure my momentum is going in his direction. The weight shift when you throw is very similar to when you're hitting. You plant your foot. As you bring back you arm, your weight goes into that back leg. Then you move your weight forward as you bring your arm around to throw." — Derek Jeter

Getting the ball to first

Shortstops often run full-out, so you must avoid tangling your legs. When you dart to your right, pivot on your right leg and cross over with your left. On balls hit to your left, do the reverse.

"When I throw to first, the first baseman's chest is the target. And I think the key is to throw through the target, not to it. That way I make sure I get something on the throw. You need a strong arm to play short. The best thing to build arm strength is playing long toss. I started doing that when I was younger and I still do it now before games. Just play catch at long distances, as far as you can throw it and as you get stronger, move back a little bit more." — Derek Jeter

"When you're in the hole and can't get on top of your throw, you might have to sidearm the ball to first base. You see a lot of inexperienced shortstops wasting a lot of motion trying to get something on that throw. If you're going toward first, get your wrist into the ball and snap off that throw. Your momentum will help put something on the ball. If I'm moving toward third when I catch the ball, I contort my body to get off a throw. I try to keep my front (left) foot closed, so my toe is pointed toward the left field stands. Then I throw against my body and use torque to propel a snap throw. On a play like that, you don't have to throw the ball all the way to first. (Former Reds Gold Glove shortstop) Davey Concepcion taught me how to bounce the ball on one hop to the first baseman. Shortstops should work on that play in practice." — Barry Larkin

If you dive for a ball — something shortstops do frequently — you must get to your feet immediately. However, don't rush the play.

"Too often, young shortstops who dive start trying to throw the ball before they really catch it. Catch the ball, hit the ground, pop up, and make the throw. When a guy tries to throw the ball before he catches it, he stands a good chance of dropping it. With practice, you'll learn to pop up quickly after a dive with the ball securely in your possession. This should leave you plenty of time to get off a good throw. Studying martial arts helped me with this. One of the first things I learned was how to roll with a fall so I wouldn't be rigid when I hit the ground. If you can learn how to roll with your dive, your momentum will help get you to your feet." — Barry Larkin

Backhanded compliments

After ranging far to your right, you may still be unable to get in front of the ball. You have to make a backhand play in those situations.

"This should always be a play of last resort. You should be trying to increase your range daily so that you don't have to backhand too many plays. If you're not rangy, play a little deeper to compensate. When you do have to backhand the ball as you go towards the hole, try to catch it just beyond your left foot. Stop your momentum, plant on your right foot, step to your left and throw." — Barry Larkin

"When I backhand, I prefer to take it off the middle of my right foot. Then I can bring my left foot over and get momentum going towards first base. You can increase your range at shortstop by doing lateral movement drills, anything that gets you moving or shuffling side to side. Have someone roll a ball to your left, then your right, then have them mix it up. As you go along, (your partner) can roll the ball wider and wider until you're covering more ground." — Derek Jeter

Figure 10-5 shows you the position for a backhand play.

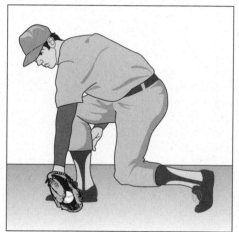

Figure 10-5:
The back-
hand play.

Illustration by Wiley, Composition Services Graphics

The wisdom of an open-glove policy

This advice should be common sense: It is much easier to catch a ball with a glove that is fully open than with one that is half or completely closed. All infielders should know this (although you would be surprised at how many Major-League infielders approach grounders with half-opened mitts), but it is especially important for the shortstop, who has little time to bobble the ball.

As you reach the ball, slow down and bend with your legs rather than your back. Lower your glove on an angle to the ground and open the glove wide. The fingers should be touching the field and your palm should be lifted up slightly toward you (see Figure 10-6).

Figure 10-6:
The short-
stop's glove
has to be
ready.

Illustration by Wiley, Composition Services Graphics

Doubling up

Like the second baseman, the shortstop can start double plays (his usual function) or act as the pivot man. If the ball is hit within three or four steps of second base, you usually don't need to involve your second baseman. Simply step on the bag with your left foot, push off, and throw off your right foot. Do this in one fluid motion. In other double-play situations, the shortstop's role changes:

✔ On balls hit near second, but not close enough to permit an unassisted play, give your second baseman a chest-high, underhanded toss. Throw sidearm to your second baseman on balls hit directly to you or just to your right.

✔ You must turn the pivot on the double play on balls hit to the right side of the infield. Get to the bag immediately.

✔ When the ball is hit so far to your right that you have to extend, take the time to plant your right foot and make a strong throw to second. You usually get only the lead runner on this play (which, by the way, should always be your priority), though the second baseman may be able to turn two if your throw is strong and accurate (and the runner heading toward first isn't very fast).

✔ On slowly hit grounders, forget about the double play. The shortstop must know the speed of each base runner so he can decide whether to attempt the force at second or get the out at first.

"When I'm the pivot man on the double play, I prefer to receive the ball on the left field side of second. As I get to the bag, I slow my momentum so that I can adjust if the throw to me isn't where I expect it. On the pivot, if the ball is to my right, I step to it with my right foot and drag my left foot over the bag. If the throw is on my left, I step to it with my left foot and drag my right." — Barry Larkin

"The biggest key to remember is you can't get the double play unless you get that first out. Make sure you catch the ball and tag second. Then you turn your body toward first base, get that momentum going towards first for the throw, and remember to avoid the runner coming in." — Derek Jeter

Chapter 11

Playing the Outfield: Where Fly Balls Go to Die

*O*h boy, do outfielders have the life. They don't have to worry about kamikaze base runners bearing down on them during the double play, hot line drives sizzling toward their craniums, or which base to cover on any given play. All they have to do is saunter after the occasional fly ball, throw it back toward the infield, and work on their suntans.

Yeah, right.

Playing the outfield is like playing any other position. It demands discipline, hard work, and knowledge. You must be able to gauge fly balls that come at you from diverse angles, understand the mechanics behind a good throw, and know what to do with the ball after you catch it. On balls hit into the gap, you must sprint full out, time your extension and catch, and then throw to the right base in one fluid move.

Infielders can afford to take their time on many plays. Outfielders are so far from the action, they don't have a half-moment to spare on any ball that sets runners in motion. Infielders can bobble or even drop a ball and still record an out. If an outfielder drops a ball, the hitter is not only on first base, but he probably takes an extra base. Outfielders don't collide with base runners, but they can run into the occasional wall. (And unlike human beings, those structures often have no "give" to them.) So you have to know what you're doing out there to avoid hurting yourself and your team.

Our chief outfield coach is Mr. Center Field, the incomparable Willie Mays. We believe that Carly Simon, a die-hard baseball fan so we're quoting her twice, was thinking of Mays corralling a fly ball when she sang, "Nobody Does It Better." Willie holds the major-league record with 12 consecutive Gold Gloves for outfield play. He's also the all-time Major-League leader in total outfield chances accepted. Runners rarely took liberties with Mays's powerful throwing arm. He once hit a long drive that fell just beyond the reach of a diving outfielder for extra bases. The broadcaster covering the game summed up Willie's fielding prowess by saying, "The only man who could have caught that ball just hit it."

Ken Griffey Sr., the 1980 All-Star Most Valuable Player, also shares his thoughts on outfield play in this section. Griffey patrolled all three outfield positions during a 19-year MLB career spent largely with the Cincinnati Reds and New York Yankees. Sparky Anderson said, "Kenny is an example of how a person can make himself into an outstanding fielder through hard work. He was a defensive weapon wherever he played, and he charged the ball as well as any outfielder of his day." We also bring in Rusty Staub, a smart outfielder whose powerful throwing arm was feared throughout baseball, for a word or two of expertise.

Setting Up for Basic Defense

Because they have more real estate to cover, outfielders have more positioning options than infielders. Where you play depends on the hitter, the pitcher, the situation, and the count. For example, Joey Votto is a left-handed hitter with good power to all fields. He can hit the ball with authority anywhere. However, against a hard-throwing right-hander like Matt Harvey, Joey is more likely to pull the ball when the count is in his favor. Conversely, if a hitter is *behind in the count* (he has more strikes on him than balls), he tends to protect the plate and hit the ball to the opposite field. So if Harvey has a 3-ball 1-strike count on Votto, Matt's outfielders should shade closer toward right field.

However, if you're playing the outfield behind left-handed pitcher Clayton Kershaw, you may not move toward right if you don't believe Votto can pull Kershaw's fastball. And even that is not an absolute. Suppose it's a close game in the late innings and Kershaw has lost some of the hop from his fastball. You may think that Votto, who is looking to drive the ball for extra bases, may now indeed be able to pull on the tiring Kershaw.

When setting up in the outfield, you must also consider your limitations and those of your teammates. Do you go back on balls well but have more difficulty on balls that pull you in? Play shallow. Do you move to your left better than your right? You have to compensate and position yourself a few steps to your right when a right-handed pull hitter is at the plate. Does your center fielder have a weak throwing arm? With the winning run on third and less than two out, you may have to take a ball that he would normally catch, so you can attempt the throw home. All of these factors — plus the field conditions for that day — determine where you play on each pitch.

Taking your basic stance

You should set up in the outfield with a square stance:

- ✔ Keep your feet parallel, shoulder-width apart, and pointed toward home plate.
- ✔ Get into a semi-crouch with your weight evenly distributed over the balls of both feet.
- ✔ Rest your hands on your knees but drop them as the ball approaches the plate.

This stance gives you momentum to chase the ball if it is hit beyond the infield as Figure 11-1 shows. Because your weight is evenly balanced over both feet, you can move to either side quickly. If it looks as if the ball will be hit over your head, put the toes of whatever foot is on the ball side behind the heel of your other foot. (This is called a *drop step.*)

Figure 11-1:
The basic outfield stance.

Illustration by Wiley, Composition Services Graphics

"Get as loose as possible before the game starts. Give yourself 15 minutes to stretch, do calisthenics, and some light running. Don't bring any tension to the outfield; it will rob you of quickness." — Ken Griffey Sr.

Getting a good jump

What is the one thing you hear said about any great outfielder? He gets a good jump on the ball. Your eyes, ears, and head determine how quickly you break for a fly ball. If you've done your homework, you should already know where the batter most often hits the ball.

"Getting a good jump on the ball starts at home plate. You have to know who is hitting. If you don't know where the hitter tends to hit the ball, how can you get a good jump on it? If you start moving as you see the ball coming over the infield, you're too late. Study the hitters so you can anticipate what will happen before a certain pitch is thrown. For example, Billy Williams (a Hall of Fame outfielder with the Chicago Cubs) was a left-handed pull-hitter. But he would take the breaking ball to left-center (the opposite field). So I had to make sure our pitchers worked him inside, but way inside or he would hit the ball out of the park. I'd play him straightaway in that spot. If I knew we were going to throw him off-speed stuff away in San Francisco, I'd anticipate going towards left. Now, if you don't know the hitter, talk to the pitcher. Find out how he's going to work him. Tell him you're going to play straightaway until you see the batter over a few games." — Willie Mays

Concentrate on the pitcher-batter confrontation. You may not be able to tell what kind of pitch has been thrown, but you can at least observe its location. Notice if the batter is getting a late hack (swing) or is in front of the ball. Your knowledge of the hitter and pitcher should then give you some idea of where the ball is likely to land.

"Depending on who was on the mound, I would key off of the pitcher's fastball and how the hitter was reacting to it. That would tell me if the hitter could pull the ball, or, if he was a little late, hit it the other way. Or just hit it back up the middle." — Ken Griffey Sr.

Another indicator of how far a ball will travel is the sound made when the bat hits the ball.

"Here's a little game my teammates and I used to play during batting practice to sharpen our ears. We would stand with our backs to home plate and try to identify where a ball would be hit without peeking. All we had to guide us was the sound of the ball against the wood. Practice that day after day and, after a while, you can take off at the crack of the bat. It becomes instinctive." — Rusty Staub

Outfielders usually move laterally on fly balls. To achieve maximum acceleration, pivot and push off the foot nearest the ball as you rise out of your semi-crouch. Cross over with your outside foot. If you must angle your run, stride first with the foot nearest the ball. Pivot on both feet whenever the batter hits the ball over your head.

"When you are going into the gap, don't keep your eyes on the ball. Train yourself to recognize where the ball will probably land and run to that area. After four or five steps, you can glance up to check the flight of the ball." — Ken Griffey Sr.

You don't have to move much on balls hit right at you, but you do have to determine whether the ball will rise or sink. Don't take a step until you can read the ball's trajectory.

Making the Catch

Pursue fly balls aggressively. If you drift over to time the catch of a ball, you aren't in position to throw. You may also be unable to adjust if you misjudge a ball's flight or a sudden gust carries it farther than you anticipated. Hustle on every play.

"The wind can be a factor when you go for a catch. You might run to the spot where you think the ball is coming down only to find out the wind has carried it another six feet or held it up so that it drops in front of you. Check which way the wind is blowing before the game starts. Then keep checking it every inning after that because the direction can change. I always looked at the flags to see where the wind was blowing. Some games would start with the wind blowing in, and then it would start blowing out after only a few innings." — Willie Mays

Using both hands, catch the ball out in front of your body and over your throwing shoulder (refer to Figure 11-2). If you're left-handed, your right foot should be forward; if you throw from the right side, your left foot is out in front. This position leaves you in the correct position to get off a good throw. Take a short hop to close the shoulders and hips on your glove side, and then move through the ball as you throw overhand with a cross-seam grip.

Figure 11-2:
Catching the
fly ball.

Illustration by Wiley, Composition Services Graphics

You will instill sound habits if you catch every ball as if you have to throw it to a base, even when there aren't any runners on the base paths.

"Before a ball is hit, you have to be thinking baseball. What is the situation? How many are out? Are you behind or ahead and by how many runs? Who comes up next? When a ball gets by you in the gap with one out, you don't want that batter to get more than two bases. He can score from third without a base hit with less than two out. So your throw is going to third." — Willie Mays

"Practice taking the ball out of your glove in a cross-seam grip until you can do it blindfolded. Do it every time you grab a baseball. For maximum power, throw the ball over the top whenever you can and have your momentum pointed towards your target. The best way to build your arm strength for these throws is to play catch as often as possible. And I don't mean just randomly tossing the ball back and forth. Play catch with a purpose. Make a game of hitting a target every time you throw. If you deliver the ball up near your catching partner's face, you get two points; at his chest, you get one. Low point man buys the soft drinks. Try to hit a specific target even when you're just loosening up." — Rusty Staub

"I tried to make my throws so that my teammates didn't get hurt. What I mean is that I would give them a ball high that they could handle. I didn't want them to have to reach down as the runner was sliding in because that's where the fielder can get injured. But on a throw to the catcher, I would throw low, even bounce the throw, because he has all that protection and if he stays low he can block the plate better. Now, when you make a throw, you're not always trying to get the base runner, you're trying to get the guy who hit the ball. If that hitter is slow, you might get him if he tries to take the extra base. So I would hit my cutoff man on purpose, try to catch that hitter running to second. I always tried to keep my throws to the cutoff man chest-high where he could handle them." — Willie Mays

Don't fall into the gap

Any time a ball is hit into the gap or power alley, one outfielder should try to cut off the ball, while another should run at a deeper angle to back up the play. Usually the fielder closest to the ball goes for it. On plays where the ball is equidistant from both fielders, the center fielder has priority. However, to avoid mix-ups, especially on balls hit between two players, you and your fellow outfielders should call loudly for any ball you pursue.

Coming in on a ball

During practice, learn how to read the trajectory of balls far in front of you so you can instantly decide if you should make the putout or catch it on a bounce. If you have to play the bounce, slow down while keeping your body and glove in front of the ball. That way, if you don't catch it cleanly, you can knock it down.

"Make sure you catch this ball belt-high or chest-high so that you keep your eyes on the ball. It will be easier to handle." — Ken Griffey Sr.

"Again, you have to know your hitter. A strong hitter might hit a line drive that will hang up a little longer; someone not as strong, the ball might just die. And the wind might blow the ball up, down, or even to the side. Which is why you have to know what's happening in the ballpark at all times." — Willie Mays

Going out on a ball

Most major leaguers will tell you the most difficult fly ball to catch is the one smacked over your head. Inexperienced outfielders often start back pedaling on that ball, which is the worst thing they can do. If you back pedal, you don't see the ball clearly because your head is bobbing up and down, you can't generate any speed (which is why marathoners do not run backward), and you can't jump if you need to.

"I would try to catch the ball like a wide receiver in football, over my left shoulder or right shoulder depending on where the ball is hit. And I'm getting in position to throw that ball while I'm making the catch. If you see a picture of my catch against Vic Wertz in the 1954 World Series, I caught the ball over my shoulder because I could see the ball better. I looked directly over my shoulder. And the left side of my body was ready to throw before I even caught the ball." (Note: Mays is referring to perhaps the most famous catch ever made. With his back to the plate, Mays galloped full speed into deepest center to catch Wertz's booming line drive some 450 feet from home plate. He then uncorked a perfect throw.) — Willie Mays

"Outfielders tangle themselves on that play when they start off on the wrong foot. If a ball is hit over your right shoulder, drop step back with your right foot. Cross over with your left foot and stay angled sideways as you go back. If it is hit over your left shoulder, do the reverse." (See Figure 11-3.) — Ken Griffey Sr.

Figure 11-3:
Going back
on the fly
ball.

Illustration by Wiley, Composition Services Graphics

Playing Ground Balls

With runners on, outfielders should charge ground balls as aggressively as infielders. They must field the ball in a position that allows them to unleash a good throw. Field the ball on your glove side with your glove-side foot down. Close off your upper body with a short hop, stride with your left foot, and throw over the top with a cross-seam grip.

"When no one is on base, all you want to do is keep the ground ball in front of you. If it gets by, the runner is taking extra bases. Get in front of it, get down on one knee, and block the ball." (See Figure 11-4.) — Ken Griffey Sr.

Figure 11-4:
Keeping the ground ball in front of you.

Illustration by Wiley, Composition Services Graphics

"You have to charge that ball and keep it in front of you like an infielder. I didn't practice doing that in the outfield. Instead, I took grounders at second or shortstop during practice. So when I went to the outfield, grounders were a piece of cake." — Willie Mays

Part IV

From Little League to the Major Leagues — Organized Baseball

The National and American League teams

NL East	NL Central	NL West
Atlanta Braves	Chicago Cubs	Arizona Diamondbacks
Florida Marlins	Cincinnati Reds	Colorado Rockies
New York Mets	Milwaukee Brewers	Los Angeles Dodgers
Philadelphia Phillies	Pittsburgh Pirates	San Francisco Giants
Washington Nationals	St. Louis Cardinals	San Diego Padres

AL East	AL Central	AL West
Baltimore Orioles	Chicago White Sox	Houston Astros
Boston Red Sox	Cleveland Indians	Los Angeles Angels
New York Yankees	Detroit Tigers	Oakland Athletics
Tampa Bay Rays	Kansas City Royals	Seattle Mariners
Toronto Blue Jays	Minnesota Twins	Texas Rangers

Check out www.dummies.com/extras/baseball for more in-depth information about what you need to know to follow the MLB.

In this part...

- Read about all levels of organized baseball, everything from the T-ball for your 6-year-old all the way up to Major League Baseball.

- Understand the ins and outs of college baseball, and why it's more popular and important than ever.

- Look at every level of professional baseball, including where in the world baseball is played, what the types of leagues are, and how those leagues operate.

- Discover information about the amateur draft — why it has gone from an obscure event for scouts to an eagerly awaited highlight of the Major League season for fans and big-league players alike.

- If you're a coach, see what Hall of Fame manager Sparky Anderson says about coaching a baseball team and what you can do to help your team reach its full potential.

- Take a closer look at who really pulls the strings for your favorite Major League team in its front office and understand why the general manager (GM) is the most important person in the organization and how scouts who work for the GM try to predict which amateur player will become the next best natural.

- Examine what the men in blue (also known as the umpires) are responsible for during a baseball game.

- Start to calculate some basic baseball math so that you won't be at a loss the next time your friends ask you to figure out their slugging percentage, batting average, earned run average, and so many other interesting stats.

- Know how to evaluate MLB players' performances with the latest sabermetric tools, including what sabermetrics are, so you can feel invincible in any baseball debate.

Chapter 12

T-Ball to College Baseball and Everything in Between

. . . .

. . . .

*W*hether you're 5 or 55, male or female, you don't have to regard baseball merely as a spectator sport. If you want to compete in an informal atmosphere, your local parks department can make a baseball diamond available for pickup games. (You should always reserve field time in advance, especially if you have a number of leagues competing in your town.) Throughout the United States and Canada, thousands of baseball leagues and associations also offer nonprofessional players of all ages and genders an opportunity for organized competition.

The league that you or your child joins does not have to be affiliated with USA Baseball (919-459-0761, www.usabaseball.com), but if it is, be assured that the organization conforms to a rigorous standard. USA Baseball is the national governing body of amateur baseball. Members include the Little League, the Amateur Athletic Union, the National High School Coaches Association, PONY Baseball, the Police Athletic League, and the NCAA. This chapter examines these levels and also discusses the amateur draft. At the start of the 2013 season, USA Baseball alumni who were playing in the Major Leagues included such stars as Derek Jeter, Matt Holliday, Chris Carpenter, Steven Strasburg, and Max Scherzer. In the land of Blue Jays, Baseball Canada (613-748-5606, www.baseball.ca) is the prominent amateur organization.

Starting with Baseball: T-Ball

T-ball is baseball's version of miniature golf. The baseball is served on a batting tee, bases are never more than 60 feet apart, and everything else is scaled down so that children (usually 8 years old and under) can experience the joys of the national pastime without risking physical harm. The **T-Ball USA Association** (203-381-1440, www.teeballusa.org), based in Stratford, Connecticut, doesn't run any leagues or teams of its own, but it does assist many leading amateur organizations with their T-ball programs.

This nonprofit association also runs clinics to teach coaches and parents the rudiments of baseball. For more information about the program, pick up a copy of *The Official Family Guide to Tee Ball* by Bing Broido (Master PR), available at any of the major online used and new bookstore sites, such as Amazon (www.amazon.com), Barnes & Noble (www.barnesandnoble.com), Alibris (www.alibris.com), or any of their affiliated sites.

Amateur Leagues for All Ages

Little League Baseball (570-326-1921, www.littleleague.org) is played in every state in the United States and in more than 80 countries. With more than two million participants (including more than 400,000 registered in softball), a million volunteers, and 7,000 leagues, Little League is the world's largest organized youth sports program. Leagues are required to play an annual schedule of at least 12 games. The program, Little League Child Protection, requires member leagues to conduct background checks on certain volunteers. The organization also maintains a museum and conducts instructional clinics for umpires and managers. It annually sponsors an international World Series in nine divisions.

Does Little League baseball provide a first step to the big leagues? An estimated 80 percent of all Major-League players participated in Little League baseball. Current Major Leaguers who played in the Little League World Series, held each year in Williamsport, Pennsylvania, include Lance Lynn, Todd Frazier, and Jurickson Profar.

You can keep up with the latest Little League events at the website and by ordering its ASAP newsletters, which offer advice on safety and instruction, or one of its several electronic newsletters. Subscriptions are free. You should also contact the Little League for a complete list of its instructional manuals and magazines.

The **Babe Ruth League** (609-695-1434, www.baberuthleague.org) operates in at least 48 states in the United States. Founded in 1951, the organization is currently composed of well over half a million players. This league stresses player participation over winning and is famous for teaching the proper way to play the game. And I (Joe) participated in the Oakland chapter of the Babe Ruth League as a member of the Qwik Way Drive-In team.

Competition is probably fiercest in leagues sponsored by the **Amateur Athletic Union** (407-934-7200, www.aausports.org), which boasts associations in all 50 states in the United States. Like professional clubs, many member teams travel out of their locales to play games. Players participate in nine divisions with ages ranging from 9 to 20. AAU championships are decided in tournaments featuring double-pool play. Teams are seeded before the first round. Winners go on to play in the National Championship Tournament, and losers participate in a consolation bracket.

Other youth baseball organizations include the following:

- **All American Amateur Baseball Association** in Zanesville, Ohio (740- 453-8531, www.hometeamsonline.com)

- **American Legion Baseball** in Indianapolis, Indiana (317-630-1203, www.legion.org/baseball). This hallowed organization registers more than 5,400 teams in all 50 states, including Canada and Puerto Rico.

- **Dixie Youth Baseball** (www.dixie.org) claims to be the leading youth baseball program in the southern United States.

- **Dizzy Dean Baseball** in Hernando, Missouri (662-429-4365, www.dizzydeanbbinc.org)

- **George Kelly Amateur Baseball Federation** in Altoona, Pennsylvania (814-944-8567, www.leaguelineup.com)

- **Hap Dumont Baseball** in Wichita, Kansas (bruce@prattrecreation, www.kansashapdumontbaseball.com)

- **National Association of Police Athletic Leagues** in Palm Beach, Florida (561-745-5535, www.nationalpal.org)

- **PONY Baseball** in Washington, Pennsylvania (724-225-1060, www.pony.org)

- **US Amateur Baseball Association** in Edmonds, Washington (425-776-7130, www.usaba.com)

- **US Amateur Baseball Federation** in Chula Vista, California (619-934-2551, www.usabf.com)

Your child and the child within you can compete in the **National Amateur Baseball Federation** (410-721-4727, www.nabf.com), which has approximately 350,000 participants in about 85 franchises across the United States. Founded in 1914, this is the only all-volunteer amateur baseball organization in the country. For younger players, classifications advance from rookie (ages 10 and under) to senior level (ages 18 and under). Players between the ages of 19 and 22 compete in the college classification. If you're over 22, you can recapture your youth at the major level, an unlimited classification. If you're under 22 and there isn't a collegiate league in your area, you also can play at the major level. Many former college players and professionals who have reacquired their amateur status by requesting a waiver compete in this division. Member teams play anywhere from 30 to 50 games per year in local competition. The best of these teams participate in round-robin championship tournaments scheduled between mid-July and late August. Two other organizations have unlimited classifications.

The **American Amateur Baseball Congress** (505-327-3120, www.aabc.us) holds July-to-August tournaments in 13 divisions, named for present and future Hall of Famers: Rod Carew (7 and under), Roberto Clemente (ages 8 and under), Jackie Robinson (9 and under), Willie Mays (10 and under), Gil Hodges (11 and under), Pee Wee Reese (12 and under), Nolan Ryan (13 and under), Sandy Koufax (14 and under), Ken Griffey, Jr. (15 and under), Mickey Mantle (16 and under), Don Mattingly (17 and under), Connie Mack (18 and under), and Stan Musial (unlimited).

The **Continental Amateur Baseball Association** (740-382-4620, www.cababaseball.com) maintains competitive balance by spreading players out among 12 classifications (ages 9 and under to unlimited).

Founded by former Detroit Tiger minor leaguer John Young in 1988, **Restore Baseball in the Inner Cities** (RBI) annually brings the national pastime to more than 220,000 youths in baseball and softball across the United States and the Caribbean. RBI teams compete to participate in an annual World Series, which is held in a major-league club city. Girls' softball has been part of the program since 1994. Major League Baseball and all 30 of its clubs have contributed more than $30 million in support of the RBI program.

Dipping into the Collegiate Talent Pool

The first baseball game played between two colleges took place on July 1, 1859, when Amherst beat Pittsfield 73–32. (Evidently, they thought they were playing football.) Only 35 feet (10.6 meters) separated the pitcher from the batter, and the bases were a mere 60 feet (18.2 meters) apart. Few of the great college players of the late 1800s ever donned a big-league uniform;

most college men didn't consider baseball to be a respectable profession. However, the ascent of Christy Mathewson of Bucknell University, the elegant and erudite Hall of Fame pitcher for the New York Giants, considerably altered that attitude. Matty had been president of his class and a member of a literary society, and he could beat ten opponents at chess simultaneously. He demonstrated that one could play professional baseball without surrendering the title "gentleman." Largely due to his influence — as well as that of other turn-of-the-century college stars who turned pro (such as Hall of Famers Eddie Collins and Harry Hooper), American campuses became incubators for Major-League talent.

Today, a majority of major-league players have a college education. Collegiate baseball provides the perfect stage for aspiring big leaguers to showcase their talents — not only to Major League scouts, who have been intensely scrutinizing them for years, but to the increasing number of pro baseball fans doing unofficial "scouting" for their home teams in anticipation of the amateur draft (refer to the next section, "The Amateur Draft: Fishing for Talent" for more information).

The National Collegiate Athletic Association (NCAA) is, of course, the big kahuna of the college game. Two hundred and ninety-three colleges compete in its Division I conferences. Other NCAA college baseball squads play in either Division II or III.

The NCAA Division I College World Series is held for approximately two weeks in the middle of June. Both championship series for the other two divisions take place during the final week of May. For decades, the NCAA had allowed only 48 teams to qualify for the tournament. But in 1999, as the event drew ever-widening public interest — helped by ESPN's televising of the entire competition and a clever marketing campaign similar to that which transformed the once-staid NCAA basketball tourney into March Madness — the NCAA added 16 teams and amped up the format. The top eight teams advance to the College World Series in Omaha, Nebraska.

If you have never thrown two bucks in your office's NCAA hoops pool or who forgot to add that calculator app to your smartphone, you can see a complete diagram of the tournament by visiting the NCAA website at `www.ncaa.com/interactive-bracket/baseball/d1`.

The Amateur Draft: Fishing for Talent

If you've ever been tempted to ask, "Daddy, where do players come from?" or some variation, here we explain it to you — and no, it doesn't involve the stork.

Players and owners: Strange bedfellows

Before 1965, amateur players could hitch their destiny to any team who had the diligence, cunning, and cash to sign them. This "policy" gave flush teams, such as the New York Yankees, Brooklyn (subsequently LA) Dodgers, New York (now San Francisco) Giants, and St. Louis Cardinals, a huge advantage. They had more money to spend on scouts, and even more to dole out to the talented players their scouts discovered. Small-market teams, such as the Boston Braves and St. Louis Browns, lacked the funds, and some big-market teams had owners who preferred to pocket most of their profits rather than spend money on potential superstars and put a winning team on the field.

Depending on whom you ask, the baseball amateur draft was created in 1965 to eliminate that big-market gold rush and promote fairness and parity among Major League franchises or to cut costs for all its teams *and* eliminate the only opportunity players had to choose their place of employment.

That was because, under the terms of baseball's *reserve clause* — a part of all player contracts — a player was bound to a single team for a long period (even if the individual contracts he signed covered only one season). So the only bargaining power the player ever had in his pro career was before he started it — that being the choice of where he'd spend the rest of his career. (Unless, of course, he was traded or released; he had no control over those possibilities, either.)

Still, in the 1940s, some owners began dispensing generous sums (bonuses) to the most promising amateur players. Their brethren stopped that in 1947 by instituting the *bonus rule,* which declared that any amateur player who received a signing bonus of more than $4,000 would be forced to stay on his team's Major League roster for two seasons before he could be even sent to the minors. If that rule were still in place, you could have the greatest young players on the planet, players who just needed a year or two of seasoning, but with the exception of prodigies, such as Bryce Harper and Mike Trout, all they could do for two years was cheer from the bench. (Even icons such as Mickey Mantle, Willie Mays, and Joe DiMaggio played in the minors.)

Finally, in 1964, a bidding war broke out over University of Wisconsin two-sport start Rick Reichardt. The Los Angeles Angels won with a record-breaking $205,000 offer, which was more than big-league superstars were making. Other owners followed suit. The 20 Major League teams at that time spent more than $7 million combined on signing bonuses for amateur players that year, which was more than they spent on major league salaries. Thus began the amateur draft.

As for the reserve clause, for most of baseball history, it was held to be essentially perpetual, so that a player had no freedom to change teams unless he was released. This clause lasted until the mid-1970s, when players — led by Curt Flood and union leader Marvin Miller — initiated a series of lawsuits and finally won the right to become free agents after a certain number of years of service (currently and for some time the magic number has been *six*) and sell their services to the highest bidder. This system has remained in place, with minor tweaks, ever since.

If you want to become an expert on the history of MLB player-owner relations, we recommend John Helyar's eye-opening book, *Lords of the Realm* (Villard), one of the most essential tomes on the sport — and a real page-turner.

Draft order: The last shall be first

The draft apportioned amateur players to teams in reverse order of the prior season's standings. If a team finished with the worst record in baseball last year, it received the very first pick in next year's draft. Although the draft originally had several phases, MLB narrowed it to one draft in June, held right after the college and high school baseball seasons. The amateur draft has 40 rounds where teams get one pick per round until the talent pool is exhausted. They must sign their fledgling pros by mid-August. That pool consists of players from the United States and Puerto Rico. Teams also sign players from a growing number of other countries (refer to the nearby sidebar about the international draft).

Teams may also receive compensation picks for losing players to free agency the previous year. These *sandwich picks* are stuffed in between the first and second rounds.

Negotiating a contract — a cat-and-mouse game

After a team drafts a player, it tries to lure him into turning pro with a signing bonus. Until he signs, the teams, the players, and the players' advisers jockey a lot. Amateur players aren't officially allowed to have agents until they turn pro, but the better prospects are usually counseled in their negotiating by the top agents, who, like the teams, also have been scouting those players since they were 16 or younger. Most drafted players sign, but some feel that by postponing signing — or even threatening not to sign — they can boost their potential worth and/or avoid being signed by a team they don't favor. This behavior often alienates some teams, who fear drafting a player they may fail to sign.

Signability — the willingness of an amateur player to sign with the team that he expects to draft him for the bonus money the team is promising — factors heavily in a team's decision of which player to draft when its turn comes around to make a selection. Players who resist signing with the team that drafted them may *drop down* in the draft (for example, a first-round talent may not be selected until the tenth round) because they've convinced all but the bravest — and deep-pocketed — teams that they're willing to wait at least another year or more, to increase their value by, say, excelling at a major college program. (Unsigned high school players may turn to junior or four-year colleges, and college juniors may return to college for their senior year, hoping to increase their bonus the following year.) Conversely, teams try to lure that centerfielder who is holding out for more money by offering him a bonus far higher than their market price.

Playing the slot machine

In 2012, MLB introduced a new wrinkle — each team is allocated a *bonus pool* — a specific dollar figure from which it can offer initial contracts to its drafted players. Each team's pool is based on its draft position and number of picks, plus the amount spent in the previous year's draft. (Players selected in the first round can earn more money than players chosen in later rounds.) If a team exceeds the total amount allotted for the first ten rounds, it incurs penalties, including a high percentage tax on the amount it overpaid, and even the potential to lose future draft picks.

This bonus pool limit inhibits *over-slot spending* — when a team tries to be aggressive in adding amateur talent by paying a player more than what MLB has mandated for that slot. This new rule may cost baseball some talented players, because athletes with college scholarships for another sport (most commonly football) are often the recipients of that over-slot bonus money, offered by teams trying to tempt them away from pursuing their other sport.

To be eligible for the draft, a player must fit the following criteria:

- ✔ Be a resident of the United States, Canada, or one of their territories (such as Puerto Rico)
- ✔ Never signed a MLB or minor league contract
- ✔ Be a high school graduate who never attended college
- ✔ Be a junior at a four-year college or at least 21 years of age
- ✔ Be a junior-college player in either his freshman or sophomore year

Players picked in the first few rounds are considered the best prospects; however, getting picked in a high round is no guarantee of success. One-third of first-round picks never play a single inning of Major League Baseball. And many late-round picks have gone on to all-star careers. For example, Mike Piazza, perhaps the greatest hitting catcher of all time, was the Los Angeles Dodgers' 62nd-round pick in 1988. That means clubs preferred more than 1,600 players — enough bodies to stock the rosters for the entire major leagues and then some — to this Hall of Fame–worthy player.

Draftology, baseball style

MLB's amateur draft, which for many years was considered such a non-event that it wasn't even televised, quickly has become an event. Draft-mania — intense scrutiny and educated guesses about the order in which each player would be taken and by whom — was initially the province of a handful of periodicals, such as Baseball America and the scouts and other members of a club's front office. (For more on what goes on in a team's inner sanctum, see Chapter 15.)

A *sabermetrician* is someone who practices *sabermetrics*, the objective analysis of the game — player performance, front-office maneuverings, and history — anything to which he can apply his computer. This person takes his or her name from the acronym of the Society of American Baseball Research (SABR), a scholarly organization formed in 1971 to put under the microscope the many axioms used by players, fans, and sportswriters, and create new, ideally more accurate, formulae for evaluating performance. (For more on *sabermetrics,* refer to Chapter 16.) So it was no surprise when sabermetricians, the same people who were hungry to re-examine the big-league game's long-cherished axioms, turned their gaze to the ways in which amateur players were evaluated. How did you know that your team picked the right players? And how did your team know which players had the talent, temperament, and determination to make the big leagues — after spending two to six years toiling in the minor leagues?

Scouts who eyeball versus scouts who use computers

A chasm quickly opened between old-school scouts and *statheads,* young, brashly brainy computer-toting statisticians. The scouts — called *bird-dogs* for their propensity to comb the nation by car in pursuit of the next natural, would give a prospect the once-or-twice over and file a report grading his five tools (running, throwing, catching, hitting, and hitting for power). The statheads sized up players using equations so complex that they'd flummox your high-school algebra teacher — often without ever seeing the player play.

The scouts scoffed at the idea that you could assess a player's potential by crunching numbers, and they had a point. The further a player was from pro ball, the less relevant the numbers became, due to everything from puberty (how tall and heavy would a 17-year-old be at 22) to the relative level of competition he faced in college and, especially, high school, to how well he would take instruction. The stat-heads countered that they could objectively analyze at least some aspects of a player's game.

Prospects were now scrutinized by not just maverick websites such as Baseball Prospectus, but by the beat writer for the paper that covered your local team. In the weeks leading up to the draft, general managers — the single-most important position in a team's organization — and scouting directors suddenly were pushed into the media spotlight from the shadows they'd occupied for more than a half-century.

Prospect experts proliferated — most from the stathead side of the aisle — and the best of them, such as Keith Law, Kevin Goldstein, and John Sickels, were taken seriously enough to be scooped up by major media outlets or advisers who would help big-league clubs make more educated guesses.

Despite the enormous growth of focus on the amateur draft, it remains a crapshoot — mostly for the same reason it always has been — because the skills in baseball are more nuanced than on other sports. It is harder to predict years in advance whether that 18-year-old out of said university who can run 60 meters in 6 seconds and hit a baseball 450 feet will turn out to be the next Ken Griffey, Jr. — who was picked first by the Seattle Mariners in the 1987 draft — or the next Mark Merchant, who the Pirates selected right after Bonds and who never played a single game in the big leagues.

Foreign intrigue: International signings

Major League Baseball wanted to institute a second amateur draft to include international players, but the players' union nixed that idea in the last Collective Bargaining Agreement (CBA). Professional players from abroad, such as those coming from the Japanese, Korean, Mexican, and other professional leagues, as well as pedigreed talent with experience playing against world-class competition (usually found in countries such as Taiwan and Cuba), are subject to another set of rules. Refer to Chapter 13 for more information.

Chapter 13

The Majors, the Minors, and Other Leagues

Major League Baseball isn't the only game in town (especially if you live in Helena, Montana, or Rome, Italy). Thousands of amateur and professional baseball leagues offer games to fans all over the globe. Japan, Mexico, Holland, Cuba, Venezuela, Italy, Korea, and China are just some of the countries that have embraced baseball. And who knows how many amateur leagues are flourishing throughout the world — the number must easily reach five figures. Baseball fever . . . it's catching and spreading everywhere! This chapter examines professional baseball and all its glory.

Eyeing the Major Leagues

Major League Baseball is an extremely complex and profitable organization with a long, illustrious history that has managed to modernize with the times. MLB's headquarters are in New York City, where Commissioner Allan "Bud" Selig, who was elected by the team owners, enforces rules and policies. MLB (www.mlb.com) has a wide variety of departments — from player relations to media — and comprises 30 teams (or franchises), each of which is an organization of its own, with hundreds of employees. The American and National leagues also maintain offices in New York City, as does the Major League Players Association — the player's union. These sections take a closer look at the game's administration and the league's teams.

Introducing MLB administration

MLB team owners officially elected Selig, the former owner of the Milwaukee Brewers, as commissioner of baseball in 1999. His office enforces rules and policies among the owners for both leagues. Future Hall of Famer Joe Torre is baseball's executive vice president who runs baseball's day-to-day business operations. Hall of Fame outfielder Frank Robinson, MLB's executive vice president of baseball development, helps Torre. Robert Manfred of the Major League Baseball Player Relations Committee represents the owners' interests in labor negotiations.

The leagues no longer have individual presidents. The baseball commissioner and his executive staff implement policy, issue directives, approve contracts, and have jurisdiction over all league matters, including player fines, protests, and other disputes.

Michael Weiner doesn't own a club, swat home runs, or throw any high fast-balls, yet he may very well be the most powerful man in baseball. Weiner is the executive director of the Major League Players Association, the baseball players' union.

Think you have the stuff to play in the big leagues? The Major League Scouting Bureau holds tryouts around the United States every June and July. To participate in a tryout camp, you must be at least 16 years old. You must bring your own equipment and sign a liability waiver before taking the field. If you're under 21, a parent or guardian must also sign the waiver. There's no fee to try out, and you can register 30 minutes before camp opens. To discover the location of the tryout camp nearest you, check out www.mlb.com.

Meeting the franchises

William Hulbert founded the National League (NL) in 1876. Chicago, New York, Philadelphia, Cincinnati, Louisville, Hartford, St. Louis, and Boston provided homes for the original eight franchises. The NL expanded to 10 teams in 1962, 12 (in two divisions) in 1969, and 14 in 1993. Table 13-1 shows the breakdown of the NL teams.

Table 13-1	The National League	
NL East	*NL Central*	*NL West*
Atlanta Braves	Chicago Cubs	Arizona Diamondbacks
Florida Marlins	Cincinnati Reds	Colorado Rockies
New York Mets	Milwaukee Brewers	Los Angeles Dodgers
Philadelphia Phillies	Pittsburgh Pirates	San Francisco Giants
Washington Nationals	St. Louis Cardinals	San Diego Padres

Ban Johnson founded the American League (AL) in 1900 and declared it a major league the following season. However, it was not officially recognized as a major league until 1903. The original eight franchises included Chicago, Boston, Detroit, Philadelphia, Baltimore, Washington, Cleveland, and Milwaukee. The league expanded to 10 teams in 1961, 12 (in two divisions) in 1969, and 14 in 1977. Table 13-2 lists the AL franchises in their respective divisions.

Table 13-2	The American League	
AL East	*AL Central*	*AL West*
Baltimore Orioles	Chicago White Sox	Houston Astros
Boston Red Sox	Cleveland Indians	Los Angeles Angels
New York Yankees	Detroit Tigers	Oakland Athletics
Tampa Bay Rays	Kansas City Royals	Seattle Mariners
Toronto Blue Jays	Minnesota Twins	Texas Rangers

Each club carries 25 players on its regular-season roster (13 to 16 position players and 10 to 12 pitchers). Rosters expand from 25 up to 40 players on September 1, when many teams give their better minor-league prospects a taste of the Major Leagues. However, only those players who are on the roster before that time are eligible for postseason play.

A club captures first place in its division by compiling the best win-loss percentage. (You can discover how to calculate that percentage by consulting Chapter 16.)

Understanding interleague play

In 1997, MLB introduced *interleague play,* in which teams from each league played each other during the regular season. Prior to that, the only interleague play occurred in the World Series, fought between the AL and NL champions, and the midseason All-Star Game, a contest between the best players from the AL and the NL (fans voted for some of the players and managers of the previous year's league champions chose the others).

As of the 2002 season, a new format to interleague play was instituted where teams play interleague games against various divisions. The number of interleague games a team played, as well as the number played against a geographical rival (such as the Yankees versus the Mets) has varied over the years. However, due to the realignment that produced an equal number of clubs in each league (15) starting in 2013, at least one interleague game will be played on every day of the Major-League season.

One for the Major-League history books

Both leagues have rich histories that have been vividly captured in countless books. The best of these include

- ✔ Harold Seymour's and Dorothy Seymour Mills' *Baseball — The Early Years, Baseball — The Golden Age,* and *Baseball — The People's Game* (Oxford University Press). Critics have hailed Seymour as baseball's greatest historian. *The Early Years* covers the game from the pre–Civil War years to 1903. *The Golden Age* follows the game until 1930. *The People's* Game is devoted entirely to the game outside the professional league, its place in institutions, the rise of women's baseball, and the struggles of black players and clubs, bringing to life the central role of baseball for generations of Americans. Seymour presents baseball against a historical backdrop that provides the reader with a sociological context for changes within the sport.

- ✔ The eighth edition of *Total Baseball* (Sport Classic Books) is the game's ultimate reference work. Esteemed baseball historian John Thorn and co-editors Phil Birnbaum and Bill Deane have loaded their encyclopedia with statistics on every Major-League player who ever pulled on a pair of spikes. This 2,600-page-plus volume contains league, team, and ballpark histories, all-time leader lists in every major category, a ranking of baseball's 100 most influential figures, and illuminating essays on such topics as the origins of baseball, the historical impact of Barry Bonds, Jackie Robinson and the breaking of baseball's color line, and the fact and fiction behind the "Moneyball" phenomenon. The new edition also includes more than 200 photos and illustrations.

HEADS UP

Joining the Society for American Baseball Research

Is Mike Piazza the best hitting catcher of all time? Did Babe Ruth really call his home run against the Cubs in the 1932 World Series? What team originally drafted Tom Seaver out of college and how did they lose him?

You can find out the answers to these and many more questions by joining the Society for American Baseball Research (SABR) (800-969-7227, www.sabr.org). Founded in 1971, SABR is a nonprofit organization dedicated to the preservation of baseball history. Its two publications, *The National Pastime* and *The Research Journal,* are, by themselves,

worth the $45 yearly membership dues. You also can get three-year memberships at a discounted rate. Family and gift memberships are also available. In addition, SABR sends out a weekly e-newsletter titled "This Week in SABR." Members also have access to the SABR Lending Library, whose comprehensive inventory includes microfilm reproductions of *Sporting Life* (1883–1917) and *The Sporting News* (1886–1957). You can also participate in various research committees with top baseball historians.

✔ In *Rob Neyer's Big Book of Baseball Lineups* (www.robneyer.com), the baseball analyst answers many long-standing baseball arguments. He starts a few new debates by presenting a series of lineups (including All-Time, All-Rookie, and All-Bust) for each MLB franchise with thought-provoking tidbits and essays on every player picked.

You can also check out Leonard Koppett's *The New Thinking Fan's Guide to Baseball* (Dutton Publishers) and *Nice Guys Finish Last* by Leo Durocher with Ed Linn (University of Chicago Press). Koppett is considered one of America's definitive sportswriters, and this book his greatest and most influential work.

Examining the American Minor Leagues

Major-League organizations often send their young players to the minor leagues to hone their talents before joining the big club. Veteran ballplayers sometimes visit the minors, too. A Major-League player usually rehabs his injuries in the minors before returning to the big leagues, and if his performance has slipped and he is trying to recapture the magic, he may step down to the minors for a while. Most minor-league players have something to prove. And while the youngsters want to show their organizations that they're ready to step up to the big leagues, declining veteran players are eager to convince a team that they can still compete in the majors.

Because nearly everyone on the field is highly motivated, you often see a hustling, rollicking brand of baseball in the minors. The level of skills on display varies from league to league, team to team, and player to player, but the level of thrills is consistently high from Triple-A ball down to the Rookie Leagues. Most minor leaguers have large dreams but small salaries. They play a game they love not for dollars but for glory. Their innocent, fervent aspirations will fail to touch your heart only if you don't have one. These sections identify the different minor leagues.

Identifying the different teams

Nineteen minor leagues were operating under the National Association in 1999. For most of the 20th century, a second umbrella organization — the American Association — also oversaw minor-league play. But at the end of the 1998 season, the American Association folded. Its member teams were dispersed among the remaining minor leagues.

The number of teams in each minor league may vary from year to year. Most minor-league clubs are owned by major-league organizations that absorb all the operating costs. A few are independent entities, though even they have working agreements with clubs that underwrite much (if not all) of their overhead costs. When the working agreement expires, a minor-league club can switch its major-league affiliation (which it might do if it has greater proximity to another big-league team).

At the end of the 2013 season, the National Association leagues and franchises were competing under the following alignments (2013 major-league affiliations are listed in parentheses):

Class AAA (Triple A)

Triple A is the highest level of play in the minor leagues, comprised of the International League and Pacific Coast League. The Triple A season lasts 144 games. Most players at this level are youngsters who are a stone's throw from the MLB, but you can also find veteran ex-Major Leaguers, as well as career minor leaguers who keep hope alive. The leagues are as follows:

✔ **The International League:** Buffalo (Blue Jays), Lehigh Valley (Phillies), Norfolk (Orioles), Pawtucket (Red Sox), Charlotte (White Sox), Gwinnett (Braves), Columbus (Indians), Indianapolis (Pirates), Rochester (Twins), Scranton/Wilkes-Barre (Yankees), Toledo (Tigers), Durham (Devil Rays), Louisville (Reds), and Syracuse (Nationals)

✔ **Pacific Coast League:** Iowa (Cubs), Memphis (Cardinals), Nashville (Brewers), Omaha (Royals), Albuquerque (Dodgers), New Orleans (Marlins), Oklahoma City (Astros), Round Rock (Rangers), Colorado Springs (Rockies), Reno (Diamondbacks), Salt Lake City (Angels), Tacoma (Mariners), Las Vegas (Mets), Sacramento (Athletics), and Tucson (Padres)

✔ **The Mexican League (ML)** is also a Triple A member of the National Association. All its teams are independent entities with no Major-League affiliations. The ML consists of 16 franchises playing in two divisions:

- **Northern Division:** Laguna Cowboys, Mexico City Red Devils, Monterrey Sultans, Monclova Steelers, Saltillo Sarape Users, Aguascalientes Railroaders, Reynosa Broncos, and Puebla Parrots

- **Southern Division:** Campeche Pirates, Ciudad del Carmen Dolphins, Minatitlán Oilers, Oaxaca Warriors, Quintana Roo Tigers, Tabasco Olmecs, Veracruz Red Eagles, and Yucatan Lions

Mexican League teams play a 110-game schedule that stretches from mid-March to mid-August.

The lower minors

We could present all the minor-league teams and their affiliations, but then this would turn into a book of lists. Instead, in Table 13-3, we present one last list of the other National Association leagues.

Table 13-3	National Association Leagues	
Class AA (Double A)	*Class A (Advanced)*	*Class A*
Eastern League	California League	Midwest League
Southern League	Carolina League	South Atlantic League
Texas League	Florida State League	
Short-Season Class A	*Rookie (Advanced)*	*Rookie*
New York-Penn League	Appalachian League	Arizona League
Northwest League	Pioneer League	Dominican Summer League
		Venezuelan Summer League
		Gulf Coast League

Nine independent minor leagues operated in 2013: the American Association of Independent Professional Baseball, the Atlantic League, the Canadian American Association of Professional Baseball, the Freedom Pro Baseball League, the Pacific Association of Professional Baseball Clubs, the Pecos League, the United League Baseball, the Frontier League, and the California Winter League. Most of these clubs operate without any Major-League affiliation. Kevin Millar,

J.D. Drew, and Ben Weber are some of the Major Leaguers who spent time perfecting their trade in an independent league, proof that independent leagues have become a formidable incubator for professional talent.

You may see some strange transactions in these maverick circuits. For instance, the Minneapolis Loons once sold reliever Kerry Lightenberg to the National League's Atlanta Braves for six-dozen bats and two-dozen baseballs. And the Pacific Suns of the now defunct Western League traded pitcher Ken Krahenbuhl to the Greensville Bluesmen for a player to be named later . . . and ten pounds of catfish.

If you want to follow the progress of your favorite club's top farm-team prospects, the bi-weekly publication *Baseball America* provides stats for every player as well as scouting reports on many top prospects at every minor-league level. If you want to know which teams are associated with any of the minor or independent leagues, search for a league or team online, or obtain the information from the most current copy of *Baseball America's Directory*.

Winter leagues

Two other leagues also supply US fans with baseball entertainment during the fall and winter months. The Arizona Fall League, which begins its 32-game season in early October, is a terrific place to watch the top prospects of some of your favorite major-league teams improve their games. All of the league's six teams (with 35-man rosters) have multiple working agreements with various major-league clubs.

Not just another minor-league team

Bill Murray, actor-comedian-Saturday Night Live alumnus, is one of the principle owners of Minnesota's St. Paul Saints, a Northern League entry. Under special adviser Mike Veeck, the Saints have proven to be as entertaining as the brilliant Murray himself. Chia Pet Night, MASH Night (featuring a give-away of balls bearing camouflage patterns), Ron Popeil Vegamatic Day, Whoopee Cushion Night . . . no promotion pushes the envelope too far as long as it pulls fans into the Saints' home park. St. Paul has also become a proving ground for former major leaguers eager to return from injury, retirement, or some other career detour. Slugger Darryl Strawberry launched his successful Major-League comeback with the Saints. Veeck's commitment to goofiness, if not downright lunacy (he once tried introducing Vasectomy Night — don't ask!), pays off at the box office. Veeck was also at the forefront of the formation of the American Association in 2005, a modern independent baseball venture in which the St. Paul franchise — as well as the Sioux Falls team (in which Veeck owns a controlling interest) — currently plays.

Slouching toward Fargo: A Two-Year Saga Of Sinners And St. Paul Saints at the Bottom of the Bush Leagues with Bill Murray, Darryl Strawberry, Dakota Sadie, And Me by Neal Karlen (Harper Paperbacks) chronicles the theater of the absurdist adventures of the Saints, who aren't likely to be canonized anytime soon.

Experience not always necessary

Few players make it to the majors without first playing in the minor leagues. However, a fair number of those who made their professional debuts in the Major Leagues and were never sent down to the minors would eventually win baseball's highest honor — induction into the Baseball Hall of Fame in Cooperstown. Their ranks include

The stars of the minor leagues

Minor-league audiences have witnessed some phenomenal performances over the years. In 1954, Joe Bauman, a first baseman with Roswell, hit 72 home runs to establish a minor-league baseball record that still stands. Tony Lazzeri, who would eventually star at second base for the New York Yankees, drove in 222 runs for San Francisco of the Pacific Coast League in 1925 (his team played 197 games that year). In 1922, pitcher Joe Boehler won 38 games for Tulsa of the Western League. In 1951, Willie Mays compiled an astounding .477 batting average over 35 games for the Minneapolis Millers. Mays was promptly summoned by his parent club, the New York Giants, and never spent another day in the minors.

Some players' lifetime totals are equally staggering. Hector Espino, a slugging first baseman, hit a minor-league career record 484 home runs, primarily for teams in the Mexican League. Bill Thomas won 383 games while pitching for various teams and leagues. Steven Fields holds the Pacific Coast League career wins record with 363. Ox Eckhardt spent parts of 13 seasons with various minor-league clubs; he retired with the highest career batting average in minor-league history — a dazzling .367. He also holds the all-time professional

baseball record for batting average, counting both Major and minor league stats. His .192 average in 57 Major-League plate appearances barely lowered his .367 career batting average in the minors (second all-time among minor league-only batting averages to Ike Boone's .370). Eckhardt ends up fractionally ahead of No. 2 Ty Cobb, whose career .366 is lowered marginally by his minor league stats.

Buzz Arlett won 108 games in his first six minor-league seasons (1918–23). He won 29 games while pitching for Oakland in the Pacific Coast League in 1920. He also enjoyed two 25-win seasons. However, after hurting his arm, he switched to the outfield and hit 432 career homers. Billy Hamilton raced his way into the record books with a minor league record 147 stolen bases in the 2012 season.

The minors have also showcased their share of legendary teams. The best of these may be the 1937 Newark Bears, a New York Yankee–affiliate that featured such future major-league stars as second baseman Joe Gordon (an eventual American League MVP), outfielder Charlie "King Kong" Keller, first baseman George McQuinn, and pitcher Atley Donald. This group won the International League pennant by 25½ games with a 109–43 record.

- Pitcher Walter Johnson (417 wins)

- Pitcher Catfish Hunter (224 wins)

- Pitcher Chief Bender (212 wins)

- Pitcher Ted Lyons (260 wins)

- Pitcher Sandy Koufax (165 wins, 3 Cy Young Awards)

- Pitcher Bob Feller (266 wins)

- Pitcher Eddie Plank (326 wins)

- Pitcher Eppa Rixey (266 wins)

- Shortstop Ernie Banks (512 home runs): Banks, who played his entire career with the Chicago Cubs, spent half of it at first base. He won two consecutive MVP awards (1958–59) while playing shortstop.

- Shortstop Bobby Wallace (the greatest fielding shortstop of his era): Wallace's glove work was so spectacular, he is one of the handful of men who played 25 years or more in the majors. In 1902, he was baseball's highest-paid player.

- Second baseman Frank Frisch (.316 lifetime batting average)

- First baseman George Sisler (.340 lifetime batting average)

- Outfielder Mel Ott (511 homers)

- Outfielder Al Kaline (3,007 career hits)

- Outfielder Dave Winfield (3,110 hits, 1,833 RBI)

Swinging the Bat in Japan

Historians credit Horace Wilson, an American professor based in Tokyo during the 1870s, as the founder of Japanese baseball. Wilson's students called the game *yakyu* (field ball) or *beisu boru*. Amateur baseball flourished in Japan during the early part of the twentieth century. American teams regularly toured the country, and many top U.S. stars — including Frankie Frisch, Babe Ruth, and Casey Stengel — helped teach the nuances of the game to an enthusiastic Japanese audience. Ty Cobb, baseball's career hit king at the time, held baseball clinics in Japan in 1928. Masanori Murakami, a left-handed reliever with the San Francisco Giants from 1964–65, was the first native-born Japanese player to play major-league baseball in the United States. These sections discuss the leagues and stars of Japanese baseball.

Naming Japan's major leagues

Japan's first professional team, Nihon Undo Kyokai, was formed in 1920. Two more professional teams appeared in 1921, but all three disbanded by 1923 due to a lack of competition. Matsutaro Shoriki, a newspaper magnate, re-introduced professional baseball to his country when he formed the all-pro team Dai Nippon (the forerunner of the current Tokyo Giants) in 1934. Two years later, Shoriki and a group of businesspeople formed Japan's first professional league. In 1950, that league split into the Central and Pacific Leagues. Today, six teams operate in each of the two leagues (see Table 13-4).

Table 13-4	Japanese Baseball
Central League	*Pacific League*
Chunichi Dragons	Chiba Lotte Marines
Hanshin Tigers	Fukuoka Daiei Hawks
Hiroshima Carp	Nippon Ham Fighters
Tokyo Yomiuri Giants	Orix Blue Wave
Yakult Swallows	Rakuten Golden Eagles
Yokohama Bay Stars	Seibu Lions

Both leagues include tie games in their standings. Foreign (non-Japanese) players may hold four of each team's roster spots. Teams play a 144-game schedule (home and away game breakdowns vary each season). Regular season games begin during the first week of April and end by the final week of September. In each of the two leagues, teams with the best winning percentage go on to the playoffs based on a *stepladder-format* (the third-place team plays the second-place team; the winner of that series plays the first-place team). Occasionally, a team with more total wins has been seeded below a team that had more ties and fewer losses and, therefore, had a better winning percentage. The winners of each league compete in the Japan Series — their version of America's World Series — in mid-October.

The quality of Japanese baseball has improved dramatically during the last two decades, though it still isn't on par with the American game. American scouts also have enormous regard for Japanese infield play, which generally equals, if not surpasses, US Major-League standards. However, Japanese outfielders and catchers lack the throwing strength of American Major Leaguers. Power hitters are scarce. Japanese pitching is impressive and, although their hurlers still rely on guile and a deeper arsenal of pitches than their Major-League counterparts, fireballers such as Yu Darvish and Hiroki Kuroda have emerged to successfully compete in the United States. Elite hitters Ichiro Suzuki and Hideki "Godzilla" Matsui have also won fame while playing in the North American Major Leagues.

Bowing to the stars

Like the United States, Japan boasts its share of legendary baseball heroes, all of whom would have been stars no matter where they played. Their numbers include

- Sadaharu Oh: He's the winner of 15 home-run titles, 9 MVP awards, 5 batting championships, and 13 RBI crowns while hitting — are you seated? — 868 career home runs.

- Tetsuharu Kawahami: Japan's "God of Batting" hit .377 in 1951 and managed the Tokyo Giants to 11 pennants in 14 years, including 9 straight Japan Series victories.

- Katsuya Nomura: The "Johnny Bench of Japan" hit 657 home runs from 1954 to 1980 while catching 2,918 games.

- Masaichi Kaneda: This left-hander posted 400 career wins and 4,900 strikeouts from 1950 to 1964 while playing with a club that finished in the upper half of the league standings only once.

- Yutaka Enatsu: He struck out 401 batters in 329 innings in 1968.

- Kazuhisa Inao: This pitcher won 42 games as the Nishitetsu Lions' ace in 1961.

Fielding in New Asian Frontiers

Over the past 25 years, professional baseball has become wildly popular in two of Japan's neighboring countries. Taiwan is home to the Chinese Professional Baseball League. Founded in 1990 and merged with the Taiwan Major League in 2003, the league's four teams play a 120-game schedule. Each team is allowed to carry a 25-man active roster, including up to three foreign players and two simultaneously on the field. The CPBL's season is separated into two halves of 60 games each with the winner of each half facing each other in a best-of-seven Taiwan Series.

The Korean Baseball Organization has been operating since 1982. Its nine clubs compete in a 132-game season and its championship is the Korean Series. Chan Ho Park, who made his Major-League debut with the LA Dodgers in 1994, was the first native-born Korean player to achieve stardom in the United States. Outfielder Shin Soo Chu, as of 2013 with the Cincinnati Reds, and starting pitcher Hyun-Jin Ryu, who made an impressive MLB debut with the Dodgers in 2013, are among the other Korean players to star in MLB.

Playing in the Tropics — The Caribbean Baseball Federation

In Mexico, Central America, and the Caribbean, baseball is nothing so sedate as a pastime; it's a passion. U.S. sailors and students introduced the game to Cuba around 1866. (See "Looking At the Cuban Juggernaut" later in this chapter.) The Cubans, in turn, brought baseball to Puerto Rico, the Dominican Republic, Panama, Mexico, Nicaragua, Venezuela, and Colombia.

With the exception of the Mexican League, which is part of the American minor leagues, most other teams south of the equator play in one of the leagues that compose the Caribbean Baseball Confederation (CBC). These associations are referred to as Winter Leagues because their seasons begin in late October or November. There is no regular-season interleague play, but the league champions do compete against each other in the Caribbean World Series held each year in early February.

The following leagues make up the CBC:

- **The Dominican League:** Founded in 1951, each of its six teams plays a 50-game round-robin schedule from mid-October through December. The top four teams engage in another round-robin schedule with 18 games per team from the end of December to the end of January; the top two teams in those standings then play a best-of-nine series for the national title. The league's champion advances to the Caribbean Series to play against the representatives from Mexico, Venezuela, and Puerto Rico. Dominican League franchises are Aguilas, Escogido, Estrellas, Licey, Indios del Cibao, and Toros del Este.

- **The Mexican-Pacific League:** Not to be confused with the Triple A Mexican League, the MPL was founded in 1958. Its eight teams each carry 30 players on its roster. They play a 68-game schedule divided into halves from mid-October to late January. Rosters are limited to 27 players. Three rounds of playoffs follow. Two finalists emerge from those series to play a best-of-seven league championship. Mexican Pacific League franchises include Culiacan, Guasave, Hermosillo, Mochis, Mazatlan, Mexicali, Navojoa, and Obregon.

- **Liga de Béisbol Profesional Roberto Clemente:** Formerly known as Liga de Béisbol Profesional de Puerto Rico, this league was founded in 1938. It was the oldest Caribbean league and for decades the premier Latin American winter league, often featuring some of the greatest stars in MLB history. However, the inclusion of Puerto Rican players in the US amateur draft in 1990 dealt it a profound blow. Puerto Rican players now had to wait until 18 to enter a Major League organization, and they had to go against players from the United States and Canada in the draft. Even more crucial, Major League teams have less incentive to cultivate talent in Puerto Rico, because those players may end up with another team through the draft.

The island's economic status — not as poor as Venezuela and the Dominican Republic, but not affluent enough to support an amateur talent development structure as in California or Texas — also hindered it. Young players got discouraged and turned to basketball. Local fans stayed home to watch their homegrown stars play in the big leagues. The league hit bottom in 2007, when it was forced to suspend operations for the first time since its creation. In 2008, the organization resumed operations, after restructuring, and in 2012 changed its name in honor of Clemente. It features six teams and a 40-game schedule that runs from early November to the end of December. At season's end, the top four advance to the semifinals, followed by a best-of-nine championship series. Puerto Rican League teams include Carolina, Criollos, Mayaguez, Ponce, Manati, and Santurce.

✔ **The Venezuelan League:** Founded in 1946, the league has eight teams in two divisions. The teams play a 62-game schedule that starts in late October and ends by New Year's Day, with the top five — each division's top two teams, joined by a wild card — advancing to a round-robin playoff schedule in which each club faces the other four times. The two teams that win that series meet in a best-of-seven playoff for the league championship. Venezuelan League teams are Anzoátegui, Aragua, Caracas, La Guaira, Lara, Magallanes, Margarita, and Zulia.

Looking At the Cuban Juggernaut

Emilio Sabourin founded *Liga de Beisbol Profesional,* Cuba's first organized league, in 1878. Cuba later had a minor-league entry, the Havana Sugar Kings, in the International League (AAA). Players from the island who went on to star in the American Major Leagues included Tony Oliva, Minnie Minoso, Camilo Pascual, Dolf Lucque, Zoilo Versalles, Luis Tiant, Tony Perez, Rey Ordonez, and Orlando "El Duque" Hernandez.

However, shortly after Fidel Castro took power in 1959, the International League transferred the Havana franchise to Jersey City, New Jersey. Castro reacted by banning professional baseball throughout the country. He disbanded all pro teams and forbade Cuba's players from signing Major-League contracts. The flow of Cuban talent to the United States was stemmed at the source. Castro, a rabid baseball fan who had once been a middling pitching prospect, sought to fill the void by establishing the amateurs-only Cuban League.

The Cuban League's regular season is called the National Series and consists of a 90-game schedule played between November and May. The 16-team circuit includes clubs in all provincial capitals and two teams in Havana. The National Series is composed of four divisions. In Group A the teams are the Industriales and Metropolitanos (Havana), Isla de la Juventud, and Pinar del Río; Group B has Camagüey, Guantánamo, Havana Province, and Villa Clara; Group C has Ciego de Ávila, Granma, Holguín, and Las Tunas; and Group D has Cienfuegos, Matanzas Sancti Spíritus, and Santiago de Cuba.

At the end of the season, the top players are chosen to the Cuban National Team, which represents the country in international competitions such as the Pan American Games, the Intercontinental Cup, the Olympics, and the World Baseball Classic (refer to the nearby sidebar for more information about the World Baseball Classic).

Most observers agree that Cuba was the world's epicenter for amateur baseball up until relatively recently. It still may be — Yasiel Puig, the latest refugee from the island — practically single-handedly led the Dodgers to the 2013 NL West division crown. But the Dominican Republic and Venezuela squads have caught up; each has fared exceptionally well in international play.

I covered the historic game between the Baltimore Orioles and Cuban All-Stars in Havana on March 28, 1999. Five Cuban players made a lasting impression on me. Jose Contrares especially looked like the real deal, gifted with a lively fastball, devastating splitter, sharp control, and genuine mound smarts. And that's what he turned out to be, pitching impressively as a spot-starter and reliever for the Yankees in 2003 and for years thereafter. As of 2013, he still was active in the MLB, as a reliever for the Pirates.

The World Baseball Classic: A United Nations of the sport

The seeds of the World Baseball Classic (WBC) were planted, unintentionally, when the International Olympic Committee removed baseball as a sport in 2005. Since 2003, MLB had been attempting to create such a tournament, patterned after soccer's World Cup, to market the game worldwide, but both the players' union (MLBPA) and its own team owners had held the plan back. Owners, notably former New York Yankees owner George Steinbrenner, had feared that their star players might become injured in international play before the beginning of spring training, when the players weren't in peak condition.

These differences were ironed out, and the WBC's debut in March of 2006 made a splash internationally. For the first time, Major Leaguers from all nations participated for and against the world's best players — both professional and amateur. (Major Leaguers had been prevented from playing in the three Summer Olympics that included baseball, due to a conflict with MLB's season.) Taiwanese fans had only speculated about how their best players would perform against Major Leaguers — most of whom were from the United States — found out. (But only to a degree, as many MLB teams ended up following Steinbrenner and holding back their star players.) Protecting pitchers was a prime concern, and pitch-count rules were introduced.

Although the 2006 and 2009 editions of the WBC were contested by a pre-selected field of the same 16 teams playing a round-robin tournament, in the 2009 tournament, they replaced the controversial round-robin set-up with a modified double-elimination format for the first two rounds (the semifinals and final game remained single-elimination). For the 2013 tournament, only the 12 teams that won at least one game in 2009 were guaranteed a berth. The other four contested a qualifying round in late 2012, along with 12 additional teams. The main tournament took place in March 2013, and ended with the Dominican Republic running the table (8–0) and defeating Puerto Rico in the final. The Dominicans, Koreans, Japanese, Cubans, and Venezuelans have the best overall records. Initially, the WBC was to be held every three years, but in 2009 the length of time between tournaments was extended to four. The next WBC will be held in 2017.

Required Reading for Minor-League Fans

Your local library or bookstore is loaded with many fine books about minor-league and international baseball. Here's a sampling:

✔ *Stolen Season: A Journey through America and Baseball's Minor Leagues* (Random House) by David Lamb. In this remarkable book, the author — a foreign correspondent — rediscovers America by traveling the minor-league circuit.

✔ *The Society of American Baseball Research's Minor League Baseball Stars* and *Minor League Baseball Stars* (SABR). Both of these books offer complete surveys of minor-league records. The two volumes include stats for 300 minor-league stars as well as profiles of the most successful minor-league managers.

✔ *The Story of Minor League Baseball: A History of the Game of Professional Baseball in the United States with Particular Reference to Its Growth and Development in the Smaller Cities and Towns of the Nation* (The Stoneman Press) edited by Robert Finch, Ben Morgan, and Henry Addington. Its title is the length of some books, but this volume delivers what it promises. Packed with records and stats, it is the most comprehensive book ever written on minor-league baseball as it was played during the first half of the twentieth century. You may have to search the Internet and look for a website featuring backlisted sports titles to find it, but this book is well worth the search.

✔ *Sadaharu Oh!: The Zen Way of Baseball (New York Times Books)* by Sadaharu Oh and David Falkner. No book offers more insight into the life of a Japanese baseball player.

✔ *Foul Ball: My Life and Hard Times Trying to Save an Old Ballpark* (Lyons Press) by Jim Bouton. A baseball love story. Bouton, a former 20-game winner with the New York Yankees and author of the baseball classic *Ball Four,* recounts how he and a few dedicated townspeople tried to save the oldest minor-league ballpark in America from the wrecking ball.

Chapter 14

The Rest of the Field: Managers and Coaches

• •

In This Chapter

▶ Understanding your players

▶ Knowing what it takes to win

▶ Getting the lead

▶ Criticizing the right way

▶ Managing the media

▶ Keeping the game in perspective

• •

*B*aseball managers are responsible for all on-field decisions affecting their teams. Professional baseball managers (usually with the help of an array of coaches) decide what to emphasize in training camp, who bats where in the starting lineup, who sits on the bench, and which players make up the team's roster.

On the other hand, the general manager (GM) is primarily responsible for personnel decisions. He decides which free agents to sign, which players should be traded and for whom, who to release or pick up on waivers, and which young players should be summoned from or relegated to the minor leagues. He also conducts contract negotiations and discusses the state of the team and any problems, as needed. In short, the GM assembles the team for the manager to manage. For more on the general manager's role, see Chapter 15.

Below the professional level, baseball managers — often called *coaches* — face even more responsibilities. In addition to making decisions about what happens on the field, they must decide how to effectively encourage younger players while still offering them sound advice and constructive criticism. In this chapter, we explore how to do all these things and still find time to enjoy the game.

Grasping What a Manager Does

During games, managers decide which strategy to employ from inning to inning (though many professional managers trust their veteran players to make those decisions for themselves). Managers call for, among other things, sacrifice bunts, hit-and-run plays, and stolen base attempts. They occasionally flash the *take sign* when they don't want a hitter to swing at a particular pitch.

Managers impact a game most dramatically with their choices of substitutions. Picking the right pinch hitter or relief pitcher often spells the difference between victory and defeat. Some people say that a great major-league manager can add six victories to a team's total during a 162-game season. That may not sound like much, but because every game you don't win is a loss, five additional wins translate into a ten-game spread in the standings. (For example, a team with a mediocre manager may go 81–81 during a 162-game season. If a great manager milks five more wins out of that team, it finishes 86–76.) That spread can mean the difference between having a disastrous season or a respectable one, between being an also-ran or a pennant contender.

Calculating how many games incompetent managers cost their teams is difficult. If a manager's strategy is unsound or the lineup selections fail to maximize a club's offensive potential, you may be looking at another ten-game spread in the other direction. However, much depends on the makeup of the club; a well-schooled, veteran team can band together to overcome a poor *skipper* (manager). But if the manager is also a divisive presence in the clubhouse, an entire season may be undermined.

Managerial responsibilities deepen and broaden below the pro and college levels. If you're coaching a high school or youth team, you must spend more time teaching fundamentals to your inexperienced charges. That task requires patience. Besides being a manager, you sometimes have to assume the role of psychologist and parent figure, especially if your players are preteens. Many of your young players may be going nose-to-nose with loss, failure, and rejection for the first time in their lives. If you guide them with compassion, each defeat becomes an opportunity for growth and insight. If you ignore their pain, or worse, exacerbate it with ridicule or cold silence, you may scar them for life. Your responsibility is nothing less than that.

Tapping into an Expert: Sparky Anderson's Winning Advice

Coaches and managers can find hitting, pitching, training, and defensive tips to pass along to their players throughout the chapters in Part II of this book. However, nothing written on any of those pages can illustrate how a manager thinks. To do that, we have brought in the most successful base-ball manager of the last 50 years. In 26 seasons as manager of the Cincinnati Reds and Detroit Tigers, Sparky Anderson won 2,194 games (only five manag-ers in baseball history have won more — and he lost only 1,834), three world championships, five league championships, and seven division titles. He had a .545 lifetime winning percentage. He's the only manager to guide teams to World Series championships in both leagues. Here you can discover how a master manager approaches the game.

Note: Although Sparky Anderson's advice stems from his experience as a manager in the Major Leagues, what he says can be applied to coaching baseball at almost any level.

web extras

You can also find additional defensive strategies that managers can use by visiting www.dummies.com/extras/baseball.

Know your players

"You should develop enough of a feel for your players that you can sense if something is off just by walking through the clubhouse. This means you have to be able to read a player's face and body language, his whole demeanor, so that you can head off a problem before it threatens the team. This also means you have to talk to your players constantly to get some insight into how they think. And that doesn't just mean talking baseball. Find out about their hob-bies, their families, the movie they watched the night before. Anything. Listen closely and you'll find out what your players are all about — that will help you deal with them.

"Don't think the players have to adjust to your personality. It's the other way around. You have to find out what inspires your players and what turns them off. Some managers say they treat all their players the same, but that's impossible. Everyone on your team is different, and they must be treated as individuals.

"Knowing your players also means understanding their strengths and limita-tions. If a left-handed junkballer is on the mound, and you send up a pinch hitter who has difficulty with slow stuff, whose fault is it when he makes an out? That's your out because you asked him to do something he couldn't do."

Avoid having a happy bench

"You hear about those utility players who play very little but are content with their role on the club. I love those guys — as long as they're on someone else's club. I never wanted anyone on my roster who was happy about not playing. You want guys who want to be out on the field, so that when you give them a chance, they're going to bring some fire to the lineup."

But don't let them get too unhappy

"Keep your bench and your regular starters fresh by weaving players in and out of the lineup all season. In 1976, the Reds had a tremendous starting lineup; we won the division by ten games and were 7–0 in the playoffs and World Series. Our eight regulars each had over 500 plate appearances, but we played them as a unit only 57 times during the season. We gave everyone a chance to contribute."

Know the elements of a winning team

"Pitching, defense, speed, and power, in that order. Power is marvelous, but when you put up eight runs and the other team puts up nine, it can be draining. When you have great pitching, you stop the other team from moving. You can create enough runs to win without using the long ball. On defense, if you give the other team only 27 outs, you have a chance. Give them 28 or 30 outs (by making errors or mental mistakes), and you're handing their big sluggers extra at-bats to beat you.

"When you have speed, you can drive the other team crazy. I'm not just talking about stolen bases here. I mean going from first to third, pulling the hit-and-run, faking steals, doing anything that injects movement into the game. When you do that, it's hard for the opposition to get set defensively. I always liked playing against teams that could only slug; if you took away their long balls, you had them. But teams that are always on the go can beat you so many different ways."

The purpose of Major-League spring training

"Number one, your team should leave camp in top physical condition. If a player is not in condition when the season starts, you're dead with him because he'll be out of shape all season. Number two, drill those fundamentals constantly. For example, in spring training games, any time a runner was on first and a ground ball was hit through to center or right, I wanted him to go to third. I didn't care if we were down by ten runs. If they got thrown out, fine, it was part of the learning process. That's how they found out when they could take that extra base and when they couldn't. I never cared if we won a single game during spring training. My whole focus was on preparation for the regular season."

Use those first five innings

"Don't get the idea I don't like power. During innings one through five, I always wanted to destroy the other team, beat them up so badly that they went home crying to Mama that they didn't want to play anymore. So we'd play for the big inning and try to blow the opposition out of the park. One of the reasons you do that is that almost every club today has a big closer. A Mariano Rivera. You don't want to get into a war with those guys because nine times out of ten, you'll lose. If you bury the other team early, the closer never even gets up from his bullpen seat. However, come the sixth inning, if you don't have a lead, you have only 12 outs left to get something going. Now you have to grind it out, steal more, sacrifice runners, do all the little things to create some runs. If your team can't do that, you're stuck."

Criticize in private

"If you want players to be loyal, don't show them up. We had a game in Houston where a player on second was thrown out on an attempted steal of third for the final out of the inning. Now, you should never make the last out of an inning at third, and when a player does it, everyone knows he pulled a rock. When the reporters asked me about it after the game, I said, 'I had a hunch and I sent him.' Well, of course I hadn't, but I was deflecting the blame away from him. Why humiliate him when he already feels bad? You can bet he and I are going to have a long discussion about the mistake, but we'll do that in private. Once a player knows you're going to protect him that way, he'll be receptive to anything you tell him; he'll give you the best effort he's got.

"When some move you make doesn't pay off, never pass the buck. I was managing the Tigers in the ninth inning of a 2–2 tie. We put men on first and second with nobody out. Nine times out of ten, your next hitter is bunting, giving himself up to move those runners into scoring position. But if Cecil Fielder was coming up, there's no way I was asking him to bunt. Cecil was a slugger; bunting wasn't something he did well. So I would just let him do his thing, swing away, to drive in that winning run. If he hits into a double-play, I'm going to take the heat. After the game, I'm going to let everyone know it was my call."

Exercise tough love

"The hardest part of managing is letting a star player know he can't do it anymore. Stars don't want to believe that. Before breaking the news, you must evaluate if the player can still contribute in a different role. For instance, maybe this person can still be effective playing in fewer games against certain types of pitchers. Perhaps he can contribute in a platoon role. Do whatever you can

Choosing a pinch hitter

"I rarely picked pinch hitters on a strict platoon basis (lefty hitters versus right-handed pitchers, right-handed hitters versus lefties). Instead, I looked at how you matched up against the pitcher's stuff. If there was a hard-throwing right-hander on the mound, and I had a lefty whose bat wasn't that quick and a right-hander who loved to hit the fastball, the right-hander is going up to the plate. I was more interested in what kind of pitches you could handle than what side of the batter's box you stood in. When I brought in relievers, I applied the same thinking, only in reverse. If I knew a hitter hated the breaking ball, I was bringing in a curveballer even if it meant bringing in a left-hander to face a righty. Now this means you not only have to know what your team can do, you have to know the opposition's personnel as well. I also always tried to save my best pinch hitter for the late innings when he could come up with the game on the line."

to get the maximum out of whatever talent remains. Then you have to discover if the player will accept this limited role. If you decide he can't perform in any role on your club, give it to him straight. Some may want you to break the news gently; others may want it without any sugar coating. That's where your knowledge of the player comes into use. I would start by asking the player, 'Have I ever lied to you?' After he said 'No,' I would continue, 'Then I'm not going to start now,' and I would give him my honest evaluation. Of course, this only works if you already built a foundation of trust with the player. That is one reason why you should never lie to your players."

Work with your coaches

"Grant them full authority in their area of expertise. Trust that they will get everything done exactly as you discussed it. Don't be checking up on them in the field. Never second-guess anyone. If your third-base coach sends in a runner and the player is thrown out by 20 feet, don't say a word. In 26 years, I never questioned any of my third-base coaches' decisions. Once when a coach tried to apologize for sending a runner who was thrown out, I said, 'Hey, I'm glad you're out there and not me.' That should be your attitude. You also shouldn't think that just because you're the manager, you're superior to your coaches. Each of them will have an area of the game where they know much more than you ever will. Use that knowledge. Go to them for advice.

"You must also back up your coaches. My pitching coach with the Cincinnati Reds, Larry Shepard, used to lace into our pitchers so badly; you could hear him from down the hall. More than once I was tempted to go down to prevent what sounded like murder. I never left my chair. Larry knew his pitchers and understood what it took to motivate them. I had to put my faith in that. And it worked. Our pitchers respected him because he got the most out of their abilities."

Managing off the field

Major-League managers must make many decisions in the course of a game, but probably 90 percent of them are almost automatic — when to pinch-hit for the pitcher, when to sacrifice, and such. However, when tough decisions have to be made, managers are put on the spot — suddenly the focus of 50,000 fans in the stadium, millions more fans tuning in via TV, radio, and Internet coverage and a growing horde of reporters, bloggers, and Twitterers. In the age of 24/7 media coverage, the ranks of the second-guessers are larger than some country's armies. And those are the people to whom the manager must answer — not just before and after but even *during* games. When analyst Tom Verducci is pumping your manager's team as his shortstop is at bat in the bottom of the eighth, just who is minding the store? What's next? On-field interviews while the ball is in play?

The pressure is enormous. How would you handle your job, knowing that your every move is subject to a performance review by not just your boss, but by millions of fanatical people (hence, *fans*) from Kansas City to Beijing? Think it might affect your performance?

Say that your manager's team is leading in that eighth inning. At that point, he's thinking about three things: which reliever to pitch the ninth because his normally lockdown closer, Doug, has let his last three consecutive blown saves visibly undermine his confidence; how to explain to Doug that he's not pitching the ninth; and how to finesse the inevitable shower of questions from the room of reporters at the post-game press conference — without spilling the beans about Doug's sudden jitters.

Say that Doug understands why the manager seems to have forgotten his bullpen phone number. So Roberto — usually the eighth-inning man — closes the game. Your team gains a much-needed win. Everybody is happy, right? Nope. The tap dancing has just begun. The beat reporter starts by asking why Doug didn't get a chance to work his ninth-inning magic. The manager will say something about wanting to keep his arm fresh for the stretch run. His own team's TV post-game reporter — fresh and ambitious, and looking to break a story — asks if Doug's arm is tired. The manager pooh-poohs that possibility, insisting that nothing is wrong with Doug. It's a reasonable answer, but not enough to prevent a blogger from trying to spark a controversy. The blogger asks if the manager has lost confidence in Doug. The manager replies no and that Doug has done a great job this year, signaling to both his players and the owners — the guys who sign his checks — that he's a company man.

Unfortunately, that answer is hardly juicy enough for the stat-bloated blogger, who demonstrates that the opposition's batters were terrible percentage match-ups for Roberto, and that the obviously correct move was to bring in the seventh-inning right-hander to get the first batter, the seventh-inning LOOGY (Lefty One-Out-Only Guy) to face the second batter, and the long man to get the third batter.

By this time, the manager starts to think wistfully about becoming a used-car dealer. But it could be worse: His team could've lost. But he's learned his lesson. The next time he's in that situation, Doug is getting the ball even if his appendix has just burst. Then all he has to

(continued)

(continued)

do is pray that Doug holds the fort, or the guy from ESPN will ask why he called Doug after he had blown three straight saves.

This scenario may seem somewhat exaggerated, but an increasing loud chorus of experts (backed by some statistical evidence) claims that managers are so cowed by this media kangaroo court that they manage to the press box. That is, they make game decisions that are the least likely to induce second-guessing — regardless of how if affects their team's chances of winning.

Think about it the next time you're watching a game and your manager makes a decision so obviously wrong-headed that you question his sanity. It may seem insane, but in the context of modern baseball, it may be the sanest thing he's done all day.

Fear nothing

"You know what made Billy Martin (the late skipper of the New York Yankees and other clubs) one of the all-time great managers? Billy was absolutely fearless. He would make moves that he knew would bring him a lot of heat from the press and fans if they backfired, but he didn't care what they said. If he thought a play would win him a ballgame, he put it on no matter how crazy it looked to everyone else. Managers can't be afraid of criticism. No one ever wins anything by playing it safe."

Keep it all in perspective

"I never knew any manager who put together a great record without great players. They are what it is all about. Once you think you're the most important part of the team, it's time to look for another line of work. If you're coaching Little League, baseball is supposed to be fun for these kids, so don't overemphasize winning or losing. The best part of your game should be the hot dogs and soft drinks afterwards. And parents shouldn't take things too seriously, either. How can any parent get upset when their child goes 0 for 4 when I can take them to Children's Hospital and introduce them to kids who have only six months to live? Wipe your little ones' tears, give them a big hug, and let them know you'll love them even if they never get another hit."

Chapter 15

Identifying the Rest of the Cast of Characters in the Ballpark

*T*his chapter intends to give you a broader vision of the many other types of participants in MLB, most of which you won't ever see on the field. They include the team's general manager and his assistants; the scouts and player development people who are in charge of molding raw amateur talent into potential players; the umpires, who have the power to affect the outcome of every play; and the behind-the-scene people whose roles may be relatively unimportant but whose presence adds color and beauty to the landscape you experience at a ballpark.

Introducing the Man Who Manages the Manager (and Everybody Else)

Not until the turn of the 21st century did the average fan fully understand that the single-most important member of a baseball organization isn't the perennial 40-home run hitter, last year's MVP candidate, or the ace of its pitching staff. It's the team's general manager (GM). And a select few GMs — namely Branch Rickey, who invented the farm system and helped integrate baseball and Bill Veeck, the maverick whose accomplishments ranged from integrating the American League, to hiring the 3-foot, 7-inch Eddie Gaedel as a pinch-hitter, and other theater-of-the-absurdist stunts to promote the woeful

St. Louis Browns — have transcended the game and become American folk heroes. These sections examine what essential skills a GM needs to do his job effectively and what his duties cover, including building a sound roster of players.

Moneyball (W.W. Norton & Company), a book by Michael Lewis that became an unlikely bestseller because of its subject matter exposed the behind-the-curtain actions of a Major League team's front office (the Oakland Athletics). It made a culture hero out of a failed big leaguer–turned general manager named Billy Beane. It also depicted the conflict between old-school scouts who canvassed the country, Willy Loman-like, to evaluate a prospect and young, brainy front office geeks (often Ivy League graduates), who felt they could find better players using algorithms instead of a stop-watch and a radar gun. (For more on this topic, see Chapter 12.)

Focusing on two skills a GM needs

In addition to the laundry list of primary duties that we discuss in the next section, a GM has to possess the following two skills:

- ✔ **Reading:** The GM must scan everything from daily scouting reports (refer to the "Scout's Honor: The Game's Unheralded Talent Spotters" section later in this chapter) to the temperature of the team's locker room.

- ✔ **People skills:** An effective GM must be a master of people skills — the ability to forge strong relationships with the team's owners and board of directors, and his own deputies, including the assistant GM, the director of scouting (and *his* scouts), the manager, players, the marketing and communications department, team physicians, local community groups, the media and, probably most important, his fellow GMs. He needs to make sure everyone is happy and on the same page.

Identifying the GM's duties

A team's general manager's duties call for a more impressive title, when you consider their sheer number and the fact that he's on call to execute them 24/7, 365 days a year. A GM is responsible for the following:

- ✔ Representing the organization at league meetings
- ✔ Preparing for amateur player drafts
- ✔ Overseeing the minor league system

- ✔ Negotiating with agents (such as discussing contracts and potential contracts for free agents)

- ✔ Representing the club during salary arbitration

- ✔ Dealing with the media

- ✔ Handling the club's payroll — in this role, especially, he must confer with the owner(s) and other senior team executives

- ✔ Making sure his club complies with both MLB rules and the Collective Bargaining Agreement (CBA)

- ✔ Hiring and firing the manager and coaching staff

- ✔ Assembling the team's roster (refer to the next section for more discussion on this topic)

Forming the organization's roster

The GM's bottom-line responsibility is to stock the organization — not just the Major-League squad, but also the half-dozen minor-league affiliates — with good players. To do so, he has to be successful at all the duties mentioned in the previous section. The GM must be aware of a million details with personnel to ensure his organization from the top MLB team down to the team in the rookie leagues has the best players who can compete and win.

Because when his team's fortunes do call for a trade, he not only has to rely on his knowledge of his team's strengths and weaknesses and that of the other 29 clubs, but also the trust he has developed with his colleagues in the game (by not, say, offering damaged goods by withholding a player's medical records). And come free-agent signing season, he must be secure that he can offer that slugging first baseman a six-year, $120-million-deal with a left heel that's hanging on by a string, without incurring the wrath of his owner.

Scout's Honor: The Game's Unheralded Talent Spotters

Scouts constitute a team's talent search party. A team's front office relies on them heavily for recommendations of which high school and college players to draft (amateur scouts) and which prospects to ask for in a trade (minor-league scouts). International scouts attempt to pan for gold in leagues from Mexico to South Africa, and Major League advance scouts — the men who travel ahead to watch their club's future opponents — file reports to help determine strategy.

Many scouts are former coaches or retired players. Others have forged careers, starting at the bottom (as unpaid or barely paid local talent evaluators) and worked their way up to state and regional scouts. A lucky few are head of international scouting and head of pro scouting (minor and big leagues).

Here's an example of the difference a scout can make on a Major-League level: Everybody remembers Kirk Gibson's two-out, walk-off, pinch-hit home run off Oakland's Dennis Eckersley to win Game One of the 1988 World Series for the Los Angeles Dodgers — a clout that propelled the underdog Dodgers to the championship. Gibson came to bat with the Dodgers trailing the Oakland A's, 4-3, in the bottom of the ninth. With one man on and two out, Gibson worked a full count. But Gibson had remembered a report from Los Angeles' advance scout Mel Didier, who had discovered that with a full count, Eckersley favored a particular pitch (a backdoor slider) to lefties. Gibson looked for that pitch, got it, and changed baseball history.

Numerous books have been written about Major League scouting, but the benchmark against which they're all measured is *Dollar Sign on the Muscle: The World of Baseball Scouting* by Kevin Kerrane (Fireside Sports Classics).

Eyeing the Front-Office Jobs

If you have ambitions of being a *general manager,* you must be willing to start at the bottom. Front-office interns and administrative assistants often work long hours for little money. Each team offers a variety of entry-level executive positions. Clubs prefer to fill these slots with applicants who possess degrees in sports administration. If you're interested in working in a front office, choose a university whose sports administration program provides interns for local teams. Internships give you the hands-on experience that stands out on your résumé. They also offer you an opportunity to network with the people who make the hiring decisions.

Anyone seeking a front office or broadcast position should attend professional baseball's winter meetings, which are usually held in December. At these meetings, you can find everyone who is anyone from the executive ranks of the big and minor leagues. As soon as you discover where the meetings are being held (the office of MLB can give you that information), book your flight and hotel reservations. Stay at the same hotel as the executives so you can do some schmoozing. Send your résumé to the team you're targeting well in advance of the meetings. You should also enroll in the employment opportunities workshop conducted annually at this gathering by Professional Baseball Employment Opportunities (PBEO), the online home of minor league Baseball's Official Employment Service. (For more information visit www.pbeo.com.) During the meetings, you can find any available front office or broadcasting jobs listed in the PBEO office.

Baseball job seekers should subscribe to *The Sports Market Place Directory*, published by Grey House Publishing (800-562-2139; www.greyhouse.com). This 1,800-page directory carries a comprehensive listing of teams and other companies involved in the sports industry. You can find listings for key contacts in each organization with their mailing, email, and website addresses as well as fax and phone numbers. If you want to contact a team to inquire about a position or send a résumé, you can also grab the latest copy of the *Baseball America Directory* (800-845-2726), which is published annually. This directory includes an Events Calendar that usually lists the dates and city for the upcoming winter meetings.

Men in Blue: Umpiring Like a Professional

Umpiring is a demanding job. Although a hitter must concentrate on maybe 15 or 20 pitches per game, a home-plate umpire must maintain his focus for 260 to 300 pitches per game. On the bases, umpires must be as precise as microsurgeons. That's because baseball is not, as some claim, a game of inches; many times a tenth of an inch is the difference between an out or safe call. So even though they never appear in a lineup, umpires make a critical difference in the outcome of a game.

If you choose to umpire, you assume a great responsibility. The job is demanding and difficult. For more than 33 years, one of the best in the business was National League umpire Harry Wendelstedt, Jr. A consummate professional respected for his fairness and integrity, Wendelstedt also served four terms as president of the Major League Umpires Association. For more information contact . . . The Harry Wendelstedt School for Umpires (386-672-4879; www.umpireschool.com)

The following sections outline the main responsibilities of an umpire. The late Mr. Wendelstedt was gracious enough to have once shared his thoughts on umpiring. Listen closely to what he said.

Considering the intangibles

"We can teach an umpire the rules and positions, but we can't teach judgment. You're born with that or develop it by the time you're ready to umpire. You have to be able to make the correct decision in stressful situations. You must be able to think on your feet. And you have to be physically fit so you can get into position in time to make the call.

"Good vision is another requirement. You can wear glasses or contacts to bring your vision up to speed, but you have to be able to see well enough to do your job. I was lucky. I had 20/10 vision for the first 25 years of my career, and then it went to 20/20. That's very helpful.

"You also have to possess the desire to do what is right. Sometimes it's easy to take the easy path. For example, if it's a tie score, two men out in the bottom of the ninth, bases loaded, the count is three balls, two strikes, and the pitcher throws a pitch that's just on the corner, you'd better be prepared to call that strike three and head into the tenth inning. If the pitch is just off the plate, again, you call it ball four, ballgame over."

Going by the book

"If you don't have a firm knowledge of the rule book and all its nuances, you will never be able to umpire on any level and do it well. I'm not just talking about memorization, either. I've had people come to my school who can quote you every rule in the book verbatim, tell you what page it's on and even the paragraph. But they wouldn't recognize that play if it happened right in front of them. You must be able to translate those words into practical application. The rule book must be firmly entrenched in your being as well as your mind."

Calling balls and strikes

"Behind the plate, you must assume a stance that allows you to watch the entire flight of the pitch without moving. A good plate umpire stays still throughout the pitch. If you have to move, it can distort your perception and cause you to miss some pitches. You sometimes hear umpires criticized for taking their time making a call. They are just doing their jobs. Good timing is a key element to good umpiring. By that I mean you have to let happen everything that can happen. When people talk about a delayed call, the umpire is just exercising good timing. There is nothing worse than a bang-bang play in which the umpire yells, 'He's out,' only to discover the ball has trickled from the fielder's glove before he made the tag."

Positioning yourself to make the call

"Establish a 90-degree angle on each play on the bases as the ball is batted. If a play is going to be made at your bag, you watch the fielder make his throw to ensure it's true. Then your eyes go directly to the bag. You're looking for the runner's foot. You should be able to pick up the flight of the throw with your peripheral vision. Then you listen for the sound of the ball striking the glove and you make your call.

"You are using your ears as well as your eyes on that call, especially on a close play.

"An umpire in the field also has to be aware of where the ball is hit. You don't want to be in the path of a ball so that it strikes your body and interferes with a play. There is one secret for making sure this doesn't happen: Get out of the way! Ballplayers are taught to move instinctively towards the ball. As an umpire, you have to give up that instinct. Learn to pivot so you can get out of the ball's path."

Determining whether a ball is fair or foul

"On a fly ball hit down or near either of the foul lines (which, by the way are really fair lines since any ball that stays on the line is in fair territory), you must straddle the line. Follow the flight of the ball in conjunction with the foul pole. If you are off that line, it can change your perception and you could very well call a fair ball foul, or vice versa.

"Any time you're not in the proper position to make a call, you're cheating yourself as an umpire. Below the major-league level, there will be times when you're the only umpire or one of only two umpires on the field. If you're working behind the plate and another umpire is at first, it may be impossible for you to assume the correct position when a drive is smashed over third. The ball just moves too quickly. But you have to get as close to the right position as possible."

Asking for help

"There will be times when your vision is blocked on a play. For instance, a coach comes over and says, 'Harry, you blew that call — the ball popped out of his glove before he made the play.' If I suspect the fielder or runner's body blocked my view of the entire play, I have an obligation to talk to my partners, who saw the play from another angle, and ask if they saw anything happen. If my partner says, 'The ball popped out, Harry, the runner was safe,' I'm going to change the call."

Dispelling a baseball myth

"You often hear that established veterans like Tony Gwynn and Greg Maddux get more than their fair share of calls in their favor. Not true. Umpires don't favor anyone. The reason Greg Maddux has more strikes called for him by the umpire is because Greg Maddux throws more strikes than any pitcher in baseball. He can paint that corner all day long, which is why he is probably the best control pitcher of this decade. And you don't have to worry about the great hitters getting any calls, because if the pitch is close, they're swinging. You're not going to have to make too many calls on Tony Gwynn with a 3–2 count and a pitch on the corner because he's going to be hacking. You'll rarely see him take a good pitch in that situation."

Surviving the pressure cooker

"I have felt butterflies fluttering in my stomach before every game I ever umpired, particularly before a World Series or playoff game. That's part of the job. If you don't feel butterflies, then you don't care enough. I wanted to do my very best every time I walked on the field, and that creates pressure. But you learn to love the excitement. I worked five World Series, and, as with any game, you have to bear down on every pitch. That high level of concentration you take to the field will help you overcome any nervousness you might feel. After you call a pitch or two, the butterflies disappear and you settle into what you normally do. All distractions phase out. When I worked World Series games, there were as many as 50,000 or more screaming fans in the stadium. I wouldn't hear them. I was too focused on the pitch and the play. You go into a zone of total concentration, just like a player."

Meeting the Supporting Cast

You don't have Chris Davis's awesome power, Cliff Lee's pinpoint control, or Andrelton Simmons's astonishing reflexes. You can still get a position in baseball if you can't make the cut as a player. You can pursue various other positions even if your batting average has never broken .100. These people may not make thousands of dollars, but they make the ballpark experience more of an experience:

- **Bat and ball handlers:** They're in charge of keeping players' equipment — particularly their bats — ready at all times. They sit in the dugouts and clear the field of any bats that players toss aside. They then store the bats in their proper slots in the bat rack. Ball boys and girls usually sit on the field in foul territory. They're always gloved because their chief job is to retrieve foul grounders and avoid searing line drives. They never retrieve fly balls because those remain in the province of the fielders.

Umpiring diplomacy

"When you find yourself in a heated dispute with a player, manager, or coach, you must try to defuse the situation. In order to control both sides, you must exert control over yourself. Don't allow yourself to be pulled into a screaming match. Keeping a level tone, calm the person down by saying something like, 'I want to hear what you have to say, but I can't do that if you're screaming. Just tell me what you have on your mind.' Get them talking in a conversational tone. Let them have their say, then move on. Don't tolerate any excessive abuse.

"With me, a person ran into trouble whenever they put the word 'you' in front of whatever they were yelling. There is profanity on the ball field; you have to tolerate some of that. But when they put a 'you' in front of an expletive,

they're making things personal. That's when they're in trouble. You allow someone to heap personal abuse on you, and you will get buried, not just by other players and managers but by your own umpiring partners who won't take that abuse. It's important to maintain the dignity of the position.

"I've met a lot of people who think umpires enjoy throwing people out of games. We don't. The art of arguing in baseball, for an umpire, is to let someone say their piece, to let off some steam, but keep them in the game. I also found that if people know you're fair and reasonable, that you give 100 percent to your job, they give you a certain amount of respect on the field. So it doesn't become necessary to toss them."

You can apply for bat- and ball-handling jobs by sending a letter to your local team's head of stadium operations. In filling these positions, clubs look for teenagers with solid academic records and glowing letters of reference from your principal and/or teachers.

✔ **Ticket takers and ushers:** Ticket takers dispense tickets at the ballpark. Ushers must correctly read those ducats and then direct their holders to the appropriate seats. Throughout the game, patrons ask ushers a bevy of questions including where the restrooms are, how to get to the parking lot, and where to go for first aid. Ushers are also the first line of defense against rowdy customers. However, if a fan gets out of line, an usher calls the head usher or security personnel for assistance. Write your local team to apply for these positions.

✔ **Vendors:** They sell a variety of foods, beverages, and souvenirs in the ballpark. Most vendors work strictly on commission. The products sold on a particular night depend on seniority or a random number drawing. How much money a vendor makes is often a matter of what product he or she draws. Selling beer or hot dogs trumps hawking ice cream sundaes on a frigid night in September. Seniority also determines which part of the ballpark you work in.

Vendors should be physically fit. Those trays strapped around your neck can be heavy, and you're on your feet for most of the game. Teams or the companies that run their concessions advertise for vendors just before the start of the season. However, referrals are key to getting these jobs. If someone who is already vending in a ballpark recommends you for a position, you have a much better chance of getting it.

✔ **Groundskeepers:** They keep the playing field smooth and dry and the grass trimmed (unless management wants it otherwise). Groundskeepers also smooth out the infield dirt in between innings. In more sophisticated parks, groundskeepers oversee a system of underground pumps and drainage devices. During rain delays they must cover the field with a tarpaulin before that downpour renders the diamond unplayable.

Maintaining healthy sod is also one of the groundskeeper's primary responsibilities. For that reason, many groundskeepers study their craft in school. Many universities feature agriculture programs that offer majors in soil science with specialties in grounds management. Most groundskeepers start off as interns through their university programs and then go on to regular positions.

If you want to apply for a job with a club, call to find out the name of its grounds crew chief and then direct your résumé to him or her.

✔ **Trainers:** They supervise a team's conditioning, strengthening, and injury rehabilitation programs. They also administer sophisticated first aid whenever someone is injured on the field (or sometimes in the stands.) Teams look for trainers who are college-educated and board certified in sports medicine. Send your résumé to a team's head trainer, but many of these jobs are snagged through referrals.

Chapter 16

Measuring Performance: Calculating Baseball's Statistics

*B*aseball fans are amazing. Math may have given them nightmares as students, but let their favorite player make a hit or an out, and they have his slugging average computed before he takes a step from the batter's box. Statistics provide the game's followers with a context that allows them to compare players and eras. To hold your own in any conversation about the sport, you have to know what the numbers mean. This chapter introduces baseball's primary stats.

If you can only own one baseball reference work, Lee Sinins's *The Complete Baseball Encyclopedia* (www.baseball-encyclopedia.com) should be your choice. Sinins has collected the complete statistical history of every Major-League player and team and packaged it in a software program that features a search engine you can use to analyze stats and create your own fun projects. When you call up a player's statistics, the encyclopedia provides his numbers in the context of league averages, so you can see how a player performed compared to his peers. We asked the search engine to compile a list of the all-time stolen base leaders among right-hand hitting third basemen under five-feet, ten inches, and born in Delaware (it was a slow writing day). In a matter of moments, the list — which would have taken more than a hundred hours to research manually — popped up with Hans Lobert sitting atop it (and we bet even ol' Hans wouldn't have known the lofty position he held unless he had the Encyclopedia loaded on his hard drive).

Calculating a Batter's Abilities

Mention the numbers 755, 4,256, and 73 to avid baseball fans, and they'll probably rattle off the famous baseball records that correspond to them. (Just for the record, Hank Aaron hit 755 homers in his career, Pete Rose had 4,256 hits in his career, and Barry Bonds hit 73 home runs in 2001.) Even if you don't feel compelled to memorize baseball's legendary numerical feats, these sections help you make some sense out of the many ways that players and fans track and measure offensive ability.

Batting average

A batting average is the statistic used to measure what percentage of a player's at-bats results in a base hit. This statistic made its first appearance in 1864. To calculate it, divide Miguel Cabrera's total hits by his official times at bat for 2013:

$$\frac{193 \text{ hits}}{555 \text{ at-bats}} = .348 \text{ batting average}$$

BASEBALL SPEAK

Yes, you may say Mr. Cabrera can hit a little. In addition to winning the batting title, he also led the league in home runs and RBI, which in baseball parlance is called the *Triple Crown* — the first time any player had done it in 45 years.

A hitter's at-bats don't include walks, sacrifice bunts, sacrifice flies, obstruction calls, catcher's interference, or being hit by a pitch. These events count as plate appearances but not as at-bats, so they aren't used to calculate the batting average. When the hitter is safe on an error, you credit him with an at-bat, but not a hit.

To qualify for a Major-League batting championship (which means leading the league in batting average over the course of a season), a player must have 3.1 plate appearances (not at-bats) for every game his team plays. In a regulation 162-game season, a hitter needs at least 502 plate appearances to qualify for his league's batting title.

On-base percentage

Branch Rickey and Brooklyn Dodger statistician Allen Roth created this statistic during the 1950s. *On-base percentage* (usually shortened to *OBP*, or sometimes referred to as on-base average, or *OBA*) tells you what percentage of a hitter's at-bats results in his getting on base by any means other than an error, interference, or fielder's choice. To calculate this figure, add a batter's hits, walks, and hit-by-pitch (hbp) totals and divide by his at-bats plus walks plus hit-by-pitch plus sacrifice flies.

$$100 \text{ hits} + 100 \text{ walks} + 10 \text{ hpb} = \frac{210}{500 \text{ at-bats} + 100 \text{ walks} + 10 \text{ hbp} + 10 \text{ sacrifice flies}}$$
$$= 620 = .3387 \text{ slugging \%}$$

In this case, the on-base percentage rounds out to .339. The average Major-League hitter is right around that number. Ideally, the first two hitters in your lineup, the players who jump-start your offense by getting on base any way they can, should produce on-base percentages of 350 or better.

Slugging average

You derive a player's slugging average by calculating how many bases he averages with each at-bat. To do so, divide the total bases he accumulated with hits by his at-bats. A single equals *one* base, a double *two* bases, a triple *three* bases, and a home run *four* bases. For example, in 2012, that same Miguel Cabrera had 121 singles (121 bases), 40 doubles (80 bases), no triples (or bases), and 44 home runs (176 bases) for a hefty total of 377 bases in those same 622 at-bats.

$$\frac{377 \text{ total bases}}{622 \text{ at-bats}} = .606 \text{ slugging average}$$

The average Major Leaguer slugs around .405. A hitter with a .450 slugging average has good power; the elite sluggers are at .490 or better. Cabrera hits as if he's from an alien planet of superior beings.

OPS and OPS+

The two most important things a hitter can do are getting on base and smacking the ball for power. *OPS* measures both these elements by combining on-base percentage and slugging average. This hybrid stat provides a much better gauge of a player's production than mere batting average. For example, in 2011, first baseman Mark Reynolds, then with the Baltimore Orioles, had only a .221 batting average — typical of a weak-hitting shortstop — but had a fairly respectable .335 on-base percentage, due to his 73 walks. Meanwhile, *OPS+* accounts for small variables that might affect *OPS* scores, such as the hitter's league and home park effects and puts the statistic on an easy-to-understand scale. A 100 *OPS+* is league average, and each point up or down is one percentage point above or below average.

An extreme example of this kind of disparity occurred in 2003. Injuries limited Yankees' first baseman Jason Giambi to a .250 batting average, a figure 18 points below the American League average. But Giambi's .412 on-base percentage (thanks to his 129 walks) and his .529 slugging average combined to give the first baseman a .939 *OPS*, the seventh best figure in the league. That high *OPS* largely explains why Giambi finished fifth in the AL in runs created.

OPS has merit as a stat because it measures all these facets of offensive performance: patience, contact, and power. The average fan can understand it; it has crept into the back of baseball cards and the vocabulary of announcers. And it's almost the only stat about which every stat head can agree. However, many sabermetricians don't like it because it treats on-base percentage as equal in value with slugging percentage, whereas *OBP* has been proven to be roughly twice as important as slugging in scoring runs (times 1.8 to be exact). It also factors in a player's league, park, and era, which allow you to compare players across time and space. So the next time you get into a discussion with a cocksure friend who thinks that his discovery of OPS makes him an Einstein, you can drop *OPS+* on him.

Runs created and weighted runs created+

Bill James originally formulated *runs created* to measure total offensive production. It measures a player's ability to reach base and move around base runners. However, Tom Tango's *weighted runs created* (wRC) and its even more refined extension, *weighted runs created+ (wRC+),* are improved versions of James's statistic. wRC+ measures how a player's runs created compares with the league average. The league average for runs created is always 100, and every point above 100 is a percentage point above that league average.

For example, a 125 wRC+ means a player created 25 percent more runs than the league average. Similarly, every point below 100 is a percentage point below the league average, so an 80 wRC+ means a player created 20 percent fewer runs than the league average.

wRC+ is also park- and league-adjusted, allowing you to compare say, Joey Votto, one of contemporary Major League ball's best run producers, to Ted Williams (Sorry, Joey, *nobody* in today's game compares to Teddy Ballgame.) There are at least 15 version of James's stat. This represents the basic formula:

$$\frac{(\text{hits} + \text{walks})(\text{total bases})}{\text{at-bats} + \text{walks}} = \text{wRC}+$$

We could give you the equation for wRC+, but first we'd have to enroll in an advanced statistics course. (For those math wizards and other brave souls, you can find out more about wRC+, *weighted on-base average+ (wOBA+),* and other esoteric stats by visiting Fangraphs, one of the stellar sabermetric websites, at www.fangraphs.com.)

Isolated power average (IPA)

Another stat created by Rickey Roth, the *isolated power average (IPA)* measures a player's power by revealing how often he reaches a base on extra-base hits, excluding singles. Award the player 0 points for singles, 1 point for doubles, 2 points for triples, and 3 points for home runs. Total his points and divide by his number of at-bats. For example, Chris Davis, who led the Major Leagues in this category in 2013, had an *IPA* of .348. He collected 42 doubles, 1 triple, and 53 home runs to amass 203 IPA points.

$$\frac{203 \text{ IP points}}{584 \text{ at-bats}} = .347 \text{ isolated power average}$$

Measuring a Pitcher's Performance

Not to be outdone by the hitters, pitchers also have a whole slew of stats to measure pitching performance. The stats covered in these sections help you determine how effectively pitchers get out opposing hitters. Although most people — fans, the media, and especially the players — feel that the critical indicator for any pitcher is wins, there are many factors over which a pitcher has no control that can affect his win-loss record. He may play most of his career for poor teams that don't give him any run support or play poor defense (especially true if he isn't a strikeout pitcher and relies on his defense to cover ground and be sure-handed). He may pitch in a bandbox stadium that turns every outfield fly into a potential home run.

Here are some other statistics that give you a more accurate indication of a pitcher's true value.

Earned run average (ERA)

This statistic measures how many *earned runs* (runs that score without benefit of an error) a pitcher surrenders every nine innings. To calculate, multiply the number of earned runs on a pitcher's record by 9 and then divide the result by his innings pitched. Consider Dodgers' Clayton Kershaw from the 2013 season:

$$\frac{48 \text{ earned runs allowed} \times 9}{236 \text{ innings pitched}} = 1.83 \text{ ERA}$$

Kershaw's *ERA* was 1.83. He allowed a meager 48 earned runs in 236 innings.

 Earned run averages have fluctuated widely over the years. When I played, an ERA under 3.50 was considered good. The offensive pyrotechnics dominated the game from the early 1990s to around 2008 (the so-called Steroid Era; see

Chapter 19 for a detailed accounting). During that era, a pitcher did well if he had an ERA of around 4.00. Now, however, the pendulum has swung back in favor of the pitchers. In 2012, the Major-League average ERA was 3.94. (ERA has dropped over 0.6 of a run since the 2006 season. Strikeouts per nine innings have increased by one full strikeout since the 2005 season.) Because of the designated hitter rule, ERAs are usually a bit higher in the American League than in the National League. In 2013, Kershaw led all pitchers with a 2.53 ERA.

Cracking the WHIP

WHIP, which is an acronym for *Walks + Hits per Innings Pitched*, tells you how many base runners a pitcher surrenders for every inning pitched. Simply add the number of hits and walks a pitcher allows and divide the total by the number of innings he throws. For example, in 2012, the Atlanta Braves' Kris Medlen was one stingy pitcher:

$$\frac{103 \text{ hits allowed} + 23 \text{ walks}}{138 \text{ innings pitched}} = 0.91 \text{ WHIP}$$

A *WHIP* below 1.20 is outstanding for a starting pitcher these days, so you can see why Medlen is considered one of the top pitchers in the National League.

Getting a decision: The pitcher's dilemma

To earn a victory, a starting pitcher must pitch at least five innings (or four if the game goes less than six innings), and his team must have the lead at the time he leaves the game. If that lead is never relinquished, he gets the win. If the game is tied when a pitcher who has pitched at least five innings is removed for a pinch hitter, and his team goes ahead to stay during the inning in which he is pulled, he gets the win.

When the starter can't get the win, the victory can go to any relief pitcher who is the pitcher of record at the time his team gains a lead it never loses. Credit a pitcher with a loss if he's charged with the run that beats his team.

If a reliever is the finishing pitcher for the winning team and does not qualify for the victory, credit the pitcher with a save in these situations:

✔ The pitcher gets the final three outs of a game that he entered with his team leading by three runs or less.

✔ The pitcher gets the final out (or more) when he inherits a situation in which the tying run is in the on-deck circle.

✔ The pitcher pitches the game's final three innings regardless of the score. (However, his pitching must be effective in the judgment of the official scorer.)

Determining a Fielder's Reliability

Fielding average reveals what percentage of attempted plays a fielder successfully completes. To calculate this percentage, add the fielder's putouts and assists, and then divide that number by his total chances for fielding a play (putouts, assists, and errors). Fielding average measures surehandedness, not range. Players who don't reach a lot of balls have fewer chances to make errors.

If you know how many innings a player has played at a position, you can determine his *range factor* by adding his putouts and assists, multiplying by 9, then dividing by his defensive innings played. In 2012, Cubs' shortstop Starlin Castro played 1,402 innings in the field while recording 266 putouts and 465 assists. His range factor was 4.69, which means he reached many more balls than the average shortstop.

However, at this point in time, defensive metrics haven't attained the consistency and accuracy as pitching and offensive metrics. Although more recently devised defensive statistics, such as Zone Rating, its refinement, *Ultimate Zone Rating (UZR),* as well as the percentage of outs from balls in play, seem at times to be the standard for judging a fielder's prowess, they suffer from too many inconsistencies. At the moment, trying to pick the best fielder at a position in a given year involves scanning three or four of these stats — and using your eyes, especially at the ballpark, where you can watch defensive alignments shift from batter to batter, pitcher to pitcher, and pitch to pitch. Then you can go have a friendly argument with your friends — another gift of the game of baseball.

Crunching Your Team's Winning Percentage

You determine winning percentage by dividing a team's wins by the number of games played. Want to see a mind-boggling win-loss percentage? Check out the 1906 Chicago Cubs:

$$\frac{116 \text{ wins}}{152 \text{ game played}} = .763 \text{ win-loss percentage}$$

Would you believe they lost the World Series that year? Every team wants to play at least .500 ball. Usually, a .550 winning percentage makes you a playoff contender. However, you can win a weak division with a relatively low winning percentage. In 1973, the New York Mets won the NL East with a .509 winning percentage and then went to the World Series by beating the — oh, must I relive this memory? — Cincinnati Reds in the league championship series.

The lowdown on statistics

Statistics are often misleading. Everyone believes that a .300 hitter is a good player and that a pitcher with a low ERA is a good pitcher. That belief is not necessarily the case. To be a good player, you have to either drive in runs or score runs (depending on where you hit in the batting order), and the great players do both. A .300 hitter makes seven outs for every ten at-bats, and if his seven outs come with men on base and his three hits come with no one on base, these hits are not very productive. Run production is crucial. Likewise, many pitchers pitch just good enough to lose. Pitchers will tell you that it's just as tough to win a 5–4 game as it is a 1–0 game, because they have to pitch out of more jams.

Chapter 17

Going All the Way: MLB Postseason Play and the World Series

In This Chapter

▶ Getting the World Series off the ground

▶ Expanding the postseason

▶ Introducing wild card teams

etting to the World Series — that's the ultimate fantasy for every Major League baseball player, manager, owner, or fan. At least it ought to be.

 I've participated in four World Series (including the Boston-Cincinnati classic in 1975, which many people have called the greatest World Series of all time) and seven National League Championship Series (NLCS). The moment I stepped on the field to play the Eastern Division champion Pittsburgh Pirates for the 1972 National League pennant in my first NLCS, I knew that the postseason is what baseball is all about. The stadiums are packed to bursting, and the spectators are continually on their feet or the edge of their seats. Adrenaline is running high in both dugouts, and the media is everywhere. It feels as if the whole world is watching. Every pitch, every at-bat, every play assumes ten times as much significance as it held during the regular season.

If you can't get excited about postseason baseball, you'd better check for a pulse. To understand what all the hoopla is about, we offer you a bit of the history of postseason play and examine the difficult path teams must tread to reach it.

Discovering How the World Series Began

People who watch very little baseball during the regular season often find themselves riveted to the television when the World Series is broadcast in late October. At its finest, this best-of-seven confrontation between the champions of the American and National leagues has a gradual, dramatic build that makes the series the most compelling event in sports.

The series wasn't always quite so compelling. Baseball's earliest "world series" took place in 1882 and consisted of two informal postseason games between Cincinnati of the American Association and Chicago of the National League. The teams split these contests, which received scant press coverage and were seen as little more than exhibitions. In fact, the National League chose not to see them at all. At that time, the National League refused to consider the American Association as a legitimate major league. A standing edict forbade National League clubs from participating in contests against American Association teams. To defy that order without risking expulsion from the league, Chicago had to release all its players from their contracts before it could face Cincinnati. (The players re-signed with their club as soon as the games ended.)

The National Agreement of 1883 brought peace between the two leagues. One year after the pact was signed, the National League champion Providence Grays met the American Association champion New York Metropolitans for a three-game set, billed as a battle for the baseball championship of the United States. However, after the Grays won, the media hailed them as world champions. Subsequently, the phrase World Series began slipping into the baseball lexicon, though the Major Leagues would not officially embrace the name until the early 1900s.

Setbacks faced by the early series

From 1885 to 1890, the American Association (AA) and National League pennant winners faced each other in series whose lengths varied from 6 games to 15. The National League won five of these six events. But friction between the two leagues forced the cancellation of the championship series in 1891, and shortly after that, the American Association folded.

In 1892, the National League expanded to 12 teams when it absorbed four AA franchises — Washington, Baltimore, St. Louis, and Louisville. The league then divided its season into two halves. Boston, the winner of the first half-season, played Cleveland, owner of the second half's best record, for the league championship and "baseball's world title." The best-of-nine series was less than a sensation. Fans generally abhorred the split-season concept (it was abandoned after this one season), so they were unable to muster much enthusiasm for the confrontation it produced. A series packed with suspense may have won them over, but it was not to be. Boston shellacked Cleveland five games to none (there was one tie). Due to the disappointing response to the matchup, no championship series of any kind took place during the following season.

Postseason blues

William C. Temple, a noted Pittsburgh sportsman, tried to revive postseason play in 1894 by offering a prize cup to the winner of a best-of-seven series between the National League's top two finishers. For the next four years, baseball hailed the winners of the Temple Cup as world champions. Again, fans failed to embrace this concept and the trophy went back to its original donor.

In 1900, a Pittsburgh newspaper, the *Chronicle-Telegraph,* offered a silver loving cup to the winner of a best-of-five series between the National League's first-place finisher, the Brooklyn Superbas, and the second place Pittsburgh Pirates. Brooklyn won the set, three games to one, but the sparse attendance (the four games attracted fewer than 11,000 fans) convinced the National League owners to once again abandon postseason play.

Success at last

Fortunately, baseball owners gave postseason play one last chance in 1903 after a new National Agreement recognized the recently formed American League as a major league. Barney Dreyfuss, owner of the National League champion Pittsburgh Pirates, challenged the American League champion Boston Pilgrims to a best-of-nine confrontation. Boston established the American League's credibility by winning the series, five games to three. More important, the series generated enthusiastic fan interest.

When the National League champion New York Giants declined to meet the American League champion Boston Pilgrims in 1904, the public outcry persuaded baseball's ruling body, the National Commission, to officially establish the World Series for the following season. The 1905 series between the New York Giants and Philadelphia Athletics officially established the best-of-seven format, which is still followed today. (The leagues experimented with a best-of-nine format from 1919 to 1921, but deemed a nine-game series too long to hold the public's attention.)

Except for 1994 when a players' strike canceled the event, both leagues have participated in the World Series — or, to use its more elegant nomenclature, the *Fall Classic* — in every season since 1905. The series has endured to become an American cultural icon.

The best of the best: The All-Star Game

Since 1933, the stars of the American and National Leagues have competed against each other in the All-Star Game, a mid-season *exhibition game* (which means it's not counted as part of the regular season records) played in a different Major-League stadium each year. The managers of the previous season's pennant winners lead the AL and NL squads. Fans participate in a nationwide poll to choose the starting lineups (with the exception of the pitchers) for both clubs. Japanese baseball fans can also participate via the Internet. After an extra-inning tie in 2002's game (which had to be stopped when both teams ran out of pitchers), Major League Baseball ruled that starting in 2003, the winning team of the All-Star Game earned home-field advantage for their league in that year's World Series.

The managers' own picks fill out the rest of their 34-player rosters. Each Major-League club must have at least one All-Star representative. The National League has a 43–39 lead in this game, but much of that bulge was built from 1965 to 1985, when the NL teams — which were then much deeper in middle infield talent and power pitchers than their American League rivals — won 18 of 20 All-Star Games. Since then, however, the AL has prevailed in most of the meetings. The AL won seven in a row from 2003 to 2009.

To find out more about World Series records, history, and heroes, check out these titles:

- ✔ *The Complete Baseball Record Book,* published annually by *The Sporting News,* contains all the essential records from both the playoffs and World Series.

- ✔ Donald Honig's *October Heroes* (Simon & Schuster) is an oral history of the World Series as told by such players as Tom Seaver, Gene Tenace, Johnny Podres, and Lloyd Waner.

- ✔ *Eight Men Out* by Eliot Asinof (Holt Reinhart Winston) is the best book ever written about the appalling scandal that occurred in 1919 when gamblers bribed members of the Chicago White Sox to lose that year's World Series against the Cincinnati Reds. The fallout nearly destroyed baseball's credibility. Director John Sayles later transformed Asinof's masterpiece into a compelling film of the same name starring John Cusack and David Strathairn. This movie is currently available on DVD.

Following the Road to the World Series

Getting to the World Series has changed over the years. Prior to 1969, a team just needed to win their league's pennant to advance to the Series. Since then, there are increasingly more obstacles to overcome. These sections explain how a team can advance to the World Series.

How expansion changed the playoffs

MLB's 1969 expansion forever altered the postseason. Franchise owners voted to divide both the American League and National League — each of which had been a single league of ten franchises — into two six-team divisions. Intradivisional opponents played each other 18 times during the season and met teams from its league's other division 12 times per year.

Both leagues also introduced a playoff format (since named the *League Championship Series* or LCS), which required the teams that ended the season with the best records in their divisions to meet each other in a best three-out-of-five series. The winner of each playoff was declared league champion and went on to the World Series. If the season ended with two teams tied for a division lead, they met in a sudden-death one-game playoff. Whichever club won that contest went on to the LCS. The survivors of those events represented their respective leagues in the World Series. Baseball tinkered with that format in 1985 when it expanded the playoffs to a best-of-seven game format.

Advancing to the playoffs: Divisional championships and wild card teams

A more startling alteration to postseason play came in 1994 when the two leagues adopted their alignment (see Chapter 13 for more details) of three divisions each. The addition of third divisions necessitated the creation of a second tier of playoffs — a three-out-of-five game series followed by a four-out-of-seven playoff to determine a league champion.

The division change also required the inclusion of a *wild card* (an additional playoff qualifier) team in the postseason mix. In 2012, MLB expanded its playoffs for the third time, this time with the addition of two more wild card teams — one from each league — and a single elimination game in each league, which increased the postseason field to ten teams, the largest in Major League history.

The three division winners in each league await the survivor of a one-game playoff between the wild card teams in each league. The division series returned to the *2-2-1 home/road format* (the team with the better record has home-field advantage in the first two games, the series shifts to the opponent's park for the next two games (if a fourth game is necessary), and if the series goes to a fifth game, it is played on the home turf of the first team). Division titles and wild card berths are now decided by a 163rd game play-in if necessary. In the past, if two teams were tied for a division lead after 162 games and the other had already clinched the wild card, head-to-head records determined the division winner. In another interesting wrinkle to the new long-term playoff rule changes, beginning in 2013, a division winner and wild card team from the same division could meet in the division series.

For example, if the Yankees have the best record in the AL and the Red Sox win their one-game wild card playoff, then they will meet in the division series. In the past, the Red Sox would have played the division winner with the league's second-best record and the Yankees would've played the division winner with the third-best mark. No one could ever understand the logic behind that now-defunct rule, and we're glad MLB straightened it out.

The additional wild cards also place a premium on winning a division title. Division winners get at least two days of rest before the start of the division series, while the wild card teams would possibly have to use their best pitchers to win an elimination game, putting them at a disadvantage, going into the division series.

The club with the best overall record in its league retains the home-field advantage throughout the playoffs. For example, in 2013, both the St. Louis Cardinals and the Boston Red Sox finished the season with 97 wins and used their respective home-field advantage to smooth their path to the World Series.

In case of a tie, scream!

What happens if two teams end the season tied for either the division title or the wild card spot? Four formulas are used to determine which team enters the playoffs as either a wild-card team or a division leader:

✔ Any two-team tiebreak — whether division winners or wild card teams that finish with the same season record — is determined by their regular-season head-to-head record.

✔ If the two teams split their games head-to-head, the tiebreak is determined by which team had the higher winning percentage in intradivision games.

✔ If the two teams had identical winning percentages in intradivisional games, the team with the higher winning percentage in the last half of intraleague games will break the tie.

✔ If they're somehow still tied, the team with the higher winning percentage in the last half plus one intraleague game, provided that such additional game wasn't between the two tied clubs. Continue to go back one intraleague game at a time until the tie is broken.

Mind you, these rules apply only to two-team tiebreakers. MLB have rules for when three, four, five, or more teams are tied for the wild card (more probably) or three or four are tied for the division winner, but they're so complex you're better off waiting for such an eventuality to happen and reading about it or watching it on MLB-TV or www.mlb.com.

Part V

The View from the Stands — A Spectator's Guide

A ballpark's perspective

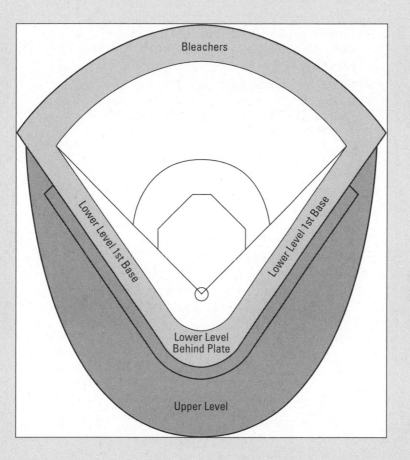

Click on www.dummies.com/extras/baseball for a thorough list of great books written about baseball, ranging from nonfiction, historical accounts to page-turning novels.

In this part...

✔ Discover the nuances of keeping score — whether at home or at the park and know how to correctly keep score.

✔ Take a closer look at all the Major-League ballparks and what makes them unique with an eye toward how they can affect player and team performances.

✔ Examine the touchy topic of steroids — inarguably the most notable and controversial phenomenon in baseball in the last 20 or so years — and read why some players may have been tempted to use performance-enhancing drugs (PEDs), how PEDs have influenced the way the game was played, and how PEDs have affected the way disillusioned fans and many writers' often view many notable players guilty of or even suspected of using.

✔ Uncover how to follow the game as a spectator — no matter where you live — and where you find game coverage and recaps in various media, including the most popular websites and blogs, as well as newspapers and magazines.

✔ Understand what fantasy baseball is and acquaint yourself with the ins and outs of how to play, so the next time your friends ask you to join, you're ready.

Chapter 18

Following the Bouncing Baseball

As a spectator, if you haven't experienced a baseball game live, well, you haven't experienced baseball. A ball field functions as more than a mere backdrop; by juxtaposing speed against distance, it provides a context for athletic miracles. Chris Davis's latest 450-foot home run is merely a ball hit a long way when seen on television. But when viewed from a stadium seat, it turns majestic, almost unsettling in its celebration of raw, human power.

Baseball is a sport of nuance, and nowhere but the ballpark can these subtleties be explored and appreciated. Is the shortstop cheating toward second to gain a step on the double play? Is the hitter choking up with a two-strike count? How will the left fielder shade this right-handed pull hitter? Sitting in the stands, you can get an immediate answer to all these questions by simply looking out at the field.

A visit to your local ballpark is also a healthful experience. You get to bond with fellow humans, soak up the sun's vitamin D (if you go during the day), fill your lungs with air made fragrant by freshly trimmed grass, and escape life's anxieties. It's sort of like going to an outdoor consciousness-raising group — only vastly more entertaining. This chapter explains some ways that you can better enjoy your experience in a ballpark.

Picking the Seat with the Best View

Given the emphasis stadium architects put on unobstructed sight lines, nearly every seat in a modern baseball park (one built or refurbished in the last 35 years) is a good one. As you move around the stadium, you may find that each section offers a different, often contrasting perspective of the game on the field (see Figure 18-1).

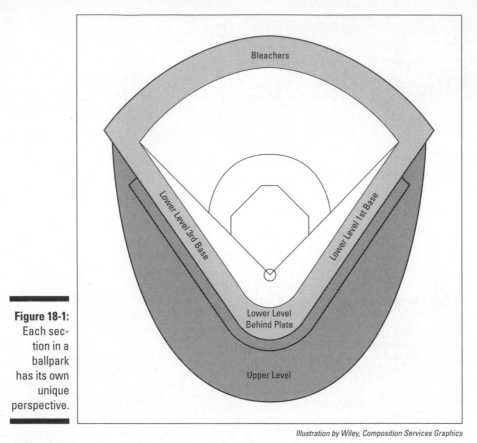

Bleachers

Lower Level 3rd Base

Lower Level 1st Base

Lower Level
Behind Plate

Upper Level

Figure 18-1:
Each sec-
tion in a
ballpark
has its own
unique
perspective.

Illustration by Wiley, Composition Services Graphics

Which perspective is best? It depends on what interests you.

✔ For the best view of the pitcher-hitter confrontation, camp out behind home plate.

✔ Want to watch the double play unfold while observing the interaction between pitcher and runner? Head for the first-base side — a seat here also grants you a bird's-eye view of most of the game's putouts.

✔ From behind third, you can watch the relay and cutoff plays evolve as the runner races toward third or home against the right fielder's throw.

✔ Visit the upper deck and you can see the field as a giant chessboard with ever-changing defensive alignments.

✔ You can form an appreciation for the various angles fly balls assume by sitting in the bleachers (if your park has them), which are located directly behind the outfield fence.

Catching a Souvenir: Where to Sit

Almost everybody who attends a ballgame fantasizes about catching a foul ball or (even better) a home run. Foul-ball hunters have their best opportunities in the upper deck or lower boxes on the first- or third-base side of the park. If you want to add a home-run ball to your trophy case, sit near the end of the foul lines (just look for the foul poles to find out where those sections are) or in the bleachers (unless you're at Coors Field, where you can just wait out in the parking lot). Figure 18-2 shows you some of the best places to sit if you want to get your hands on a baseball.

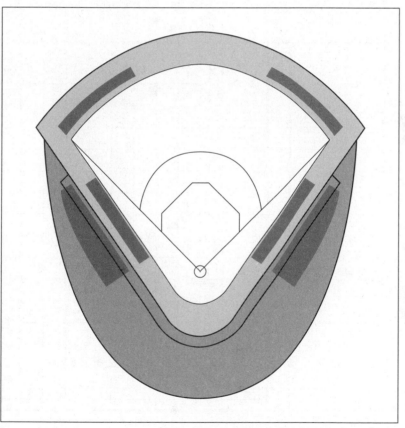

Figure 18-2: Where to await a chance for a free souvenir.

Illustration by Wiley, Composition Services Graphics

You're free to do whatever you want with any ball you catch, but you should know that in many ballparks, such as Chicago's Wrigley Field, hometown fans expect you to throw any home runs hit by the visiting team back onto the field.

You should never attempt to catch any ball while it remains in play because you could be guilty of fan interference and influence the outcome of the game.

Knowing How to Keep Score

Nothing focuses your full concentration on a baseball game like keeping score. You can purchase *scorecards* from stadium vendors (who sell cards for each game) or at almost any sporting goods store and via certain websites (where they are sold by the book). Or you can make your own. For every game you score, you need two cards — one for the home team, another for its opponent. Figure 18-3 shows what a typical, blank scorecard looks like.

	P	1	2	3	4	5	6	7	8	9	10	11	AB	R	H	RBI	E
TOTALS	R H																

Figure 18-3: A blank baseball scorecard.

Illustration by Wiley, Composition Services Graphics

To score like a professional, the first thing that you should do is write the date, the weather, and whether the game is a day or night game (or the first game of a doubleheader, and so on) on the top of your scorecard, along with the names of the teams competing. Many fans keep their scorecards (and ticket stubs) for a lifetime of memories.

Sticking to ballpark etiquette

When you visit a stadium, have fun. Just make sure you mind your ballpark manners in the following ways:

✔ Refrain from using foul language (because children are usually nearby).

✔ Don't drink to excess. (In fact, why drink at all?)

✔ Never, ever throw an object onto the field, run onto the diamond, or do anything that interferes with play.

✔ Don't block the view of the folks sitting behind you.

The numbers running across the top of the grid represent innings. Spaces on the left-hand side of the grid are reserved for the players' names, positions, and uniform numbers. You summarize a team's output of hits and runs for each half-inning in the spaces provided at the bottom of the scoring columns. When the game ends, record the player and team totals (at-bats, runs, hits, runs batted in, and errors) in the grid's right-hand columns. These sections provide more information you need to know in order to score a baseball game.

Using a scorekeeper's codes

The first time you encounter a completed scorecard, it may look as if some ancient sage has scribbled on it in hieroglyphics. Don't be intimidated. The scribbling becomes decipherable after you learn the basic symbols. Numbers represent the position players (not to be confused with their uniform numbers), as Table 18-1 shows.

Table 18-1	The Numbers Assigned to Each Player
Player	*Number*
Pitcher	1
Catcher	2
First baseman	3
Second baseman	4
Third baseman	5
Shortstop	6
Left fielder	7
Center fielder	8
Right fielder	9

All scoring systems adhere to this numerical code. The symbols and abbreviations used to record the outcome of each at-bat, however, can vary from scorer to scorer. Novice scorers should stick to the basic abbreviations shown in Table 18-2.

Table 18-2	Baseball Scoring Abbreviations
Event	*Abbreviation*
Single	1B
Double	2B
Triple	3B
Home run	HR
Base on balls	BB
Intentional base on balls	IBB
Balk	BLK
Caught stealing	CS
Double play	DP
Error	E
Fielder's choice	FC
Force-out	FO
Fly out	F
Ground out	G
Hit by pitcher	HBP
Interference	I
Strikeout	K
Line drive	LD
Passed ball	PB
Stolen base	SB
Sacrifice hit	SH
Sacrifice fly	SF
Triple play	TP
Wild pitch	WP

Combine the position numbers and abbreviations to record the sequence of an out — which tells you who got the *assist* (a throw by a fielder that leads to an out), if anyone, and who made the putout. You can also pinpoint the location of a hit or assign blame for an error. For example, if a leadoff hitter flies out to left field, mark F-7 in the first inning grid alongside the batter's name. If that ball drops just in front of the left fielder for a single, the proper notation is 1B-7. However, if the official scorer deems the ball catchable, enter an E-7. A double-play ball that is fielded first by the second baseman, who throws it to the shortstop for the relay throw to the first baseman, is scored 4-6-3 DP (second-to-short-to-first double play).

Tracking the runner

Most scorecards have tiny diamonds within the scoring blocks. (If yours doesn't, you can draw them.) Use the diamonds to record the progress of the base runners. Treat the lower point of the diamond as home plate and work around the box counter-clockwise.

For example, if a batter singles to center field, darken the line of the diamond leading from home to first while recording the circumstances that put him on base in the lower right-hand corner.

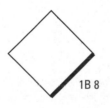

If the same player then advances one base on a wild pitch, darken the line from first to second and put the abbreviation WP in the upper right-hand corner.

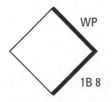

When a short single to right moves this player up one more base, darken the line from second to third and note 1B-9 in the upper left-hand corner.

After a sacrifice fly to left field scores the runner, darken the line from third to home, fill in the diamond (to signify a run scored), and put a dot in the box of the batter who drove in the run. The result is a snapshot of a batter's entire one-inning history.

When the half-inning ends, draw a slash across the lower right-hand corner of the scoring block for any batter who makes the last out of a team's turn at-bat.

After mastering the rudiments of scoring, you can adopt such advanced techniques as color coding — which requires you to record walks in green, strikeouts in red, and hits in blue. (You'd better own one of those multi-barreled pens, or you may need an extra seat at the ballpark just for your office supplies.)

Many books explain the various scoring systems. But if you're looking for one that entertains as well as informs you, purchase Paul Dickson's gracefully written *The Joy of Keeping Score* (Harcourt Brace). (You can get it at www.acebooks.com.)

Looking At the Stadiums

We think of the player who hits 40 home runs while playing half his games in Coors Field as a fearsome slugger. But would we hold him in such high regard if his club's home address was AT&T Park and he struggled to hit 25 home runs a season? Conversely, the Colorado Rockies' pitcher whose *earned run average* (ERA) hovers near 5.00 appears to be one step away from his release.

However, let him pitch half his games in San Diego's Petco Park, and he may find himself among the league's ERA leaders. (See Chapter 16 for more information on ERAs.) Ballparks matter. They not only provide a pleasant setting to watch a game, but they also profoundly affect run scoring and our assessment of a player's ability. In these sections, we examine the impact each Major-League stadium has on performance and perception.

The National League stadiums

For years, National League stadiums tended to be a bit larger than their American League counterparts. These NL parks were built with pitching and defense in mind. But many of the newer parks in this league — Coors Field, Miller Park, and Chase Field — favor hitters. We used statistics from 2010–2013 when we discuss these stadiums.

Chase Field: Arizona Diamondbacks

When I (Joe) first saw the model for this new park, its dimensions suggested a neutral field with perhaps a slight bias toward the pitcher. Forget it. This park is a hitter's paradise. When Chase's retractable roof is open — which is most of the time — long balls positively soar through Arizona's warm desert air. Chase's deep outfield features a lot of quirky angles so triples come relatively easy here. Center field is large, and the overhangs can produce some challenging caroms. When the roof is closed, the sod in the outfield loosens and breaks away in clumps that can make running treacherous. Management equipped the stadium with a family-friendly play area that features a swimming pool.

Chase Field produced 112 runs for every 100 runs produced in the average MLB park, and 112 home runs for every 100 homers, for a mean park factor of 112. *Park factor* are the effects of a park's dimensions, weather, wind, architectural quirks, and grounds. Park factors can be determined for every statistic. The two most common park factors are run factors and home run factors. However, other factors affect play, specifically strikeouts, walks, and errors. A park factor of 100 means that park is *neutral,* meaning it gives no advantage to either pitcher or hitter. If the park inflates a particular statistic by 10 percent, the park factor is 110. Similarly, if the park deflates that stat the same amount, the corresponding factor is 90. For example, if a player were to hit 20 home runs in a neutral park, he would hit 22 in a park with a factor of 110 but only 18 in a park with a factor of 90, because 10 percent of 20 is 2.

Turner Field: Atlanta Braves

Pitchers love working in the Braves' home digs, Turner Field. The park's spacious foul territory allows fielders ample room to convert lazy pops into outs before they drop beyond reach into the stands. During the spring, the strong cool wind blowing in from center field often stops fly balls that will rocket out of the park when the temperature rises.

Turner will increase the batting averages for players who can consistently drive the ball into the vast expanse of right field. Playing a strong-armed speedster in right field is practically a must in the ballpark. If your right fielder fails to cut off a base hit on the first or second hop, the ball can roll behind him forever. However, in more recent years, although it still suppresses the long ball, Turner Field has become less a pitcher's Valhalla and more like a Supreme Court — neutral. It has produced 100 runs for every 100 runs produced in the average MLB park, and 95 HRs for every 100 homers, for a mean park factor of 97.

Wrigley Field: Chicago Cubs

I hit my first Major-League home run in this park. Since its opening, Wrigley has been considered a hitter's paradise, but the park is deceptive. When the wind blows in early in the season, this stadium favors pitchers, particularly those who are adept at inducing batters to hit ground balls. And during the late innings of day games, hitters can have a tough time picking up pitches coming out of the shadows.

However, when the wind shifts outward from late June into mid-September, scoring rises nearly 40 percent, and a batter's chances of hitting a home run double. One of the smallest foul territories in the Major Leagues also aids the hitters by allowing fielders less room to convert foul balls into outs, thus prolonging at-bats. Nonetheless, pull hitters can still struggle here, because Wrigley features the third-longest distances right down the right- and left-field foul lines. Their best shots often end up as harmless fly balls.

In 2013, Wrigley Field produced 104 runs for every 100 runs produced in the average MLB park, and 103 HRs for every 100 homers, for a mean park factor of 104. So although overall Wrigley plays as a neutral park, run scoring often depends on which way the wind blows.

Great American Ballpark: Cincinnati Reds

When this park opened in 2003, well, the hits just kept on coming. It was a hitter's paradise — for every kind of hitter. However, in recent seasons, the Reds' ballpark, while still heaven for home run hitters, has become less friendly to gap hitters and so plays more like a neutral park.

The Great American's home run index is 122, but its doubles index is 94 and its triples index is 93, which makes it close to neutral for run scoring. Overall, Great American's park factor for runs was only 102 in 2012, which suggests that most fly balls that don't go over the fence get caught, as opposed to bigger parks where the outfielders have to cover more ground. Although it's optimal to start ground-ball pitchers in the GAB, a manager shouldn't be overly concerned about starting fly-ball pitchers, especially if their walk rate is low and/or their strikeout rate is high. Routine fly balls still can carry into the seats in both straight-away left and right, and the strong prevailing winds will blow the ball over the fence even in dead center field, but it's not as hazardous as most people think.

Coors Field: Colorado Rockies

Coors Field is baseball's black hole for hurlers. Pitchers who visit Coors are often never heard from again. This is the greatest hitter's park of all time. In fact, it produced 143 runs for every 100 runs produced in the average MLB park and 145 HRs for every 100 homers for a mean park factor of 144.

However, the Rockies' hitters aren't taking advantage of this luxury. In 2013 the Rockies scored 706 runs, 434 at home (an average of 5.3 per game) but only 272 on the road (3.35 per game). (Because 2013 is the second straight year the team had such a disparity, we're guessing that the Rockies need some vitamin B shots.) Still, Coors has increased Colorado's run production by a large margin in most, if not every season since the field opened in 1995. Because it favors hitters, the park's dimensions often surprise people. They expect Coors to be a bandbox, but its playing field is actually slightly larger than average. Home runs launch themselves into orbit thanks to the thin, mile-high atmosphere — despite a failed attempt in the 2000s to deaden the balls by placing them in a humidor prior to each game.

And this isn't just a home-run park. Because the visibility at Coors is excellent, you can get a good read on a pitcher's offerings. The spacious playing field inflates extra-base hit totals and batting averages. Teams whose outfielders possess below-average speed and weak throwing arms are at a particular disadvantage here.

Coors Field also features two defensive quirks. First, the thin, arid atmosphere retards grass growth; hard hit grounders zoom past even the quickest infielders. And second, during the mid-summer months, the setting sun shines directly into the first baseman's eyes, at times making it difficult to pick up throws.

You will rarely witness a complete game at Coors. Few pitchers dare throw anything near the heart of the plate, and all that "nibbling" at the corners results in deep pitch counts. Pitching up in the strike zone at Coors invites disaster because every fly ball is a candidate for the seats. The thin Colorado atmosphere also robs the bite from many a pitcher's best curveball. (This accounts for its below-average strikeout factor of 94.) Any Rockies pitcher who maintains an ERA under 4 should be congratulated. Jhoulys Chacin, the Rockies' star young right-hander, allowed more than twice as many runs a game at Coors than he did on the road.

Miller Park: Milwaukee Brewers

Any hitter who puts the ball in the air in Miller Park has an excellent shot at an extra-base hit. The corners are deep, the power alleys are short, and the fielders have a lot of ground to cover in what looks like the widest outfield in major-league baseball. Anyone patrolling center field can rob enemy base hits by playing shallow, but he must possess excellent lateral range or the sky will start raining doubles. The ball carries well to right field, so left-handed sluggers pose a particular danger in this stadium.

Miller Park features North America's only fan-shaped convertible roof, which can open and close in less than ten minutes. In its early years, maybe when the roof was closed, pitchers gained advantages at Miller. Former Brewers' ace Ben Sheets learned to neutralize left-handed hitters by developing a groundball-inducing changeup in 2003, and Yovani Gallardo, the Brewers' ace lefty, has had some excellent seasons here.

Things have changed; in 2012, more runs were scored in Miller Park than any other park in the MLB, and it was in the top five in 2013. Miller Park produced 107 runs for every 100 runs produced in the average MLB park and 131 HRs for every 100 homers for a park factor of 119.

New Marlins Park: Florida Marlins

The Marlins' new park in Little Havana, square on the site of the old Orange Bowl, is a major departure from the team's old football-stadium home. Its seating capacity — 36,742 — the smallest-capacity park in the Major Leagues, helps disguise the public's indifference to the team in recent years. The park looks fuller, and at least when they play ball, the Marlins feel a bit more like practicing entertainers than actors in a perennial rehearsal.

Despite a very new look, actual baseball dimensions are very similar to Pro Player Stadium, the Marlins' old home that also served as home to the National Football League team, Miami Dolphins. The new park is complete with the Bermuda Triangle alley in left, which has resulted in the new field playing much like the old — as a fair-to-strong pitcher's park. In its debut season, 2012, Marlins Park was 23rd in total runs scored. New Marlins Park produced 101 runs for every 100 runs produced in the average MLB park and 72 HRs for every 100 homers for a mean park factor of 86. The fences are the same or a bit deeper than the old park: 340 feet in left, 335 feet in right, 420 feet to dead center, with power alleys swooping out to 384 feet and 392 feet in left and right.

The new southeastern alignment should have an impact on the prevailing winds, although we don't yet know exactly how, and the retractable roof will neutralize or redirect most of it. Park factor data isn't accurate or reliable, of course, until the stadium logs another season or two.

Minute Maid Park: The Houston Astros

Want to see a Major-League hitter salivate? Just drop him off in Minute Maid Park and place a bat in his hands. This stadium is the anti-Marlins Park. The left-field fence sits only 315 feet from home plate, and 326 feet to right field represents little more than a chip shot for an average left-handed slugger. Even though these dimensions make Minute Maid a home-run haven, pitchers can survive in these confines by inducing batters to hit the ball to the wide, deep piece of real estate called center field — the longest in the Majors at 436 feet (including an uphill slope and a flagpole that is in play, so outfielders can salute while chasing down triples).

Left fielders must stay alert in this ballpark. Balls often carom at eccentric angles off the seats jutting out along the left-field line, one reason why the 'Stros have hit nearly twice as many triples at home as on the road during the last three seasons. Obviously, pitchers are best served by keeping the ball down in this stadium — and even more, striking people out, which is why Roy Oswalt thrived there for years. Minute Maid Park produced 97 runs for every 100 runs produced in the average MLB park and 108 HRs for every 100 homers for a mean park factor of 102.

Dodger Stadium: Los Angeles Dodgers

One of the reasons the Dodgers have had great pitching year-in and year-out is their ballpark. (Signing talented pitchers like Sandy Koufax, Fernando Valenzuela, Eric Gagne, and Clayton Kershaw are another reason.) The park doesn't appear cavernous, but at night, the dense, moist air floating in from the Pacific Ocean prevents hard hit balls from traveling far.

Hitters don't see the ball well here even during the day when glare and smog are often factors to contend with. As the summer wears on, bad hops abound after the intense heat hardens the infield; even the best fielders become error-prone on this surface. They also must cover an unusually large foul territory.

Fly-ball hitters languish in Dodger Stadium, though the stiff breezes that often blow out in right field provide some relief for left-handed sluggers. Yet, whether it's the beefy Dodgers lineup of late or some hot air emanating from Hollywood, Dodger Stadium has become a more neutral park. It produced 91 runs for every 100 runs produced in the average MLB park and 102 HRs for every 100 homers for a mean park factor of 97.

Nationals Park: Washington Nationals

From 2005, when the Montreal Expos moved to Washington and renamed themselves the Washington Nationals, they played in RFK Stadium, which once served as home to the now-defunct Washington Senators of the American League, from 1962 to 1971 as well as home to the NFL Washington Redskins.

In the 2005 season, the stadium was renovated as a stopgap home for three seasons, until the Nats moved into the spanking-new Nationals Park in 2008. Their new home is a 41,000-seat ballpark grazing the Anacostia River, less than a mile from the Capitol. Labeled the first green-certified park in MLB (we thought they were all green), the stadium had a park factor of 102 when it produced 98 runs for every 100 runs produced and 105 HRs for every 100 homers. The park has standard dimensions and no special on-field elements. Although it plays offensively neutral, winds and humidity can greatly impact the ball's flight. None of this fazes either Stephen Strasburg or Bryce Harper in the slightest.

Citi Field: New York Mets

Shea Stadium, the Mets' home from 1962 until 2009, was a tough park for home-run hitters. The team decided to maintain the status quo — with a vengeance — when it built Citi Field, which opened in 2009. Offense was so curtailed by the new park that Mets' hitters did everything but go on a hunger strike until management yanked in the fences in 2012. Ironically, it didn't help; fewer homers were hit that season. It's called being a Mets' fan.

Winds in the park vary widely from day to day, but no conditions ever offset the pitching advantage the park provides. The field is asymmetrical: 335 feet to the (orange-colored) left-field foul pole but only 330 feet to the one in right. The 415-foot right-center alley is even deeper than the fence in straightaway center (408 feet). The outfield fences are also high down the foul lines — 16 feet in left and 18 feet in right — which further robs the park of offense. The angles, nooks, and crannies in right field, which were built to resemble those of the old Brooklyn Dodgers' stadium, Ebbets Field, make it even harder to go long in right than in any other part of the outfield. Just as in Shea, adjacent to which Citi Field was built, the winds off nearby Flushing Bay continue to knock down many fly balls before they can reach the seats. Mets' announcers have mentioned that it's very difficult for hitters to pick up the ball leaving the pitcher's hand. It may be due to the color or depth of the background.

All of this resulted in Citi Field's dungeon-like park factor of 87, one of the lowest in the league. Giving rookie ace Matt Harvey a home like this is like placing a jewel in a crown.

Citizens Bank Park: Philadelphia Phillies

Unlike the Phillies' old park, Veteran Stadium, which was blanketed in punishing artificial turf, Citizens Bank Park has more grass than Woodstock. Its neutral park factor of 102 comes as a surprise to the casual fan who was used to seeing the Phillies and their opponents racking up runs with the cool efficiency of a champion pool player.

However, despite its coziness for both fans (seating capacity: 43,000) and right-handed pull hitters (329 feet down the left-field line), the misconception that CBP is a bandbox is due to the lineup of slugging uber-stars the team fielded almost from the park's onset from 2004 until a couple of years ago, when age sapped the pop from its sluggers. The park gives up more home runs than the average NL ballpark (HR factor of 105), but thanks to its generous center field and power alleys, it actually plays as only a slightly above-average offensive park, especially because the walls were adjusted to deeper positions in 2007.

PNC Park: Pittsburgh Pirates

The Pirates' ballpark opened in 2000. Along with the Giants' AT&T Park, it's often declared the loveliest in MLB, due to a view of the Allegheny River, right behind the outfield stands, shared by both fans and the home team, whose dugout is unorthodoxly situated along the third base line. The park seems to favor pitchers, with a depressed park factor of 83, although undoubtedly the Pirates' anemic lineups made a hefty contribution to that number. Left-handed sluggers love it because a shot down the right-field line clears the fence at only 320 feet. But the fence angles off as far as 410 feet in left center, making it difficult for right-handed hitters to smack home runs, though they will get their share of doubles in the gaps. All-Star centerfielder Andrew McCutcheon covers more ground than Middle East peace negotiators. Infielders complain that the dirt infield has no give; the surface is hard on the knees and produces an inordinate number of bad hops.

Busch Stadium: St. Louis Cardinals

Busch Stadium, sometimes called New Busch or Busch II to set it apart from the Cardinals' older home, also called Busch Stadium, opened in 2006. It features small foul areas, short fields, steep and clear seating, and spacious but typical dimensions (336 feet in the corners, 375 feet in the alleys, and 400 feet to centerfield). An expanse of foul territory behind and around the plate gives All-Star catcher Yadier Molina more help than he needs — added room to snatch popup outs — but the foul area tapers to near nothing in the corners.

People often overlook it when they talk about pitchers' parks. Busch Stadium's park factor was 88. It produced 94 runs for every 100 runs produced in the average MLB park and 82 HRs for every 100 homers. You may presume that Albert Pujols left St. Louis for Los Angeles after the 2012 season because he thought he had a better shot at the all-time home run record there. We hope his agent has proprietary information that contradicts the fact that "The Big A" is worse (it's so hitter-hostile, only a team of celestial beings — plus Mike Trout — can thrive there).

Petco Park: San Diego Padres

Petco has the rep of being the ultimate fan-friendly park. The Padres gave their followers a cutting-edge venue with all its seats angled toward the pitchers mound to provide optimum sight lines. Some boxes feature computers so that patrons can surf the Internet, check stats and out-of-town game scores, or order concessions without leaving the comfort of their seats.

In an unusual move, Padres' management has designated an area just beyond center field for lawn seating. Fans can watch games from there for free. But its center field is situated unconventionally — due north of home plate — to calm the ocean's winds. Although you may think the location can serve to allow fly balls to leave the park more comfortably, think again. Petco Park produced 85 runs for every 100 runs produced in the average MLB park and 78 HRs for every 100 homers for a park factor of 82. Pitchers pray that when they die, they'll spend the rest of eternity in Petco Park.

AT&T Park: San Francisco Giants

Fans and aesthetes alike consider AT&T Park (formerly SBC Park) set in the historic Mission District with a view of San Francisco Bay as the most beautiful in the game. The field has more green than the St. Patrick's Day Parade, and more angles than a geometry textbook — asymmetrically shaped by its proximity to San Francisco Bay. Left-handed pull-hitters are probably the only batters who look forward to an evening's swings at AT&T, because the park's right-field line is a short 309 feet, fully 30 feet shorter than the left-field corner. A steep angle, however, makes the right-field, power alley deeper than the left (421 feet compared to 404 feet), and the sharp angles make the 400 feet to dead center closer to home plate than the alleys.

A Willy Mays high wall (24 feet) in right field helps balance the short porch, and balls aimed at McCovey Cove (a body of water just beyond the fence) have to first get over that wall. (Fans float out there in rowboats and kayaks, hoping to retrieve home runs that soar from the park. Fishing isn't nearly as plentiful as when Barry Bonds played there.)

The right-field wall itself contains many arches and odd angles, however, which have caused enough bad bounces to earn it the nickname, Triples Alley. Though the fence down the right-field line is only 309 feet from home plate, the wall is high and gale-force winds usually blow in over it from left to right. For this reason, power pitchers who induce fly balls thrive in AT&T. (Paging Tim Lincecum and Matt Cain.)

AT&T Park produced 81 runs for every 100 runs produced in the average MLB park and 67 HRs for every 100 homers for a mean park factor of 74. For hitters, it's the ninth circle of hell.

The American League stadiums

For a long time, the American League was known as more of a hitter's league, but not just because the league used a designated hitter to bat instead of the pitcher. It was also because the AL was home to some of the best hitters' parks in baseball, such as Fenway Park, Camden Yards, and the Hubert H. Humphrey Dome (also known as the Homerdome). But in the last decade or so, just as in the NL, new pitcher-friendly parks such as Comerica in Detroit have sprouted up. In addition, for a variety of reasons, former hitter-friendly parks such as Camden Yards and Progressive Field in Cleveland have become more neutral, favoring neither the hitter nor the pitcher.

Oriole Park at Camden Yards: Baltimore Orioles

When Camden Yards first opened, the Orioles scored so many runs there that the stadium earned a reputation as an extreme hitter's park. Turned out that the high-octane offense was due to all the power in the O's lineup rather than some home field advantage. But parks, like people, constantly evolve. After a span of years when hitters wandered the offensive desert, they've returned to the Promised Land.

Camden Yards produced 109 runs for every 100 runs produced in the average MLB park and 124 HRs for every 100 homers for a mean park factor of 117. In 2013, the Orioles led the Major Leagues in home runs, with 212.

Home runs are plentiful at the Yard, but the park's configurations diminish a batter's chances of hitting a double or triple. Fly balls carry deep to left field during the warmer months. In the past, Orioles groundskeepers have kept the infield grass unusually high, reducing ground-ball hits by a substantial margin.

If you attend a game at Camden Yards, keep an eye on the right fielder. The ball can take any number of crazy hops off that tall wall and scoreboard that stand behind him. Left-handed power hitters such as Chris Davis flourish in this park.

Fenway Park: Boston Red Sox

Think Fenway and you think of the Green Monster in left field, Ted Williams, Jim Rice, Carl Yastrzemski, Manny Ramirez, Nomar Garciaparra, and Big Papi David Ortiz and 10–9 slugfests. Despite many renovations to a park that was built before World War I (1912 to be exact), Fenway has been the best AL park for hitters for a century now, although that primacy has been threatened in recent years.

Although the 2005 perching of new seats above the famous left-field wall known as the Green Monster seems to have reduced home run totals — Fenway's home run factor over the last three years is a below-average 95. It's still a good place for enhancing your batting average (the small foul territory contributes to that). Outfielders have to be quick to cover the vast real estate in Fenway's right field. If you're playing shallow and a ball gets past you, it can roll into Triple City. Left fielders must contend with the crazy caroms balls take off of that Green Monster (see Figure 18-4). Fenway Park produced 115 runs for every 100 runs produced in the average MLB park and 95 HRs for every 100 homers for a mean park factor of 105. A hitter's park — yes — but it ranked tenth in MLB over the last three years.

Figure 18-4:
The Green
Monster
looms at
Fenway.

Photo courtesy of National Baseball Hall of Fame Library, Cooperstown, N.Y.

US Cellular Field: Chicago White Sox

US Cellular is what Fenway used to be. It was a pitcher's paradise until the 2001 season when management pulled in the fences, so it's now one of the top home-run parks in the Major Leagues. It has produced 137 four-baggers for every 100. It also created 113 runs for every 100 runs produced in the average MLB for a mean park factor of 125. (How does Chris Sale do it?)

Those short fences are a blessing and a curse for the White Sox. Some of the team's hitters fall into the habit of swinging for the long ball on every pitch only to see their batting average whittled down by a lot of harmless fly balls. However, the park should warm the heart of any second baseman. The grounds-keeping crew maintains the infield so meticulously that the ball rarely takes a bad hop.

Progressive Field: Cleveland Indians

If it's late or early in the season, bring an overcoat. The wind off the nearby lake can be frigid. Progressive Field once had a well-deserved reputation as a hitter's park, but in recent years has played close to neutral. The park is hospitable to pitchers during those cold spring and fall evenings. Many make the mistake of calling Jacobs Field a home-run hitter's park. It really isn't. Balls don't carry well to left field under any conditions — deterred by Lake Erie's capricious winds and weather, and the 20-foot high left-field wall prevents many long drives from reaching the seats. Not to mention random Biblical mosquito plagues. (Tiny flies called *midges* threw the Yankees' pitcher Joba Chamberlain off his game and led to Cleveland winning the 2007 AL Divisional Series.)

Lefty batters prosper by hitting the ball in the air into a jet stream blowing out to right in Cleveland (11th highest home run rate in 2012), while righty batters curse the 19-foot wall in left field (28th highest home runs rate). Progressive Field produced 94 runs for every 100 runs produced in the average MLB park and 98 HRs for every 100 homers for a mean park factor of 96.

Comerica Park: Detroit Tigers

Comerica was such an extreme pitcher's park when it first opened in 2001 that the Tigers front office was afraid hitters would be wary of signing with the team. So, the left-field wall came in more than 20 feet just prior to the 2003 season, and the home-run totals ticked upward. And smart hitters are learning to drive extra-base hits into the long, wide gaps in left- and right-center field. With most of the fences so far back, you can't hide any slow, weak-armed hitters in the outfield when your team plays in Detroit. Fly-ball pitchers can challenge sluggers with impunity here. Comerica Park produced 104 runs for every 100 runs produced in the average MLB park and 98 HRs for every 100 homers for a mean park factor of 101. Of course, these numbers don't apply to Miguel Cabrera, who is using Comerica like a toy stadium.

Kauffman Stadium: Kansas City Royals

Line-drive hitters who can drive the ball into the gap for doubles and triples fare best in this ballpark. George Brett, who hit nearly everything on the line, almost hit .400 while playing here. His teammate Hal McRae, a similar hitter, won the American League RBI crown at the age of 37. More recently, Eric Hosmer and Billy Butler have taken similar advantage of the gaps. Management completely renovated Kauffman from 2007 to 2010, but kept the dimensions almost exactly the same. Still, balls often hug the wall down the lines and scoot past outfielders, turning singles into doubles, and doubles into triples. Kauffman Stadium produced 101 runs for every 100 runs produced in the average MLB park and 88 HRs for every 100 homers for a mean park factor of 95. Generally speaking, pitchers travel first-class at Kauffman.

The Big A: Los Angeles Angels

A brief history of Angels Stadium in Anaheim illustrates the extent to which architects fundamentally can alter the game: For years, the former Edison International was a pitcher's park. Then in 1979, the Angels erected three-tier seating behind the outfield walls. That construction enclosed the stadium, cutting off the wind. As a result, the ball started flying out of there. From 1994 to 1997, the Angels played in the best home-run hitter's park in the American League. However, in 1997, management started a second renovation that opened up the center-field area. The wind once again became a factor as home-run totals dropped, particularly for left-handed hitters. However, winds gusting about in right-center field still aided some right-handed sluggers. The Big A also depresses batting averages because visibility is poor.

The Big A has continued to be a pitcher's park. It produced 84 runs for every 100 runs produced in the average MLB park and 79 HRs for every 100 homers for a mean park factor of 81.You could even call it an extreme pitcher's park. AL hitters call it Public Enemy No. 1.

Target Field: Minnesota Twins

Target Field in Minneapolis, the team's relatively new open-air stadium, is a distinct improvement over the hideous Hubert H. Humphrey Stadium (often called the Homerdome), in which the Twins played until 2010. So far, it appears to be heavily tilted toward hurlers, though it will take some time before enough data rolls in to confirm that early indication.

The park has medium-deep dimensions (339 feet to the left-field corners, 328 feet to the right-field corners, and a 411-feet center field), but it does compensate hitters, especially lefties, with a short porch in right center. (Never mind that the 365-feet alley is capped with a higher than average wall to prevent home runs from coming too cheaply.) The absurdly wide range of Minnesota weather (from lows of 40 in April to highs of 110 in July) gives the park multiple personalities during different months of the season. However, over the last three years, Target Field produced 98 runs for every 100 runs produced in the average MLB park and 86 HRs for every 100 homers for a mean park factor of 92.

(New) Yankee Stadium: New York Yankees

Despite the legacy of Babe Ruth, Joe DiMaggio, Mickey Mantle, and Reggie Jackson — the old, fabled Yankee Stadiums (the original, built in the early 1920s, was completely renovated in the 1970s) were actually pitcher's parks. (Old-time fans remember the 463-feet sign in left center. And Dodger great Don Drysdale likened it to pitching in an airport.) The old Yankee Stadium favored left-handed pull hitters. That hasn't changed.

If you can jack the ball down the line in the new stadium, you'll get some extra short-porch home runs. Left-handed Yankees' sluggers who often hit the ball to the opposite field — Ruth, Lou, and Jackson come to mind here — usually stroked more home runs on the road than at home. The park aided hitters like Oscar Gamble and Tino Martinez, though they were powerful enough to hit the ball out of any park. However, the new park is even more hitter-friendly overall than its predecessor. It retains the beckoning siren of a right-field porch, and the ball seems to fly out there as if shot from a cannon. Newly arriving hitters fall under its spell; think Curtis Granderson. With his former Tigers' team, he never hit more than 30 homers in a season. But he eloped with the short porch in 2010 and the two have been happily married since; he slugged more than 40 homers the next two years. Conversely, it's bad news for fly-ball pitchers. Just ask Phil Hughes. New Yankee Stadium has produced 110 runs for every 100 runs produced in the average MLB park and

128 HRs for every 100 homers for a mean park factor of 119. And Hughes's career, once so promising, reminds one of a silent movie star who just couldn't adjust to talkies.

Oakland County Coliseum: Oakland Athletics

The Coliseum continues to be among the American League's stingiest pitcher's parks. Because the outfield gaps are wide, speedy slap hitters can serve the ball to either side of the field and run all day. Groundskeepers maintain the infield and outfield in a neat buzz-cut; groundballs scoot past any lead-footed fielders for base hits. Oakland County Coliseum produced 93 runs for every 100 runs produced in the average MLB park and 78 HRs for every 100 homers for a mean park factor of 86. Only two AL stadiums were stingier when it came to runs from 2010–2012.

Safeco Field: Seattle Mariners

Safeco Field is one tough park to hit in. The glare in center field can blind hitters. In 2003, the Mariners heeded that old Rolling Stones song and painted the wall behind center black to remedy the problem. The dark backdrop helped somewhat, but it remains difficult to pick up pitches during day games. Sluggers find it difficult to pound the ball through Seattle's cool, damp atmosphere. Pitchers such as Felix Hernandez will challenge hitters with high fastballs, knowing that even the hardest hit fly balls rarely leave the field.

Safeco features a three-paneled retractable roof; it doesn't seal the stadium, but it covers it like a gigantic umbrella so that an open-air environment is sustained even during inclement weather.

Opposing teams never relish visiting the Mariners' home field. Seattle's fans were once the most raucous in baseball. They electrified their team with their cheering while taking the opposition out of the game. During recent, losing years, however, during a game you can hear the Space Needle drop a millimeter. Safeco Field produced an ungodly-low 79 runs for every 100 runs produced in the average MLB park and 77 HRs for every 100 homers for a mean park factor of 78. All hail, King Felix!

Rangers Ballpark in Arlington: Texas Rangers

Teams seldom win in this stadium without playing long ball. Doubles and triples flourish in the roomy power alleys, and home runs are practically a long check-swing down the short right-field line for most left-handed hitters.

Players call the rock-hard infield the worst in baseball; grounders that would be outs in most stadiums rush past infielders for singles or down the line for doubles. When the sun resides in the gap between the Ballpark's upper and lower decks, outfielders can easily lose sight of the ball. For example, the

Rangers made 114 errors in 2012 — among the most in the AL — though the Rangers have been a team of sure-handed fielders over recent seasons. The Ballpark in Arlington produced 123 runs for every 100 runs produced in the average MLB park and 128 HRs for every 100 homers for a mean park factor of 125. Yu Darvish must have a taste for that thin Texas air.

Rogers Centre: Toronto Blue Jays

It's all about the dome — the retractable dome at Rogers Centre. It's a haven for home runs, and many observers attribute it to a boost fly balls get when the roof is open. When closed, they cite a wind scoop caused by the stacked components of the dome that they suspect keeps those flies in the park. However, the website Baseball Prospectus (www.baseballprospectus .com) did an analysis of this theory and found no difference in homers whether the roof was open or closed. The main reason that the dome plays as a hitter's park isn't about wind scoops, but the fact that the roof's mere climate-controlled environment eliminates any cold-weather games (which suppress scoring), which makes Rogers Centre look more hitter-friendly by comparison with other cold-weather teams.

Rogers Centre's artificial-turf infield — thankfully, one of the last remaining from the Astroturf era — may be the truest in baseball (probably because it's held together by Velcro rather than the zippers used to bond other turfs.) You get the feeling that customs officials turn away bad-bounce base hits at the border. Rogers Centre has produced 107 runs for every 100 runs produced in the average MLB park and 119 HRs for every 100 homers for a mean park factor of 113. Jose Bautista, Edward Encarnación, and crew make this park feel like their neighborhood pub.

Tropicana Field: Tampa Bay Rays

Tropicana Field is such a morosely unnatural environment for baseball that the team discourages its fans from attending. Okay, not really, but before the 2013 season, it covered many empty seats in the outfield to make the park look fuller. If you're wondering why fans don't clamor to get into the Trop, despite the Rays being perennial contenders, it could be due to the nonretractable dome (thus, indoor baseball in the land of sunshine, which many people would rather bask in directly), artificial turf, and a catwalk over the outfield.

The park's asymmetrical design doesn't favor righties or lefties. Outfielders can lose balls in the stadium lights or against the background of the ivory roof. And those balls that wildly carom off the catwalk above the field remain in play. (Catwalks belong in Fashion Week, not in a Major League ballpark.) The Rays play on artificial turf, which means that ground balls that fielders might easily glove on grass often shoot through the infield for base hits. The Trop features one of the smaller outfields in all of baseball, but the Rays have drafted and developed many good young pitchers who know how to avoid giving up too many fly balls. Hitters who can drive the ball into the gap benefit. The front office is composed of extremely smart people who know how to minimize the park's weaknesses and field perennial contenders. In the David Price, James Shields, and Matt Moore era, Tropicana Field produced an average park factor of 85, meaning that for every 100 runs scored in an average park, only 85 were tallied in the Trop.

Looking Closer at Stadium Statistics

Table 18-3 gives you the lowdown on all the major-league stadiums. (Because of space limitations, all these dimensions are in feet. If you want to talk meters, just divide the feet by 3.28.)

Table 18-3			Major-League Stadium Statistics				
Park	**LF Line**	**Left CF**	**Center**	**Right CF**	**RF Line**	**Surface**	**Capacity**
Chase Field	328	376	402	376	334	Grass	49,033
Turner Field	335	380	401	390	330	Grass	50,097
Wrigley Field	355	368	400	368	353	Grass	39,241
Great American Ballpark	328	379	404	365	325	Grass	42,263
Coors Field	347	390	415	375	350	Grass	50,490
Miller Park	344	371	400	374	345	Grass	41,900
Marlins Park	340	385	416	392	335	Grass	37,000
Minute Maid Park	315	362	435	373	326	Grass	40,950
Dodger Stadium	330	385	395	385	330	Grass	53,275
Nationals Park	335	377	402	370	335	Grass	41,888
Citi Field	338	378	410	371	338	Grass	41,800
*Citizens Bank Park	329	374	401	369	330	Grass	43,647
PNC Park	325	389	399	375	320	Grass	38,496
Busch Stadium	336	375	400	375	335	Grass	46,861
Petco Park	334	367	396	387	322	Grass	42,445

(continued)

Table 18-3 *(continued)*

Park	LF Line	Left CF	Center	Right CF	RF Line	Surface	Capacity
AT&T Park	335	364	404	421	309	Grass	41,915
Oriole Park at Camden Yards	333	364	400	373	318	Grass	48,876
Fenway Park	310	379	420	383	302	Grass	37,402
US Cellular Field	347	377	400	372	347	Grass	40,615
Progressive Field	325	370	405	375	325	Grass	43,545
Comerica Park	345	395	400	365	333	Grass	41,782
Kauffman Stadium	330	375	400	375	330	Grass	39,000
Angel Stadium of Anaheim	333	365	400	365	333	Grass	45,483
Target Field	339	377	411	365	328	Grass	39,504
(New) Yankee Stadium	318	399	408	385	314	Grass	50,291
O.Co. Coliseum	330	375	400	375	330	Grass	35,067
Safeco Field	331	390	405	387	327	Grass	47,116
Rangers Ballpark in Arlington	332	390	400	381	325	Grass	49,170
Rogers Centre	328	375	400	375	328	Artificial	50,000
Tropicana Field	315	370	410	370	322	Artificial	36,973

Indicates new stadium; dimensions are estimated.

Chapter 19

Tackling Baseball's Steroid Controversy

*E*ven the casual fan of baseball probably has many questions about what has become the most discussed topic in baseball: the use of anabolic steroids, human growth hormones, and other performance-enhancing drugs (PEDs). That's why we decided to include this chapter in the newest edition of *Baseball For Dummies.* These chemical agents have cast a huge shadow on the entire sport and its players, and PEDs will continue to influence voting for the Hall of Fame for years — even decades — to come. In fact, most fans and writers already are referring to the offensive explosion of the mid-1990s through the mid-2000s as the *Steroid Era,* and not approvingly. So this chapter provides you with a brief primer on this thorniest of subjects.

I'm vice chairman of the board of Hall of Fame. Any statements I make here in this chapter are from Joe Morgan, Hall of Fame member, not in my official capacity with the Hall.

PEDs have tarnished the game because baseball has always been about numbers. When I was growing up, I knew what 714, 56, and 61 meant. *(Note:* 714 was Babe Ruth's all-time record for home runs, 56 referred to Joe DiMaggio's consecutive-game hitting streak record, and 61 was Roger Maris's single-season home-run record.) PEDs destroyed the credibility of numbers compiled during the Steroid Era. I think the numbers put up by today's hitters, and the hitters who played before the introduction of PEDs, more accurately represent their true level of performance.

Recognizing the Lowdown on PEDs

Although innumerable performance-enhancing drugs (PEDs) are used across the sporting spectrum, the most commonly abused substances in baseball are *anabolic steroids* and *human growth hormone (HgH)*.

- **Anabolic steroids:** These are *synthetic steroid hormones* — derivatives of testosterone — that are used medically, especially to promote tissue and muscle growth. Some physicians, self-proclaimed health practitioners, and dealers also illegally prescribe or sell them on the black market. These substances come in oral, injectable, and cream forms. Their side effects include damage to the liver and reproductive system, hair loss, and acne. In large doses or combinations known as *stacks,* they may injure the cardiovascular system.

- **Human growth hormone (HgH):** HgH was developed in 1985 to spur growth in children and adolescents. It also helps to regulate body composition, body fluids, muscle and bone growth, sugar and fat metabolism, and possibly heart function. HgH is found in products that are available via the Internet. The people selling these products tout HgH as a fountain of youth, but no scientific evidence supports those claims. Side effects, however, are real, and include nerve, muscle, or joint pain; swelling due to fluid in the body's tissues (*edema*); carpal tunnel syndrome; numbness and tingling of the skin; high cholesterol levels; and an increased risk of diabetes and cancerous tumors.

Grasping Why Athletes Use PEDs

Since the dawn of competitive sports, athletes have sought an edge, whether legal or illegal in their society or banned or accepted in their sport. According to the World Anti-Doping Agency (WADA), Thomas Hicks ran to victory in the 1904 Olympic games marathon in St. Louis, with the help of raw egg, injections of strychnine, and doses of brandy administered to him during the race. (***Caution:*** Don't try this at home — or anywhere else, for that matter. Strychnine is a deadly poison.)

At the elite level of any sport, especially a sport such as baseball that requires both athletic tools and finely nuanced skills, adding to your hit, home run, or win totals can mean extra millions in salary and increased playing time. Some players mistakenly decide that the extra money they can make by taking PEDs provides enough incentive to cheat, even though the evidence indicates taking those drugs puts your health at risk.

For its first 150 years, baseball enjoyed a squeaky-clean image. It's true that some Major Leaguers threw spitballs, corked their bats, and used other ploys to gain a competitive edge, but PED use was relatively unknown. However, ever since the 1950s, we've heard stories that some players regularly used amphetamines that, according to Jim Bouton's book *Ball Four* and other sources, were often made available in clubhouses and dugouts.

Those pills were commonly known as *greenies*, and they supposedly kept players more alert and helped them stave off the fatigue of a long season. Estimating how many players regularly took amphetamines in any era is difficult, because the evidence of use is largely anecdotal, and the sources of the stories are often anonymous.

I won't deny that players took greenies, but they only helped make you alert. They didn't make you hit the ball farther or more often. When comparing greenies to steroids, they're apples and oranges. One thing I read that was totally inaccurate was that in the big-league clubhouses they had two pots of coffee: one with plain coffee and one pot laced with amphetamines. I never saw anything like that, and I played in the Majors for more than 20 years.

Exploring What PEDs Do for Baseball Performance

Because anabolic steroids, testosterone, and HgH had been proven to build muscle mass and quicken muscle recovery, baseball players presumed that more and bigger muscles would allow them to hit the ball harder and longer. They also thought it would make their bodies better able to withstand the rigors of a 162-game season.

Were they right? Some people who cover the game don't believe that PED use was completely responsible for the long-ball outburst of the Steroid Era. One writer claimed that the ball was changed, which made it travel farther, but Major League Baseball denied that theory. Others claimed that the wave of new ballparks built in the 1990s — small, intimate with shorter fences and otherwise favorable hitting conditions (think Coors Field) — caused the upsurge in offense.

There is no telling how large a role those factors played, but there remains this one undeniable fact: Offense has dropped precipitously since Major League Baseball started testing for PEDs and imposing penalties, including suspensions. Babe Ruth's single-season home record (60) stood for 34 years, until Roger Maris broke it in 1961. In one four-year period (1998 to 2001) during the height of the Steroid Era, Sammy Sosa, Mark McGwire, and Barry Bonds topped Maris's total six times. During the Steroid Era, players who never had hit even 20 home runs in a season were suddenly hitting 40 or even 50 homers. Batters uniformly slugged at record-breaking levels. In 2013, baseball started testing players for HgH, and run production fell even further. It's highly unlikely that the curtailment of PED use and the decreased power we see throughout the game are unrelated.

Here's another undeniable fact: Forget the theories about changed balls and smaller parks. If PEDs didn't help players hit the ball farther and more often, they wouldn't have been taking them. And, players believe PEDs helped the cheaters. I was broadcasting college baseball for ESPN and noticed athletes who were taking some supplement that was building them up and making them decidedly more muscular. One team had a second baseman who looked like Arnold Schwarzenegger. I realized that players were trying to enhance their body strength and performance by using some substance. The first time I started thinking about the type of substance it could be was in 1998, when a baseball writer reported seeing androstenedione (commonly referred as andro) on a shelf in the locker of St. Louis Cardinal first baseman Mark McGwire. At the time, McGwire and Sosa of the Cubs were both closing in on Babe Ruth's single-season, home run record, a chase that caught the imagination of the fans and the media. I later was asked about the story, and I said I didn't think it was wrong because it wasn't illegal.

My eyes were really opened when I was in a golf tournament in Florida playing with slugger Jose Canseco, and he said, "Joe, a lot of guys shouldn't be sleeping well tonight." I said, "What do you mean?" and he replied, "I'm going to write a book about steroid use." I said, "Are you sure you want to do this?" and he emphasized, "I have to." (In 2005, Canseco published the book *Juiced*, in which he not only celebrated the benefits of steroids, but he also claimed that most big-league ballplayers used them, including numerous MLB stars he cited by name. Canseco's book brought steroid use in baseball to the public's attention.)

Whatever its veracity, Canseco's book caused a sensation. I started wondering if one guy was using it or how many others were. At that time I was broadcasting, and I wanted to know what I was talking about when it came to steroids. I'm not a scientist, so I had lunch with the head of the WADA. He told me what steroids did to an athlete's body and psyche and led me to believe that they could help someone become a better baseball player by giving him greater strength, faster recovery time, and a sense of invulnerability. They didn't let you get mentally down. I was convinced. Although people say they didn't help you hit a baseball, I believe that they helped you hit it farther and harder.

A history of baseball's performance-enhancing drug scandals

The 1990s and early 2000s were a golden age for the game. An offensive explosion enticed fans in droves, and everybody — players (including their union), agents, and especially owners and Major League Baseball itself (through massively increased television contracts, profitable new stadiums, increased ticket prices, and ancillary benefits) — was raking in the gold. It seemed that a week didn't go by without some long-cherished record falling by the wayside. Mark McGwire didn't just break Roger Maris's single-season home-run record; he splintered it into a million pieces when he hit 70 in 1998. Three seasons later, Barry Bonds hit 73 homers to break McGwire's record. Barry followed that by surpassing baseball's most hallowed statistic of all: Henry Aaron's career home-run record of 755 in 2007. (Bonds finished his career with 762.)

To give you some perspective on how the issue of steroids (and other PEDs) came to dominate baseball conversation — and how MLB dealt with them — here's a timeline of the most important events:

- **1998**: After a baseball writer reported seeing a jar of androstenedione in McGwire's locker, the Cardinals' first baseman admitted that he used the steroid precursor (which wasn't banned under the rules of baseball), and then went on to hit a record 70 home runs. Although then-MLB Commissioner Fay Vincent had called for a ban on PEDs in 1991, neither the baseball owners nor the players' union tried to implement a testing program or penalties.

- **2002**: At a Senate Commerce Committee hearing in Washington, DC, Senators Byron Dorgan (D-North Dakota) and John McCain (R-Arizona) told Commissioner Bud Selig and MLB Players Association executive director Donald Fehr that they had to negotiate a strict drug-testing program during collective bargaining for a new basic agreement, which was about to expire. Up to this point, no MLB player could've been tested for drug use without probable cause.

- **2003**: MLB and the players' union negotiated a policy banning players from using steroids for performance enhancement. No testing existed during the off-season, and penalties were light (for example, it took five positive test results to warrant a lifetime ban).

The steroid ban didn't yet apply to andro or other over-the-counter steroid precursors, which would come the following year, when President George W. Bush signed into law the Anabolic Steroid Control Act of 2004. The bill added hundreds of steroid-based drugs and precursors, such as andro, to the list of anabolic steroids that were now classified as Schedule III controlled substances — those that are banned from over-the-counter sales without a prescription. MLB and the players' union agreed that all the drugs banned by Congress should also be banned by baseball.

- **2004**: As an outgrowth of an inquiry into use of an array of elicit substances (including steroids and HgH) by members of the US Olympic track-and-field team, Victor Conte, owner of BALCO Labs, was indicted before a grand jury. Within a matter of months, Gary Sheffield accused Barry Bonds of supplying him with steroids, and fellow Yankees' slugger Jason Giambi admitted injecting himself with HgH in 2003 and using steroids that he obtained from Barry Bonds' trainer, Greg Anderson, for at least three seasons. Although claiming little knowledge about the dissemination of steroids in baseball, Conte admitted he gave them to Anderson.

(continued)

(continued)

Still in 2004, the *San Francisco Chronicle* reported more grand jury testimony from Bonds, who claims Conte supplied him with steroids but without informing him of the nature of the substances.

✔ **2005:** The growing steroid controversy drew the attention of Congress. Numerous current and former MLB players, including McGwire and Jose Canseco, testified in front of the House Government Reform Committee on steroids in baseball.

Later in 2005, Conte pled guilty to steroid distribution and money laundering. He was sentenced to four months in prison as part of a plea deal for his role as ringleader of a scheme to provide professional athletes with undetectable PEDs. However, Conte denied giving steroids to Barry Bonds.

2007: A report on PEDs by former senator George Mitchell, commissioned by MLB, implicated 103 players, including such stars as Roger Clemens, Andy Pettitte, Chuck Knoblauch, and Mo Vaughn. Clemens' attorney denied that his client ever used PEDs, and observers questioned the use of evidence — the testimony of Kirk Radomski (former New York Mets' bat boy and PED dealer) and Brian McNamee (Roger Clemens' trainer). The players' union refused to cooperate with Mitchell's investigators.

✔ **2008:** Congress asked the US Department of Justice to investigate Roger Clemens for perjury.

✔ **2009:** MLB and the Major League Baseball Players Association agreed to amend MLB's Joint Drug Prevention and Treatment Program to include testing of some amateur players and broaden the scope of PEDs to include numerous other drugs.

Later in 2009, *Sports Illustrated* reported that Yankees' superstar Alex Rodriguez had failed a drug test in 2003. Rodriguez publicly denied

using steroids, and then admitted that he did so but was naive about their purpose.

✔ **2011:** MLB became the first sport to ban HgH but agreed that testing would only be held in spring training and the off-season. After seven years, a federal jury convicted Bonds only on the obstruction of justice charge. A judge declared a mistrial on the three remaining charges.

✔ **2013:** After a Hall of Fame vote in which the first-time candidacies of Bonds and Clemens were rejected because their names have been linked to PEDs, MLB and the Players Association agreed to implement more stringent PED policies regarding PED use. They also announced the following stricter penalties for positive steroid test results. (Refer to the later section, "Facing the Consequences: MLB's Rules Regarding PED Use" in this chapter for more information.)

Later in 2013, the Biogenesis Clinic began doing business in 2009, and according to MLB, Rodriguez was one of its biggest clients, possibly even recruiting other players there. Rodriguez allegedly attempted to acquire some of the paperwork from the clinic so that MLB's investigators, who also were trying to obtain it in an effort to discipline Rodriguez, couldn't get their hands on it. Baseball suspended Milwaukee Brewers' outfielder Ryan Braun for the final 65 games of the season, 12 more players for 50-games each, and threatened an unprecedented 211-game suspension for Rodriguez. (At the time this book went to press, Rodriguez was appealing the suspension and playing for the Yankees.) For the first time, in a major change that threatened to splinter the players' union, the great majority of its members supported the suspensions, as well as advocated lifetime bans and the voiding of guaranteed contracts for violating MLB's drug policy.

Although I knew then that a lot of players were taking PEDs, what many baseball fans and the press seem to miss is that not everybody was taking them. No one knows what the percentage was; I don't think it was even 50 percent, so the rest were being cheated. But it made money for everyone — players, owners, and TV networks. It enhanced players' stats, which gave them a better chance of making the Hall of Fame.

And, not just the hitters were taking PEDs. The drugs may have helped relief pitchers more than starters because it gave them a chance to rebound more quickly and pitch more often — four or five days straight. Starters were helped, too, though, because PEDs helped them work harder in between starts and be more prepared. Although both pitchers and hitters were taking PEDs, PEDs probably favored hitters.

Facing the Consequences: MLB's Rules Regarding PED Use

MLB has a drug prevention and treatment program that stipulates all the things players can or can't do. For example, a player can either test positive or violate the program in other ways, such as possessing HgH or syringes. If a player refuses a test, he can get suspended; MLB treats a refusal as a positive test.

The basics of the program are as follows:

- A player's first offense (such as failing a drug test) garners a 50-game suspension without pay.
- For a second offense, the player is suspended for 100 games without pay.
- A third offense results in a lifetime ban.

Every player is now tested twice during each baseball season. Plus, there are an unlimited number of random, unannounced in-season tests for steroids and HgH, and MLB takes baseline testosterone readings for all players to help detect the use of synthetic testosterone, a substance growing in popularity because it doesn't stay in the body long. The actual testing regimen — scheduling the tests, supervision of the sample collection, transportation of samples to a lab, oversight of the lab work, and reporting of positive test results to MLB and the players' union — is handled by an independent program administrator. However, MLB sends its own staff to the ballpark, where the testing is done.

Ridding the Game of PEDs

When the steroid scandals first came to light, someone from MLB asked me what I thought the penalties should be. I replied that a first offense mandated a 50-game suspension, a second offense a 100-game suspension, and a third offense a lifetime suspension — three strikes and you're out. MLB eventually implemented that, but players didn't stop taking PEDs.

During the 2013 offseason, players who recently had incurred suspensions for PED use received lengthy, lucrative contracts. So, I feel that the current penalties are too lenient. Major League Baseball must figure out a way to make the risk outweigh the reward. The only way to do that is if you get penalized, you risk forfeiting your contract, or a large chunk of it. Perhaps they should limit players who are suspended for PEDS in the final year of their contracts to initial one-year deals when they become free agents. Having said that, MLB must produce evidence that can withstand a challenge before penalizing any player for using PEDs.

Chapter 20

Keeping Up Online, on the Air, and on the Newsstand

The enormous amount of media coverage devoted to baseball reflects the sport's enduring popularity. And the coverage doesn't end with the regular MLB season. You can lounge in front of the fire in the dead of winter and still enjoy plenty of baseball action — without leaving the comforts of your living room. This chapter provides many ways you can follow your favorite team.

Baseball in Cyberspace

Thousands of baseball websites abound on the Internet. You can get scores, news, and a wealth of other information at the click of a mouse. These sections highlight some of the most popular ones.

Baseball Prospectus

If you're a baseball zealot, you should subscribe to Baseball Prospectus (www.baseballprospectus.com) and then bookmark it as your homepage. You can find many of the best young analysts in the game sharing their cutting-edge insights on everything from the myth of clutch hitting to the effects ballparks have on player performance (something we touch on in Chapter 18). BP not only provides but also has fathered advanced statistics that have become commonly accepted among statheads — as well as player and team performance projections. They visit, revisit, and re-revisit every aspect of the game from how to interpret minor league statistics, to just how effective an infield shift is, to how some seemingly minor player transactions turn out to pay unexpected dividends.

There's no aspect of the game BP doesn't turn its gaze to; BP staff watches prospects and chart injuries, gives you daily updates on not just the results but also the impact of yesterday's games and late-season call-ups, and provides postseason analysis. No infield rock is left unturned: international baseball and the economics and business of baseball (valuation of players, team and stadium finances, the player marketplace). If that weren't enough, BP is also the home of the former website, Cot's Baseball Contracts. Want to figure out how much A-Rod earns per hour? Grab your calculator and then visit this site, which breaks down the annual salaries, including bonuses, for every MLB player — even Bud Selig.

Since 1996 the BP staff has also published an annual *Baseball Prospectus* as well as numerous other books devoted to baseball analysis and history. BP also hosts a Sirius radio show.

MLB.com

In 1995, baseball became the first major-league sport to go on the Internet (and the Seattle Mariners was the first team to have its own website). All 30 Major-League franchises now boast websites. To keep up with your favorite team's latest doings, you only have to access www.mlb.com and pick a club from its pull-down menu. Then get ready to dive into a treasure trove of baseball delights.

During the regular season, you can enjoy such goodies as the latest standings, league leader boards, up-to-the-moment scores, great play highlight reels, and live broadcasts of games you can't see anywhere else. You can also access stadium-seating charts, check the schedules of every Major-League team, and purchase tickets for select games. We once ventured onto this site and even stumbled upon a live conference call between all 30 Major-League managers.

Come here during the off-season if you want to get the facts behind the latest trade or check the results from one of the winter leagues. The site also lets you play general manager by offering one of the best fantasy baseball games in cyberspace.

Bleacher Report

Since its founding in 2007, Bleacher Report (www.bleacherreport.com) has become the upstart in the room of sports websites — if you consider a multimedia company owned by Time Warner that delivers curated content on hundreds of teams in baseball and the other — ahem, less major — sports across the globe. The site has received justifiable criticism for open-source publishing (meaning all registered B/R users were permitted to publish articles on the site without editorial oversight), which made it hard for discerning fans to separate the credible analyst from the blowhard fan.

It does host one must-read: Will Carroll. Practically everyone acknowledges him to be the nation's leading writer on sports injuries. Carroll's "Under the Knife" column (which he took with him from his first home, Baseball Prospectus), in which the author analyzes players' injuries and physical vulnerabilities, is worth visiting the site alone.

SBNation (BaseballNation)

SBNation is a conglomerate that includes 300 websites. For our purposes, we stick to one — www.baseballnation.com — and its chief of baseball writer, Rob Neyer. A former protégé of stathead Bill James, Neyer wrote more words than anyone during his long stint at ESPN.com, and most of them were elegant, incisive, and lively.

Fangraphs

Fangraphs (www.fangraphs.com) now occupies the position Baseball Prospectus had in its first years. In fact, two of its leading writers — Dave Cameron and Dayn Perry — were former standouts at BP, and its content is almost as solid. The website offers a daily spate of articles on the game, and among other things, plots the course of every game, showing which hits and outs changed outcomes.

You can rest assured that, whether you agree or not with a given article, the data on which it is based — including pitch type, velocity, batted ball location, and play-by-play — is rock-solid. It's provided by Baseball Info Solutions, whose services are sought by a wide range of elite clients, including *The Bill James Handbook*. Traditional fans might find this counterintuitive, but BIS's scouts don't sit in the stands at live games, but record information from satellite video feeds of each game, allowing them to rewind and review each play as often as necessary to record accurate information. The results of all this satellite gazing is expected to drastically improve the accuracy and objectivity of hitting, pitching, and fielding analysis.

The Negro Baseball Leagues

James A. Riley, director of research for the Negro Leagues Baseball Museum, is the editor of this website (www.blackbaseball.com). The site is an archival resource that acquaints you with the rich history of the various Negro leagues, their players, managers, owners, and teams. This site also provides video biographies (via YouTube) of famous Negro League teams, such as the Homestead Grays and Chicago American Giants, and sells various books on Negro League history and its stars.

The National Baseball Hall of Fame and Museum

The National Baseball Hall of Fame website (www.baseballhalloffame.org) can't give you the same thrills as an actual visit to Cooperstown, but it's the next best thing. This site offers users an online tour of the Hall of Fame, its museum, famed bronze player plaques, and library. You can purchase baseball books, prints, videos, and other merchandise through the Museum Shop.

CNNSI

Sports Illustrated is the most hallowed name in sports journalism. Its baseball website (www.cnnsi.com) features dogged reporting by Tom Verducci, plus top-of-the-line analysis by former Baseball Prospectus luminaries Joe Sheehan and Jay Jaffe, whose path-breaking analysis of just what makes a Hall of Famer — called *JAWS* — has been most influential for analysts and fans taking a second or third look at HOF criteria. JAWS compares a potential HOF-er to the players at his position who are already enshrined, using advanced metrics to account for the wide variations in offensive performance levels throughout the game's history. Jaffe's intention has been to improve the Hall of Fame's standards, or at least not erode them, by admitting players who are at least as good as the average Hall of Famer at the position, combining stats from a player's peak years with his longevity.

Baseball Reference

How many games did Babe Ruth win as a pitcher? The best place to find out is this website (www.baseballreference.com), an online encyclopedia that contains the records for every player who ever pulled on a pair of big-league spikes. When you access a player's stats, you not only find his regular season numbers, you also discover how he fared in postseason play. Each player profile includes his fielding stats as well as a comprehensive list of where he finished in the voting for any major awards. (By the way, the answer to the trivia question is 96 wins for the Babe.)

Ballparks of Baseball

Are you a ballpark buff? Does just a glimpse of Wrigley Field's near-mythic ivy-covered walls set you to swooning? Do we have a website for you! Ballparks of Baseball (`www.ballparksofbaseball.com`) has all the information you could ever want about Major-League ballparks present, past, and future — including seating plans, field dimensions, interior and exterior photos, turf type (for example, the Baltimore Orioles play on Maryland Bluegrass in Camden Yards), and historical summaries. Looking for the ideal gift for that Red Sox fanatic in your life? You can purchase a 3-D scale model replica of Fenway Park (complete with Green Monster) from a catalogue of great baseball venues past and present.

Skilton's Baseball Links

This website (`www.baseball-links.com`) links fans to 12,574 baseball sites and updates. Talk about a baseball cornucopia! Visit this site when you want to find out whether your favorite team in the Federation de Baseball du Luxembourg won its big game last night. If you can't find a baseball site here, it probably doesn't exist.

MLB.TV

Concerned relatives may have to pry you from your laptop, smartphone, or tablet after you bookmark this site (`www.mlb.com`) to your favorites. The cybernetwork streams every out-of-market game live online and on 350 different mobile and connected devices, from Sony PlayStation to Android tablet to your washer-dryer (well, maybe someday). A high speed broadband Internet Connection (Cable, DSL, T1) is required to stream MLB.TV content, and all live games are subject to local blackout restrictions. You can order the service through `www.mlb.com` or call 866-800-1275.

Other sites to check out

You can find out tons of more information about baseball on the Internet. Table 20-1 lists some of our other favorite sites.

Table 20-1	Other Baseball Websites	
Name	*Address*	*Neat Features*
Baseball Cube	www.thebaseballcube.com	The homepage lists "Active Batting Streaks." How cool is that? Find complete listings of the amateur drafts dating back to 1965 and comprehensive player records, including hard-to-find minor-league statistics.
Baseball Plays	www.jes-soft.com	You can find training drills to improve the performance of any team, from Little League to the big leagues. Coaches can download a free baseball playbook that features color graphics and animated plays.
Baseball Think Factory	www.baseballthinkfactory.org	In "The Transactions Oracle," columnists analyze the latest trades, signings, and other transactions, and then they invite readers to post their comments. The chats are often exhilarating.

(continued)

Table 20-1 *(continued)*

Name	Address	Neat Features
Beckett Marketplace	www.beckett.com	*Beckett Marketplace* is a guide to the fluctuating baseball card market (the Dow Jones often exhibits less volatility) by the leaders in the industry. Beckett content establishes the market for cards and other baseball collectibles.
The Sporting News	www.sportingnews.com	The Sporting News — once known as the Bible of baseball, ceased print publication in 2012. Its website still covers all the Major-League teams throughout the year, as well as other sports.
ESPN	www.espn.com	This site is full of info, including Jayson Stark's "Rumblings and Ramblings," covering all 30 MLB teams, Keith Law's scouting reports on minor league prospects, and "The GM Office" by ex-Major League general manager Jim Bowden. To get the whole ball of wax, you need to subscribe to the "Insider" package.
The Exploratorium	www.exploratorium.edu	Consider this Baseball Science 101. This site contains thoughtful essays that explain, in layman's language, what makes a curveball curve, a slider slide, and a home run.

(continued)

Table 20-1 *(continued)*

Name	Address	Neat Features
High School Baseball Web	www.hsbaseballweb.com	Top high school coaches share tips on how to enhance your chances of making the team, whereas college scouts reveal what you have to do off the field to merit a baseball scholarship.
Dr. Mike Marshall's Pitching Coach Services	www.drmikemarshall.com	Former L.A. Dodgers' reliever Mike Marshall, who set a Major-League record by pitching 106 games in 1974, shares his secrets for pitching durability. You can download this baseball brainiac's (Dr. Marshall has a PhD in physiology) primer on pitching mechanics free of charge.
Minor League Baseball	www.milb.com	This site features a list of the top 100 minor-league teams of all time, plus comprehensive histories (including rare player photographs) and statistics for each club. You can also subscribe to a package — similar to MLB.com's — to watch your local minor league club on all your gadgetry.
Retrosheet	www.retrosheet.org	For baseball researchers, this is what the Field of Dreams resembles. It's a resource for box scores, rosters, play-by-play accounts, schedules, and game logs for Major-League games dating back as far back as 1871.

(continued)

Table 20-1 *(continued)*

Name	Address	Neat Features
Society for American Baseball Research	www.sabr.org	Although the late Detroit Tigers' broadcaster Ernie Harwell called SABR the "Phi Beta Kappa of baseball," the organization founded in 1971 is more like baseball's think tank. Its 6,000 members — players, analysts, and regular fans — can read the voluminous amount of information on the site, and convene in small groups or national meetings.
Web Ball	www.webball.com	You can find a weightless training center, a guide to conditioning exercises for the pre-adolescent set. "Your Brain on Baseball" explores the parts of the brain engaged in processing baseball events, the signals generated, and the paths they take from brain to body. (Bring your own neurologist.) The site also offers advice on how coaches can help kids overcome fear and build confidence on the ball field. Our favorite tip: Learn to duck!

Watching Baseball on TV

If you're like most fans, you see the majority of your baseball on television, which is a terrific way to find out more about the sport. When you watch games on TV, you don't have to do any work. The camera people direct your attention to all the important action. If you miss a critical event — a fielding gem, a clutch hit, or dramatic strikeout — replays give you multiple chances to view it. Stop-action and slow-motion shots help you to dissect a play from a variety of angles.

All the major networks use computer graphics to analyze pitch locations, *hit spreads* (those places on the field where a batter's hits are most likely to fall), defensive alignments, and batter-pitcher matchups. The latest technological gizmos will reveal pitch location as well as velocity and bat speed. Cool, huh? You don't have to look at a single scouting report. The announcers always have a wealth of data at their disposal, so you get information you'd have to go searching for on the Internet. And, best of all, if there's a rainout, you're already home. The following is a guide to get you pointed in the right direction — toward your television screen.

ESPN

This cable network, based in Bristol, Connecticut, begins its regular-season baseball coverage on opening day. ESPN and its younger sibling ESPN2 broadcast Sunday night games as well as games during the week, while ESPN *Deportes* carries a regular slate of games broadcast in Spanish. You can access the schedule for each of these networks at www.espn.com.

Fans can get the latest scores and game gossip on *Baseball Tonight,* which airs every evening throughout the baseball season. The ESPN sports ticker runs during the station's broadcasts of other sports, offering you up-to-the-minute game scores, transactions, and additional bits of news.

ESPN also affords baseball wide coverage all year round on its flagship news program, *Sportscenter.* The show appears at regular intervals throughout each day. ESPN2 covers some off-field baseball events, such as the Futures Game, which features the game's best minor league prospects and the World Baseball Classic. Both networks also broadcast college baseball games. Consult your schedule to find out who plays and when.

ESPN's Classic Sports Network

Even when the snow is piled up to your rooftop, you can still watch baseball. Tuning in to the Classic Sports Network is like stepping into a time machine. The cable network doesn't carry any live baseball telecasts, but it does bring you some of the greatest games ever played, in their entirety. You'll see the Brooklyn Dodgers win their first and only world championship, Nolan Ryan pitch a no-hitter, the storied sixth game of the 1975 World Series between the Red Sox and Reds, and much more. Check your cable listings to see if your carrier provides the network.

FOX Sports

FOX Sports brings you 12 regular-season games on Saturdays, two league division series, and one league championship series. Each year, it alternates leagues with Turner Broadcasting in the postseason — one year it will carry the AL postseason games and the next, NL postseason games. It also has full rights to televise the World Series.

Other telecasts

Many Spanish-speaking networks carry baseball from the Caribbean leagues during the winter months. You can watch players like Juan Gonzalez, Bernie Williams, and Ivan Rodriguez strut their stuff while you wrap Christmas presents. Consult your local TV listings for times and schedules.

Reading about Baseball in Print

If you don't want to play or watch baseball (or look for it on the Web), perhaps you'd like to read about it. This section describes some great starting points for you. (You can find contact information for these publications in Appendix B.)

- ✔ *USA Today* provides fans with excellent daily coverage of national baseball. Unlike many local papers, it rarely brings a hometown slant to a game or story. *USA Today Sports Weekly* is an excellent source of week-to-week coverage, particularly during the off-season. You can call the paper's fine back-issues department to research any articles you may have missed on the stands.

- ✔ *Sports Illustrated* provides comprehensive coverage of particular baseball news stories or events.

✔ *Baseball America* publishes every two weeks; therefore, many of its Major-League stories are old news by the time a copy reaches your hands. However, no publication can surpass its coverage of minor-league and college baseball. If you're in a fantasy league and want to chart the progress of an up-and-coming prospect, a subscription to this magazine is a shrewd investment. (See Chapter 21 for more information on fantasy leagues.)

Other publications for your baseball reading pleasure include

✔ *Baseball Digest:* A monthly compendium of baseball articles written by leading sportswriters from around the country.

✔ *ESPN, The Magazine:* A sports fanzine (published every two weeks) whose mesmerizing graphics and illuminating sidebars pull the reader into the text.

✔ *Street & Smith's Baseball:* Among the most respected of the pre-season baseball annuals.

✔ *Street & Smith's Sports Business Journal* and *SportsBusiness Daily:* Gives you the story of the game off the field while offering a glimpse of the economic hardball played in front offices throughout both leagues.

✔ *Who's Who In Baseball:* This annually updated publication contains the complete minor- and Major-League records of nearly every current major-league player. Its current author, Pete Palmer, is one of the founding fathers of sabermetrics. His book, *The Hidden Game of Baseball*, written with John Thorn, is one of the two foundation stones of advanced statistical analysis — the other being *The Bill James Baseball Abstract*s.

Chapter 21

Playing Fantasy Baseball

*A*ccording to an article in *Forbes* magazine in 2009, 11 million people play fantasy baseball every year. "What's the big deal?" you ask. Fantasy leagues let you act as general manager for a team of Major Leaguers in a baseball universe of your own creation. You get to pit your executive skills against an entire league of virtual general managers who try to guide their teams to the pennant. After scouting and signing players, you spend the entire season modifying your club through trades, free agent drafts, and other transactions. If you win a championship, you get to take home a little prize money, bask in the applause of family and friends, and have a bottle of chocolate milk poured over your head.

Believe it or not, but the first fantasy league baseball game was created by an IBM computer programmer in 1961 and then adapted into a Pittsburgh radio show that same year. Ah, the days of radio! (Even more implausibly, Beat Generation icon Jack Kerouac created his fantasy league in the 1940s, although it wasn't based on actual Major-League stats.) Daniel Okrent — whose contributions to baseball literature include the aptly named *Ultimate Baseball Book* (Houghton-Mifflin) — created the first fantasy league in 1980 while dining in the Manhattan bistro La Rotisserie Française with several other devotees of the national pastime. The originators named the game *rotisserie baseball* after the restaurant.

Explaining What Fantasy Baseball Really Is

Fantasy baseball is simulated baseball, a game you play with 10 to 12 people, also known as *team owners*. Each team selects anywhere from 20 to 32 Major-League players who compete against other teams of an equal number of players; all players are based on real-life players and their regular-season statistics. For this discussion, we set the number at 23, which was the standard for many years.

The week before the start of the Major-League season, you gather with the other owners in your league and hold an auction-style draft in which each owner purchases players. After each of you fills his roster of players, the competition begins. Your team battles against the other teams based on the real-life statistics of the players drafted. You don't play individual games in fantasy baseball; instead, you try to accumulate the best totals possible in each statistical category.

Most fantasy leagues use the eight statistical categories (four hitting, four pitching) shown in Table 21-1.

Table 21-1	Fantasy Baseball Scoring Categories
Offense	*Pitching*
Total runs batted in (RBI)	Team Earned Run Average (ERA) (See Chapter 16 for information on calculating ERA)
Total home runs	Total wins
Team batting average	Total saves
Total stolen bases	Walks plus hits divided by innings pitched ratio (WHIP)

The goal is to select players who will amass the highest totals in the categories (except for ERA and WHIP, where the lowest total wins). You're not restricted to using these stats; some of the more sophisticated leagues are replacing team batting average with team on-base percentage, and many leagues take advantage of ever-powerful computers and the reams of Internet stats to use more than a dozen categories to decide their championships. Scoring can be done entirely by computer, which allows leagues to develop their own scoring systems, often based on these more esoteric stats. Find out more about scoring in the section "Figuring your point total and winning," later in this chapter.

Examining How You Play

These sections help you figure out how to begin a league, draft a team, complete your roster, and make adjustments. Basically they give you an overview to the world of fantasy baseball.

Covering all the nuances of fantasy baseball in a single chapter is impossible, so you get only the general stuff here. A plethora of excellent books on the subject are available, from *Fantasy Baseball for Beginners: The Ultimate How-To Guide* by Sam Hendricks (Extra Point Press), to annual guides produced by Rotowire and Baseball Prospectus. All the major baseball websites, as well as others, such as Yahoo!, offer their own game and rules. They can help you discover more about fantasy baseball, establish the official rules for your league, and even give you an insider's edge.

Starting a league

Starting a league is easy. Here's what you do:

1. **Recruit 11 friends.**

   Twelve is the usual number of teams for a fantasy league, but you can play with fewer. If you can round up more than 12 participants, you may have to open the bidding to include players from both leagues.

2. **Select a date to hold your annual player draft.**

   Most leagues hold the draft the weekend before the MLB season begins. If this date doesn't work for your busy schedule, try to hold the draft two weeks before the start of the season or the weekend after baseball's Opening Day.

3. **Choose to play with either National League or American League players.** (See Chapter 13 for more information on the two leagues.)

   Limit your fantasy league to selecting players from only National League teams or only American League teams. Nearly all fantasy leagues choose only one league.

4. **Agree on an entry fee.**

   This dollar amount can be as high or low as you like. Pool the entry fees to form the pot — the cash paid out to the winners at the end of the season. (Many leagues are free and only involve imaginary dollar figures.)

That's it. Start gathering information on your favorite players and get ready to draft!

Drafting a team

Before you start drafting your team, set a salary cap for your fantasy league. For example, you and your fellow owners may decide to limit each team's payroll to $260 (or some other affordable sum). You don't have to play with actual money, however; you may credit an imaginary $260 to each team. But you must keep the $260-to-23-players ratio. (See the next section, "Filling out your roster," for the position-by-position breakdown of the 23-player roster.)

Although the league can't require any team to spend its entire budget, spending less isn't wise. Always try to spend all your money on draft day to maximize your chances of getting all the players you want.

Assign a drafting order for calling up players to the auction block. Picking first doesn't ensure that your club will acquire the player of your choice. Team A may start the draft by saying, "Miguel Cabrera for $1." The other owners begin calling out bids, always upping the bid in increments of at least $1. When the bidding slows, the owner who started the bidding, in this case Team A, gives fair warning. ("Cabrera going once, going twice . . . "). If no other owner ups the bid, the last bidder wins the Tigers' future Hall of Famer. Team B then calls up a player, and then Team C, and so on until all teams have drafted 23 players. Setting up a draft order ensures fairness because all owners get equal opportunity to call up players for auction.

Designate two people as official secretaries to record all the players, dollar amounts paid for each player, and remaining dollar amounts for each team. Accurate records help to resolve any potential conflicts.

Filling out your roster

Your roster should consist of the following:

- Two catchers
- One first baseman (first and third basemen are also known as corners)
- One second baseman
- One shortstop
- One third baseman
- A back-up second baseman or shortstop
- A back-up first or third baseman
- Five outfielders
- Nine pitchers

If you're playing with American League rules, you need to also draft a designated hitter. (See Chapter 3 if you don't know what a designated hitter is.) If you play by National League rules, draft a utility player (an extra outfielder, infielder, or catcher).

A player qualifies at a certain position by playing at least 20 games at that position during the previous year. If a player appeared in at least 20 games each at second base and shortstop last year, you may play him at either position. If a player played 125 games at catcher and 15 at first base, you may only draft him as a catcher. The position-qualifying rule varies widely from league to league; for example, in 2003, Álex Rodríguez played all his games for the Texas Rangers at shortstop, but he started 2004 as the New York Yankees' third baseman. Many leagues would allow you to put Rodríguez at short or third during the 2004 season, but you might be limited to using A-Rod at third in 2005. Confer with your fellow fantasists and agree upon your league's position-qualifying rule.

Nearly all leagues also draft a group of reserves. Use these players to fill in for injured or traded players. Because so many leagues treat the reserve list differently, refer to the website your fellow owners agree upon to serve as your league's bible or formulate with them a reserve list policy for your league.

Managing your team after the draft

After the draft, you can kick back, relax, and watch your team in action. Or, to really have some fun, you can start calling fellow owners to make trades. Trading players with other owners adds spice to any league and can help you improve your team in the process. For every player you trade to a team, you must get a player in return. After completing a trade, all teams involved (yes, you can negotiate multi-team deals) must have 23 players on their rosters.

Your league may decide to charge a nominal fee ($1 is the usual tariff) for every trade transaction. These fees can be added to any prize money your league awards at the end of the season.

When a flesh-and-blood Major-League player is traded out of his league, released, put on the disabled list, or dispatched to the minors during the actual season, you can replace him in your lineup. For example, if Yankees' first baseman Mark Teixeira tears his thumb in spring training and misses the rest of the season, you can replace him with a player from your reserves or acquire a new player. That new addition doesn't necessarily have to be a first baseman. If your roster is deep with first-base candidates, you can draft a player who mans a different spot, provided he keeps you within your league's position requirements. In the case of the Teixeira injury, if your team drafted

Albert Pujols to play third base, your league might allow you to switch him to first (two of the five positions Albert has played during his MLB career) so you can sign a third baseman to replace Teixeira on the roster.

Once again, thousands of rule variations exist for handling player movement during the season. Refer to the rules of your league — whether it be a book or a website — to help your league adopt a policy for picking up new players during the season.

Taking care of administrative tasks

As you may have guessed, running your own fantasy league involves some work. Here are some tips for minimizing the work and maximizing the fun:

- ✔ **Adopt a written set of rules.** Absolutely, positively do this or you'll face dozens of arguments throughout the season. Take an existing set of rules and use them exactly the way they are or modify them to meet your league needs.

  Don't be afraid to tweak the so-called traditional rules of fantasy baseball. Create whatever rules you think will make the game as fun as possible.

- ✔ **Appoint a commissioner.** Choose someone, preferably the most ethical owner in your league, to wear the commissioner's hat and enforce rules and arbitrate all disputes.

- ✔ **Agree upon the statistics you'll use in your league.** Most existing leagues provide free in-depth and up-to-date stats, and many even provide advice on managing your team, such as which players are hot and undervalued (or cold and overvalued). For example, Yahoo! Fantasy baseball provides all of the above. If you're starting your own league, you may agree to appoint a league statistician to retrieve the data from a service such as Yahoo! Fantasy or choose to have each team be responsible for checking the latest stats provided.

  Search the Internet under "Fantasy Baseball" to see what's available in existing leagues or, if you're starting your own, which reliable sources of statistics are available.

Figuring your point total and winning

Rank teams throughout the season from first to last in each of the scoring categories. In a typical 12-team league, you award 12 points for every first place finish, 11 for second, 10 for third, and so on down to 1 point for 12th place. For example, say your team has the rankings shown in Table 21-2 in a 12-team league.

Table 21-2	A Scoring Example	
Category	*Place*	*Points*
Total home runs	First	12
Total RBI	Third	10
Batting average	Sixth	7
Stolen bases	Fifth	8
Pitching wins	Second	11
Pitching saves	Tenth	3
ERA	Eighth	5
WHIP ratio	Twelfth	1
Total		**57**

You then compare your 57 total points to the other teams' total points. At season's end, the owner with the most points finishes first. If you play for cash, award the prize money as follows (or create your own prize money distribution plan):

✔ 50 percent of the total prize money pool for the pennant winner

✔ 20 percent for second place

✔ 15 percent for third

✔ 10 percent for fourth

✔ 5 percent for fifth

Being Successful in Fantasy Baseball

Use the following information to keep your team near the top of the standings and your sanity on an even keel:

✔ **Gather info, more info, and even more info.** Gather as much information on players as you possibly can. Information gathering is the key to drafting success.

✔ **Check out as many pre-season publications as you can.** *Sporting News,* available online or at the newsstand, is an excellent source of fantasy baseball info. You should also read John Sickels' "Down on the Farm" column featured on ESPN.com to get the latest skinny on up-and-coming minor leaguers.

✔ **Carefully monitor your money during the draft.** Remember, you have only a limited budget to spend on 23 players. Plan wisely.

✔ **Choose players who stay healthy.** Injuries can destroy even the strongest team. Try to avoid the injury-prone and aging players.

✔ **Beware of Spring Training phenoms.** Just because a rookie has a great Spring Training (baseball's pre-season) doesn't necessarily mean his success will carry over into the regular season. Don't overbid for a player based solely on his success in the preseason. Put a premium on consistency, players who come close to replicating their performances season after season.

✔ **Watch out for the World Series factor.** If a player had a great World Series the year before, chances are owners will overbid for him in the next year's draft. World Series heroes usually remain fresh in everyone's mind on draft day. Don't get suckered into overbidding for them.

✔ **Remember, there's always next year.** Is your team mired in last place? Don't worry, hope springs eternal; next year could be the year you win it all.

Economics 101: Supply and demand in fantasy baseball

Here's where you finally find a practical use for that high school or college economics course you took years ago. Just as a scarcity of oil in Saudi Arabia causes gasoline prices to rise in the United States, supply and demand of players dictates the prices paid in fantasy baseball drafts. A short supply of certain types of players sends bids soaring through the roof. For example, each team in the majors typically includes a closer (a relief pitcher who finishes off games). Because closers accumulate most of the saves (one of the scoring categories in fantasy baseball), most drafts place a premium on the short supply of each league's outstanding closers. (Count on paying $25–$35 for each closer.) Similarly, demand rages for four-category players — offensive players who excel in all four scoring categories: batting average, home runs, RBIs, and stolen bases. For example, in 1999, Chipper Jones hit .319 with 45 homers, 110 RBIs, and 25 stolen bases — the type of season that fantasy owners drool over. Expect to pay around $35–$45 for scarce, four-category players like Jones.

Unique events during your draft may cause player values to fluctuate as well. For example, if three teams still need a first baseman and only one good first baseman remains available, you'll pay a pretty penny for him or else get stuck with a lousy first baseman. Also, watch out for the favorite team factor: If most of your league's owners follow the Cubs, for example, expect a high demand and overbidding for Cubs players.

Playing Baseball on Your PC

Not content to draft a team of players and then follow their progress through the daily box scores? Want to know the thrill of managing your club to a World Series title? Computer baseball games put you right in the dugout, where you can watch the teams you draft and manage battle their way through a full season of competition. More than 100 such games are on the market today. The best of them include the following:

✔ **Diamond Mind Baseball:** You practically take a seat in a Major-League dugout when you play this game. Easily the most sophisticated baseball simulation on the market, the game is surprisingly easy to master. Diamond Mind lets you utilize the most intricate strategy options while matching your managerial expertise against a human opponent or the computer.

Nearly anything that happens in a baseball game can occur in Diamond Mind. Umpires eject feisty players, home-plate collisions can leave players injured, and your fielders might blow a sure out by running into each other. Batters are rated for speed, production against righties and lefties (you can call up their stats with a click of the mouse), bunting ability, clutch-hitting production, injury vulnerability, and base-stealing (game designer Tom Tippett and his crew even rate what kind of jump a runner gets). Fielders are rated on range, fielding average, and throwing arm strength. Pitchers are rated for endurance (pitch counts matter here) as well as their ability to subdue right-handed and left-handed batters.

No matter how many talents your players possess, the decisions you make play a critical role in your team's success. For example, we blew one game against the computer when we forgot to properly warm up Eric Gagne before bringing him in for a save. Our opponents lit up the usually invincible Dodger closer like he was a cheap birthday candle. Ballparks also exert considerable impact on player performance in Diamond Mind competition. That pop fly that carries over the fence for a home run in Colorado's Mile High Stadium ain't nuthin' but a can o'corn in San Francisco's SBC Park.

Unlike other PC baseball games, Diamond Mind's rosters are deep enough to let each franchise carry more than 40 players (something that lets you wheel and deal like a big-league general manager). You can replay past seasons, order all-time all-star teams for nearly every franchise, or create your own leagues and teams and then dump the players into a talent pool for a draft. You can even play head-to-head against other gamers online. Our favorite Diamond Mind feature is the Projected Season Disk. It utilizes a complex rating system that allows you to play with current team rosters while the actual season is in progress. So we don't have to watch the World Series this year — we already know who won. To order, visit its website at www.diamond-mind.com.

✔ **Strat-O-Matic Computer Baseball:** Designer Hal Richman's baseball simulation offers an extensive range of managerial and general managing options. You can replay entire seasons dating back to the dead ball era of the 1900s or create a draft league. The Swap-O-Matic feature lets you match your trading skills against the computer (which told us, in so many words, to take a hike when we offered it a back-up catcher in exchange for Magglio Ordonez). Colorful pie charts help you manage by indicating who has the advantage in pitcher-batter matchups.

Playability remains one of Strat-O-Matic's most attractive features. First-time users can have their leagues up and running in less than half an hour. In just minutes, you can play a nine-inning game against a friend, the computer, or solo. Clicking the Quick Play option lets you replay a full day's schedule of games in seconds or an entire MLB season in less than ten minutes (depending on the speed of your computer). Want to abandon the dugout for the field? With the Create A Fringe Player option, you can put yourself on a team's roster and lead it to the pennant. An encyclopedia allows you to keep a permanent record of each player's seasonal and cumulative career performance. To order, visit its website at `www.strat-o-matic.com`.

✔ **Dynasty League:** Beautiful high-definition graphics represent a hallmark for creator Michael Cieslinksi's baseball simulation. Each stadium, from the golden oldies like Ebbets Field and the Polo Grounds to Cincinnati's Great American Ballpark, resembles an oil painting. Bang-bang calls at first, that shortstop's diving stop and throw, the deep drive bounding through the gap — Dynasty depicts all the heart-stopping plays (as well as the routine ones) with a verisimilitude that makes it the next best thing to an ESPN highlight reel. This game rates players on the usual skills, but it also takes into account intangible qualities such as team chemistry, clutch performance, a catcher's game-calling proficiency, and umpire judgment. Bizarre plays can also contribute to outcomes. Every now and again, a ball bounces off a player's head and into the stands for a home run. You can almost hear him cry, "Ouch!" Recent and past seasons are available, and the Greatest Teams discs give you an opportunity to match the best clubs and players of all time in league or tournament competition. To order, visit its website at `www.designdepot.com`.

Part VI
The Part of Tens

the part of tens

web extras

Refer to www.dummies.com/extras/baseball for a couple bonus Part of Tens lists that cover Joe's favorite ten nicknames in baseball and Joe's top legends in Negro League baseball.

In this part...

- ✔ Discover the ten toughest pitchers Joe has ever faced — and just what made them such a challenge.

- ✔ See who Joe identifies as his ten smartest players he played with and against.

- ✔ Meet ten of the greatest Negro League players from the days before Major League Baseball integrated.

- ✔ Read about some of the most creative and interesting nick-names in baseball.

- ✔ Find out what different baseball jargon terms mean and start using them adeptly the next time you're around the diamond.

Chapter 22

Joe Morgan's Top Ten Toughest Pitchers He Batted Against

Pitchers come in all sizes and shapes, with a variety of mechanics, windups, release points, mannerisms, and eccentricities that exceeds that of any other athlete in any sport. Good, bad, or mediocre, they're all a delight and a fascination to watch. Their battle of wits with each hitter is the crux of baseball and more than any other factor make it a chess game on grass.

Although some pitchers are tougher to hit than others, the greatest pitchers are universally the hardest to hit. The reasons range from the pitcher's velocity, movement, control, and command, to his repertoire and pitching IQ.

During my storied 21-year career, I faced hundreds of hurlers. This chapter describes ten of the best, and what it felt like to stand 60 feet, 6 inches away from greatness.

Sandy Koufax: The Left Arm of God

I never saw Sandy Koufax when he didn't look like he was going to pitch a no-hitter. The first pitch that he would throw in a ballgame always looked like the fastest pitch he would throw that night. It was his way to not so subtly intimidate his opponents. I asked him about that last year, and he just looked at me and smiled.

Hurling his flaming fastball and drop-dead, 12-to-6 curveball Sandy was the most dominant pitcher of his time. After six years with the Dodgers — first in Brooklyn and then in Los Angeles — Koufax became master of his tool kit by 1961, launching a six-year run as dominating as any in the game's history. He became the first pitcher in MLB history to toss four no-hitters (one of them a perfect game), and the only pitcher to win three Cy Young awards during an era when there was just one such award for all of MLB (not one for each league). Koufax also won the pitcher's triple crown three times by leading the league in wins, strikeouts, and earned run average (ERA).

Koufax pitched with pain in his left elbow throughout much of the 1966 season. The injury convinced him to retire at the peak of his career, and in 1972, at age 36, he became the youngest player ever elected to the Baseball Hall of Fame.

I chatted with Sandy at a recent Hall of Fame gathering, and he told me that if Tommy John surgery had been available when he was playing, he could have pitched several more years. Who knows how many records he might have set?

Bob Gibson: Master of the Brushback

Bob Gibson of the St. Louis Cardinals was the toughest competitor I ever faced. Most fastballs that attain their highest speeds are high fastballs, but his fastball was low, which should have made it easier to hit, but it wasn't. Gibson's facial expression said, "You can't hit me." I still managed to fare well against him.

Gibson's pitching attack backed up a near-belligerent facial glare. He used a fastball-slider combo to tally 251 wins, 3,117 strikeouts, and a 2.91 ERA during his 17-year career. A nine-time All-Star and two-time World Series champion, he won two Cy Young Awards and the 1968 National League MVP award. In that year Gibson set a modern record for lowest ERA, a microscopic 1.12. In Game 1 of the 1968 World Series, Gibson set a record by whiffing 17 Detroit Tigers.

For the statheads, Gibson threw almost 4,000 innings and finished with a career ERA+ of 127, meaning he was 27 percent better than the average pitcher — quite a lofty perch. Refer to Chapter 16 for what the different stats mean.

Tom Seaver: Thinking Man with a Power Arm

Tom Seaver, whose career included stints with the Mets, Reds, White Sox, and Red Sox, had great mound presence and a deep understanding of how to get hitters out. He always tried to make me think that I was a better inside hitter than anything else by saying so in the papers, but then he always pitched me inside.

"Tom Terrific" won 25 games to lead the Mets to their first world championship in 1969. He had already won the Rookie of the Year award in 1967, and three Cy Young awards followed. During his 20-year career, Seaver used his powerful legs in the classic "drop and drive" delivery to uncork his rising fastball and a slider right-handed hitters couldn't hit with an oar. He also developed a fine changeup and used impeccable mechanics to compile 311 wins, 3,640 strike-outs, 61 shutouts, and a 2.86 ERA. He had nine consecutive 200-strikeout sea-sons and was a 12-time All-Star. He is one of only two pitchers (the other being Walter Johnson) to have 300 wins, 3,000 strikeouts, and an under 3.00 ERA.

In 1992, in his first time on the ballot, he was inducted into the Hall of Fame by the highest percentage ever recorded (98.84 percent). He has the only plaque at Cooperstown, wearing a Mets' hat.

J.R. Richard: He Could Have Been the Best Ever

J.R. Richard may have ended up being the best pitcher of them all if he had remained healthy. He was six-foot, eight-inches, his fastball was in the high 90s, his slider was in the mid-90s, and at times his stuff was unhittable. He had great movement on all his pitches. We played a game in the Astrodome one night, and after he got Pete Rose and me out, I came back to the bench and said, "We need to get a hit tonight." And we only got one — by Bill Plummer, a blooper over first base.

If only . . . those two words were never more apropos than when applied to Richard's career. If only the Astros hadn't limited him to spot duty for his first four years. If only he hadn't suffered a near-fatal stroke in 1980 — a stroke that snuffed out a career that was just blossoming after only eight years.

Observers, including myself, felt that right before his body betrayed him, Richard was improving each year, as he developed better command of his pitches. Always a high-strikeout pitcher, he had blown away 313 batters in his final full season, and he is only one of three pitchers in MLB history to have struck out 300 batters in consecutive seasons (Sandy Koufax and Nolan Ryan are the other two). Richard attempted a comeback a year after the stroke, but he spent a few years in the minors before hanging up his spikes forever.

Juan Marichal: The Dominican Dandy

Juan Marichal, whose stints included the San Francisco Giants, Boston Red Sox, and LA Dodgers) had the greatest repertoire. He had five pitches: a fastball, curve, slider, change-up, and screwball. The number of different pitches he could deliver at different speeds and with different motions and release points could keep you off balance better than any pitcher I faced. I had trouble with him. He even had a screwball to use against lefties, which is highly unusual for a right-handed pitcher. In one bat at Candlestick, he threw me one of those screwballs, which he thought was a good one, but I got a hit, and he stopped throwing it. But he was still tough — he went inside with me and I had trouble. Later, he told me he'd learned a lot about how to pitch me.

Despite the fact that he won more games than any pitcher of the 1960s, threw 244 complete games (more than half his starts) and 52 shutouts, and was probably the greatest All-Star Game pitcher in history, Marichal was overshadowed by Koufax and Gibson, whose teams won more pennants and championships. His high leg kick, combined with pinpoint control, made it hard for batters to recognize the oncoming pitch. He twice won 25 or more games, tossed a no-hitter, and finished with a lifetime record of 243–142.

Marichal didn't compile the highest strikeout numbers, but he hardly walked anyone. In 1983, he was enshrined into the Hall of Fame.

Steve Carlton: The Lefty

Steve Carlton was one of the true power pitchers. He had the greatest hard slider, and he located it well. In fact, everything he threw was hard. One of the greatest at-bats I ever had was against him; he threw a slider diving down and away, and I didn't know how, but I hit a liner over third base for a double. Later, when I played behind him with the Phillies, I realized he was even better than I thought.

In a 24-year career, Carlton played for the Cardinals, Phillies, Giants, White Sox, Indians, and Twins. He amassed some of the most astounding numbers of any pitcher: 329 wins (the second-most lifetime wins of any left-handed pitcher and 11th overall), 44,136 strikeouts — the second-most lifetime strikeouts of any left-handed pitcher (fourth overall) — and, oh yeah, four Cy Young awards. "Lefty" also completed one of the most remarkable feats in baseball history by accounting for nearly half of his team's wins when he won 27 games for the last-place 1972 Phillies. He was elected to Cooperstown in 1994 with 96 percent of the vote, among the highest percentages of all time.

Nolan Ryan: The Ryan Express

Nolan Ryan was aptly named "the Ryan Express." His fastball exploded and because I wasn't a very good high fastball hitter (who is?), he was especially hard on me. One night when I was with the Phillies, in the eighth inning of a game in Houston, I was in an 0-for-30 slump. Ryan had gotten me out all night with fastballs, but this time he threw me a curveball, and I hit a homer and we won 1–0. Afterward he said, "Well, you make a dumb pitch to a good hitter and you pay the price." I think he thought it was stupid to get hit with his second-best pitch. By the way, that kind of thinking isn't true of today's pitchers. Even if they make a batter look sick with two straight curves, say, they'll think, "I don't want to throw him three straight curves. So instead they might throw the batter a pitch he can handle instead of waiting for the hitter to *prove* he can hit that curve."

Nolan Ryan, who played for the Mets, Angels, Astros, and Rangers, just blew batters away. With a fastball that reached 100 miles per hour — and whose velocity he maintained into his 40s during a 27-year career — and a jaw-dropping 12-to-6 curve, Ryan amassed a Major League career record of 5,714 strikeouts. He and Koufax are the only Hall of Fame pitchers who had more strikeouts than innings pitched. He also threw seven no-hitters. In 1973, his first season with the Angels, Ryan also set a still-standing Major League record by allowing only 5.26 hits per nine innings.

Ferguson Jenkins: Iron Man
in Wrigley's Shadows

Ferguson Jenkins pitched magnificently in Wrigley Field, the toughest park for a pitcher, and he had exceptional control, much like Greg Maddux, only Jenkins threw harder. He could warm up on a matchbox. His control of the outside corner was the best I've ever seen. He also had a great slider, and right-handed hitters were at a disadvantage because he could pinpoint the outside corner. A lot of people thought he was underrated, but he wasn't by the hitters.

Some people who underappreciated Jenkins were the Hall-of-Fame voters, who didn't vote for him until three years after his initial eligibility. Besides spending the majority of his career at Wrigley Field, Jenkins lacked a dominant pitch, but he had a deep repertoire of stuff, which he threw with dart-like command; he averaged exactly 2 walks per game over his 19-year career. He won the Cy Young award in 1971 and finished his career with 284 wins and a staggering 4,500 innings pitched. In addition to the Cubs, he played for the Rangers, Red Sox, and Phillies.

Vida Blue: Flamethrower Extraordinaire

When I first faced Vida Blue in the All-Star game and 1972 World Series, he had an exploding fastball; it had a couple of extra stages. He didn't pitch at the highest level as much as some others in this chapter, but on his best day, he was as good as anybody. Even when he wasn't at 100 percent, you could tell he was special. He had confident mannerisms. He would challenge anybody. He'd throw you his best fastball and challenge you to hit it. Vida was a great athlete and an excellent defensive pitcher. I don't think he realized his full potential, due to holding out early in his career (he held out for more money from A's owner Charlie Finley for much of 1972) and injuries.

Blue was the 1971 Cy Young and MVP winner, when he went 24–8 and led the league in ERA (1.82), hits-per-nine innings, and strikeouts per nine innings. He also was an All-Star six times in his 17-year career, in which he played for the A's, Giants, and Royals.

Roger Clemens: The Rocket

When he first came up to the Major League, Roger Clemens could just blow the fastball by you. Early in his career, he was a thrower. He then developed a great, biting slider and got better with age as he added a devastating split-fingered fastball to his repertoire. He could throw all of his pitches for strikes at any point in the count.

You could make a convincing case that Clemens was the greatest pitcher who ever lived. Over a 24-year career, Clemens compiled a lifetime record of 354–184, won seven Cy Young awards, and led the league in ERA+ (adjusted for parks) an incredible *nine* times. He pitched for five pennant-winning teams and two World Series winners. He collected 4,672 strikeouts, the third-most of any pitcher in history, and he was an 11-time All-Star.

Chapter 23

Joe Morgan's Ten Smartest Players

In This Chapter
▶ Recognizing the savviest players Joe played against
▶ Identifying what made them so smart

*A*lthough the scouting ideal is a five-tool player — someone who can run, throw, play defense, hit, and hit for power, the great players had a sixth tool — intelligence.

The ten players listed in this chapter may not have been Phi Beta Kappas off the field, but on the field they were. They all had baseball intelligence, which means that they knew themselves well, their strengths, and their weaknesses. You're not a smart player unless you know your weaknesses. For example, if you can't hit the low strike, don't swing at it. Or if you have to protect yourself from a possible strike three, foul it off and wait for a more suitable pitch. If you don't have speed, develop anticipation. Know where fielders are playing, both when you run out a batted ball and when you're a base runner. When on base, the smartest players study the nuances of each and every pitcher, as well as each fielder. They figure out how to distinguish a pitcher's good pickoff move from his bluff move — and the precise moment when he plans to deliver the ball to home plate.

Because baseball doesn't have any stats for baseball smarts, here are why these ten players make my all-time list of smartest players. I limit my list to position players, who have to make adjustments from at bat to at bat and have many more variables to handle. (For my favorite pitchers, check out Chapter 22.)

Willie Stargell: "Pops"

When I played, there were 600 baseball players, and 599 of them loved Willie Stargell. He's the only guy I could have said that about. He never made anybody look bad, and he never said anything bad about anybody. He was one of the great leaders and smartest players I've ever met. People follow smart leaders, and Willie was one of the smartest. Most fans know him as a slugger, but he understood all aspects of the game. He knew the role of all his teammates and what they were supposed to do. He came down hard on them if they didn't follow team rules, yet he rewarded them with embroidered "Stargell stars" for their caps after a nice play or a good game. So he demonstrated intelligence using both intimidation and finesse.

As a first baseman (he started his career as a leftfielder), when a runner reached his bag, he altered his positioning. For example, instead of anchoring himself to the base, he stationed himself off the baseline and away from the bag so I couldn't see the pitcher, and I had to stand behind him, because technically the fielder has the right of way. This made me strain to watch the action and delayed my taking off for second. Eventually, I found a way to get around this maneuver.

Stargell was a great leader of men, which he demonstrated while leading the Pittsburgh Pirates — the team with whom he spent his entire 20-year career — to six NL East division titles, two NL pennants, and two World Series (1971 and 1979) while earning the nickname "Pops."

He was a seven-time All-Star and finished in the top ten in MVP voting another seven, winning the award in 1979 with the Cardinals' Keith Hernandez. Stargell led the league in home runs and on-base plus slugging twice each, and bashed 475 career home runs — many of the most massive ever struck, including two of the only four balls hit out of Dodger Stadium in its 50-plus year history. Stargell was inducted into the Baseball Hall of Fame in 1988.

Cito Gaston

When I played against Cito Gaston when he played with the Padres, Braves, and Pirates, I realized he knew all aspects of the game. And as a manager of the Blue Jays, he knew how to get the most out of his personnel — you don't train to be a manager the moment you become one. You do it while you're playing. I watched him watch our pitchers and adjust at the plate.

Although he played for 11 years, he only had one above-average season. It was as a manager that Gaston shined. He managed the Toronto Blue Jays from 1989–1997, and again from 2008–2010. During this time, he led the Blue Jays to four AL East division titles (1989, 1991, 1992, and 1993), two AL pennants (1992 and 1993), and two World Series titles (1992 and 1993).

Gaston was considered a player's manager: a steady, soft-spoken, and quiet leader. Outfielder and 1993 World Series hero Joe Carter said of Gaston that he knew how to work with each individual, treated everyone like a human being, and knew exactly what to say, when to say it, what moves to make when.

Gaston was fired by the Blue Jays in 1997, after the team's fortunes declined due to aging players and new ownership. He went 11 years without another managerial job until the Jays, now under different management, rehired him in 2008. He revived the team's fortunes before retiring in 2011.

Johnny Bench

Considered the greatest catcher in baseball history, Johnny Bench was extra-smart. Johnny could read not only his pitchers, but also every nuance of his opponents — their motions and whether they could pitch inside or not. He became an excellent base stealer by recognizing the moment the opposition wasn't paying attention. He also could anticipate when the opponents would decide to try to steal a base against us — that's how he was able to throw out so many runners.

In addition, he was an exceptional game caller: Outside of Don Gullett and, in 1970 Wayne Simpson, the Reds' starters aren't overpowering, but they had great command. They needed a savvy game general to guide them through starts. Bench knew how to pitch to everyone.

Bench, a 14-time All-Star selection and a two-time NL MVP, was a key member of that Cincinnati squad named the Big Red Machine that won six division titles, four NL pennants, and two World Series championships in the 1970s. He was voted into the Hall of Fame in 1989.

Pete Rose

Pete Rose had great instinct and intellect. He just knew what was going on at all times and felt he could outhustle everybody else. He had a dim view of pitchers and would say, "If all pitchers could think, we'd all hit .100." He used his intellect to play mind games with a pitcher, taking pitches he'd otherwise swing at. For example, early in the game he'd take a fastball down the middle as if not expecting it, allowing the pitcher to think he could get away with it later in the at-bat, or even a subsequent at-bat later in the game (or season). Of course, if the pitcher wasn't smart enough to realize this and threw him another fastball, he'd be ready to smack it.

Rose played with the Reds, Phillies, and Expos. He managed the Reds from mid-1984 to mid-1989, with a 426–388 record. During his four full seasons at the helm (1985–1988), the Reds posted four second-place finishes in the NL West division. His 426 managerial wins rank fifth in Reds history.

Willie Mays

Willie Mays made his work sound easy. He once said, "They throw the ball, I hit it. They hit the ball it, I catch it." Mays — like too many black and Latino players — is too often considered to have been a wunderkind, a "natural" who didn't have to work or study to attain his transcendent greatness. But that acumen put him in the genius category. As a centerfielder, he always seemed to be in the right spot. He studied the hitters and could see to what part of the plate the pitchers were going to throw, and he adjusted his positioning accordingly.

Mays displayed just as keen an intellect as a base runner. In a meaningless 1967 game against the Dodgers, he walked, then scored on Jack Hiatt's single to right field — a play that just doesn't happen unless the fielders botch the play. Only they didn't. He must've been moving on the pitch. He must've noticed exactly where the outfielders were playing and where the cutoff man was set up.

Hank Aaron

Hank Aaron, who played for the Milwaukee/Atlanta Braves and the Milwaukee Brewers, could do most of the things Mays could do, except without the flair. He was the supreme hitter — he could go to any part of the field with power. Even when he was going after Ruth's record and trying to pull the ball, he would fake you out by suggesting he wasn't able to get around on a pitch — and then clobber that same pitch a minute later. He also knew where to position himself in the outfield.

In 1957, the year after he won the NL batting title, he began using a 34-ounce bat instead of the 36-ounce model he'd previously used to increase his bat speed. The results: He led the league with 44 home runs, a career-high 132 RBI, batted .322, and won his only NL Most Valuable Player award.

Bob Lillis

Bob Lillis had no power and didn't get on base much, but he played ten years in the Major Leagues as a shortstop/utility infielder. Lillis spent six years as a player, five years as a scout, 11 years as a coach, and three full seasons as a successful manager for the Astros. How? By using his brain and his instincts.

He made himself a big league player by using his intellect — hitting behind the runner, bunting people over, executing the hit-and-run, and stealing signs. He didn't have the talent to achieve the big things, so he mastered the little things. Lillis and my teammates Nellie Fox, Eddie Kasko, Walt Bond, Joe Gaines, and Lee May taught me how to play winning baseball.

Frank Robinson

There's a reason why the Cleveland Indians chose Frank Robinson to be the first African-American Major League manager (he was a player-manager from 1984–1986). It wasn't just that he was one of the top 20 greatest players in MLB history. I'd played against and for him for years, and it was clear that no one knew more about every part of the game than Frank — pitching, hitting, fielding, throwing, *and game strategy*.

Robinson was the ultimate leader and competitor, both as a player and manager. He proved this after being traded at age 30 by the Reds to the Orioles. Reds' owner Bill DeWitt said Robinson was "an old 30." But in his first year in Baltimore, he won the Triple Crown and the MVP award, with a .316 batting average, 49 home runs, and 122 RBIs, while leading the team to a World Series victory over the Dodgers. He continued to pound AL pitching; the Orioles won three consecutive pennants between 1969 and 1971 and the 1970 World Series over his old club. Robinson was a 12-time All-Star and the only player to win the MVP award in both leagues.

He was the first black man to manage in both leagues — he was named AL Manager of the Year in 1989 for leading the Baltimore Orioles to an 87–75 record, and in 2002, MLB, which managed the Montreal Expos, chose him to manage the beleaguered franchise. The 2002 Expos surprised everybody, finishing second in the NL East.

Dusty Baker

Dusty Baker was an excellent player for the Dodgers, Braves, A's, and Giants; he told me he learned a lot from Aaron, who taught him how to play the game. He came up in the Dodgers' organization, which made a mastery of baseball fundamentals a mantra.

But as a manager (for the Giants, Cubs, and Reds), he has proven to be his own man. What he's really smart at is getting all his players playing hard every day. We assume all players do this, but the reality is that they don't. Players love to play for him, because they knew he'd been through the grind and pressure of a big-league season — and they know he'll give every player, including the roster's 25th man — a chance to help the team win. He also constantly gauges the temperature of his players. It's more important than ever today for a manager to have been a player — the better player you were, the more you'll get the attention of young players — many of whom have no sense of baseball history.

Nellie Fox

I grew up idolizing Nellie Fox and had the opportunity to play with him in the early years of my career. During my first year, he told me that the players who stay in the big leagues the longest do the most to help their team win. He did exactly that. Only 5-foot-9, he had minimal power but he had a keen batting eye — he was one of the toughest batters to strike out, fanning just 216 times in his career (once every 42.7 at-bats, which is third all-time).

A solid contact hitter (with a lifetime .288 batting average) he batted over .300 six times, accumulated 2,663 career hits (leading the league in that category four times), and was a 12-time All-Star when he played for the Philadelphia Athletics, White Sox, and Houston 45s/Astros. He didn't have a strong arm, but he made himself an exceptional fielding shortstop by knowing how to position himself for every batter so that he'd have time to make the play. He won the 1959 MVP award and led the White Sox to the AL pennant. He was enshrined in the Hall of Fame in 1997.

Appendix

Baseball Speak: A Glossary

● ●

*I*n this glossary, you discover the most common baseball terms (as well as a few uncommon terms here and there!) to help you in any baseball-lingo jam.

Ace: The top card in a deck, the top gun on a pitching staff. Strikeout kings and 20-game winners like Felix Hernandez, Max Scherzer, and Clayton Kershaw are all considered aces. Teams can have more than one. The 2013 Detroit Tigers' staff featured a fistful of aces: Justin Verlander, Scherzer, Anibal Sanchez, and Doug Fister.

Across the letters: Any pitch that passes the batter chest high.

Activate: To return an injured or suspended player to your team's active roster (in the Majors, a 25-man squad).

Adjudged: Any judgment call made by the umpire, such as declaring a runner out at second base on a close play.

Advance: For a runner, to move along the base paths. ("Jeter advanced from first to third on Rodríguez's single to right.") For a hitter, to move the runner at least one base. ("Cabrera's groundout to Pedroia advanced Jackson from second to third.")

Advance sale: The number of seats sold before game day.

Advance scout: A scout who follows opposing teams, trying to spot their strengths and, more importantly, their weaknesses.

Airmailed: "He airmailed it" refers to a high throw over another player or players' head(s).

Ahead in the count: If you're a pitcher, you have more strikes than balls on the hitter you're facing. If you're the hitter at the plate, the count contains more balls than strikes.

Alive: An inning that is extended by the offense after two outs. ("Base hits by Walker and Alvarez kept the inning alive.")

Alley: The section of outfield real estate between the center fielder and the left or right fielders. It is also called the *power alley* (where hits go to become doubles or triples) or the *gap*.

Alley hitter: A batter who is an expert at driving the ball into the alleys for extra base hits. Among current players, Matt Carpenter has been one of the better alley hitters.

Allow: To surrender hits or runs. ("Chad Billingsley allowed three runs on five hits in the first.")

All-Star: Any player voted by the fans or chosen by the manager to appear in an All-Star Game.

All-Star Break: A three-day hiatus in the major-league schedule; break occurs in mid-July and coincides with the All-Star Game.

All-Star Game: The annual interleague contest between players representing the American League and National League. The league that wins the game earns home field advantage in the World Series in October. Fans wishing to choose the starting lineup for both teams can vote in major-league ballparks or online at www.mlb.com.

Alphonse and Gaston act: Two fielders charging after the same ball suddenly pull up short when they each think that the other is going to make the catch. The ball drops or goes through for a base hit. They just pulled the old Alphonse and Gaston act. The name comes from two turn-of-the-19th-century cartoon characters, Alphonse and Gaston, whose deference to each other was so extreme, simple tasks like getting through a doorway took an eternity. ("After you, my dear Gaston." "No, after you my dear Alphonse." "No, I insist.")

Appeal: When a player who has been fined or is subject to some other disciplinary action asks to plead his case to the league president or commissioner's office.

Appeal play: The defensive team's attempt to reverse a safe call by contending that a runner missed a base or left a base too early on a fly ball. An appeal must be called for immediately following a disputed play and before the pitcher throws another pitch toward home plate. Major-League protocol requires the pitcher to step off the mound and throw to the base in question. The umpire at that base then rules if the runner was indeed safe or out.

Appearance: Taking part in a baseball game, either as a pitcher, fielder, or hitter.

Around the horn: A double play that goes from third base to second to first. The phrase comes from a time before the

opening of the Panama Canal when ships had to sail around South America's Cape Horn to reach the Pacific from the Atlantic.

Artificial turf: Any playing field surface that isn't made of grass.

Assist: A throw from one fielder to another that puts out the batter or a base runner.

At 'em ball: A ball that is hit directly at a fielder.

At-bat: Any time the batter gets a hit, makes an out, or reaches base on an error or fielder's choice. If the batter draws a walk, is hit by a pitch, completes a sacrifice, or reaches base on catcher's interference, he is credited with a plate appearance but not an at-bat.

Attempt: The act of trying to steal a base. ("He has 33 steals in only 40 attempts.")

Automatic out: A weak batter who has such a poor sense of the strike zone that he rarely hits or walks. Most pitchers are automatic outs when they come to the plate.

Away game: When your team plays on your opponent's home field.

Babe Ruth's curse: The jinx that supposedly haunted the Boston Red Sox, who until 2004, hadn't won a World Series since the team sold Babe Ruth to the dreaded New York Yankees in 1920.

Back through the box: A ball hit sharply through the pitcher's mound.

Backdoor slide: A difficult maneuver in which the runner reaches out to touch the base with his finger or hand as his body slides past the bag.

Backdoor slider: A slider that appears to be out of the strike zone as it approaches the batter, but then breaks over the plate.

Backstop: The screen that sits behind and extends over the home plate area. It protects fans from foul balls. Major-League backstops must stand at least 60 feet from home plate.

Backup: When one fielder runs behind another who is about to field a ball or receive a throw so he can catch the ball if it eludes the primary fielder.

Bad ball: A pitch thrown out of the strike zone, but just close enough to invite the batter to swing.

Bad bounce or bad hop: A batted ball that eludes the fielder when it takes an unexpected hop, usually because it has struck an object on the field such as a pebble.

Bad call: A call that the umpire misses.

Bad hands: An affliction attributed to poor fielders.

Bad-ball hitter: A batter who is adept at hitting pitches outside the strike zone. New York Yankee catcher Yogi Berra used to get base hits on balls thrown nearly over his head.

Bag: A term often used in place of *base*.

Bail out: What a hitter does when he falls away from a pitch that appears to be coming toward his body.

Balk: A pitcher's motion that is deemed deceptive by the umpire. Runners who are on base when a balk is called get to advance one base.

Ball: A pitch out of the strike zone that the batter doesn't swing at and the umpire does not call a strike.

Ball boy or ball girl: The person who retrieves foul balls.

Ballclub: A baseball team.

Baltimore chop: A batted ball that bounces so high it cannot be fielded before the hitter reaches first base. Wee Willie Keeler, John McGraw, and the cagey Baltimore Orioles popularized it during the 1890s.

Bandbox: A small ballpark that favors hitters.

Bang-bang play: The base runner and ball reach a base or home plate at nearly the same moment.

Barber: A pitcher who throws close to the batter's chin and "gives him a shave."

Barrel: The thickest part of a bat.

Base: The 15-inch (38-centimeter) square white marker found at three of a baseball infield's four corners. (Home plate is five-sided.) Bases are placed 90 feet (27.5 meters) apart from each other.

Base on balls: What a pitcher surrenders whenever the umpire calls four of his pitches out of the strike zone (balls) during a hitter's time at bat. The batter takes first base, the errant hurler's manager takes a Maalox, and, if the pitcher allows very many of these, he takes a trip to the showers. Also known as a *walk*.

Base runner interference: The act of a base runner deliberately preventing a fielder from completing a play by making bodily contact, deflecting the ball, or blocking the fielder's vision. If an umpire calls the play, the runner is ruled out.

Baseball: The white, red-stitched sphere that pitchers throw, fielders catch, and hitters whack during a baseball game. It is composed of a cork core under layers of rubber, yarn, and cowhide.

Baseball mud: Umpires rub this auburn mud into new baseballs to remove the sheen from the leather. Why? So that pitchers can get a better grip on the ball. Also known as rubbing mud.

Bases juiced: Bases loaded.

Basket catch: A catch made with your glove at belt level. Coaches frown on the practice, but Willie Mays won 12 consecutive Gold Gloves with his signature catch.

Bat: The sculpted, wooden implement (usually fashioned from pine or ash) that hitters use to assault a baseball.

Bat around: What a team does when its entire lineup bats during an inning.

Batboy (or girl): The players' valet during the game. The batboy (or girl) picks up the hitter's bat and helmet when the hitter's turn at bat ends. He or she also brings new balls to the umpires between innings.

Bat check: When an umpire inspects a player's bat, usually upon the request of an opposing manager, to verify that it meets Major-League specifications.

Bat speed: The time it takes a hitter to get his bat through the hitting zone.

Batter: What a player becomes when he steps into the batter's box to take his swings.

Batter's box: The rectangle, marked by chalk, on both sides of home plate. The batter must stay within that box when hitting.

Battery: A team's pitcher-catcher combination for any given game.

Batting cage: A metal cage placed behind home plate during batting practice. It protects bystanders from being hit by foul balls.

Batting eye: A player's ability to judge the strike zone. Batters who average 80 to 90 or more walks per season have excellent batting eyes.

Batting glove: Batters usually wear this soft leather glove on their bottom hand (right for left-handed hitters, left for righties), though some batters wear them on both hands. Batting gloves prevent blisters and give the hitter a better grip on the bat handle. Some fielders wear batting gloves underneath their fielding gloves to soften the impact of hard-hit balls.

Batting helmet: Hard plastic helmet that protects a hitter's cranium from errant pitches.

Batting order: The sequence in which a team's hitters appear at home plate during a game.

Bazooka: A fielder with a strong throwing arm.

Beanball: A pitch that is deliberately thrown to hit the batter.

Beat out: When a runner reaches base just ahead of a throw, as in "Ellsbury beat out that grounder to short for a base hit."

Bench: What players sit on while they are in the dugout. Players who are *benched,* or have been forced to *ride the pines,* have been indefinitely removed from a team's starting lineup.

Bench jockey: A player, usually a sub who rarely appears in games, who hurls insults from the dugout at opposing players on the field to break their concentration.

Bender: A curveball.

Bereavement list: A team can place a player whose family member or friend has died on the bereavement list and fill his roster spot with another player. The grieving player must stay on the list for at least three days and his team must reactivate him within ten days.

Big leagues: The Major Leagues.

Bird dog: A part-time baseball scout.

Black seats: Seats located behind center field that management keeps empty so batters can see the white ball better against the dark background.

Black, The: The outer edges of home plate. Balls that are *on the black* are strikes and difficult to hit squarely. Control pitchers are often said to *paint the black* with their pitches.

Bleachers: The least expensive seats in the park. Located behind the outfields of most Major-League parks.

Bleeder: A base hit — usually one that barely makes it through the infield. It can also be a weak pop fly that falls in front of an outfielder.

Block the plate: When a catcher positions his body in front of home plate to prevent a runner from scoring. The catcher must have the ball in his position when he starts the play in order for it to be legal.

Bloop: Or blooper. A weakly hit fly ball that just makes it over the infield. Also known as a *dying quail* or *Texas Leaguer.*

Blown save: Any time a pitcher enters the game with his team leading by three runs or fewer and allows the opposition to tie the score or go ahead.

Bonehead play: A mental error. A typical error by a player who rarely makes one:

Babe Ruth made the final out of the 1926 World Series when he was caught trying to steal second with the score 3–2.

Book, The: A mythical compendium of traditional baseball strategies. Managers who *go by the book* play to tie in the ninth at home, bring in left-handed relievers to get out left-handed hitters, and have their pitchers bunt with none (and often one) out and runners on base. The best managers often go against The Book.

Boot: A fielding error. Also known as a *muff.*

Bottom dropped out: A sinking pitch that dives down as it comes to the hitter.

Bottom of the inning: The second half of an inning.

Box score: The statistical record of a baseball game.

Breaking pitch: Any ball that curves.

Brushback: A pitch aimed at a batter, not to hit him (though they sometimes do, often to the pitcher's chagrin) but to move him off the plate. Also known as a *purpose pitch* or *chin music.*

Bullpen: The area where pitchers warm up before entering a game. In most stadiums, it is located behind the outfield fence. In other parks, the bullpens can be found in foul territory along the left and right field lines. The term is also used to refer to the collection of relievers on a club. ("The Cincinnati Reds have a deep bullpen.")

Bunt: An offensive weapon in which the hitter holds his bat in the hitting zone and lets the ball make contact with it. If he is bunting for a hit, the batter tries to get to first before an infielder fields the softly hit ball and throws him out. If he is bunting to move a base runner up a base, the hitter only needs to push the ball to a spot where a play at first base is the infielder's sole option.

Bush: Any amateurish action or behavior. Publicly criticizing a teammate for a failed but honest effort is considered *bush*.

Butcher: A poor fielder.

Cadillac trot (or Cadillacing): A slugger's trot around the bases after hitting a home run. From a quote by Ralph Kiner, a homer king of the late 1940s and early '50s: "Singles hitters drive jalopies, home-run hitters drive Cadillacs."

Call: The umpire's declaration of safe or out, ball or strike, fair or foul. The term also refers to the official score's ruling on a play (hit or error, wild pitch or passed ball, and so on).

Call up: Summoning a minor leaguer to the majors.

Called game: A game that has been terminated by the umpire-in-chief before its completion. Umpires usually call games due to inclement weather or curfews.

Called out looking: What is said to have happened to a batter when he takes strike three without attempting to swing at it.

Camp under: What an outfielder does when he positions himself under a fly ball.

Can of corn: An easy fly-ball out.

Career year: The best season of a player's career.

Carry a club: To be the leading force behind your team's victories over an extended period. ("Soriano's home-run splurge has carried the Yankees for the last ten days.")

Castoff: A player cut from a team.

Catch: The act of a fielder getting secure possession of the ball in his glove or hand. Whether you have secure possession is sometimes obvious, but it is often a subjective call by an umpire.

Catcher's box: The area behind home plate where the catcher must stand until the pitcher delivers the ball.

Cellar: Last place in your division or league.

Cellar dweller: The team in last place in the league.

Challenge the hitter: To throw your best pitch, usually a fastball, to the hitter, daring him to make contact.

Challenge the outfielder: To test an outfielder's throwing arm by trying to advance to the next base.

Chance: Any opportunity for a fielder to catch a ball.

Change-up: A slow-pitch thrown with the same motion as a fastball, meant to throw off a hitter's timing.

Cheat (shade): When a fielder sets up a few steps to the left or right of his normal fielding position in anticipation of where the batter is mostly likely to hit the ball.

Checked swing: A swing that is terminated before a batter *breaks his wrists* (brings his top hand over the bottom hand while taking his swing). Whether the hitter went around too far is the umpire's subjective call.

Choke hitter: A hitter who grips the bat at least an inch or two from the bottom of its handle. Using an extreme version of this grip (four inches or more) sacrifices power for contact. Rarely seen in today's game.

Choose-up sides: A method for determining the rosters for teams in an informal baseball game. Two team captains alternate picks from among the available players.

Circus catch: A spectacular, unusually acrobatic fielding play.

Cleanup hitter: The number four hitter in a lineup. He is expected to *clean* the bases by driving in runs.

Closed stance: A hitting stance in which the batter's front foot is nearer to the plate than the back one.

Closer: The relief pitcher who finishes games, usually in *save* situations. Mariano Rivera, Craig Kimbrel, and Rafael Soriano are all considered premier closers.

Clubhouse lawyer: A player who is outspoken and critical about club, league, or union policy.

Clutch: A situation when the outcome of a game or series is on the line. It often occurs in the late innings of an important ballgame.

Collar: From *horse collar* (which resembles a large 0). A batter who doesn't get a hit in a game is *wearing the collar.* Collars come in all sizes — size 3 when the batter is hitless in three at-bats, size 4 when he suffers a quartet of failures, and so on.

Comebacker: A ball hit back to the pitcher.

Conceding the run: What a team does when its manager orders his infielders to remain in their normal fielding positions with a runner on third and less than two outs, rather than move in close to home plate. This maneuver makes it easier for the runner to score on a ground ball while enhancing the defensive team's chances of turning a double play.

Corked bat: A bat with a deep hole drilled into the center of its barrel. The perpetrator (corked bats are illegal) fills the hole with cork, shredded rubber, or mercury, and then plugs it with glue and sawdust to make the bat appear normal. Bats filled with these substances propel the ball faster and farther than those made strictly from wood.

Count: The numbers of balls and strikes called on a hitter during a time at bat. The balls are always listed first. A 2–1 count means the batter has two balls and one strike.

Cousin: A pitcher who can't get a particular hitter out with any regularity.

Cup of coffee: A brief stay in the Major Leagues. A minor-league player who fills in for an injured major leaguer for a few weeks and is then sent back down has been up for *a cup of coffee.*

Curtain call: What a player takes when he comes out of the dugout to bow or wave to the crowd; it usually occurs after a player hits a home run in front of the hometown crowd.

Cutoff: When an infielder or pitcher intercepts an outfielder's throw.

Cutter: A fastball that breaks late, often to the side.

Cycle: When a hitter hits a single, double, triple, and home run in the same game. Of these four, the triple is the hardest to collect.

Dead ball: A ball that the umpire has ruled is no longer in play because play has been suspended. (A base runner is *dead* when a fielder throws him out.)

Dead from the neck up: A phrase used to describe a player who is gifted physically but is intellectually challenged.

Dead pull hitter: A right-handed hitter who always hits the ball to the left side of the field or a left-handed hitter who always hits the ball to the right side of the field.

Deep in the count: Two balls and two strikes or three balls and two strikes against a batter.

Defense: The team in the field.

Defensive indifference: An undefended stolen base. The defensive team makes no attempt to throw out the base stealer.

Defensive interference: Any act by a fielder that interferes with a batter's swinging at a pitch.

Designated for assignment: When a team designates a player for assignment, management has ten days to decide to return him to the active roster, demote him to the minors, trade him to another team, or give him his outright release. A player may only be designated for assignment when the team wants to add a player to the 40-man roster that is already full.

Designated hitter (DH): The hitter in the American League lineup who bats without having to take the field. He always bats in place of the pitcher, though the rules state he may bat in any position in the batting order.

Diamond: A baseball field (more correctly, the *infield*).

Dig out: To successfully field an inaccurate throw.

Dinger: A home run.

Disabled list: Teams can place an injured player on this list only after receiving a medical doctor's diagnosis. Players placed on the disabled list must remain inactive for 15 to 60 days. Players on the 60-day DL don't count against the 40-man roster. A team can place a player on the DL retroactive to any date after the last date he appeared in game.

Dish: Home plate.

Doctored ball: A ball that the pitcher has scuffed, scratched, or coated with an illegal substance, such as petroleum jelly or saliva. Doctored balls tend to break erratically.

Donut: Weight put on a bat for practice swings that, once removed, helps a hitter with his bat speed.

Double: A two-base hit.

Double play: A single defensive play that produces two outs; it usually occurs in the infield. In an unassisted double play, one fielder records both outs.

Double steal: Two base runners attempting to steal on the same pitch.

Double-header: Two consecutive games played between the same teams on the same day.

Down the line: A hit that closely follows the foul line.

Downtown: The place where Petula Clark hangs out and where deeply hit home runs are said to land. During the late 1960s, a San Diego Padres outfielder was known as "Downtown" Ollie Brown.

Dribbler: A slow bouncing ball in the infield.

Drilled: When a pitcher hits a batter with a pitch. Also when a batter hits a ball with great force, he is said to have "drilled" it.

Ducks on the pond: Base runners.

Earned run: Any run charged to the record of the pitcher. These runs can develop as the result of a hit, a sacrifice fly, a fielder's choice, a walk, a hit batsman, a wild pitch, or a balk. Runs that develop as the result of an error, passed ball, or catcher's interference are *unearned*. (See Chapter 16 for how to figure a pitcher's earned run average, or ERA.)

Ejection: Banishment from the field of a player, manager, or coach by an umpire.

Erased: A runner on base that gets out trying to advance. "He was erased."

Error: A defensive misplay.

Even count: One ball and one strike or two balls and two strikes against a batter.

Even stance: A hitting stance in which both of the batter's feet are equidistant from the plate.

Everyday player: A player who appears in his team's starting lineup for most of its games.

Exhibition games: Any game that does not count in the season's standings. All spring training games are exhibition games.

Expansion: Adding new franchises to a league. The first Major-League expansion in the 20th century occurred in 1961, when the Los Angeles Angels and new Washington Senators (the old Senators had moved to Minnesota) joined the American League. During the last MLB expansion in 1998, Tampa Bay joined the American League, and the Arizona Diamondbacks joined the National League.

Extra-base hit: Any base hit other than a single.

Fadeaway: The original term used for what we now call a screwball. Hall of Famer Christy Mathewson reportedly created the appellation.

Fair ball: A batted ball that: 1) Settles in fair territory between the foul lines; 2) Remains in fair territory until it passes first or third base; or 3) Stays within the foul lines while it passes over the outfield fence for a home run.

Fair territory: The part of the playing field between and including the first and third base lines, from home base to the outfield fences.

Farm system: A Major-League team's system of minor-league clubs.

Fielder's choice: When a fielder handles a ground ball and attempts to throw out a base runner other than the hitter.

Fighting off a pitch: When a hitter has (usually) two strikes on him and is trying to *stay alive* by fouling off a pitch.

Finding the handle: Getting a firm grip on the ball before throwing it.

Finesse pitcher: A hurler who gets hitters out more with guile and control than speed. Greg Maddux is arguably the greatest finesse pitcher in baseball history.

Fireballer: The opposite of a finesse pitcher, this stud overpowers hitters with a blazing fastball.

Fireman: A relief pitcher, usually one who is brought into a precarious situation. He is there to put out the fire.

First ball hitter: A batter who usually swings at the first pitch. Such hitters rarely walk and usually have low on-base percentages.

Five o'clock hitter: A low-average hitter who hits his best shots during batting practice.

Five-tool player: A player who runs the bases quickly, fields his position expertly, demonstrates a strong, accurate throwing arm, and hits for both power and average. Matt Kemp, Andrew McCutcheon, and Carlos Gonzalez are five-tool players.

Flake: Any player who behaves eccentrically.

Flare: A looping fly ball hit to the opposite field, just beyond the infield. It usually plunks in for a base hit.

Flashing the leather: A fielder who makes a spectacular, if not flamboyant, play.

Fly ball: A ball hit into the air on an arc.

Force-out: When a batted ball forces a runner to advance to another base and the fielder possessing the ball tags that base before the runner reaches it.

Forfeit: A game terminated by the umpire upon the violation of a rule, with the victory going to the offended team.

40–40 club: That group of rare players who have hit 40 home runs while stealing 40 bases in the same season. Oakland's Jose Canseco became the first 40–40 man in 1988. As of 1999, Barry Bonds, Alex Rodríguez, and Alfonso Soriano were the only other three members of this select group.

Foul pole: The yellow poles along the outfield walls that mark the end of the foul lines. They indicate whether a ball hit into the seats is foul or a home run. Balls hit to the left of the left field foul pole are foul, as are balls hit to the right of the right field pole. A ball that hits either pole is, for reasons no one understands, called fair. (That being the case, why don't they call it the fair pole?)

Foul strike: A strike charge to the batter when he hits a foul ball that is not caught with less than two strikes. After two strikes a

hitter can foul off as many balls as he wants without the umpire calling strike three.

Foul territory: The section of the playing field outside the first and third base lines.

Foul tip: A batted ball that careens sharply toward the catcher's mitt and is caught. It is a foul tip only if it is caught. Any foul tip is also a strike. The ball is in play. If the catcher catches a foul tip with two strikes on the batter, the batter has struck out. If a foul tip is not caught (in which case it remains a foul ball), the pitch is called a strike if the batter has less than two strikes. With two strikes on the batter, the count holds and the at-bat continues.

Franchise player: A star player, usually young, around whom management can build a team. Pittsburgh's Andrew McCutcheon and the Angels' Mike Trout are both franchise players. When the young Tom Seaver was leading the New York Mets out of oblivion in the 1960s, he was nicknamed "The Franchise."

Free agent: A player who is not contracted to play for any team. He is free to negotiate with any club interested in his services.

Full count: When the pitcher has three balls and two strikes on the batter.

Fungo: A long, thin bat used by a coach or player to hit grounders or flies during fielding practice. The hitter tosses the ball into the air before striking it.

Game face: A look that tells you a player is all business.

Gamer: A player who thrives in pressure situations, handles adversity well, or has a high threshold of pain. Also, the bat a hitter uses during a game. Out of every dozen bats he orders, the average major leaguer usually finds three or four gamers. He uses the other bats during batting practice or gives them away as souvenirs.

Games back: The number of games your team is out of first place.

Gap: The area between the left fielder and center fielder or the right fielder and center fielder. See *alley*.

Gap shot: An extra-base hit that lands in the gap and usually rolls or bounces to the wall. Also called a *tweener* or *gapper*.

Get a piece of the ball: When a hitter is just trying to make contact with a pitch, usually with two strikes on him.

Getaway game: The final game in a series for the visiting team.

Glove: The padded leather covering that protects a fielder's hand and makes it easier for him to catch a baseball. All fielders use gloves except the catcher and first baseman, who wear *mitts*. (The difference between a mitt and a glove? Mitts have more padding.)

Glove man: An expert fielder. Often used to describe a weak hitter whose fielding prowess keeps him in the lineup.

Go deep: To hit a home run.

Go yard: To hit a home run.

Goat: A player who makes a glaring mistake that contributes to a defeat. It's a term used almost exclusively by reporters and fans. Most professional players will tell you that no one play ever costs a team a game.

Gold Glove: The annual award given in the Major Leagues (AL and NL) to the best fielding player at each position.

Goose egg: A scoreless inning. ("Josh Beckett has put up nothing but goose eggs through seven.")

Gopher ball: A pitch that is hit for a home run.

Grand slam: A home run with the bases loaded. (*Note:* The popular phrase "grand slam home run" is a redundancy.) Also known as a *grand salami* (a term popularized by broadcaster Tim McCarver).

Green light: Not an actual sign. When a player has the green light, his manager has told him he can steal a base whenever he chooses, or he can swing away on 3–0 and 3–1 counts.

Ground ball: A batted ball that rolls or bounces on the ground. Also known as a *grounder*.

Ground-rule double: A fair ball that goes over the outfield fence on a bounce. The runners take two bases.

Guarding the lines: When an infielder positions himself close to the first- or third-base line to stop fair balls from shooting into the corners for extra-base hits.

Gun: A fielder's strong throwing arm. The term is usually applied to an outfielder, shortstop, third baseman, and catcher. ("Cardinals' catcher Yadier Molina has a gun behind home plate.")

Gun shy: Being fearful of getting hit by a pitch.

Hack: To swing at a pitch ("take a hack").

Handcuffed: What an infielder becomes when a ball is hit so hard that he can't handle it, even though it was hit right at him. Also, when a pitcher throws an inside pitch to a hitter and it causes a short, bunched-up swing.

Handle: The end of the bat gripped by the hitter. It is the thinnest part of the bat.

Hanging curve: A curveball that breaks little except a pitcher's heart. Hanging curves don't hang for very long; hitters usually quickly deposit them into the upper decks for home runs. Also *hanger,* for any pitch — curve, slider, or change-up — that doesn't drop or break as intended and stays up in the hitting zone.

Happy zone: The portion of the strike zone where a batter is most likely to hit a pitch hard, which makes it the unhappy zone if you are a pitcher.

Headhunter: A pitcher who throws at hitter's heads.

Heads-up play: A smart maneuver on the base paths or in the field.

Heat: An above-average fastball. Also known as *cheese, high cheese, smoke, gas, high heat,* and *hummer.* Dennis Eckersley used to call his fastball a *yakker.* Want to flash some retro-cool? Try on a term popularized by the Cincinnati Reds pitchers during the mid-1960s. That hard-throwing lot — they led the National League in strikeouts four times in five years — measured their fastballs by how much *hair* they had. The faster the pitcher, the more hair he had on the ball. ("Did I have much hair out there today?" "You were positively shaggy, son.")

Hill: The pitcher's mound.

Hit: A ball batted into fair territory, which allows the hitter to reach base safely without benefit of a fielding error or a fielder's choice.

Hit behind the runner: When the batter hits the ball to the right of a runner advancing to first base.

Hit by pitch: A plate appearance that results in the batter being hit by a pitch. The batter is awarded first base. It's also known as *taking one for the team.*

Hit-and-run: An offensive strategy called by a manager with a runner on first. As the pitcher winds up, the runner takes off for second base. The batter must make contact so that the runner can safely take second on an out or go for extra bases on a hit.

Hitch: The term used to describe a hitter's habit of dropping his hands just prior to swinging his bat. It disrupts the timing of most batters, though for some players a hitch is part of their timing mechanism.

Hitter's count: A ball-strike count that favors the hitter by forcing the pitcher to throw a fastball over the plate. 3–0, 3–1, and 2–0 are all considered hitter's counts.

Hold: When a relief pitcher comes in while the team has a lead, gets at least one out, and doesn't relinquish the lead, but doesn't finish the game to get a save.

Hole: In fielding, the term refers to an area deep and to the far right of the shortstop or deep and to the far left of the second baseman. In hitting, when a pitcher has a ball-strike advantage over a hitter, the batter is said to be *in a hole.* ("Cain has Kemp in an 0–2 hole.") Also, a batter who doesn't make contact often is said to have a lot of holes in his swing.

Home plate: Home plate is a 17-inch (43 centimeter) square with two of its corners removed to leave a 17-inch-long edge, two 8½-inch (21.5 centimeter) adjacent sides, and two 12-inch-long (30.5 centimeter) sides angled to a point. The result is a five-sided slab of white rubber with black borders. A runner scores by safely rounding all bases and touching home plate.

Home run: A fair fly ball that travels over the outfield fence. An inside-the-park home run doesn't leave the playing field; it is a fair ball that eludes fielders for so long that the hitter is able to circle the bases before a play can be made on him. Other terms for the home run include *homer, dinger, jack,* *going yard, dial 8, long-ball, round-tripper, 'tater, four-bagger, going downtown,* and *clout.*

Home team: The host team in a baseball game. Mutual agreement determines who will be the home team when a game is played on neutral ground.

Homestretch: The final month of a season.

Hot corner: Third base.

Hot dog: A player who shows off. (For example, a hitter who stands at home plate admiring his own home run.) Players who field their positions with flamboyance are often said to be *hot-dogging* or *cutting the pie.*

Human rain delay: A hitter who takes a long time settling in the batter's box.

Ice cream cone: A ball caught in the top of a glove's webbing so that the top half is visible.

In his kitchen: A pitch that jams a hitter on the bat handle. Yankee outfielder Lou Piniella once hit such an offering from Red Sox left-hander Bill Lee for a game-winning double. Afterwards Piniella told Lee, "Bill, you can come into my kitchen, but don't sit down to eat."

In the dirt: A pitch that bounced before it got to the catcher.

Incentive clause: A clause in a player's contract that awards him for achieving certain goals.

Incomplete game: Any game that ends before the visiting team finishes batting in the fifth inning.

Indifference: Allowing an opposing base runner to advance a base without attempting to stop him.

Infield fly rule: With less than two outs, a fair fly ball (that is neither a line drive nor an attempted bunt) that can be caught with ordinary effort by one of the infielders when first base and second base are occupied by runners (or when runners are on all the bases). The umpires call this rule. The batter is automatically out even if the fielder misses the ball. (This rule is designed to keep infielders from missing fly balls on purpose to make an unfair double play; with less than two outs, runners don't try to advance if they think a ball is going to be caught!)

Inning: A unit of a baseball game consisting of a turn at-bat and three outs for each team. Regulation games consist of nine innings. A game can have fewer innings if the umpire calls (cancels) the game (due to inclement weather or some other circumstance) or can have more innings if the game is tied after the regulation nine innings.

Inside baseball: Strategy such as the hit-and-run, stealing, bunting for base hits, squeeze plays, sacrifices, hitting the cutoff man, and defensive positioning. All involve a degree of savvy and teamwork. Also known as *small ball.*

Inside-the-park home run: A home run that does not leave the playing field. To achieve it, a batter must race around all four bases before the fielder's throw beats him to home plate. During the last game of the 1999 season, Tampa Bay's Randy Winn smacked a genuine rarity against the New York Yankees: an inside-the-park grand slam.

Insurance runs: Any runs scored in the late innings by the team that is already ahead.

Interference: A situation in which a person illegally changes the course of play from what is expected. Interference might be committed by players on the offense (preventing a defender from reaching a ball), on defense (preventing a runner from advancing), players not currently in the game, catchers, umpires, or spectators.

Jamming: When a pitcher throws the ball inside and near the batter's hands, he is *jamming* the batter.

Journeyman: A serviceable player, rarely a star, who bounces around from club to club. The prototypical journeyman: right-handed pitcher Robert Miller, who was traded or sold 12 times to ten different teams.

Juggle: To mishandle a throw or a fielding chance.

Junk: Off-speed pitches such as the change-up, the slow curve, the palmball, and the knuckle ball. Relief pitcher Stu Miller was a renowned junkballer during the 1960s. He was said to throw at three speeds: slow, slower, and slowest.

K: Another term for a *strikeout*.

Keystone: Second base. A team's short-stop and second baseman are known as the *keystone combination* for their double-play collaboration.

Knock: A base hit. ("Robinson Cano had five knocks today.")

Laugher: A lopsided victory, as in "The Braves won an 11–1 laugher." Also known as a *blowout*.

Launching pad: A ballpark where home runs are plentiful. Modern players consider Colorado's Coors Field the ultimate launching pad.

Lead: The distance between a runner and a base.

Leadoff hitter: The hitter who bats first in the batting order.

Left-handed specialist: A relief pitcher who is usually brought in solely to get out one to three tough left-handed hitters. A variation is LOOGY (a left-handed, one-out specialist).

Leg hit: What a hitter earns when he gets a single on a batted ball that doesn't travel beyond the infield. Also, an *infield hit*.

Let the ball play him: Said of a fielder who waits for a batted ball to reach him rather than aggressively charging it.

Line drive: A ball that is hit, usually hard, on a straight line. Also known as a *bullet* or *frozen rope*.

Lineup: The nine players (or ten if you are using a designated hitter) who start a game.

Live arm: A pitcher who throws with excellent velocity.

Live ball: A ball that is in play.

Long reliever: A relief pitcher who enters in the early innings after a starter has been bombed or injured. Also known as the *long man,* he usually pitches three innings or more.

Looper: A fly ball that carries just over the infield for a base hit.

Lord Charles: Uncle Charlie has long been a nickname for the curveball. Lord Charles is the *curveball maximus*. It doesn't merely break; it dives and is as fast as most pitchers' sliders. The phrase was first used during the early 1980s to describe New York Mets pitching ace Doc Gooden's phenomenal curveball.

Loud foul: A ball that is hit hard and far, but foul.

Lumber: A baseball bat.

Magic number: You hear this term mentioned frequently as the season winds down. The number represents any combination of wins and losses by the first- and second-place teams (fighting either for the division lead or a Wild Card berth) that clinches the top spot in the standings for the first-place club. For example, the Atlanta Braves lead the National League East with a record of 100–60; the Florida Marlins are in second at 99–61. With only two games left in the 162-game season, Florida can't possibly win more than 101 games. Therefore, the magic number for the Braves is two; if Atlanta wins both of its remaining games, it will have 102 wins, a total Florida can't reach. Atlanta can also clinch by winning one game while Florida loses once because the Braves would have 101 victories while the Marlins could not win more than 100.

Make-up call: When an umpire makes a bad call, realizes it later, and issues a make-up call on a borderline play to make it up to a team. Umpires will never admit to doing so.

Make-up game: A game that has been rescheduled due to inclement weather or some other postponement.

Men in blue: Umpires.

Mendoza line: A batting average in the vicinity of .200. Kansas City Royals third baseman George Brett is said to have coined the term in "honor" of Mario Mendoza, a light-hitting shortstop with the Seattle Mariners who compiled a career batting average of .215.

Mental error: A mistake made by a distracted player, such as forgetting the number of outs.

Middle reliever: A relief pitcher who enters (usually) in the fifth or sixth inning of a close game.

Money player: A player who performs his best in critical games.

Mop-up man: You don't want to see him pitching too often for your favorite team. Mop-up men pitch when their team is losing by a lopsided score.

Mr. October: A player who excels during postseason play. The nickname was first hung on Yankee right fielder Reggie Jackson after he clouted three successive home runs in the final game of the 1977 World Series. Additional playoff rounds added to the contemporary game may stretch the season into November. Yankees' shortstop Derek Jeter is known as *Mr. November* for his clutch performance in that month.

Must-win: A game a team must win to stay alive in the pennant race or postseason play.

Nab: To throw out a runner, usually on a close play.

National pastime: Another name for the sport of baseball.

Nightcap: The second game of a doubleheader.

No man's land: An area on the base paths so far from any base that the runner is usually tagged out when he hazards into it.

No-hitter: A nine-inning complete game in which a pitcher does not allow a hit to the opposing team. The opposition can have base runners through fielding errors or walks. See *perfect game.*

Nonroster invitee: A player who is invited to spring training by a team, without any guarantee of a roster spot.

No-pitch: The umpire's call whenever he rules that a pitch is neither a ball nor a strike, usually because the pitcher released the ball after the umpire called timeout.

Obstruction: A call made by the umpire when a fielder, who neither possesses the ball nor is about to field the ball, impedes the progress of the runner.

Offensive interference: Any act by the offensive team that interferes with or confuses a fielder attempting to make a play, such as if a base runner deliberately runs into the second baseman while he is fielding a ground ball.

Oh-fer: What a batter takes when he fails to hit in a game or series. ("Jones took an oh-fer last night when he went 0-for-five.")

On-deck circle: The circle between the dugout and home plate where a player awaits his turn at-bat.

Open stance: A hitting stance in which the front foot is farther away from the plate than the back foot.

Opposite field: The side of the field that is opposite the batter's hitting side. For example, left field is the opposite field for a left-handed hitter like Joey Votto, who bats from the right side of home plate.

Out: One of the three required retirements of an offensive team during its half-inning turn at bat.

Out pitch: A pitcher's best pitch; the one he is most likely to throw to get an out or finish off a hitter.

Outright: To sever a player from a team's Major-League roster, either by sending him to the minors or releasing him.

Overslide: The act of a base runner sliding past and losing contact with a base.

Passed ball: Any ball that eludes a catcher, which, in the official scorer's opinion, he should have controlled with ordinary effort.

Payoff pitch: A pitch thrown on a full count (three balls, two strikes).

Peg: A fielder's throw.

Pennant: The flag awarded to the champion of each league.

Pepper: A fast-moving (soft) hitting and fielding game designed to improve a player's reflexes. The fielder and hitter stand 20 feet apart. The hitter hits the ball to the fielder, who catches it and immediately pitches it back. The hitter hits that offering, and play continues.

Perfect game: A complete game in which the pitcher does not hit any batter with the ball and does not allow any hits, walks, or errors.

Phantom double play: A double play called by the umpire, even though the second baseman or shortstop did not step on second base for the force-out.

Phenom: An ultra-talented rookie. In 2013, Miami Marlins' pitcher Jose Fernandez was a National League phenom. Also spelled *pheenom*.

Pick it: To catch a ball. Players who can really pick it are good fielders.

Pickoff: A throw by a pitcher or catcher to nab a runner off base.

Pinch hitter: A hitter who substitutes for a teammate in the batting order. Managers often ask this hitter to come through in a pinch (a crucial situation).

Pinch runner: A runner who substitutes for a teammate on the bases.

Pine tar: A dark, viscous substance spread on the bat handle so that a hitter can get a better grip.

Pitch around: Refusing to throw a pitch into the strike zone of a dangerous hitter so the pitcher can then face a less-threatening batter.

Pitcher of record: A game's winning or losing pitcher. You must throw at least five innings in a game to qualify for a win.

Pitcher's duel: A low-scoring game usually decided in the late innings.

Pitching rotation: The order in which a team's starting pitchers start games. Most modern teams employ five-man rotations, allowing each starter at least four day's rest in between starts.

Pitchout: When a pitcher intentionally throws the ball outside the strike zone so that his catcher has a better chance to catch a base runner trying to steal.

Plate appearance: Any trip to the plate by a hitter. Plate appearances include at-bats, walks, sacrifices, interference calls, and hit-by-pitches.

Platoon: A system in which players are alternated at a position, usually based on what side of the plate batters swing from. Left-handed platoon hitters generally start against right-handers; their right-handed counterparts usually take the field against lefties.

"Play!" or "Play Ball!": The umpire's order to start the game or to resume play following a dead ball.

Play-by-play: Any verbal or written account of every play that occurs in a given game. Also, a broadcaster's verbal description of a ballgame broadcast on TV or radio.

Player to be named later: The term applied to any player ineligible to be traded at the time a trade is consummated, such as a player who is on the

disabled list or a recently drafted player who cannot be swapped until a year after his signing. The term is also used when a team submits a list of players for its trading partner to choose from at some future date. In 1984, the St. Louis Cardinals traded shortstop Jose Gonzalez to the San Francisco Giants. Upon joining his new team, Gonzalez legally changed his surname to Uribe, inspiring baseball curmudgeon Don Zimmer to quip, "I guess he really is the player to be named later."

Player-manager: A player who also acts as his team's manager. No one has held that title in the Major Leagues since the Cincinnati Reds' Pete Rose in 1986.

Pop fly: A high but weakly hit fly ball that rarely goes beyond the infield.

Portsider: A left-handed pitcher.

Productive out: Some define this as any out that advances a runner, or even better, scores a run. Others believe a batter can make a productive out only when his team is behind by a run, tied, or in the lead. But a third school of thought holds that the term "productive out" is a misnomer because any out that does not result in a run reduces your team's chances of scoring. Outs that move base runners along without scoring are merely less damaging than outs that do not advance runners.

Protest: Managers play games *under protest* when they believe an umpire has made a call that contradicts the rulebook. No one can protest an umpire's judgment call. Managers must announce their protests to the umpire immediately following the disputed action, before the next play begins. The Commissioner's Office is the arbiter of all protests. Protests are rarely allowed.

Pull: To hit the ball early enough so that the bat meets the ball in front of the hitter. Right-handed hitters pull the ball to the left side; left-handers pull to the right. Pull hitters usually hit for power.

Pull the string: To throw an off-speed pitch.

Punch-and-Judy hitter: A batter who sprays softly batted hits to all fields; also known as a *spray hitter*.

Punchout: A strikeout. Also called a *whiff* or a *K*.

Purpose pitch: A pitch thrown close to the batter with the purpose of moving him off home plate.

Putout: A fielder is credited with a putout when he possesses the ball that retires a runner or hitter.

Quality start: Any game in which the starting pitcher works six or more innings while allowing three or fewer runs.

Question mark: A player whose status with a team is uncertain because of injury, a recent poor season, or a general decline in skills.

Quick pitch (or quick return): A pitch made before the batter is set. An umpire must judge whether the batter was set. A quick pitch is illegal. If the umpire rules that the pitcher threw the ball before the hitter was set in the batter's box, he can declare the pitch a ball (if no runners are on base) or a balk (if a runner is on base).

Radar gun: A device used by baseball scouts to measure the speed of pitches, the most famous of which is known as the *JUGS gun*. Scouts refer to these guns as either fast or slow, depending on their make and how they record ball speed. Some radar guns measure the speed at which the pitcher releases the ball; others measure its speed when it crosses home plate.

Rain check: The detachable portion of a ticket that guarantees you admission to another game in case the contest you're attending is rained out or postponed.

Regular season: In the Major Leagues, the 162-game season that determines each division's final standings and playoff participants. One playoff game that decide the winner of a division or Wild Card lead between two or more teams tied for the same are considered part of the regular season.

Regulation game: A baseball game that is played to its completion.

Release: A pink slip. What a player reluctantly obtains when he is permanently cut from a team's roster.

Release point: The point at which the ball leaves a pitcher's hand. Good pitchers consistently release the ball from the same point.

Relief pitcher (reliever): Any pitcher who enters a game after the *starter* (the starting pitcher) has been removed.

Retired number: A uniform number worn by some baseball immortal that is no longer available to current players. A team or the entire league can retire a number. All Major-League teams have retired number 42, Jackie Robinson's number.

Retiring the side in order: When a pitcher retires three batters in an inning without surrendering a base runner.

Retouch: The act of a runner returning to a base.

Rifle: A powerful throwing arm.

Rookie: A first-year player. For the purpose of picking its Rookie of the Year award winner, the Baseball Writers Association of America has deemed that a player will retain his rookie status as long as he has not pitched 50 innings or accumulated 130 at-bats or 45 days of service time (excluding September call-ups) before a particular season.

Rosin bag: A cloth bag containing a powder called rosin. Kept at the side of the mound, it is used by pitchers to dry their fingers to improve their grip on the ball. Applying rosin directly to the ball is illegal.

Rubber: A 6-x-24-inch (15.5-x-61-centimeter) rubber slab on top of the pitcher's mound.

Rubber game: The third game of a three-game series in which the opposing teams have split the first two contests.

Rule 5 draft: Any player is eligible for the Rule 5 draft provided his team does not carry him on its 40-man roster and 1) He was 18 or younger when he signed his first pro contract and three Rule 5 drafts have occurred since his signing; or 2) He was at least 19 when he signed his first pro contract and two Rule 5 drafts have occurred since that signing. When a team drafts a Rule 5 player, it must keep him on its 25-man roster or the disabled list for the entire following season or offer him back to his original team.

Run: A scoring unit posted by an offensive player who touches first, second, third, and home plate in that order.

Run Batted In (RBI): A batter is credited with a run batted in when he drives a runner home (helps him score a run) via a hit, a sacrifice bunt or fly, a walk, a hit batsman, a fielder's choice, or on an error if the official scorer rules the run would have scored had the error not been made. (For example, a runner scores from third with less than two out on a long, catchable fly ball that is dropped by the center fielder. The center fielder is charged with the error. However, the official scorer

credits the batter with a run batted in after deciding that the runner would have scored on a sacrifice fly had the ball been caught. Had the ball been hit to shallow center, and the scorer ruled it was not hit far enough to score the runner without the error, the batter would not receive an RBI.) You also credit a batter with an RBI if he drives himself in with a home run. Batters do not get ribbies when they drive runners in while grounding into double plays.

Rundown: Members of the defense chase a runner back and forth on the base paths in an attempt to put out the runner.

Runner: An offensive player who is advancing toward, returning to, or occupying a base.

Sacrifice bunt: When the hitter willingly bunts into an out in order to advance a base runner. Also known as "giving yourself up."

Sacrifice fly: A ball hit deep enough to score a runner from third base with less than two outs.

Save: The statistical credit awarded to a relief pitcher who finishes a game on the victorious side but does not get the win. (To discover how saves are calculated, see Chapter 16.)

Scatter arm: A pitcher or fielder who throws wildly.

Scorecard: The graph that allows you to track every play in a game, inning by inning.

Scoring position: A runner on second or third base, where he can score on almost any hit to the outfield. (Sluggers like Chris Davis, Miguel Cabrera, and Pedro Alvarez seem to be in scoring position the minute they step in the batter's box.)

Scout: The person who evaluates talent for a professional baseball organization.

Most scouts scour high schools, colleges, and minor leagues for players. *Advance scouts* monitor other major-league clubs to pinpoint opposing players' strengths and weaknesses.

Scratch run: A run produced by a sacrifice grounder, an infield hit, or ground-ball out.

Season tickets: Tickets for an entire season of home games.

Seeing-eye grounder: A ground ball that barely eludes an infielder for a base hit.

Set position: The position the pitcher takes on the pitching rubber just before going into the windup.

Set the table: To get on base for the power hitters in your team's lineup.

Set-up man: A relief pitcher who usually arrives in the seventh or eighth inning, preferably when his team is winning. He sets up the ninth inning for the closer.

Seventh-inning stretch: A brief pause in the action between the top and bottom of the seventh inning. It allows time for fans to stand and stretch their legs. One story, perhaps apocryphal, claims that the practice began in 1910 when President William H. Taft stood up to stretch in the seventh inning of a Pittsburgh Pirates game. The rest of the crowd stood up with the president out of respect. However, research has uncovered numerous earlier references to the ritual.

Shoestring catch: A running catch made at the top of a fielder's shoes.

Show, The: The Major Leagues. A term popularized in the film *Bull Durham,* starring Kevin Costner.

Shutout: A pitcher's complete game victory in which the opposition doesn't score.

Signs: Managers, coaches, and players use these coded signals to pass information to each other during a game. The term is also used to describe the hand signals catchers use to call pitches.

Single: A one-base hit. Also known as a *knock.*

Slugfest: A high-scoring game.

Slugger: A hitter who is usually among the home-run leaders. Babe Ruth, who led the American League in home runs 12 times, was the quintessential slugger.

Solo homer: A home run with the bases empty.

Southpaw: A left-handed pitcher.

Spectator interference: What an umpire should call when a fan reaches out of the stands or enters the playing field and touches a ball that's still in play.

Split-fingered fastball: A pitch thrown by placing the ball between the first two fingers. When thrown by a master such as Isashi Iwakuma, the pitch approaches home plate on a high plane and then dives precipitously.

Squeeze play: When a hitter attempts to score a runner from third with a bunt. If the runner leaves third before the hitter makes contact with the ball, it is called a *suicide squeeze;* if the hitter misses the pitch, the runner is dead. In the *safety squeeze,* the runner waits for the hitter to make contact before racing toward home.

Stay alive: For a hitter, it means to keep an at-bat going by fouling off tough pitches. For a team, it means to keep from being eliminated in a pennant race or postseason series.

Starting rotation: A team's group of regular starting pitchers who pitch in sequence.

Strawberry: A pinkish abrasion on the hip or leg, usually caused by sliding.

Stretch drive: The final lap of a horse race, or the final weeks of a season when teams are driving toward the pennant.

Strike: What occurs when a) a batter swings and misses the ball; b) the batter hits a foul ball (unless he already has two strikes on him); c) the ball crosses the plate in the strike zone and the batter doesn't swing; or d) the players' union and the major-league baseball owners can't reach an agreement and the players refuse to come to work or the owners lock them out.

Strike zone: The area a ball must pass through to be called a strike by an umpire. According to the rules, this zone is the width of home plate and extends from the bottom of the kneecap to the uniform letters across a player's chest. In practice, it varies, sometimes widely, from umpire to umpire.

Strikeout: An out made by a batter who accumulates three strikes during an at-bat. Also known as a *K* or a *whiff.*

Striking out the side: Perhaps the most misused phrase in baseball. To strike out the side, a pitcher must strike out every batter he faces in an inning rather than merely strike out three batters in an inning. If the pitcher allows a base runner of any kind during the inning, the phrase does not apply.

Suspended game: A game that is called but is scheduled to be completed at some future date.

Sweet spot: The best part of the bat to hit the ball. The sweet spot is a few inches from the end of the barrel.

Switch-hitter: A batter who hits from both sides of the plate.

Tag: The act by which a fielder retires a base runner. The fielder either touches a base with his body or the ball before the runner arrives, or the fielder touches the runner with the ball (which can be in the fielder's glove or hand) before the runner reaches the bag.

Take: To let a pitch go by without swinging.

Tape-measure home run: A long home run, usually one that travels 450 feet or more. Pedro Alvarez and Miguel Cabrera regularly hit tape-measure shots. The term was first applied to the long home runs hit by Mickey Mantle in the 1950s.

Ten-and-five rule: Any player who has ten years of major-league service time and has spent the previous five years with the same team has the right to veto any trade. Teams will often try to trade players before they achieve this status.

Time: The umpire's declaration that interrupts play. The ball is dead.

Tools of ignorance: The catcher's equipment. The term implies that one has to be lacking intelligence to want to wear them. Actually, the converse is true. A good catcher is usually one of the smartest people on a team.

Trade: An exchange of players between two or more teams.

Trading deadline: Major-League baseball imposes two trading deadlines during the regular season. July 31 is the last day teams can transact a talent swap without passing the players through waivers. The second deadline occurs at midnight on August 31 when teams must set their postseason rosters. Any players acquired after that date are ineligible for postseason play.

Triple: A three-base hit.

Triple play: Any defensive play that produces three outs on the same batted ball. In an *unassisted triple play,* one fielder records all three outs.

Triple-double: When a player attains at least ten doubles, triples, and home runs in the same season.

Twin killing: A double play.

Umpire: The on-field baseball official who declares whether a batter is safe or out, a pitch is a ball or a strike, or a batted ball is foul or fair. He also interprets the rulebook on all plays.

Umpire's interference: An act by the umpire that obstructs a catcher as he's attempting to throw out a base stealer. This call is also made when a fair ball strikes an umpire in fair territory before passing a fielder. The ball is dead.

Uniforms: What players wear on the field.

Utility player: A player, usually a substitute, who has the versatility to play more than one position. Though it rarely happens, utility players can get enough plate appearances at their various positions to qualify as regulars. Billy Goodman started at six different positions for the 1950 Boston Red Sox and won an American League batting title.

Walk: When a hitter receives four balls during a plate appearance, he is entitled to take first base. All other base runners advance if the walk forces them in. See *base on balls.*

Walk-off homer: A home run that ends the ballgame; it can only be hit by a home team player. In May 2003, Chicago Cubs shortstop Alex Gonzalez accomplished a rare feat by hitting two tenth-inning walk-off homers within six days of each other.

Warning track: A dirt path in front of the outfield fences, which warns the outfielders of their proximity to the walls.

Waste pitch: A pitch deliberately thrown outside the strike zone in the hope that the batter will chase it. Pitchers usually throw them if they are ahead of the batter in the count (on 0–2 or 1–2 counts). This pitch really is a waste if you throw it to a *bad-ball hitter* who hammers it for extra bases.

Wheelhouse: A hitter's power zone — an area that is usually waist-high and over the heart of home plate.

Wheels: A player's legs.

Whiff: A strikeout.

Whitewash: A shutout.

Wild pitch: A pitched ball that is thrown so far from the target that it gets past the catcher. If the official scorer decides the catcher should have caught the pitch, he can rule it a *passed ball.* Wild pitches and passed balls are charged only when they advance a base runner or allow a batter to reach base safely on a third strike.

Winter league: A baseball league that plays during the winter months. Most winter leagues are based in Florida, Arizona, or Latin America. Many Latin American big leaguers play winter ball for their hometown teams as a matter of local pride. American major leaguers usually play in these leagues to sharpen their skills after an injury-plagued season or to learn a new position.

Worm-burner (worm-killer): A ground ball that rolls over the infield without taking a bounce.

Index

batter's box
  accelerating out of, 84–85
  defined, 330
  overview, 51–53
battery, 330
batting. *See also* hitting
  abilities needed for, 46–47
  batter's box, 51–53
  body positioning, 55–56
  fair and foul balls, 33
  getting on base, 34
  gloves for, 25, 330
  helmet for, 330
  holding bat, 47–49
  judging pitches, 60
  outs, 32–33
  overview, 32, 45–46
  stance for, 53–54
  stride, 56–59
  strike zone, 59
batting around, 330
batting average, 242
batting cages
  defined, 330
  purchasing, 28
batting eye, 17, 74, 330
batting order, 11, 330
batting tees, 75, 196
Bauman, Joe, 213
bazooka, 330
BBCOR (Ball Coefficient of Restitution), 20
beanballs, 330
Beane, Billy, 232
beating out, 330
Beckett Marketplace website, 295
behind in the count, defined, 184
beisu boru, 214
Beltre, Adrian, 114
Bench, Johnny, 99–100, 145–146, 321
bench attitude, 225–226
bench jockeys, 330
benched, defined, 330
benders, 330
bent-leg slide, 93–94
bereavement list, 331

BESR (Ball Exit Speed Ratio), 20
Big A Stadium, 275–276
big leagues, defined, 331
The Bill James Handbook, 291
bird dogs, 203, 331
the black, defined, 331
black seats, 331
Bleacher Report website, 291
bleachers, 258, 331
bleeders, 331
blocking the plate, 154–156, 331
bloops (bloopers), 331
blown saves, 331
blowouts (laughers), 340
Blue, Vida, 318
boa constrictor handle, 18
bobbing head, 77
Boehler, Joe, 213
Bonds, Barry, 285–286
bonehead plays, 120, 331
boning bats, 21
bonus pool, 202–203
bonus rule, 200
the book, 236, 331
boots (muffs), 331
Boston Red Sox, 273–274
bottom dropped out, defined, 331
bottom of the inning, defined, 331
box scores, 331
breaking pitches, 331
Brett Brothers Bats company, 18
Brock, Lou, 93
brushbacks, 331
bullpen
  defined, 123, 331
  warming up in, 40
bunting
  catching bunts, 156–157, 163–164
  defined, 331–332
  overview, 67–72
Burleson, Rick, 119
Busch Stadium, 271, 279
bush, defined, 332
butchers, 332

• E •

earflaps, 25

earned run average (ERA), 245–246, 264, 302

earned runs, 335

Eckhardt, Ox, 213

economics, in fantasy baseball, 308

Eight Men Out (Asinof), 252

ejection, 335

Enatsu, Yutaka, 216

ERA (earned run average), 245–246, 264, 302

erased, defined, 335

errors

  abbreviation for, 262

  avoiding, 120

  defined, 34, 335

  overview, 119

  short-legging, 119

Espino, Hector, 213

ESPN, The Magazine, 300

ESPN network, 298

ESPN website, 295

ESPN's Classic Sports Network, 299

even count, 335

even stance, 53–54, 335

everyday players, 335

exhibition games, 252, 335

expansion, 335

The Exploratorium website, 295

extra innings, 9

extra-base hits, 73, 335

• F •

fadeaways, 335

fair balls, 33, 237, 335

fair territory, 11, 335

fake steals, 103–105

faking bunts, 72

Fall Classic, 251

Fangraphs website, 244, 291

fantasy baseball

  administrative tasks, 306

  being successful in, 307–308

  drafting team, 304

  economics in, 308

  filling out roster, 304–305

  managing team, 305–306

  overview, 301–303

  starting league, 303

  totaling scores, 306–307

  Walks + Hits per Innings Pitched, 302

farm system, 335

Fenway Park, 273–274, 280

field

  equipment for, 28–29

  overview, 10–11

fielded, defined, 11

fielders, 12

fielder's choice

  abbreviation for, 262

  defined, 335

fielding

  average of, 247

  cutoff throws, 164–165

  fly balls, 122

  grounders, 120–121

  line drives, 122

  pop-ups, 156

  when pitching, 140

Fields, Steven, 213

fighting off a pitch, defined, 335

finding the handle, defined, 335

finesse pitchers, 335

fireballers, 335

firemen, 335

first–ball hitters, 335

first–base position (1B)

  abbreviation for, 9

  bunts, 163–164

  catching throws, 162

  covered by pitcher, 165

  covered from second base, 171

  double plays, 165–166

  fielding cutoff throws, 164–165

  gloves for, 111

  holding runners on, 162–163

  leading off of, 85–87

  number assigned to, 261

  overview, 112, 159–160

  setting target, 161–162

  stance for, 160–161

• S •

About the Authors

Joe Morgan, one of six children born to Leonard and Ollie Morgan, moved from Bonham, Texas, to Oakland at the age of 10 in 1954. His principal residence has been in the East Bay Area since that time. Joe was an active participant in sports and social programs at the Brookfield Community Center. He continued his education in the Peralta College District, attending Merritt College from 1961 to 1963 and graduating with honors and an AA degree. He also attended California State University at Hayward, earning a bachelor's of science in Physical Education. Both scholastic and athletic honors were accorded him. Entering the ranks of professional baseball in 1963, Joe signed with the Houston Colt 45s. He participated with their farm club for approximately two seasons and became a regular player for the Astros in 1964. He was named Rookie of the Year in 1965 by both the National League and the *Sporting News,* and his exceptional performance continued with the Astros until 1972 when he was traded to the Cincinnati Reds. He continued to be a dominant factor in the ranks of professional baseball throughout his career. Honors accorded him during this period are numerous. These honors include Most Valuable Player in the 1972 All-Star Game; Most Valuable Player in the National League in 1975 and 1976; the Commissioner's Award in 1976 for most votes by the fans for the All-Star Game; and the Comeback Player of the Year award in 1982. Before ending his career in 1984, Joe established a new career home-run record for a second baseman; played in a record 92 consecutive games without an error (by a second baseman); played in four World Series, winning two championships; played in seven League Championship Series; and established an All-Star record by playing in seven consecutive games with a hit. In addition, he won five Gold Glove Awards, played in ten All-Star Games, and recorded 692 stolen bases. These honors are clearly indicative of his great abilities. He was elected to the National Baseball Hall of Fame in 1990 on the first ballot, and was named to Baseball's All-Century Team. The Cincinnati Reds unveiled a statue of him in front of their stadium, the Great American Ballpark, on September 7, 2013.

Richard Lally's articles and columns on baseball, business, film, and the arts have appeared in publications throughout the world. He has served as the author, collaborator, or ghostwriter for 19 books, including *The Wrong Stuff* and its sequel, *Have Glove, Will Travel,* a pair of baseball autobiographies written with legendary major league pitcher Bill Lee. In 2002, Princeton University named his book, *Bombers: An Oral History of the New York Yankees,* to its prestigious Dixon Collection, a compilation of books. He currently works as the Content Curator for Demand Media.

Dedication

I dedicate this fourth edition to my father, Leonard, who passed away on May 18, 2004. My dad taught me everything I know about baseball. He always stressed that I should devote myself to excelling in all facets of the sport, rather than trying to be the best in only one or two departments. One of his proudest moments came when I was voted the most complete player in the game. I couldn't have won that award without his guidance.

— Joe Morgan

Author's Acknowledgments

Joe Morgan: I want to thank my parents Ollie and Leonard Morgan for molding me into the person I am today. Without their love and guidance I wouldn't have been able to reach the goals we set for me both on and off the field. My family and my friends are the most important people in my life, and I thank them for celebrating my life with me. Thanks to the rest of the GREAT 8: Pete Rose, Tony Perez, Johnny Bench, George Foster, Ken Griffey, Dave Concepcion, and Cesar Geronimo. A shout out to the pitchers who were a part of the Big Red Machine. And to Theresa, Lisa, Angela, Ashley, and Kelly: I love you.

Richard Lally: We did not have a staff of researchers, but whenever data proved elusive, I was always able to turn to one of my gang of Usual Suspects: Billy Altman, the late Bill Shannon, Jordan Sprechman, Bill Daughtry, Rob Neyer, and John Collett (Our Man in the Ballparks). Willie Mays, Bob Gibson, Rusty Staub, Bill Lee, Sparky Anderson, Johnny Bench, Willie McCovey, Barry Larkin, Ken Griffey, Sr., Derek Jeter, Keith Hernandez, and Harry Wendelstedt, our "all-star" team of advisors, could not have been more generous with their time and insights. I'd also like to thank Chad Sievers, the editor of this edition.

Every writer should be blessed with the friends and relatives who have encouraged me, many of them from the first time I picked up a pen. I thank and love them all: My partner-in-crime, Marie Bresnahan, whose heart is as warm as her laughter; my brothers Joseph and Sean; my late parents Richard and Anne, who instilled in me my love for baseball; the late Brother Leo Richard, who taught me to dream in wide-screen Technicolor; my Aunt Kathy, who inexplicably keeps getting younger;

the Bresnahan clan: Joan-Marie, Danny, Joann, Haley, Luke, Shane, and Talia; Eve Lederman, a fine writer and the second best second baseman I know; my pal for life Al Lombardo and his wife Cathy; my buddy Charlie Ludlow ("Stay in the boat, young captain!") and his wife, Gabby; Joyce Altman (who doesn't seem to mind when her husband Billy and I spend hours on the phone talking about this great game); Richard and Jessie Erlanger; and my second family in Sweden, the fabulous Budnys: Alecks, Michaela, Rasmus, Paulina, and Mathilda. I love you all.

Publisher's Acknowledgments

Acquisitions Editor: Lindsay Lefevere
(Previous Edition: Kathy Cox)
Project Editor: Chad R. Sievers
(Previous Edition: Natalie Harris)
Copy Editor: Chad R. Sievers
(Previous Edition: Elizabeth Rea)

Technical Editor: John Froedge
Art Coordinator: Alicia B. South
Project Coordinator: Phil Midkiff
Cover Photos: ©Tetra Images/Getty Images
Special Help: Jim Gerard

pple & Mac

Pad For Dummies,
th Edition
978-1-118-49823-1

Phone 5 For Dummies,
th Edition
978-1-118-35201-4

MacBook For Dummies,
th Edition
978-1-118-20920-2

S X Mountain Lion
or Dummies
978-1-118-39418-2

Blogging & Social Media

Facebook For Dummies,
th Edition
978-1-118-09562-1

om Blogging
or Dummies
978-1-118-03843-7

Pinterest For Dummies
978-1-118-32800-2

WordPress For Dummies,
h Edition
978-1-118-38318-6

Business

Commodities For Dummies,
nd Edition
978-1-118-01687-9

Investing For Dummies,
h Edition
978-0-470-90545-6

Personal Finance
For Dummies,
7th Edition
978-1-118-11785-9

QuickBooks 2013
For Dummies
978-1-118-35641-8

Small Business Marketing Kit
For Dummies,
3rd Edition
978-1-118-31183-7

Careers

Job Interviews
For Dummies,
4th Edition
978-1-118-11290-8

Job Searching with
Social Media
For Dummies
978-0-470-93072-4

Personal Branding
For Dummies
978-1-118-11792-7

Resumes For Dummies,
6th Edition
978-0-470-87361-8

Success as a Mediator
For Dummies
978-1-118-07862-4

Diet & Nutrition

Belly Fat Diet For Dummies
978-1-118-34585-6

Eating Clean For Dummies
978-1-118-00013-7

Nutrition For Dummies,
5th Edition
978-0-470-93231-5

Digital Photography

Digital Photography
For Dummies,
7th Edition
978-1-118-09203-3

Digital SLR Cameras &
Photography For Dummies,
4th Edition
978-1-118-14489-3

Photoshop Elements 11
For Dummies
978-1-118-40821-6

Gardening

Herb Gardening
For Dummies,
2nd Edition
978-0-470-61778-6

Vegetable Gardening
For Dummies,
2nd Edition
978-0-470-49870-5

Health

Anti-Inflammation Diet
For Dummies
978-1-118-02381-5

Diabetes For Dummies,
3rd Edition
978-0-470-27086-8

Living Paleo For Dummies
978-1-118-29405-5

Hobbies

Beekeeping
For Dummies
978-0-470-43065-1

eBay For Dummies,
7th Edition
978-1-118-09806-6

Raising Chickens
For Dummies
978-0-470-46544-8

Wine For Dummies,
5th Edition
978-1-118-28872-6

Writing Young Adult Fiction
For Dummies
978-0-470-94954-2

Language & Foreign Language

500 Spanish Verbs
For Dummies
978-1-118-02382-2

English Grammar
For Dummies,
2nd Edition
978-0-470-54664-2

French All-in One
For Dummies
978-1-118-22815-9

German Essentials
For Dummies
978-1-118-18422-6

Italian For Dummies
2nd Edition
978-1-118-00465-4

e **Available in print and e-book formats.**

Math & Science

Algebra I For Dummies,
2nd Edition
978-0-470-55964-2

Anatomy and Physiology
For Dummies,
2nd Edition
978-0-470-92326-9

Astronomy For Dummies,
3rd Edition
978-1-118-37697-3

Biology For Dummies,
2nd Edition
978-0-470-59875-7

Chemistry For Dummies,
2nd Edition
978-1-1180-0730-3

Pre-Algebra Essentials
For Dummies
978-0-470-61838-7

Microsoft Office

Excel 2013 For Dummies
978-1-118-51012-4

Office 2013 All-in-One
For Dummies
978-1-118-51636-2

PowerPoint 2013
For Dummies
978-1-118-50253-2

Word 2013 For Dummies
978-1-118-49123-2

Music

Blues Harmonica
For Dummies
978-1-118-25269-7

Guitar For Dummies,
3rd Edition
978-1-118-11554-1

iPod & iTunes
For Dummies,
10th Edition
978-1-118-50864-0

Programming

Android Application
Development For
Dummies, 2nd Edition
978-1-118-38710-8

iOS 6 Application
Development For Dummies
978-1-118-50880-0

Java For Dummies,
5th Edition
978-0-470-37173-2

Religion & Inspiration

The Bible For Dummies
978-0-7645-5296-0

Buddhism For Dummies,
2nd Edition
978-1-118-02379-2

Catholicism For Dummies,
2nd Edition
978-1-118-07778-8

Self-Help & Relationships

Bipolar Disorder
For Dummies,
2nd Edition
978-1-118-33882-7

Meditation For Dummies,
3rd Edition
978-1-118-29144-3

Seniors

Computers For Seniors
For Dummies,
3rd Edition
978-1-118-11553-4

iPad For Seniors
For Dummies,
5th Edition
978-1-118-49708-1

Social Security
For Dummies
978-1-118-20573-0

Smartphones & Tablets

Android Phones
For Dummies
978-1-118-16952-0

Kindle Fire HD
For Dummies
978-1-118-42223-6

NOOK HD For Dummies,
Portable Edition
978-1-118-39498-4

Surface For Dummies
978-1-118-49634-3

Test Prep

ACT For Dummies,
5th Edition
978-1-118-01259-8

ASVAB For Dummies,
3rd Edition
978-0-470-63760-9

GRE For Dummies,
7th Edition
978-0-470-88921-3

Officer Candidate Tests,
For Dummies
978-0-470-59876-4

Physician's Assistant Exam
For Dummies
978-1-118-11556-5

Series 7 Exam
For Dummies
978-0-470-09932-2

Windows 8

Windows 8 For Dummies
978-1-118-13461-0

Windows 8 For Dummies,
Book + DVD Bundle
978-1-118-27167-4

Windows 8 All-in-One
For Dummies
978-1-118-11920-4

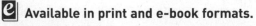 **Available in print and e-book formats.**